RELATIVE CREATURES

RELATIVE CREATURES

Victorian Women in Society and the Novel

Françoise Basch

SCHOCKEN BOOKS • NEW YORK

To my sisters, brothers, fathers and mothers

Contents

List of Illustrations

viii

Acknowledgements

I would like to thank all those without whose help and advice I would never have been able to finish this book: Vincent Brome, who for four years stood by patiently and offered much useful advice; Jean-Jacques Mayoux, whose penetrating criticisms (not always as well received as they deserved) substantially improved the book; Pierre Grappin, who one day on a bus worked out an outline plan for me; Peter Fryer, who put me on the track of valuable material; Raphael Samuel, who read part of the text; Martine Aquistapace, who managed to decipher a manuscript scored and corrected to the point of illegibility; Ian Willison, and the staff of the British Museum, guardian angels, all of them, of the solitary scholar; Madame Raïssa Tarr, who read and corrected the complete typescript; John Edwards, who revised the text; Michael Young, who added the final touches.

1. 'The "Bloomers" in Hyde Park, or an Extraordinary
Exhibition for 1852.' Caricature by George Cruikshank
from *The Comic Almanack*

La femme est une esclave
qu'il faut savoir mettre sur un trône

Balzac *La Psychologie du Mariage*

Introduction

The French writer Taine in an imaginary homily to the public urged the Victorian novelist to 'Be moral, since your novels must be suitable for young women to read ...'[1] Angus Wilson is no less ironical about the characters of the Victorian novel in the context of the contemporary domestic ideal: the taste for wedding bells, and the obsession with chastity. For him, these elements are associated with the literary convention of the happy ending.[2] The happy ending, marriage seen as the point of no return, and the culmination of heroes' and heroines' tribulations, severely restricts the world of the novelist and reveals characteristic attitudes towards society. 'George Sand portrays passionate women; portray good decent women for us. George Sand encourages us to be in love; encourage us to marry ...'[3] This is how Taine's homily went, thus stressing the opposition between the cult of marriage and the subversive force of passion and love.

But too often such analyses fail to point out that, generally speaking, the hegemony of this domestic and family ideal, this amenable and disciplined vision of human relations, has one chief victim, the heroine. Most females in English fiction of the first part of the Victorian era are caricatured or idealized figures; at any rate they are simplified, and seem to conform to a few stereotypes inspired by a tyrannical and narrow ideal of the woman in the home. Forced into a system that takes no account of the complexity of human behaviour and, simultaneously, enhanced by emotional connotations deriving from the intrusion of a sacred or symbolic dimension, the female characters appear for the most part to be deprived of that internal dialectic, social and psychological, which, according to Lukacs, is a prerequisite for the independent existence of the characters in great realistic novels.

A reading of the contemporary novels in France and Russia confirms this impression. The period 1837–67, to which this study is limited, saw the appearance of the masterpieces of Stendhal, Balzac and Flaubert in France and of Turgenev, Dostoevsky and

Tolstoy in Russia.[4] La Sanseverina in *The Charterhouse of Parma*, Balzac's Cousine Bette and Esther Gobseck and Madame de Nucingen, Emma Bovary, Elene in *On the Eve*, Madame Odintsova in *Fathers and Sons*, Natasha and Princess Mary in *War and Peace* – all these characters are endowed with a life of their own that allows the twentieth-century reader to be involved in their experience, if not actually to identify with them; which is, to say the least, difficult with the heroines of Dickens, Thackeray, Charlotte Brontë, Elizabeth Gaskell and of the early novels of George Eliot. If Jane Eyre, Becky Sharp and Maggie Tulliver are exceptions, they are ones that illustrate the rule.

While the anaemic heroine of the Victorian novel is in striking contrast with her French and Russian counterparts, she is equally pale when compared with her native ancestors. Although the change in the code of female behaviour took place as early as the beginning of the eighteenth century and is already perceptible in the novels of Richardson, the secondary female characters in the novels of Smollett and Fielding, notably in the latter's *Tom Jones* (1749), have an intense carnal presence. Even in Richardson's novels, women are far from being ethereal: the body is beneath the clothes. As for Defoe's heroines, they are energetic and realistic: Moll Flanders marries several times and has no qualms about selling her favours. In order to keep her economic liberty Roxana refuses to marry a nobleman. Prior to *Clarissa Harlowe* (1748), no feminine character in a novel loses her life as well as her virginity. The tragic choice between purity and death, found for the first time in Richardson's novels, continued in vogue for more than a century. Pamela succeeds in imposing marriage on her seducer, and in escaping from her humble condition. She emerges victorious from the battle; the gentleman marries the servant, thus legitimating both her virtue and her social ascent. Clarissa, on the other hand, succumbs to the antagonism between her family and her seducer: she is crushed between her own puritan morality and the materialism of two social classes – the upper-middle class enriched by trade with the Indies, and the unscrupulous aristocracy. Even though raped by Lovelace, who has previously drugged her, symbolically she remains pure. The novelist nonetheless decrees her death; though in no way herself responsible, the heroine could not survive the outrage even if she had no part in it except as victim.

The Vicar of Wakefield (1776) marks a new stage in the analysis of seduction and its social implications. Two classes and two systems of morality confront each other. The whim of the unscrupulous and dissolute nobleman, a sort of Don Juan figure, becomes law in his fief; the seduction of the vicar's daughter symbolizes the feudal power of the one man who owns the land, the place of residence, the animals, the very person of the vicar and his family. The vicar has only his faith as spiritual resource and rule of conduct, and the rape of his daughter and of his values destroys him. If the novelist had not, by a trick in the plot (the symbolic meaning of which is nevertheless profound), held off dishonour and death by revealing that Olivia and the nobleman were married without knowing it, she and the vicar would have perished. With Pamela, Clarissa Harlow and Olivia, Richardson and Goldsmith introduced into English literature the stereotype of the fragile heroine, pure and innocent, more attached to virginity than to life: a stereotype which was to dominate the Victorian novel.

At the beginning of the nineteenth century, just before my period, Jane Austen created remarkable female characters within the setting that she knew as a spinster daughter of a country vicar. Paradoxically a contemporary of the Romantic poets and the Napoleonic Wars, Jane Austen created a marvellously prosaic fictional universe. Charlotte Brontë did not hide the distaste she felt towards a vision of the world so lacking lyricism.[5] But what she took for a description, at once superficial and detailed, of the ways of genteel people is also a penetrating study of a definite social class. Jane Austen's irony went very deep, in exposing the influence of wealth, fashion and snobbery and their effect on women's psychology. Her field of exploration is narrower than that of the Victorian novelists; but the heroines are not mythical, idealized or caricatured.

With George Eliot, after 1860, and then in the novels of Meredith, Hardy, George Moore, Bennett and Wells, there is continuing progress towards more complexity and a final abandonment of the Victorian stereotype.

It is always difficult to establish a precise historical period and a 'generation' of writers. Any definition of an era is arbitrary, since it is unusual for the lives and careers of writers to coincide exactly in time. Moreover, this study is not exclusively literary. It has to consider literary history and groups of writers along with stages in feminism and historical processes and events. After Romanticism and the Napoleonic wars, the first thirty years of Victoria's reign have a certain unity: it was an age of underlying ferment preceding the intellectual, religious and political crisis of authority which, from the 1860s, and before the political outbursts of feminism, was to destroy, among other things, the myth of the woman that had previously prevailed. 1837 was the year of Victoria's accession to the throne. Coming a few years after the Reform Act of 1832 – marking the first stage in the sharing of political power by the landed aristocracy and the newly affluent members of the middle classes, the commercial and industrial magnates – it coincided with an economic and social crisis which brought forth two very important pressure groups, the Chartists[6] and the Anti-Corn Law League. 1837 was not, however, in any way prominent in the history of feminism, which got under way later: ten years later, 1847 saw the first restriction on working hours for women and in another decade, 1857, the new divorce law was passed and the *English Woman's Journal* came into being. But the beginnings were there, in 1837 Caroline Norton was already fighting for the rights of the wife, and for a reform of the law on the custody of children after divorce.

Though historians naturally differ on how to divide up the Victorian era, there is general agreement that 1860–70 marked a turning-point. Long before the establishment of universal suffrage (Acts of 1918 and 1928), the second Reform Act of 1867 was the main step taken towards democracy. The 1867 Act, though still with property qualifications, granted the franchise to the lower-middle class and to a small privileged section of the working class. It was a sign of the times, and a portent of the future, that John Stuart Mill moved an amendment to that same Bill for the extension of the right to vote that would substitute the asexual word, 'person', for 'man', thus opening the door to votes for women. The amendment was defeated, but 73 had voted in favour and the philosopher had the opportunity of defending in public the equality of the sexes.

In so far as dates matter, 1867 can be held to be a crucial date in the history of feminism. The report of a commission inquiring into schools (1867–8), before which Emily Davies, Frances Buss and Mill gave evidence, sharply accelerated the improvements in secondary and higher education for women. Two years later Girton College opened its doors. 1867 saw the Factory Acts regulating the work of women and children extended to non-textile industries and craft occupations.[7] In 1868 the problem of birth-control was publicly raised for the first time in connection with the Amberley affair; and between 1864 and 1869 the Contagious Diseases Acts were passed that were to provoke a new feminist offensive, the Great Crusade. In 1866, after the election of Mill to the House of Commons, the first association for female suffrage was created, three years before the appearance of *The Subjection of Women*.

In the literary world, Charles Dickens's career was drawing to an end; it was the year in which *Middlemarch* was conceived and in which there first appeared a new generation of novelists, notably Thomas Hardy and George Meredith. The question arises – how to choose the novelists to be dealt with? It would be impossible, and pointless anyway, to cover the entire production of fiction during a period of thirty years. Some choose themselves. Thackeray, Mrs Gaskell, the Brontë sisters and Dickens were all writing at this time, and all were dead by 1870. But others, like Trollope, Meredith and George Eliot, overlap with the next generation. Trollope and Meredith have practically been excluded, which is perhaps arguable in Trollope's case. Trollope (1815–82) and George Eliot (1819–80) were near-contemporaries. But if it be granted that Trollope's first important novel is *The Warden* (1855) his work is almost as important in quantity and quality after 1867 as before, which removes him appreciably from Dickens, Thackeray and the Brontës. As for Meredith, by 1867 he had already published four important novels, and *Modern Love*. But Meredith (1828–1909) nonetheless belonged to another generation, as is particularly shown by the way he portrays women.

George Eliot is very much present in the book if only because the majority of her novels 'are primarily concerned with the tragic heroine instead of the hero'.[8] These heroines form an admirable transition between the Victorian stereotypes of the wife-mother, the old maid, the impure woman, and the characters of self-conscious feminists, such as Sue Bridehead in *Jude the Obscure* and H. G. Wells's Ann Veronica, who attack the traditional role of the woman as well as other fundamental social institutions. George Eliot, who in 1857–8 at the age of thirty-six launched out into novel writing with *Scenes of Clerical Life*, at a time when the position of women was fast changing both socially and legally, is in all ways a key figure for my purpose. She dwelt in a psychological and intellectual world more complex and more modern than that of the other novelists who concern us here, and had already before 1858 made a long intellectual and religious journey. She had translated Feuerbach and Strauss's *Life of Jesus*, and had written articles for the *Westminster Review*, edited by the publisher, John Chapman. In this circle of intellectuals, whose emancipation in the world of ideas sometimes went with an unorthodox private life, George Eliot, who had abandoned Evangelicism for agnosticism, absorbed an avant-garde atmosphere receptive to new philosophical approaches: Comte's positivism, Spencer's evolutionism and, in the literary sphere, the reflections of G. H. Lewes on realism. Her novels, which generally combine 'a contemporary moral story' with a sociological study, reflected the new climate. Their realism, in Frank Kermode's opinion, has echoes of the naturalistic credo of the Goncourts.[9] At all events it prefigures the aesthetic of the late Victorian novel.

It should also be said that the book will only deal with the main novelists of the time: those who as a rule come into the same class as the great Russian and French contemporary realists.

Although the study of the woman in society, a particular society, is fundamental to this book, this is not to say that the fictional characters can be considered, or will be considered, simply as reflections of reality. Without falling into the fashionable cult of formalism the impossibility must always be borne in mind of reducing a fictional character, an integral part of everything that makes up the novel, to a social reality, even if one was confident that one understood that 'reality'. At the same time the work of a novelist in particular is not only an individual creation *ex-nihilo* but comes from deep within the culture and ideology of a period; and the ideology is in part determined by the economic and social infra-structure. The fictional characters will therefore be considered against a triple background: first, the contemporary system of values and what it prescribes for individuals, especially women, as their function and purpose; next a description of the conditions of life and social segmentation of the time; finally, the work of the author and his or her psychology.

First, the values. The emergence of a disembodied figure, with symbolic references to the Virgin Mary, was perhaps the most obvious result of an historical and ideological change which began in England well before Victoria, with the gradual climb to power of a middle class imbued first with Calvinist Protestantism and, later, with Methodism. If this was not, properly speaking, a Victorian phenomenon alone so much as a long-term process, it was, I think, in the early and mid-Victorian age, that the cultural expression of this image reached its climax. It affected not only the novel but all other forms of art and thought as well. The industrial revolution of England marked the advent of capitalism in Europe and of the eventual ascendancy of those classes which throughout the eighteenth and nineteenth centuries fought against the landed aristocracy for their share of economic, social and political power. The system of values of the middle classes was determined, in an individualist perspective, by the demands of work and productivity. The close relationship between the capitalist mode of production and the protestant ethic has been demonstrated by Weber and Tawney. It was Protestantism, in its seventeenth-century Puritan version, and later as expressed in the Methodist evangelical movements at the end of the eighteenth and beginning of the nineteenth centuries, that characterized the ethic of bourgeois individualism as well as contemporary feelings about sex and its association with 'sin'. The cult of family, home and marriage which so astonished Taine was linked with the increased emphasis laid on individual effort and achievement, in other words self-help. In the eighteenth-century novel (Defoe, Richardson, Goldsmith) it was contrasted with the way of life and lack of values of the declining aristocracy, all idleness and debauchery. Chastity for men and, even more, women was regarded as a force for action, as a means to avoid wasting time and energy. The marital partnership pursuing maternal and social progress and bearing children to inherit the fruit of these efforts was the best guarantee against any kind of wasted energy. By her very nature and also as a result of the functions attributed to her by ancient and deep-rooted myths and centuries of Christian theology, woman's stage was within the home and family. This is what we shall examine in the next chapter. The feminine ideal was an essential factor in the evolutionary dynamic of the middle classes. Like all ruling-class values, its effect permeated the whole of society. The artisan William Lovett – although a militant trade-unionist and Chartist – paid homage to his wife in her role as guardian angel, and glorified 'woman's mission' in terms worthy of Mrs Ellis or Ruskin in *Of Queen's Gardens*.[10]

This book considers Victorian women in fiction from three points of view which are, as it were, the three panels of the mythical triptych of the woman. The model, the revalued and even sanctified image of the wife-mother, is compared with two negative images that are the reverse of this ideal: that of the single woman, debased and largely caricatured, and the impure woman, condemned and even damned.

In pointing out the similarities and differences between the position of women and the way it is represented in the novel, that is to say the selection used by the novelist, the aim is to get a better grip on the relationship of the creator to his work and society. This attempt at 'demythification' should help throw light on certain aspects of Victorian values and culture. I have not made extensive use of the research of the late Lucien Goldmann ('genetic structuralism') on the dialectical links between literature and history that would account for fictional creations and the relationship between novel and society. This study may however help to define more clearly the role of the novelist in England at that time, his attitude towards the reading public and his view of the function of the novel.

[1]

WIVES AND MOTHERS

Contemporary Ideologies

In two centuries an agricultural nation with feudal structures was transformed into a great industrial capitalist power characterized by the economic, political and ideological hegemony of the middle classes. For middle-class women liberation from the most arduous domestic slavery, and the acquisition of leisure, were part of an evolution that began around the beginning of the eighteenth century. From that period onwards more and more girls attended institutions that claimed to prepare them for marriage, teaching them the rudiments of French, reading, writing, arithmetic, and more general accomplishments, in short the elements useful for a role of 'display'. New periodicals such as the *Ladies' Magazine*, began in 1770, and the *Annuals*, which lasted until 1840, testify to the existence of a female reading public regularly provided with edifying nourishment that was intended to '... confirm chastity and recommend virtue ...'[1]

Even before 1800 manuals of etiquette and conduct exalted the ideal of the woman in the home, and they flourished even more in the very early years of the nineteenth century. They met the needs for the codification of social behaviour on the part of a middle class that was becoming ever more prosperous but which was still not confident about the practices of good society.[2] Equally, they were in keeping with the new wave of strict non-conformist Protestantism among the rising classes. Even before Victoria's reign, reactionary conservatism, which at the turn of the century reacted alike against the freedom of aristocratic morals and the French revolution's threat of subversion, created a climate favourable to a traditionalist conception of woman under the sway of man and enclosed within the family.

One belief that had been particularly powerful in medieval Christianity was still there: woman's inferior and imperfect if not completely evil nature.[3] It was fitting, explained Mrs Sandford, the author of a treatise written in 1831, to protect this creature of instinct ('weaker vessel'), characterized by vanity, instability and lack of judgement,[4] from herself and to prevent her from coming to harm, by confining her in the home. This was the teaching of Saint Paul; there she would be sheltered behind the rampart of religion. The daughter by Paul out of Eve, corruptible and corrupting, was no spectre. In a work published a few years later, where she still writes at length on the importance of religion in female education, Mrs Sandford suggested that woman could choose between a brief and selfish butterfly existence and an altogether nobler Christian vocation – to exercise a beneficent influence on her neighbour.[5] The change of emphasis is significant: we pass from religious and family restraints upon the freedom of a fundamentally dangerous nature to framework for the accomplishment of a mission. Mary is super-imposed on Eve.

This does not mean, however, that the arguments in favour of the ontological inferiority of woman disappeared altogether after 1840. In 1869 John Stuart Mill still went to the trouble of systematically refuting them in *The Subjection of Women*. John Maynard's tract on marriage, before enumerating the wife's duties of 'unqualified sub-mission, ready and cheerful obedience', specifically recalled that man's authority flows naturally from Adam's having been created before Eve.[6] And Sarah Ellis, that ever-dutiful advocate of women's duties, urged her readers to fight the three specifically female faults – selfishness, indolence, vanity – by cultivating 'habits of industry, feelings of benevolence and Christian meekness'.[7] In general, how-ever, arraigning woman's nature was in decline. Until the seven-teenth century the Pauline conception of the tempting and sinful woman, a permanent threat to spirituality and mysticism, was more or less universal. It was to be definitively abandoned in nineteenth-century England. The Victorian advocates of woman's subjection, the adversaries of her emancipation, elaborated an image both subtler and better adapted to the times than the diabolical female anxious to turn man aside from sanctity. The feudal anti-feminist of *The Princess* was already anachronistic in 1847:

> Man is the hunter; woman is his game:
> The sleek and shining creatures of the chase ...[8]

The new and triumphant model of the woman recovers some essential elements of the courtly love of eleventh-century Provence, notably the cult of the idealized lady which, during the era of the middle class, evolved within the strict and narrow framework of the family. On the doctrine of the inferiority of the temptress based on biological arguments and the literal interpretation of Genesis was superimposed a theory of the different aptitudes and roles of the two sexes. The theory rested on the self-evident contrast between the active nature of the one and the passive nature of the other. Man was the 'architect'; woman 'the soul of the house'.[9] The offensive and even aggressive role of the man, of '... the doer, the creator, the discoverer ...'[10] is justified by his intellectual capacity for creation, invention and synthesis, of which the woman, who can only exercise her judgement on details and insignificant things, is deprived.[11] As a result of these allegedly natural differences the role best suited to woman was, in the eyes of W. R. Greg, a menial occupation, which though menial ideally fitted her dependent nature.

... they (female servants) are attached to others and are connected with other existences, which they embellish, facilitate and serve. In a word, they fulfill both essentials of a woman's being: *they are supported by, and minister to, men.*[12]

In herself the woman was nothing: 'they are ... from their own constitution, and from the station they occupy in the world ... relative creatures.'[13] This established, the woman can only justify her presence on earth by dedicating herself to others; through deliberate self-effacement, duty and sacrifice she will discover the identity and *raison d'être* of which, by herself, she is deprived.

In this perspective, education takes its proper place. According to *The Daughters of England* the acquisition of knowledge must aim only to dispel the most glaring errors that crowd the woman's weak brain, encourage the worship of the Creator, and make her a more enlightened companion for the male.[14] According to Ruskin, the acquisition of wisdom must not aim at 'self-development' but 'self-renunciation' relieved by the ability to understand and help the man in his task.[15]

When the woman is denied all capacity for creation, action and authority, her contribution in the masculine world becomes the emotional and moral guidance which are her vocations as wife and mother. On the basis of her physical and intellectual weakness, a theory of her power was constructed which commanded general assent perhaps just because of the paradox. Mrs Ellis and Mrs Beeton placed the wife at the centre of the family as the source of all thought, all feeling, all influence.[16] Ruskin invested her with an absolute power over the spirit of man, peace, war, and the fate of humanity.[17] According to Charles Kingsley, the woman is '... the natural, and therefore divine, guide, purifier, inspirer of the man'.[18] Formerly man's slave, woman was promoted to the rank of guide and inspiration, but we are not generally allowed to forget that her power was the fruit of subjection and submission. 'A true wife, in her husband's house, is his servant; it is in his heart that she is queen, ...'[19] wrote Ruskin, and elsewhere he specified that the guiding function of the woman was perfectly 'reconcilable' with 'a true wifely subjection'.[20] This creature's power, which was in inverse ratio to her weakness and subjection, could only be of a religious and spiritual dimension. She has the capacity to intercede in the mystical hierarchy. Religious symbolism was still very much of the fire. Woman was evoked in the form of an angel by Coventry Patmore[21] and Tennyson,[22] a madonna by Ruskin,[23] the Virgin Mary by Sarah Ellis,[24] representations which together sum up the contemporary ideal: chastity, humility and transcendence. The myth of Mary, whose meaning Simone de Beauvoir has brilliantly analysed, was triumphant in the Victorian era; it was indeed as a servant that '... a woman is entitled to the most magnificent apotheoses'.[25]

The moral power so often evoked, the vocation of maintaining 'love's fountain',[26] devolved upon girls, wives and mothers in a home that had been considerably transformed by the rise in the standard of living and the physical emancipation of the middle class. Freedom from household drudgery was provided by a large staff of servants. In *The Book of Household Management* (1862),[27] on whose front page a non-exhaustive list of sixteen categories of servants was drawn up, Mrs Beeton explicitly connected the new role of the mistress of the house – 'commander of an army' or 'leader of any enterprise' – with her moral responsibility towards this community.[28]

But the moralists had also to attack the newly acquired idleness. It clashed with the contemporary worship of effort and work. It was no coincidence that the inscription on Mrs Beeton's book evoked the 'virtuous woman' who 'eateth not the bread of idleness'. In order that the noble task of mistress of the house may be performed, Mrs Beeton and Mrs Ellis both insisted on the need for their readers to have 'a knowledge of household duties' from the practical point of view and 'to be acquainted with the best method of doing everything upon which domestic comfort depends'. Addressing herself explicitly to the middle classes and anxious to combat an idleness that would be harmful to their physical and moral health, Sarah Ellis tried on many occasions to rehabilitate housework.[29] In the context of her diatribes against the surrounding materialism, against the need the middle classes felt to imitate the ways of the upper classes,[30] this reminder of the dignity of humble tasks, these exhortations to 'industry', represented a typical reaction of non-conformist Protestantism against the dangers of a softening occasioned by the general rise in the standard of living, and against the sentimental, refined, imaginative, dreamy image of the heroine immortalized by the *Annuals*, by Mrs Hemans and by Laetitia Landon at the beginning of the century.[31]

The new ideal of the woman as 'helpmate', extolled by Tennyson, A. H. Clough and the progressive philanthropists who supported women's labour, cleverly fused all these elements. A primordial mission of moral inspiration, purity, generosity and altruism was linked to her maternal, physiological function. In short, the woman became an active kernel of Christian ethics, supposed to radiate beyond the confines of the home as a result of her twofold nature which, according to the moralists, ordained a double duty for her: 'a personal work ... relating to her own home ... and a public work ... which is also an extension of that ...'[32] It was on the basis of the woman's double role and her particular aptitudes (Anna Jameson's theory of the 'Communion of Work' was a variant of this) that philanthropic activities would be assigned to her as her privileged domain.[33] How much nearer could one get to bliss on earth than that?

The idealization of the wife as inspirer of humanity belonged with the Victorian conception of the Home and its meaning within the contemporary system of values. The home, a feminine attribute as it were, the 'outermost garment of her soul',[34] which surrounds the wife worthy of the name wherever she may be found,[35] is like a temple of purity, a haven of peace in a hostile and impure world. It falls to the man, the active ingredient, to take risks outside the sanctuary or bastion and to pit himself against his peers in a bitter struggle that often leaves him wounded, weakened, disenchanted. Ruskin evoked this role in symbolic terms. Mrs Ellis, whose ambition was to defend the 'nation of shopkeepers', the 'intelligence and moral power'[36] of the English middle class, was more explicit. The warrior of modern times, daily seeking comfort and inspiration from his wife, was none other than 'the man of business in the present day',[37] obsessed by the acquisition of wealth. 'The Moloch of this world' which devoured him, through ruthless competition engendering envy and hate, was the commercialism and capitalism of the nineteenth century. It was for the middle class industrialist and businessman impelled by the 'economic motive' that the wife played the double role of agent of peace and 'second conscience'. Her mission was to help him resist the 'snares of the world around him, and temptation'.[38] In 1869 Sarah Ellis again wrote about the threat to the moral and spiritual integrity of individuals resulting from bitter economic competition and material and technical progress, and urged the mother to arm her children against temptation.[39] Thus the woman, the very ideal of mother and wife, source of all virtue and purity, appeared as the good conscience of Victorian society. Poets, moralists and philosophers embellished the domestic and family role of the woman with a universal and transcendental dimension. But the mutation of the Eve myth into the Mary myth, of temptress into redeemer, implied a fundamental process of de-sexualization of the woman, who was bit by bit deprived of her carnal attributes: the housewife became at once the pillar of the home and the priestess of a temple. Some even went so far – whether or not under pretext of a scientific investigation – as to affirm categorically the absence of sexual instinct in woman. 'In men ... the sexual desire is inherent and spontaneous. In the other sex, the desire is dormant, if not non-existent ...'[40] wrote W. R. Greg. Thus it would depend largely on circumstances whether the 'sensual impulsions' broke through to the surface. Some women had no knowledge of them all their lives. The absence of desire attributed to the majority of women was used by those who pleaded the cause of the prostitute, the victim both of society and masculine appetites. Most often the cause of the 'fall' would not be desire but the sacrifice to the loved man of what was most precious to her.[41]

William Acton was elected to the Royal Medical and Chirurgical Society in 1842. He was the author of a treatise on diseases of the urinary and sexual organs (1841) and, above all, of a work on prostitution. In 1857 he published *The Functions and Disorders of the Reproductive Organs*. Contrary to the implication of the title, the anatomy and physiology of the reproductive organs of the woman were omitted from this study. Acton argued as if the said organs did not exist in the woman or, if they did, were lacking in both functions and disorders.[42] When he did evoke female sexuality it was in relation to the man, his desires, his apprehensions and his attitudes towards marriage.[43] Anxious to reassure those young men fearful of not proving themselves virile enough with their new wives, Acton presents the reader with a fascinating portrait of female

8

sexuality and the sexual life of the couple. On the one hand is the handful of mistresses and courtesans the young man has known before his marriage, who, being in Acton's view unbalanced and nymphomaniac, are completely marginal, and on the other the cohort of future wife-mothers who by definition are ignorant and incapable of any sexual impulses: 'Love of home, children and domestic duties, are the only passion they feel ...'[44] For them, consumation of the marriage meant only suffering and distress.[45] But let the husbands be reassured: 'the act of coition takes place but rarely'[46] in the life of the couple, for in a normal marriage, explained the expert, the woman conceives about every two years and feels no sexual desire during the period of pregnancy and suckling. In any case, Acton, who recommended continence to the young man both before and after marriage, advised him more specifically not to have intercourse on average more than once every seven or ten days. But even practised at these rare intervals, relations for the wife consisted of submitting to her husband, impelled by the spirit of sacrifice and the desire for motherhood. Acton found it difficult to reconcile woman's natural purity, to vindicate female nature from the vile aspersions cast on it (by ungoverned lust),[47] and the goodwill required from her in face of the demands of male instinct – even when strongly disciplined by sports, cold baths and religious readings – and procreation. The exemplary attitude was doubtless the one corresponding to

... the perfect picture of an English wife and mother, kind, considerate, self-sacrificing ..., so pure-hearted as to be utterly ignorant of and averse to any sensual indulgence, but so unselfishly attached to the man she loves, as to be willing to give up her own wishes and feelings for his sake ...[48]

Acton's treatise, which asserts the absence of sexual instinct in any healthy child, even a male one, describing the dangers of masturbation for the physical, mental and moral well being of the adolescent in terrifying terms, admirably sums up the obsessive linking of sin, punishment and sex. It was the wife's mission to save the man from himself and his carnal appetites. Her sacrifice helps the man to sublimate his instincts while doing the minimum to perpetuate the race within the framework of the family.

In his study of *The Princess* John Killham sets out to demonstrate a feminist trend that might have influenced the genesis of Tennyson's poem. Our respective researches provide abundant proof that alongside the apostles of an idealized but still essentially family role for the woman there was a growing counter-current, notably in the Unitarian periodical, *The Monthly Repository*, in the 1830s, and in the *Westminster Review*, in the shape of biographies and critical reviews, before its more direct expression in the writings of Harriet Martineau, Anna Jameson, Barbara Bodichon and Mrs Hugo Reid.[49] But the arguments of these first feminists only very rarely and incompletely called the old idea into question. The feminism of the years 1830–70 aimed less at elaborating a new female image than remedying certain particular injustices,[50] essentially those concerning the spinster without means of support and the unhappily married. Unlike the contemporary protest of French feminists such as Flora Tristan and Pauline Roland, the essentially pragmatic reformism of the first half of the Victorian era hardly questioned the woman's vocation in the family, nor her 'special' aptitudes.

Feminism, couched in the widest cultural sense, appeared towards the end of the seventeenth century. But its first truly 'modern' manifestations were Mary Wollstonecraft's *A Vindication of the Rights of Woman* in 1792 and, in 1825, a more ambitious and subversive text: *Appeal of One Half of the Human Race, Women, Against the Pretensions of the Other Half, Men, to Retain them in Political, and thence in Civil and Domestic Slavery: in Reply to a Paragraph in Mr Mill's Celebrated Article on Government*. While *A Vindication* ... did not fall into a total vacuum – a third edition of the work appeared in 1796 – the hostility to this type of protest is well attested by the even greater success of conservative works. *An Enquiry into the Duties of the Female Sex* by T. Gisborne went into nine editions between 1797 and 1810.[51] Despite the way the doctrines of Saint-Simon and Fourier sprang into life in France and their kinship with the theories of Robert Owen in England, particularly on women, early nineteenth-century public opinion in England was antagonistic to anything tainted with socialism[52] and did not approve of the really subversive feminism that was fighting for political and social emancipation (William Thompson) or sexual emancipation (the pioneers of contraception, F. Place and R. Carlile).[53] These ideas were limited to a narrow circle of socialist sympathizers.[54]

Between the appearance of the two great texts, William Thompson's *Appeal* ... in 1825 and John Stuart Mill's *The Subjection of Women* in 1869, the ideal of an exclusively family vocation and transcendental mission for women was exposed to many criticisms and attacks but ones that generally stopped short of being systematic and radical.

2 . 'My wife is a woman of mind.' Caricature by George Cruikshank from
The Comic Almanack

The concepts of woman's 'influence' and 'sphere' were the most
tempting targets. In her chapter on women in *Society in America*
Harriet Martineau had nothing but sarcasm for the notion of '... the
virtual influence of woman; her swaying the judgment and will of
man through the heart ... One might as well try to dissect the
morning mist.'[55] F. R. Parkes also laughed at 'this mysterious moral
fluid'.[56] And by contrasting the 'all-powerful so-much-talked-of
influence' with the deprivation of political and social rights,[57] Mrs
Hugo Reid revealed the mystification that went with the idealization.
George Eliot considered that in France, a country where woman
played a more active part in cultural life, one could just about speak
of some feminine influence, at least in the literary sphere. And while
refraining from adopting the views of French 'morality' the author
suggested that, however regrettable they might be, love-affairs and
intrigues constituted an undeniable field of influence.[58]

As for the 'spheres and duties' of the woman, narrowly defined as
an acceptance of family vocation, early feminists considered that no

3. ' "The Rights of Women" or the Effects of Female Enfranchisement.'
Caricature by George Cruikshank from *The Comic Almanack*

one had the right to enclose her within this.[59] The daily reality of
spinsters without support or family, or even supporting a family,
belied the theory. Every individual, man or woman, had a duty to
work.[60] Generally speaking, Harriet Martineau, and B. R. Parkes,
like John Stuart Mill later, rebelled against the narrow definition of
a particular 'sphere' reserved for women and asked that they be left
free to try their hands in wider fields.

But even though the restrictive and metaphysical aspects of
feminine influence and the feminine sphere were often ridiculed,
their existence was rarely denied. Even when it was stated that
women were treated like children and slaves,[61] or like cattle;[62] even
when, for example, Barbara Bodichon illustrated in a long and
erudite article the enslavement of women over the centuries and the
fact that their sanctification in the form of an angel or heavenly
queen had not, generally speaking, diminished their oppression;[63]
attacks against the prevailing model were few and far between until

12

the end of the 1860s and the type of systematic and rigorous analysis by John Stuart Mill and F. P. Cobbe.[64] Harriet Taylor made an accurate assessment of protest during this period when she wrote: '... (they) do not complain of their state of being degraded at all – they complain only that it is *too much* degraded.'[65]

The radicalization of the theory corresponded to the radicalization of action. Anxious to put right particularly urgent abuses and injustices, pragmatic feminism before 1865 hardly paid any attention to women's political rights; the franchise was demanded neither frequently nor systematically. Before *The Subjection of Women* the only texts that dealt seriously with female suffrage were Harriet Taylor's article in the July 1851 issue of the *Westminster Review*,[66] and Mrs Hugo Reid's *A Plea for Women* (1843). While John Stuart Mill and Harriet Taylor seem to have shared a belief in the complete equality of men and women, including political equality,[67] Mrs Reid on the whole saw women's suffrage as their only recourse against the

13

injustice they suffered in civil rights and education, as the only way of putting an end to the oppression of one half of humanity by the other.[68] Furthermore, exercising her civic responsibility would give woman an increased sense of the 'scope of her mission'.

The first woman's suffrage society was set up in 1866 following a communication by Barbara Bodichon on the franchise. At a meeting organized in November 1865 by the Kensington Society most of the prominent feminist pioneers (in education, medicine and legislation), Emily Davies, Frances Buss, Dorothea Beale, Sophia Jex-Blake and Barbara Bodichon, participated. The influence of this first suffrage society showed that public opinion was ripe. It was galvanized by the election of the first eminent feminist to Parliament – Mill in 1865. As early as 1866 the society collected 1,500 votes in favour of the right of female householders to vote, and it rapidly gained ground in Manchester where, in 1867, it collected 13,500 signatures.[69] The first public meeting was held in London in 1869.[70] Participation in the new suffrage societies and the signing of the petition were encouraged by the first important public statement on the question, Mill's in the Commons on 20 May 1867.[71]

Thus it was in the years immediately following Mill's election that feminism took on a political character and its enemies were obliged to take it seriously. On 15 January 1867, an anti-feminist aristocrat, Lady Frederick Cavendish, wrote in her journal: 'The subject of female suffrage (odious and ridiculous notion as it is) is actually beginning to be spoken of without laughter ... I trust we are not coming to that.'[72]

In 1869 public opinion appears to have been mature enough to receive Mill's message in *The Subjection of Women* (written as early as 1861) and his systematic, historical and philosophical questioning of women's subservience.

But by and large the feminism of the first part of the Victorian era was of a limited character. It sprang from a few middle-class individuals, even though their audience appreciably increased between 1830 and 1869. They recorded the growing gap between a theory of woman's family vocation, an ideal of the wife-mother dependent on the man, and the reality of her condition. The reasons that drove them to underline the contrast between the idealization of the woman and her subjection, were often of a personal kind: unused talent, repressed vocation, obligation to earn her living.

The family vocation of the woman, raised by her contemporaries to the high position of 'helpmate', no longer appeared as exclusive even if it naturally remained primary. It was well recognized that society had to admit the existence of and make a place for those who could not fulfil this vocation; but the highest value was still placed on the image of the wife-mother. It was generally by virtue of her specific nature that the 'partner'[73] helped the man in the realization of a joint task. And this image was not fundamentally questioned by the feminists. Any more radical criticism had to wait on the global political and social protest that, after a brief appearance at the beginning of the century,[74] had been repressed in the conservative years that followed. The political and sexual dimension of female emancipation could only be asserted as a consequence of a general liberalization which had hardly started before 1870.

⌈2⌉

The Legal Position

When Taine visited England in the 1860s he was struck by the contradiction between the universal obsession with marriage and the
wife's dependence. 'She is nothing but a mother superior, she must
only concern herself with her household and her children ...'[1] It is
the condition of the wife-mother in society (her position before the
law and in daily life) and its relation to the prevailing female ideal
that is the subject of this chapter.

On 21 April 1851, one month before his marriage with Harriet
Taylor, John Stuart Mill solemnly denounced in writing 'these
odious powers' conferred on him as husband by marriage. As well as
being a personal commitment, this text of 6 March 1851 – directly
inspired by his preparation of an article on the emancipation of
women that was to appear in the *Westminster Review* in July 1851 –
was a protest against the general subjection of women, as illustrated in particular by the wife's legal status. In one sentence Mill
summed up the system in force, which '... confers upon one of the
parties to the contract legal power and control over the person,
property, and freedom of action of the other party ...'[2]

The legal position of a wife between 1837 and 1865–70 continued to be defined as under Roman law, which enjoined the
omnipotence of the head of the family, and the corresponding
physical and mental inferiority of the woman. The first Matrimonial Causes Act of 1857, like the Infants' Custody Act of 1839,
was the earliest step to protect the victims of the existing system,
women and the poor. But for the most part, in those areas where the
subjection of women was most obvious – such as education and
political rights – important changes in the wife's status only came
about after 1870 in the Married Woman's Property Act, under
pressure from a feminist movement that had crystallized.

The girl who contracted a marriage – which the entire weight of
nineteenth-century ideology put forward as being the culminating
point of a woman's life – lost at one stroke all her rights as a 'feme
sole', that is to say a free and independent individual.

A woman, in law, belonged to the man she married; she was his chattel.[3]

He is the absolute master of her, her property, and her children ...[4]

a contemporary could still say. The principle on which the bondage was based is that on marriage, man and woman become one. But, as Barbara Bodichon[5] and Caroline Norton[6] emphasized – the latter, inspired by her own marital unhappiness, pursued an indefatigable crusade for a reform of married women's legal status – it was the wife who paid the price for the alleged unity. Treated as a minor, she entirely lost her own legal existence, and with it, any legal recourse against her husband or anybody else.

But the concept of the wife's 'non-existence' in the eyes of the law, derived from the legal fiction of the unity of husband and wife, began to be opposed in the 1850s. It became increasingly unacceptable that the fiction should continue to hold after the spouses had been separated. At this point, the legal non-existence of the wife – denounced by Caroline Norton, Harriet Martineau, Barbara Bodichon, J. W. Kaye, Harriet Taylor and John Stuart Mill – turned her into the powerless slave of a husband who might be guilty of desertion, adultery and cruelty. Commenting on Mrs Norton's *Letter to the Queen on Lord Chancellor Cranworth's Marriage and Divorce Bill* of 1855, and the crimes of her husband, J. W. Kaye insisted on the need for reforms that would make such abuses impossible.[7] It was almost unnecessary to point out, like Mrs Norton in her *Letter*, the grotesque anomaly which ordained that married women should be 'non-existent' in a country governed by a female sovereign.[8]

What did non-existence mean? The husband had rights over the very body of his wife if necessary; he could force her to live with him by sequestrating her. This right came increasingly under attack. In 1840, a certain Cochran, summoned before the courts for imprisoning his wife, was upheld by the judge, who cited Bacon: 'He may beat her, but not in a violent or cruel manner ... and may, if he think fit, confine her, but he must not ... imprison her.'[9] But in a similar trial in 1852 the judge decided against the husband and refused to liken the wife to a recalcitrant child whom the law can insist on returning to his parents.[10] It was not, however, till 1844 that a clause in the new Matrimonial Causes Act decreed that a husband could not force his wife to return home.[11]

The same conception of the wife's bondage was widespread among the common people. Articles attributed to John Stuart Mill

4. 'As it ought to be or – The Ladies trying a Contemptible Scoundrel for a "Breach of Promise".' Caricature by George Cruikshank from *The Comic Almanack*

and Harriet Taylor[12] give details of serious cruelty (blows, wounds, even murder) towards a mistress or wife.

... The shoes on their feet, or the cudgel in their hand – the horse or ass that carries their burdens, and that dies a lingering death under their cruelties – the wife and children – all are 'theirs' ... It is the universal belief of the labouring class, that the law permits them to beat their wives ...[13]

Non-existence also meant that it was impossible for her to take even the smallest legal step, such as signing a contract or a lease,[14] to institute proceedings for the collection of debts, to sue for libel or to be sued. In such complete impotence, which continued even after separation,[15] the wife, bound hand and foot, was easy game for her husband or anyone else in a position to attack her. As J. W. Kaye emphasized, the consequences of this inequality need not brutalize a united couple. But, declared Lord Lyndhurst, to the

House of Lords in 1856 during the debates on the Divorce Bill, the oppression of a separated wife by the entire legal and social apparatus was unworthy of a civilized society. 'From that moment the wife is almost in a state of outlawry ... The law, so far from protecting, oppresses her. She is homeless, helpless, hopeless ...'[16] Thus when the *British and Foreign Quarterly Review*, which wrongly believed Mrs Norton to be the author of a particular article, called her a 'She-Devil' and 'She-Beast', she discovered that she could not institute proceedings for libel. Being married she was consequently non-existent.

According to certain jurists, this legal incapacity for initiative and responsibility was based less on the metaphysical argument about the woman's 'lack of discretion' than on the tangible fact that *nothing* belonged to her in her own right after marriage. The doctrine of the union of man and woman amounted to placing all the wife's possessions at the disposal of the husband, in return for which he was supposed to guarantee her his protection and provide for her needs. Everything belonging to the wife at the moment of marriage, chattels and real estate, became, with few exceptions, the husband's property, as well as anything she might acquire later on: annuities, personal income, gifts and emoluments.[17] In order to parody this handover Mrs Hugo Reid brought the Anglican marriage ritual into line with the truth.

Instead of 'with all my worldly goods I thee endow', a bridegroom, to speak in accordance with the laws, ought to say: 'what is yours, is mine; and what is mine, is *my own*'.[18]

Before the 1857 Act these dispositions were maintained even in the event of separation or the husband's desertion.[19] It seemed natural to J. W. Kaye that of the couple it should be the husband, as bread-winner, who has

the responsibility of providing sustenance for the household, and the penalty of not paying for it being solely his, it would hardly seem that the wife, so long as their common wants are to be provided for by a common purse, can justly claim any exclusive property in what either accident or exertion places in her hands.

But it seemed iniquitous to him that the husband could continue appropriating to himself the proceeds of the work of a wife whom he might have deserted, betrayed or ill-treated.[20] Repeatedly Caroline Norton explained, particularly in her *Letter to the Queen* ..., that not only did she receive nothing from her husband, but he refused to hand over personal articles which her mother or family had given her, books belonging to Lord Melbourne or things bought with the fruit of her labour. Norton also kept for himself the interest on the inheritance from his wife's father. Copyright, royalties from books and articles, 'were no more legally mine than my family property'.[21]

Mrs Norton's case received vast publicity as a result of the notoriety of her relationships, especially with Lord Melbourne, and her literary and reforming activities. But contemporary newspapers cite many abuses of the same kind. Mrs Glover, the famous actress, stood up on stage to feed her children; her husband appropriated her salary despite the theatre manager's resistance. Fortune-hunters made off with their wives' dowries, leaving them penniless. One of them left his wife's fortune to his illegitimate children.[22]

While the law exposed well-to-do wives, or those with a professional activity, to various wrongs,[23] J. W. Kaye and the authors of the 1856 Petition, drawn up by Barbara Bodichon, which asked the legislators to protect the assets of married women, emphasized that the working-class wife was even more of a victim. On the one hand female labour (seamstresses, dressmakers, washerwomen, housemaids) was then more widespread in that class; on the other, wrote J. W. Kaye, wives were not protected by '... the forethought of their relatives, the social training of their husbands, and the refined customs of the rank to which they belong ... In such a condition of life the man has more temptation to lay a violent hand on the earnings of the woman ...'[24]

Equally, poor women were deprived of the rare safeguard, that well-to-do families could provide, either in the shape of a marriage settlement (an agreement between the husband and the wife's family concerning a sum for the exclusive use of the wife) or of a certain control by the wife over lands belonging to her. The husband could draw on the revenue but had no right to sell without her agreement.[25]

The first feminists concentrated their offensive on the legal status of the wife. This was especially so with Barbara Bodichon, who saw woman's claim for financial independence, whether she was married or not, as inseparable from the demand for education, professional training, and access to various trades.[26] The Married Women's Property Bill, put before the Commons in May 1857, was rejected on the third reading; for members' opinion had not evolved sufficiently to see the principle of the economic unity of man and woman abandoned, to question male supremacy within the couple, and thus the foundations of the patriarchal conception of the family.

But protest and agitation had some appreciable successes to show, notably with some of the clauses in the 1857 Matrimonial Causes Bill. The new Bill, which entirely modified divorce procedure, stipulated that a legally separated woman would be considered a 'feme sole' in regard to assets acquired by inheritance, by gift or in remuneration for work. A woman deserted by her husband could also ask for protection of her assets through a magistrate.[27] *The English Woman's Journal*[28] noted that this clause in the 1857 Bill was an essential step towards recognition of the wife's role as bread-winner. Nevertheless, as the same journal emphatically stated, the new law '... makes provision for no case where desertion has not taken place, thus leaving unprotected a large class of sufferers who are subjected to the daily loss of their property or earnings by the presence of a dissolute or unprincipled husband.'[29]

The 1857 Bill didn't, therefore, go so far as the scheme of Lord Brougham and Erskine Perry which sought to guarantee every woman the right to what she owned.[30] It was necessary to wait until 1870 for the promulgation (thanks to the activities of the Married Woman's Property Committee founded after two aborted Bills in 1868), of a Married Woman's Property Act which guaranteed the wife personal enjoyment of her earnings, investments, inheritance, rents, revenues and any money gifts over two hundred pounds.

In 1837 the husband, since he was in complete control of his wife's assets and person, also enjoyed unlimited rights over the children. Here too the law did not recognize the mother. It stipulated that children owed obedience only to their father. 'During the father's life, the mother, as such, is entitled to no power ... but only to respect,'[31] which was a succinct indication of the real meaning of the 'female influence' so widely exalted at the time. The father could sequestrate the children, punish them, take them away from their mother, entrust them to a third person of his choice, including his mistress, and refuse their mother the right of visit. Before 1839 the law did not guarantee a separated mother's rights over her children.[32] Caroline Norton devoted all her energy to changing this law that had deprived her of her own children, and published three articles on the question.[33] She demanded that in the event of separation children of less than seven years be automatically entrusted to their mother, and that for children older than seven the right to visit be regulated by a court decision, and not left to the discretion of the father. The new law of 1839 meant a step forward, but it merely allowed the mother to *solicit* from the court the custody of children under seven, and the right to visit older ones. It was still very little. The right of custody reverted *a priori* to the father.[34]

Even this reform, timid as it was, met with opposition. Its adversaries demanded that a woman must provide proof (*sic*) of her innocence in order to obtain the right of petition. As J. G. Perkins observed, no one seemed to take exception to the father tearing away his children from a virtuous mother and entrusting them to his mistress.[35] Here too, progress was unbelievably slow. As a result of a law passed in 1873, the court *could* entrust the mother with the custody of children up to sixteen. In 1878 the custody of children under ten only fell to the mother in the event of 'aggravated assault' by the father.[36]

Even though it failed essentially to alter the position of the wife, the Matrimonial Causes Act, as it applied to divorce and separation, was the outstanding event in the century. Prior to 1857 the wife could only present a petition for separation where there had been adultery and cruelty to her person, a matter of varying definition during the nineteenth century. In 1811, it referred only to 'actual terror and violence'.[37] The innumerable testimonies and protests against the widespread practice of wife-beating, cruelty and murder point to a plague hardly tackled by the magistrates.

From 1850 onwards John Stuart Mill pointed to the cruelties working-class women suffered from brutal husbands, emphasizing their need of special protection, such as the right of separation from a husband guilty of cruelty and the termination of any obligations on the wife's part.[38] But only in 1878, after an article by F. P. Cobbe,[39] did the law change along these lines.[40]

Theoretically both husband and wife could bring an action for separation or divorce because of the spouse's adultery. But this was 'tedious, costly ... revolting'.[41] Indeed, separation 'a mensa et thoro', granted exclusively by ecclesiastical courts before 1857, did not permit remarriage. True divorce 'a vinculo matrimonii' could only be brought about by a Private Act of Parliament using standardized procedure and standing orders from the House of Lords, which declared not the wife but the marriage non-existent. This procedure, which could cost up to £800 or £900, was obviously available only to the very rich.[42] The husband who sought a divorce by this means had to begin by taking proceedings against the man whom he accused of 'criminal conversation' with his wife, in order to obtain damages and benefits as compensation for wrongs suffered. Theoretically, an Act of Parliament dissolving the marriage could be promulgated at the request of one or other partner, in fact it was hardly ever at the woman's behest.[43] Out of 200 divorces adjudged before 1857, roughly 6 were at the request of the wife.[44]

The 1857 Law made provision for new courts intended to replace the Ecclesiastical Courts in the realm of divorce and empowered to grant both judicial separation (which replaced divorce 'a mensa et thoro' through the Eccesiastical Courts) and the decree of divorce 'a vinculo matrimonii'.[45] It was a procedural reform that worked in favour of married women, greeted by all who had protested against the old system which was doubly inaccessible to poor women.[46] Under the new regulations the legal expenses had to be much lower and within reach, since as a *principle* the court could sit outside London. There were persisting doubts, however, about the fairness of the procedure. These were expressed by J. W. Kaye in 1857, and they were confirmed by the findings of a court of inquiry in 1909. Two systems continued to exist in practice: one for people rich enough to initiate divorce proceedings in London, the other for the less privileged.[47]

The suppression of actions for 'criminal conversation' brought by the husband in order to obtain damages and benefits from the presumed lover of his wife was very important for the cause. This procedure, called by Lord Lyndhurst a 'scandal to a civilized country, and which excites the horror and disgust of other countries',[48] and by Lord St Leonard 'a disgrace to the country'[49] revealed in the cruellest way possible the law's non-recognition of the woman. Indeed, in such actions, where her honour, reputation and future were at stake, a woman had neither the right to defend herself nor to summon witnesses in her defence. She was the most important person involved, but she did not exist. Since what was at stake in the proceedings was compensation for the wrong suffered by the husband in respect of what belonged to him, it was in the interest of the other party to prove that this asset had no value. And while the law considered infidelity by a wife to be an attack on the rights of the husband, a loss susceptible to financial compensation, this revolting equation did not exist in the case of a similar wrong suffered by a wife. The husband's privilege indirectly confirmed one of the fundamentals of the double standard which prevailed in the Middle Ages, and in patriarchal societies generally: the man's right, as husband or father, to ownership of the person, in particular the virginity, of the woman.[50] The 1857 Act wiped out the worst effects of such legal actions.[51]

In terms of the 1857 Act, the grounds for divorce remained cruelty and adultery, to which, later, was added unmotivated desertion for two years or more. We have already seen that separation at the woman's behest as a result of her husband's cruelty was practically a dead letter before 1857 because of the courts' vague interpretation and above all because the poorer classes, where physical cruelty on the part of the husband was most frequent, had no real access to divorce. Thus poor women were doubly powerless.

As for suing for divorce on account of adultery, the new law stipulated that the man could ask for a divorce because of his wife's adultery, but the wife had to prove adultery aggravated by desertion, cruelty, rape, buggery or bestiality![52] This double standard remained until 1929, when the grounds for divorce became the same for both partners. A study of the comments of legislators and individual reactions to the discrimination that ratified the same inequality as the Contagious Diseases Act shows that public opinion was generally in favour of differential treatment, and supported a philosophy and practice that had been in force in Europe, since the Middle Ages, and in the majority of other societies, whether Hindu, Muslim or Jewish.[53] Certainly, in 1857, in a Christian society undergoing a new wave of puritanism, it was very widely believed that divine retribution would come down equally on adulterers of both sexes and that morally, in the words of Caroline Norton, 'the sin of adultery is the same in man and woman'.[54] But the law itself had to underline that the woman's sin was socially infinitely more serious.[55] Like the members of the court of inquiry of 1850, J. W. Kaye leaned on the authority of Dr Johnson to insist on the very different consequences of the man's sin and the woman's. Though a champion of female education and of making divorce procedures more democratic, Kaye developed an odd theory of the sexual inequality of men and women.

... equality there is, and can be, none, so long as the infidelity of the wife inflicts upon the husband so much larger an amount of suffering than, in ordinary cases, the infidelity of the husband inflicts upon the wife.[56]

Whatever the complexity of the elements entering into the double standard, the social consequences resulting from the woman's adultery, as Lord Cranworth asserted during the debates, were the risk of 'spurious offspring',[57] who would flaw inheritance in a capitalist society based on respect for private property.

Thus, as regards custody of the children, the grounds and initiative for separation, and mutual property, even after 1857, male supremacy within the couple remained overwhelming. The Act's one improvement worthy of note concerning the rights of the wife was the protection of her earnings in the event of separation. Only after 1870 did the law little by little establish some equality for the partners concerning assets, rights over children, and the grounds for divorce.

[3]

Daily Life

ARISTOCRATIC AND MIDDLE-CLASS WOMEN

Public opinion placed the wife at the centre of 'the mighty influences that cluster around the domestic hearth',[1] made her queen of the hearth's 'circle of gold',[2] but by law she was entirely subject to the head of the family in that 'domestic sphere' to which she had been relegated. In 1857 society finally admitted, *in the event of separation*, the injustice that a separated or divorced woman should not be able to earn her living, but until quite recently a married woman was deprived of any rights over her assets, her money and her children.

How then did married women in the Victorian era actually live out their glorified and dependent condition, and fulfil the triple role which, in the eyes of their contemporaries, was the essence of their deepest nature and dignity: husband's helpmate and inspirer, soul of the home, and mother of a family.

The importance of money in any decision to contract or postpone a marriage hardly needs stating. Although marriages of convenience, arranged by parents, were previously more common,[3] economic considerations, accentuated by status-seeking, continued to dominate. This aspect was often emphasized in satirical literature and caricatures of the marriage-market.[4] 'Prudent marriages' and 'a proper time to marry' were key-notes of the age. Contemporary pamphlets[5] exhorted young people not to allow tender feelings to gain the upper hand over more down-to-earth considerations. One issue of the *Ladies' Companion at Home and Abroad* paints a horrible picture of the fate in store for couples embarking on 'imprudent marriages': '... let the young and romantic ponder on these things, and take warning ere they rush upon a fate from which there is no retreating.'[6] In 1858 there was a fascinating correspondence in *The Times* about the budgetary needs of married couples and whether one could reasonably live off an income of three hundred pounds a year.[7]

One solution was to put off marriage until the couple could stand the costs of respectability. To counter this obsession with social position, some, like William Acton and a group of 'clergymen and gentlemen' in *The Times*,[8] besought young couples to do without 'a Belgravia house ... a footman ... and a brougham'.[9] Elizabeth Barrett Browning could not find words harsh enough to condemn marriages of convenience, which she considered '*legal* prostitution'.[10] When, following in her footsteps, her younger sister came up against paternal opposition to her marriage to Surtees, she encouraged her not to agree to this 'long dreary waiting', and to refuse to sacrifice their mutual affection for material considerations.[11] 'What is called an "improvident marriage" often appears to me a noble, righteous, and prudent act',[12] she wrote. But those who, like Emily Winkworth, William Shaen and Elizabeth Barrett herself, opted for the romantic solution at a sacrifice to their standard of living, were rare. Families exerted all kinds of pressures on the romantic individualism of the young. In 1864 Lord Amberley was still speaking of being 'crushed by the great monster "conventionality"', when his mother admonished him to be 'prudent' and, given his youth, not 'to get involved' in a precocious marriage with Kate Stanley.[13]

What was the relationship between wife and husband in marriages most often governed by financial considerations? Personal testimony in the form of correspondence reveals the whole gamut, from harmony to its opposite. There can be no doubt that Queen Victoria and Prince Albert were at one extreme. However, while Albert was getting used to his role of Prince Consort and Victoria to hers as a wife who must share responsibilities with, if not cede them to her husband, frictions occurred that were perhaps glossed over by biographers.[14]

The impression of rare marital happiness, of complete fulfilment and exceptional mutual understanding, comes over more strikingly in the letters of Elizabeth Barrett Browning. In the fourth month of their marriage she observes with some astonishment that no shadow has yet fallen between them, despite a 'perpetual *tête-à-tête*'[15] that could often be a trial. Loves like that are rare at any time. Both queen and poetess were intensely conscious of their exceptional privilege. '... All marriage is such a lottery – the happiness is always an exchange – though it may be a very happy one – still the poor woman is morally and bodily the husband's slave ...'[16] Victoria wrote to her elder daughter. The Queen's reservations particularly concerned maternity, but the use of the word 'lottery', like her remark about the frequency of unhappy marriages,[17] bears witness to a more general scepticism. As for Elizabeth Barrett Browning, the wonderment she felt at her marital happiness was enhanced by her doubts concerning the majority of marriages. '... When I look at the histories of my own female friends – ... to see the marriages which are made every day! Worse than solitude and more desolate!'[18] she wrote to Robert the year before their wedding. Two years of marriage only strengthened her conviction that theirs was an exceptional case: 'women generally *lose* by marriage, but I have gained the world by mine.'[19]

Attested cases of total disharmony or persecution are rare. The misfortunes of Caroline Norton or Lady Lytton received publicity which was generally provoked by the vicissitudes of separation. But the echo of complaints by Henrietta, Lady Stanley, neglected wife, mother of Kate Amberley, grandmother of Bertrand Russell, only sounded in her letters to her husband. Edward Stanley, whose own mother recognized his aversion to family life,[20] tended to relegate his wife to the country, while he led the gay life, hunting and carousing in London or in his friends' mansions. His dry, indifferent letters deal with his hunting exploits and the brilliant company he honoured with his presence. It is hardly surprising that Henrietta moans and groans, throughout the letters of her exile in sumptuous and more or less well-heated residences, about her solitude in the country,[21] and the icy void of the solitary bed where she caught cold. 'I believe it is all owing to my cold bed, I really cannot keep warm alone.'[22]

Between the extremes of lasting harmony and desertion or cruelty the majority were naturally in between – the average happy or unhappy, silent wives who have left no trace. But some information on them can be gleaned from Mrs Gaskell's correspondence. Mrs Gaskell's critics and biographers have conjectured about her relationship with her husband but, as her letters to him have disappeared,[23] their answers can only be speculative. It is clear from her general correspondence that husband and wife were fairly independent. Mr Gaskell was absorbed by the multiple functions of his astonishingly full life: he was attached to a parish but often visited others, taught privately, lectured in New College and Owen's College, The Mechanics' Institute, edited the *Unitarian Herald*, and simultaneously remained a member of numerous philanthropic committees. To cope with all that he visibly sacrificed his family life, and when he happened to be at home he was reluctant to leave his office, only appearing at meal times.[24] Two months before her death, Elizabeth Gaskell had to give up a tour around Switzerland as she had no money and did not know how to contact him. Despite this independence, which sometimes visibly irritated her, there are many examples of Elizabeth Gaskell's solicitude for her husband. She was always worrying about his health and exhausted much energy upon organizing his bachelor holidays. On the whole a considerable degree of harmony was evident even if on occasion one can discern a hankering after a dominating and jealous husband,[25] or to be '... back in the darkness where obedience was the only seen duty of women ...'[26]

The couple's money problems seem to have been fairly harmoniously resolved thanks to Elizabeth's growing financial independence. Certainly, she was sometimes obliged to ask her husband for money and had to display the patience of any financial dependant. During a period of reduced literary activity (1850), she was astonished to receive £20 for *Lizzie Leigh*, which sum William '... has composedly buttoned up in his pocket. He has promised I may have some for the refuge.'[27] Subsequently she would sometimes have to wait for the right moment and mood to obtain funds for her daughter.

However, on the whole she seems to have gained a financial independence. Though obviously inexperienced in the beginning, she herself would argue with her publishers, Edward Chapman and George Smith.[28] Although William pocketed the twenty pounds for *Lizzie Leigh* in 1850 and seems also to have collected fifty pounds from Chapman in 1851,[29] Elizabeth Gaskell not only financed, out of her earnings, the holidays and journeys she and her daughters adored, but also some current expenses such as doctors' bills.[30] And it was she who negotiated and financed completely (obtaining a loan on mortgage) the purchase of their house at Alton.[31] When, in 1856, Eliza Fox asked her to sign the petition demanding that wives be guaranteed the enjoyment of their own earnings, she signed without enthusiasm, sceptical as to the effectiveness of legislation in a question that touched on an intimate relationship.[32] Another woman of letters, Mary Howitt, showed more enthusiasm for this sort of female effort.[33]

The example of Jane Welsh Carlyle and Lady Stanley illustrates the humiliation of the wife reduced to begging. It seems that Jane had the responsibility not only for managing the household, but also for all kinds of financial dealings with tradesmen and even the tax-collector. If she was away, Carlyle did not bother with these things.[34] In 1855, as in previous years, Carlyle gave his wife fifty pounds a quarter for household expenses, a sum that was supposed to cover everything: bills, insurance, taxes.[35] When she could no longer meet her expenses, knowing that Carlyle hated being asked for money, she decided to ask for an increase, by means of a humorous written request (backed up by proof of all her additional expenses) entitled 'budget of a *femme incomprise*'.[36] Amused by this Carlyle paid up and fixed the quarterly sum at £58.

Jane Carlyle was successful. But what can one say of the total and degrading financial dependence imposed by Edward Stanley on his wife deported to the country? Whether for children or household, Henrietta could incur no expenses at all without reference to her husband. She asked him, for example, to authorize the spending of six guineas to repair her daughter's saddle.[37] Whether through greed or absentmindedness, or to show her dependence on him, Edward Stanley would sometimes forget to settle what they owed the governess, the servants and even the school-fees of his son Johnny, and Henrietta had often to press him about it.[38] 'I have borrowed all the money each individual has in the house to pay Clarke ...'[39] (an old and faithful retainer), she wrote in 1848. It is not surprising that she constantly complained about monies if it is true that her fixed allowance for a household of nine children and several servants came to £100 a year (at a time – 1849 – when Jane Carlyle had more than £200 for three or four people). All the more so when, as she bitterly reminded him, he as the head of the family had an income of £3,800 a year.

These few soundings indicate that, however complex these relationships may seem, we are a long way from the idyll in which the female press and the sermons of moralists delighted. It is clear that the wife's dependence – financial as well as in other ways – in which she was supposed to find self-fulfilment often prevented it.

Her kingdom was, as we have seen, the HOME, raised to a 'delightful retreat' 'surrounded by ... hallowed influences'.[40] J. A. and Olive Banks have studied the rise in the standard of living, income and expenses in the middle classes half-way through the nineteenth century. The content of women's magazines, *The Ladies' Companion at Home and Abroad* and *The British Mothers' Magazine*, whose columns for the most part were devoted to domestic tasks (needlework, embroidery, gardening), to culture (art, languages, music) and to the mother's role as educator, also illustrates the evolution from 'the perfect wife to the perfect lady'.[41] This inflation in life-style is certified by the particularly marked increase in household expenses between 1850 and 1870, an increase that was not due to rising prices[42] but to the expansion of domestic service, the development of expensive leisure pursuits (social events, entertainment, travel) and to the education of children.[43]

Mrs Beeton's *Book of Household Management*[44] speaks of the wife as commander of an army of servants. The army's size varied considerably according to the circle and income of the family.[45] Lady Frederick Cavendish could be quite pleased with hers. When she went to Hardwick Hall after her marriage, she wrote: 'Fred and I came here alone [*sic*], under the ducal circumstances of a special train, 22 servants ...'[46] The following year she mentions 'all the servants' attending prayers for whom she reserved pews in St Martin's Church and she congratulates herself on having persuaded some of them to renounce 'crinoline during their work'.[47] Lady Stanley had a large and conspicuous retinue of servants, but the number is not specified. Margaret Jeune asked that a cook and chambermaid be engaged for her during her holidays in France, but in view of the huge reception she held (100 people in 1858) the addition of a cook and chambermaid-governess for her daughters[48] seems to imply a large staff.

Henrietta Lady Stanley, Lady Frederick Cavendish and Lady Jeune were members of a moneyed aristocracy. The importance of domestic staff in the more modest circles of the Manchester Unitarians, those of Mrs Gaskell, is more surprising. In 1860 Mrs Gaskell was in correspondence with a Mrs Fielden concerning a cook and she declares that she will allow her to go to church: '... all our servants go there ...' Indeed a little later on she describes the family: '... Mr Gaskell, myself, and four daughters, not always at home, cook, housemaid, waiters, nurse and sempstress.'[49] In the annals of Victorian servants, Jane Carlyle's misfortunes with her twenty-four servants, who succeeded each other regularly in Cheyne Walk over a period of thirty-two years,[50] are well known. Apart from a few exceptional periods when, for reasons of health or because of the age of the servant, she engaged a second one,[51] Jane was generally satisfied with one servant who, given the dimensions and discomforts of the house (three floors and a kitchen in the basement) and the demands of her employers, seems not to have been underworked.[52] The niggling side of Jane Carlyle was well known to her friends; Robert Browning had the occasion to come up against it.[53]

Small or large, there always was a staff. However, domestic duties remained for a wife. In Mary Howitt's life, fitting up different homes played an important part and took up precious time. 'When we first came here', she wrote on 9 February 1837, 'establishing us and helping to do the upholstery work quite filled up my time'. Made late by these tasks, she had to immerse herself in her sewing: '... from morning till night, and never reading a word of any book. I never led so unintellectual a life.'[54]

Elizabeth Gaskell was also absorbed with the furnishing of her successive residences, with needlework and gardening. In 1850 she had to refuse an invitation from Eliza Fox: she was organizing things at her new house in Plymouth Grove. Although she was amply supported by a gardener and a needlewoman, the countless anxieties of a mother of four children (clothes, illnesses, correspondence)[55] sometimes seemed to overwhelm her days and years. 'I go on much as usual; swallowed up by small household cares...'[56]

Jane Carlyle's range of household tasks was wider still. She seems to have put all her strength into them, as well as all the emotional potentialities that she could not devote to her children or to professional activity. Her letters are full of her burdens. Needlework, buttons to sew on to Carlyle's jackets, the laborious making up of a black silk morning-coat, and a scrap screen of which she felt very proud.[57] But the best part of her time was spent engaging, supervising, organizing and dismissing servants, settling bills and inspecting the numerous household fittings intended to protect Carlyle from noise. In a letter written after Jane's death, Carlyle sadly drew up a balance-sheet of his wife's skills as 'commandress ... and manager.'[58] On several occasions we do indeed see Jane supervising workmen, moving out furniture, doing tapestry, covering armchairs and divans, sewing curtains. Her domestic activities belonged to her role as 'helpmate' to a neurotic, tyrannical, inspired husband, whom she served as secretary, housekeeper, bailiff and factotum. She sometimes complained:

... For Mr C, being a man, cannot understand to exact the least bit less attendance, when we are reduced to one servant again ... So I have all the valeting, and needle-womaning, and running up and down to the study for books ... besides having to superintend the Welsh girl.[59]

What a pleasure it is when one is away from home and has no servants to manage, and no food to provide. Mr C. gets more and more difficult to feed, and more and more impatient of the imperfections of human cooks and human housewives. I sometimes feel as if I should like to run away. But the question always arises, where to?[60]

Then there were the sexual and emotional frustrations of her marital life. Her dissatisfaction, in a woman endowed with such intelligence and vitality, was emphasized by the emptiness of her existence – with no children into the bargain. It was evident not only in her frantic and often unnecessary state of excitement, but also in the countless psychosomatic symptoms that poisoned her life: acute stomach trouble, repeated influenza, atrocious migraines, neuralgia, and even very marked depression.[61] 'Blue pills', castor-oil and heavy doses of morphine were very little use in alleviating a life-weariness that Geraldine Jewsbury had already diagnosed as unemployed energy. She advised Jane to throw herself into her work and not allow herself to be influenced by her husband.[62] Her vehement declarations of independence were not to the taste of Carlyle, who in 1846 violently denounced both 'George-Sandism' and Geraldine Jewsbury's influence on his wife.[63]

What about the role of Mother? The moralists invested that revered figure with an unlimited influence over the younger generations. In the female press, in particular the *British Mothers' Magazine*, the religious aspect of the educator's function played a leading part. The objectives of the Maternal Societies were 'to unite godly and praying mothers', 'to awaken the careless to a sense of their duties and position as mothers of immortal souls'.[64] Titles of articles in the *British Mothers' Magazine* between 1845 and 1849 reveal the obsessive concern with religion.[65] Around 1850, the magazine seems to have evolved a little towards wider cultural preoccupations and one finds more articles on education, reading, the organization of a household budget, and how to behave towards governesses.

Understanding of children and maternal love were natural to Elizabeth Gaskell and Elizabeth Barrett Browning. Elizabeth Browning's wonderment at the gestures and utterances of her only son fill whole pages of her letters. Elizabeth Gaskell had four daughters and was constantly harassed by the usual round of family problems: medical, educational, clothing amongst other things. Her attitude towards her daughters was both lucid and kind. Sometimes she drew portraits of them for Eliza Fox which had the ring of truth: the eldest, Marianne, 'a law unto herself', displays a precocious sense of family duty and a disquieting passivity in other realms. Meta, who is endowed with a richer inner life, wastes time, reads and draws.[66]

But Elizabeth Gaskell, Mary Howitt, and Elizabeth Barrett Browning were not mothers of large families. J. A. Banks places the average number of children per couple around 1860 between five and six.[67] Kate Dickens, for her part, had ten children in fifteen years, not to mention the premature births, whose number is difficult to assess. The fact remains that between the date of her marriage, 2 April 1836, and 1852, the year of Edward's birth, Kate was constantly pregnant; her first son Charles was born on 6 January 1837. She miscarried in June the same year.[68] A gap of less than two years between the birth of Sidney, their seventh son, on 18 April 1847 and Henry, the eighth, on 15 January 1849, seems, according to Dickens's letters, to tally with one or two miscarriages.[69] Dickens frequently mentions her indispositions, sometimes with impatience.[70] Kate suffered constantly, was overweight when young,[71] and had a rather apathetic temperament, so it is not surprising that she was completely taken up with child-bearing, left the education of her children more to her sister Georgina Hogarth, and became less interested in the social, worldly and intellectual preoccupations of Charles Dickens.[72]

Henrietta Lady Stanley was even freer from material cares than Kate Dickens, since she could raise her children on the family's lands and in the family's mansions, with the ample support of an enormous staff of servants, housekeepers, tutors. Nonetheless, she was overwhelmed and exasperated by the difficulties of bringing up her brood of nine children born between 1827 and 1844. On the birth of the eighth, her mother-in-law wrote, not without humour:

> I think Henrietta expects she has a patent for producing children without trouble or delay ... now she has four couple, a very pretty collection ... I wish she would be content, especially as she has had as many as anybody in the family now, for I know she does not like to be outdone ...[73]

Lady Stanley's letters to her husband are filled with complaints: the difficulty of finding competent housekeepers, complaints about the illnesses and caprices of the whole household: '... Johnny's knee is swelled and stiff, Blanche of course is suffering very much, Lyulph has got a boil on his leg ... Alice's cold is worse.' The same month, December 1846, she wrote that she and 'half a dozen children' had colds, and demanded a small stove.[74] The worries, bitterness and

5. 'The Happy Family. "A Quiet Hint to the Wives of England".' Caricature by George Cruikshank from *The Comic Almanack*

frustration were aggravated by her awareness that the sacrifices she made for her children were partly or totally caused by her husband's absence. She envied the freedom of Lady Ashburton.

Although Lady Stanley felt that her family responsibilities and worries enslaved and alienated her, she seemed undisturbed by her pregnancies. It is Queen Victoria who provides a realistic and fierce critique of the calvary of pregnancy, from which, by her own admission, she suffered less than the average woman.[75] Between 1840 and 1857 the Queen brought nine children into the world. 'What made me so miserable was – to have the two first years of my married life utterly spoilt by this occupation! I could enjoy nothing – not travel about or go about with dear papa ...'[76] she wrote to her eldest daughter, Vicky, who was married on 25 January 1858. She urged her daughter, without success, to space out the births before losing her freedom for ever in the process of procreation and education of numerous children. She recalled with horror those '9 times 8 months' of 'real misery',[77] the many physical hardships that obliged her to forgo the pleasures of existence,[78] and to live a dull and diminished life.[79] She hated the condition that reduced her to a heavy, suffering body. Joy at the awakening of a new life and all feeling of creative and triumphant motherhood seem to have been foreign to the Queen. She wrote prosaically to her daughter:

What you say of the pride of giving life to an immortal soul is very fine ... but I own I cannot enter into that; I think much more of our being like a cow or a dog at such moments; when our poor nature becomes so very animal and unecstatic ...[80]

Exasperated by the discomforts of pregnancy, the Queen also feared the pains of childbirth, and was amazed by the effects of chloroform with which she became acquainted at the birth of Leopold on 7 April 1853.[81] What she modestly called the 'Schattenseite' or 'the dark side' of married life must also have included physical relations and everything that, according to her, constituted an outrage to feminine refinement. The violence that nature and men inflicted on 'the modesty of a young girl'[82] was one of the themes of her letters to her daughter. It is not surprising to find that the Queen declared she was absolutely opposed to large families. In January 1841, when she only had one child, she wrote:

I think, dearest Uncle, you cannot *really* wish me to be the '*Mamma d'une nombreuse famille*', ... men never think ... what a hard task it is for us women to go through this *very often*. God's will be done, and if He decrees that we are to have a great number of children, why we must try to bring them up ...[83]

Later, her personal experience only confirmed her horror of breeding like rabbits. In 1859, two years after the birth of Beatrice, her last child, this woman, who over a period of seventeen years had given birth to so many children, wrote: 'I positively think those ladies who are always enceinte quite disgusting.' Similarly, writing about a 'Lady Kildare who (had) two a year, one in January and one in December', she enlarged on the damage to the mother as well as to the child wrought by births so crowded together.[84] Lady Stanley did not enter into any details but when she met the possible fiancée of her eldest son Henry, she stated with satisfaction: 'She is older than I thought, one comfort is she could have fewer children.'[85]

Thus there was a highly critical attitude towards large families on the part of many women, whether or not they themselves had many children. Elizabeth Browning took pity on a certain Maria who had just delivered her sixth child. 'Poor children, poor mother.'[86] And she tried to persuade her sister, who had just miscarried, to be content with her two children, and proclaimed that she was delighted to be the mother of a single Penini.[87]

The trend against large families in aristocratic and middle-class circles was significant in many different ways. There was a steep decline in the birth-rate in the nineteenth century. The average number of children per family dropped from 5 or 6 in the middle of the Victorian era to 2.2 in 1925–9. As J. A. Banks suggests, this decline, which started in the 1860s in well-off circles,[88] was connected with an increasingly ambitious style of life, impossible to reconcile with large families. The point is borne out by the difference, until then negligible, between the number of children in middle-class and working-class families, which became more marked between 1881 and 1886.[89]

While between 1840 and 1860 the birth-rate began to decline, and social pressures encouraged smaller families, there was no question yet of proper birth-control.[90] The solution seems to have been postponement of marriage. There had been clandestine propaganda for contraception by Francis Place[91] and Richard Carlile[92] between 1820 and 1826. But until 1868 it was not widely disseminated; only a few works on contraception were published between 1835 and 1868.[93] Then the propaganda picked up again in the early 60s among a small circle of the Malthusian League, with Charles Bradlaugh and George Drysdale in the lead. The principal steps in the resumption of contraceptive agitation were, first, the Amberley affair in 1868 which provoked fury in medical circles and cost Lord Amberley his South Devon parliamentary seat,[94] and then, in 1877, the Bradlaugh-Besant trial.[95]

The feminists, not only during their pioneering days (infiltration into higher education and the professions, and struggle for the vote), but even after 1870, were opposed to any voluntary restriction on births. All their efforts concentrated on the plight of the single woman, whether unmarried, divorced or widowed, rather than on the position of the wife.[96] It remains true, however, that on an individual level, the reactions quoted earlier formed part of a revolt against the definition of the mother as, primarily, a reproducing animal (Victoria's images are significant: cow, dog, rabbit, guinea-pig). They belong to an essential aspect of female emancipation, particularly in well-to-do circles where the economic argument in favour of limiting the size of families was not all-important.

Weariness, revolt and disgust at the accelerated rhythm of pregnancies, and the physical and intellectual diminution resulting from it were necessary but not sufficient conditions for an initiative to limit births.[97]

A glance at the medical press shows that the most primitive form of birth-control, abortion, was widely practised from the 1860s.[98] One can learn from the published correspondence of Lady Stanley that this mother of nine children (who underwent eleven pregnancies), the last born in 1844, provoked a miscarriage in 1847 on her own initiative, and with the approval of her husband.[99] Although the technique might give rise to some scepticism (a very hot bath, a powerful purgative, a very long walk), not only did it succeed, but this reassured Henrietta 'for the future by the efficacy of the means'.[100] In 1849, however, Lady Stanley gave birth to a child who died soon after. Remorse grew out of the grief for the dead child, in all likelihood punishing an outcome that had given effect to the simply expressed desire not to have any more children. These reactions were surprising after the 1847 incident. However, there is no question that she saw the death of the last born as 'punishment for having said I did not wish for a child'.[101]

Such examples of life in well-to-do-circles before 1860 provide a considerable corrective to the exalted vision of the wife-mother. They echo Taine's fear of family tribes and the father's role, which were also humorously evoked in *Punch* illustrations:

... 6, 8 or 10 children, who sometimes come in annual succession; he is fifty years, his head is getting bald, his proportions are becoming aldermanic, and his youngest has just been weaned.[102]

The duties of a wife in such a family did not end with the home. They ranged from the social events required by her position in society, to the cultural display necessary to demonstrate the status of the family, involving anything from amateur philanthropy to paid literary work.

Meetings, dinners, receptions and visits kept the aristocracy busy. Lady Jeune in Oxford seems to have been caught up in a whirlwind of aristocratic-university social events. She mentions a dinner at New College on 17 November 1858, a dinner at Blenheim Palace, several receptions and ceremonies in honour of the Prince of Wales in 1859, the Oxford fêtes and Commemoration balls.[103] Certain manifestations had a cultural character, like a reading by Dickens, and the 'Museum Soirées' in 1860 that were devoted to remarkable people. The variety and richness of her society life are shown by the 100 guests invited to her 'at home': 'not so many as on a former occasion.'[104] In February 1865 in London, Lady Frederick Cavendish appeared at a ball given by the Prince of Wales, 'with all the diamonds on my head'. In May of the same year she was present at a 'drawing-room' of the Queen '... in gorgeous array of white lace ... and white moiré train, with my beautiful diamond tiara'.[105]

In a completely different setting, Elizabeth Gaskell as citizen of Manchester, writer, and wife of the Reverend Gaskell, was intensely involved in the cultural and social life of this important provincial centre. Her friends in Manchester included the Kay-Shuttleworths, the Shaens, and Charles Hallé. She also received illustrious visitors: Charles Dickens, the Carlyles, Mark Lemon, R. Monkton-Milnes, Charlotte Brontë, and Harriet Beecher-Stowe. She dined with Darwin and the poet A. H. Clough in 1851. In her turn, she travelled abroad (Cologne, Heidelberg, Paris and Rome), which enlarged further the circle of her acquaintances. Her cultural activities were varied: 1857 Exhibition, concerts conducted by Hallé, lectures by Thackeray.[106]

Perhaps the only common denominator in the existence of these women and of women in general in this age of philanthropy, was the practice of charity. The charitable tradition in spheres as diverse as workhouses, schools, and reformatories, gave a certain notoriety to Mary Carpenter, Louisa Twining, Frances Cobb and Octavia Hill.[107] What was done by Elizabeth Gaskell partly as wife of a Unitarian minister, partly from personal interest, was astonishingly varied, and provided material for some of her novels. She concerned herself with a sixteen-year-old girl who 'had led the most miserable life' and whom she enabled to emigrate, with the help of Dickens and Miss Burdett-Coutts.[108] She belonged to a mutual aid establishment of 'Invalid Gentlewomen' where she got to know Florence Nightingale. The latter interested her in the 'Soldier's Home'[109] in Gibraltar. She embroiled herself in the fate of seamstresses and factory workers.[110] She also taught, and a list of all the works she took part in would be very long. Whatever reserves one may have about the portrayal of working life in *Mary Barton*, there can be no denying that, for her sex and her epoch, she had an exceptional knowledge of the way workers lived. On the other hand, the first accounts by Mary Howitt, the Quaker woman of letters, of her 'works' displayed astonishing naïvety, which doubtless was more typical. Her visits to the poor on behalf of the 'Nottingham Provident Society' were a revelation for her.

... one looks on them as a flock of sheep. All seem alike. All have many children, little leisure, poor clothes, and all are more or less dirty. But one does not sit with them many five or ten minutes once a week without soon detecting very marked and curious varieties.[111]

From philanthropy to politics is a short step and Mary Howitt was a militant member of an anti-slavery committee in 1852–3, and in favour of the Married Women's Property Bill in 1856.

Between her receptions and balls, Lady Frederick Cavendish dashed from one charitable work to another: she attended the inauguration of a diocesan charitable committee, a meeting of a society of mothers, took food-baskets to the hospital, visited a workhouse with Gladstone where the rather repugnant sight of the 'poor old goodies' destroyed for ever in her any romantic illusion about such objects of charity. She also taught at Sunday school, and read to female prisoners.[112] Mrs Gladstone's life followed a similar pattern: mother of seven, she still managed a wide social life, listened to debates in the House of Commons for four or five hours on end, and in the mornings visited workhouses or hospitals in the East End.[113]

We shall see presently how 'good works' – which were the private activity of the weaker sex in the privileged castes, and supposedly manifested the specifically female virtues of charity and sacrifice – were the starting-point for certain professional activities, whether paid or not. Sarah Austin's experiences in Malta, as early as 1837–9, illustrate this development.[114] Her husband, a well-known jurist, went to Malta in 1836 as a member of a commission instructed to 'enquire into the nature ... of the grievances ... of the natives'. She considered it her duty to devote herself to their welfare, and at the beginning of her stay undertook charity sales of locally produced handicraft, school-inspections, and visits to native families. Eventually, her charitable activities turned into an organized offensive against illiteracy that was both effective and scientific – she made use of statistics on the extent of literacy and emigration among the Maltese. Two years later she stated that 'my schools ... are flourishing, about 1,000 boys and 500 girls are being taught, where before our arrival there was not one.'[115] As her correspondence and contacts with Gladstone in February, May and June 1839 prove, she was, in her own words, 'regarded as quite an

authority about public instruction'.[116] For this intelligent and cultivated woman philanthropy led to a genuine role of technical adviser
though it was of course unpaid.

As the century advanced, so did female education, especially in
the aristocracy, and social problems changed, good works became
more technical or militant and less bound up with the more traditional female occupations. The change can be seen in the mode of
life of three generations of women of the landed aristocracy, Lady
Stanley, the mother of Edward; Henrietta Stanley, her daughter-
in-law; and Kate Stanley, daughter of Henrietta and Edward
Stanley. In 1848 Lady Stanley campaigned among her poor tenants
in favour of smallpox vaccinations for children.[117] Around the same
time Lady Henrietta dispersed clothing to the poor, distributed
'emigration circulars and ventilation tracts',[118] and obtained relief
from the emptiness and frustration of her marital and family life
through her success in sending twelve children to school. Above all,
she campaigned for 'the amelioration of the working classes'.[119]
This was the germ of the preoccupations that were to make of this
woman in 1869, after the death of her husband – whose total slave
she had been – 'a pioneer of women's education' and one of the
founders of Queen's School and Girton College.[120] Reading her
moans about her children's illnesses and her husband's indifference,
one would not expect to see her in the belated role of feminist and
free-thinker – she forbad the building of a chapel at Girton College
during her lifetime.

In the next generation, her daughter Kate Amberley, who was
better read, freer in her movements, and more politically conscious,
continued the family tradition. In 1865 she gave courses for working
girls, in hygiene and the domestic arts: the benefits of fresh air, the
damage wrought by too tight lacing, and the power of 'soap and
water'.[121] One significant symptom of progress even in male attitudes: her husband gave similar courses to young men.[122] The
exchanges of ideas between these two, who were obviously far
more progressive than the average couple, not only included training
courses for adults, philosophical and political discussions with John
Stuart Mill and Harriet Taylor, but also went so far as to involve the
details of childbirth. Lord Amberley could describe the difficulties
of breast-feeding and the taste and appearance of the mother's
milk.[123]

In the same year, 1865, Lady Frederick Cavendish joined in her
husband's political activities. Receptions, balls and good works did

not prevent her from visiting the House of Commons. In 1866 she was very struck by Mill's speech in favour of the Franchise Bill. The woman who, in April 1865, regretfully admitted her interest in politics, one which she hoped would not make her '*necessarily* an odious woman!',[124] was capable of interpreting her philanthropic activity in a political way after hearing Mill:

... coming straight out of one of the depths of misery and pauperism, to hear the claims of the people so grandly brought forward: those 'dumb thousands' ... and voiceless in the nation whom they might help to rise to the most noble of battles.[125]

It is also worth considering what was being read within a single family, from one generation to the next, to see how the standard of instruction and the relations of the couple developed. In 1841 the grandmother, Lady Stanley, mentioned Dickens's serial, *Master Humphrey's Clock*, and, with a delicious sense of guilt a few French novels that she was reading. She asked her daughter-in-law to suggest to her titles of '... *proper* French books ... but no Reine Margot please.'[126] But Kate and her husband read together various magazines such as *Fraser's*, the work of John Stuart Mill and *Wilhelm Meister* in German.[127] Lord and Lady Frederick Cavendish spent hours on their estates studiously reading *On Liberty*, Carlyle, The Iliad (in translation), and sermons. Between reading two novels, *The Vicar of Wakefield* and *Martin Chuzzlewit*, Lady Frederick Cavendish studied art books and a 'course of English history'.[128]

Thus the wife's sphere gradually extended socially and culturally: many engaged in paid work, generally of a literary nature, for the simple reason that it did not tear the wife away from her husband and was, to a certain extent, compatible with a role of wife and mother.

Elizabeth Rigby was already active as a woman of letters before her late marriage (in 1849 at the age of forty) when she became Lady Eastlake. Travel books, especially *A Residence on the Shores of the Baltic Told in Letters*, published by John Murray in 1841 and swiftly reprinted, as well as numerous articles in *The Quarterly Review* between 1842 and 1848, had already made her famous.[129] When she married the painter Charles Eastlake in 1849 (who became Director of the National Gallery) she specialized more in the history of art, published a fierce criticism of Ruskin's *Modern Painters* in *The Quarterly Review*, edited and finished a work by

Mrs Jameson, *History of Our Lord in Art* in 1860, and wrote a biography of the sculptor, Gibson.[130]

Sarah Austin was known above all for her translations from the French and German, particularly for *The History of the Popes* by L. von Ranke in 1839; the author complimented her on her translation which gave her considerable prestige. A fourth edition of the work in 1865, supplanted another cheaper translation.[131] Her journalism was prolific: she wrote for the *Athenaeum, The British and Foreign Review* and *The Edinburgh Review*. Sarah Austin and Elizabeth Rigby never mention money. Before and after the deaths of their husbands, both were ladies of considerable affluence. They wrote out of taste, marital devotion, and a need for intellectual activity.

By contrast Elizabeth Gaskell, Mary Howitt, and Elizabeth Barrett Browning frequently refer to financial pressures which alternate or blend with their creative impulses. With Elizabeth Gaskell there was often a direct relationship between a particular financial requirement and a particular work. Thus she wrote the stories, 'Round the Sofa', in order to finance a holiday on the continent. In 1859, she prolonged a tour from Heidelberg to Dresden by writing two stories for *Household Words* and asked to be paid immediately. She was sent forty pounds.[132]

Literary work was the very foundation of Elizabeth Barrett's life, and later of the Brownings'. Before their marriage, Robert recalled his desire for a shared life of work, of mutual encouragement in their individual efforts.[133] At certain periods their labour was intense: particularly before one trip to England, in 1855, when they had 16,000 verses to finish between them! Next she put the finishing touches to *Aurora Leigh*, while Browning finished *Sordello*.[134] In 1861 she was still working steadily and prepared a literal Italian version of her 'Italian poems' for a Venetian poet who was unfamiliar with English.[135] As in any truly professional activity, work was bound up with money, which she spoke about often enough: the amount Elizabeth Gaskell received for *Mary Barton*, the respective profitability of fiction and poetry, Tennyson's income and the payment agreed for five or six lyric poems sent to America.[136] The Brownings' financial situation was far from good until the Kenyon inheritance.

Mary Howitt's literary work was intense, often under financial pressure and eclectic, which it had to be in order to make the trade a profitable activity. In collaboration with her husband she translated the novels of Frederick Bremer from the German as well as poems of Brentano and Heine.[137] In 1846 William Howitt had for a time refloated *The People's Journal* (henceforth *Howitt's Journal*) with the intention of urging the working classes to improve their lot through sobriety, education and morality.[138] Mary Howitt was closely involved in this undertaking, which proved a failure. But she had other accomplishments in the world of journalism: five articles, for example, in *The Chamber's Journal* in February 1839. In 1850 Charles Dickens asked both Howitts to contribute articles for *Household Words*; in November 1850 she wrote a ballad for the magazine and prepared others for the Christmas number of *The Illustrated News* and for *The Ladies' Companion*. The financial insecurity of this type of work, by definition irregular and subject to the whim of editors and the fluctuations of literary fashion, was particularly evident in 1848: 'Times are so bad that publishers will not speculate on books; and when I have finished the work I am now engaged on, I have nothing else certain to go on with.'[139]

Her work depended more on commercial demand than on artistic inspiration. She wrote for unexpected publications such as Bradshaw's Railway Library.[140] In 1848 she was asked to collaborate regularly on a collection of edifying pamphlets, with plots to be seasoned with religion and death-beds.[141] She was visibly overworked: '... I am so deadened and stupefied often ... I sit down after breakfast and work, work, work; then when the usual stint is done, I only want to be quiet and sleep.'[142]

The overwork of course was the result of combining the tasks of mother, wife and woman of letters, and she complained frequently of having to work in the dining-room, exposed to interruptions. 'The greatest want to me is not having a little working-room to myself ... The poor mother of a family learns to be patient.'[143]

The demand for 'a room of one's own', the symbol of women's equality for Virginia Woolf, was not expressed so clearly by Elizabeth Gaskell. While the Reverend Gaskell isolated himself in the peace of his study, his wife wrote amidst the confusion and constant excitement of a house filled with children and servants, constantly interrupted by the problems of all and sundry, the kitchen, the garden, clothes, receptions, meetings and unexpected visits. Only when she was away from home and during the rare stays with friends was she free from overwhelming family cares. She could discover the joys of regular work in silence and isolation, and the pleasure of 'not having the sick wearied feeling of being overworked'.[144] She envied Caroline Norton the peace of her library where, she wrote, she herself could 'outdo Rasselas in fiction'. The excitement, the responsibility for the well-being of six people, and above all being torn between family life and the writer's work inevitably produced tensions as shown by her rather rare complaints of fatigue, overwork and frequent headaches.[145]

Even Elizabeth Browning, working in her own room in unusual conditions of comfort, isolation and calm, with an attentive husband and one child, could not always escape the whirl. Before their journey to England in 1855, when she reckoned on presenting her publisher with 8,000 verses (*Aurora Leigh*) she too had to make numerous preparations: shoes and stockings for the trip, Penini's clothes to iron and sew, twenty letters to answer, visits into town (Florence), Penini's homework to supervise. 'My head swims and my heart ticks before the day's done, with positive weariness.'[146]

The motives behind literary activity, one of the few careers open to women, included a sense of vocation and sheer need of money. This activity became overwhelming when combined with family duties. However, can anyone conceive people of the calibre of Sarah Austin, Elizabeth Browning, Elizabeth Gaskell and Mary Howitt being wives and mothers only? For all four, writing had deep intellectual and emotional significance. Mary Howitt chafed when, swamped by vast amounts of needlework, she had no time to read. During her husband's and son's long absence in Australia, she recognized that 'we should have felt the separation appalling but for the wholesome panacea of the work'.[147] Elizabeth Browning overcame her grief at losing her brother – which was threatening her sanity – through a frenzy of work.[148] As Alethea Hayter has emphasized, with excellent quotations, the poet's creative activity was her reason for living.[149] Elizabeth Gaskell, perpetually torn by the conflict between the 'duties of the wife and the writer', recognized the priceless value of 'the hidden world of art' in a woman's life, which fortified her against the wear and tear and greyness of a thousand daily cares.[150] The case of Jane Carlyle and Henrietta Stanley gave her ample justification, as did all those who saw a wife's professional activity as a source of independence and enrichment. Nonetheless, while the entire life of Elizabeth Gaskell denied the incompatibility between the life of the artist and that of a mother of a family, she was always tormented by the contradiction between what she defined as 'home duties and the development of the individual'.[151] The same conflict between lived experience and principles tormented Queen Victoria, who declared more than once that she was convinced that a woman worthy of the name was not made for the job of monarch.[152]

It seems clear that one of the reasons for the upright Elizabeth Gaskell's[153] admiration for Charlotte Brontë was the latter's sharpened sense of family duty. When she included in her biography Charlotte's correspondence with Southey,[154] and Charlotte's letters describing the anguish she suffered when living with her father at Haworth, it was still the woman of duty she was praising to the skies; duty towards her family and not towards herself. This was the woman without other identity than that of Mother, Wife, Daughter, as extolled by the Victorian moralists. In Charlotte Brontë she found her own problem of the hierarchy of duties experienced more acutely, resolved more fanatically. Did she not always put the family first herself? She noted with approval, in a sermon of F. D. Maurice and in *Sartor Resartus*, the exhortation for a woman to fulfil her most immediate obligation, that of wife and mother. '... I am always thankful to him that I am a wife and a mother and that I am so happy in the performance of those ... defined duties.'[155] The remark recalls a passage in *The Life of Charlotte Brontë* where she affirms that no one can fulfil the duties of daughter, wife and mother as well as she whom God has placed in this role and that a woman is not in a position to choose her task on this earth.[156] The practical advice she gave in 1862 to a mother of a family tempted by the literary life left no doubt as to her theoretical position on this point: family duty comes before everything,[157] and literature is a luxury. Though she admired duty less enthusiastically than Charlotte Brontë, Elizabeth Gaskell always gave priority to duty towards human beings, 'real persons', whom she opposed to the fictional persons that totally absorb the writer during literary creation. She resolved the conflict between literary and family vocation that she found in Charlotte Brontë, as she did the class struggle, by means of a Christian formula, the parable of the Talents: like men, women are obliged to develop the gifts that can contribute to the building of the Kingdom of God. Thus more or less unconsciously she took the Christian and orthodox argument used by feminists like Anna Jameson and Barbara Bodichon to justify and encourage work for women – an argument which, given the intellectual and moral climate of the period, was tactically excellent.

This conflict of duties did not arise for Elizabeth Browning, a non-conformist in more ways than one. Her letters seem to reveal an exceptional flowering of family and artistic life simultaneously. The ethical contradictions in work for women did not exist for her. She saw the exaltation of the traditional virtues of the nurse (in the cult of Florence Nightingale, for example) as retrograde and ana-chronistic step. 'Every man is on his knees before ladies carrying lint, calling them "angelic she's".'[158] Extolling female virtues in the sister of charity surely amounted to denying women any other role. As artists, Eizabeth Browning and her mouthpiece Aurora Leigh, demanded autonomy and the individual's absolute right to self-fulfilment, whether married or not. Her exchange of letters with Thackeray about a poem she had sent to *The Cornhill Magazine* reveals what scant respect was given to a woman poet, even one as eminent as Elizabeth Browning. In order to spare the feelings of his prudish readers, Thackeray decided not to publish the poem; but his rejection was profuse with embarrassed protestations concerning the irreproachable virtue of 'one of the best wives, mothers, women ... Browning's wife and Penini's mother'. The unconscious insolence of these remarks did not escape Elizabeth Browning.[159] However great the wife's professional success and her personal independence it was not going to be easy for her to escape the designation of wife-mother.

It is not surprising that faced with the universal and limiting nature of an imposed identity, even the most advanced among women had to struggle continuously to find any other with less social dictatorship in it. But feminist protest about the position of the wife in society did not take any organized form before approxi-mately 1868. Even then it remained vague on the very points where wives suffered most: rights over possessions, earnings, children, and suing for divorce. As for the fundamental right of birth-control, it did not become a feminist objective until the end of the century.

THE WORKING CLASSES

The gap between reality and myth in the lives of middle-class wives and families was considerable, but for the working classes the gap was a gulf. There is much less information about family life in these classes.[1] Better-off wives could – relatively speaking – express themselves, but elsewhere the silence was almost total. The interviews and inquiries of factory inspectors and members of Royal Commissions were conducted within their own ideological framework, not that of those whom they were inquiring into, and no documentation exists in the form of correspondence or personal diaries. In newspapers aimed at the working classes, and in novels, the effort to apprehend a very different way of life frequently became a projection of the attitudes and desires of one class on to the others. Nevertheless, it is possible to give some idea of the life of proletarian women. When in 1856, J. W. Kaye drew the public's attention to the legal impotence of the ill-treated wife, he drew a distinction between the refined, verbal, emotional and usually private torture by bad middle-class husbands, and the blows and cruelties generally and unrestrainedly inflicted by bad husbands in the less privileged classes.[2] 'The most constant sufferer from domestic brutality',[3] wrote J. S. Mill. 'Miserable squaw',[4] wrote another contemporary, and this was how the working-class wife often appeared. Indeed, the cruelties inflicted by husband or lover became notorious, and kept the newspapers well supplied: kicks and punches,[5] brutalities causing the death of the victim,[6] attempted murders.[7] In 1851, Mill listed examples of this kind of cruelty: a bulldog set at the heels of a wife, attempted murder by hanging, stabbings, blows with the poker, murder in a fit of drunkenness.[8] 'You hear of men occasionally leading out their wives with a halter round their neck, and selling them amid shouts of laughter, not of disgust', wrote a journalist in *Eliza Cook's Journal*.

The victim of male brutality was also exposed in even more serious ways. It is generally agreed that the wife's 'chastity' was as meaningless among the common people as 'the respect' her husband was supposed to show her. W. Gilbert related a conversation that left no room for doubt about the husband's intention to make his wife turn prostitute.[10] 'The general degradation' of men and women began in earliest childhood[11] in the slums, and was noted in the factories by Elizabeth Gaskell and other observers.[12] The employer-seducer did not spare even married workers.[13]

The fickleness of the women, whether married or not, and the brutalities vented on the weakest ones, were already considered a social problem, a symptom of a 'great disease'.[14]

The disease was the total misery which the industrial revolution brought to the working classes. Its worst symptom was the housing problem, which challenged the very idea of the 'Home', and the wife's role as 'Homemaker'. The records of the Metropolitan Police

Courts, explained J. W. Kaye, prove that cruelty towards women was linked with overcrowding. Parliamentary reports and other contemporary evidence[15] vouch for the atrocious housing conditions of the poor in the towns and in the countryside. The most interesting attempt at making the well-do-do understand that this misery had implications for the traditional virtues of the home was Henry Mayhew's essay, 'Home is Home, be it Never so Homely'. His analysis of the concept of 'Home', a refuge where comfort, well-being and affection reign – 'sanctuary – a spot sacred to peace and goodwill, where love alone is to rule and harmony to prevail' – was followed by realistic descriptions of the 'homes' of the poor: the silkweaver, the dock-labourer, the needlewoman. In conclusion Mayhew asked the reader himself to compare ideal and reality.[16]

In the slums, those 'homes' that were nothing of the kind, the function of 'homemaker' was derisory, all the more so as contemporaries were in full agreement as to working-class women's lack of household skills. 'They do not know how to sew, knit, cook or wash', wrote Engels.[17] Taine cited the example of a family of fourteen children where neither the mother nor the eldest daughter '... knew how to make soup, a roast ... everyone in the family knew how to clean a field, no one knew how to grill a chop.'[18]

It was the ignorance of many a working class wife about the domestic arts, that for some explained, if not justified, the brutality of a husband, denied the comfort, 'a comfortable arm-chair, a singing tea-kettle, a tidied room' that he had the right to expect on returning home from work.[19]

The majority of observers persisted in laying the responsibility for the happiness, or unhappiness, of the home on the working-class woman herself. J. W. Kaye urged the rich to help the poor, like the characters in *Sunbeams in the Cottage*, a moral novel by M. M. Brewster.[20] An edifying serial in the *British Mothers' Magazine*, 'Cottage Readings',[21] described a 'good employer' who fitted out and improved the cottages of his workers, and his charitable wife, who visited the needy. But the most striking aspect of this literary treatment is the sharpness of the distinction made between the good poor and the bad poor. For example, the virtuous and hard-working widow Scott,[22] who taught child-rearing to the girls of the village, is set against the bad, poor, lazy wife, full of complaints and envy. The wife should remove the bread from her own mouth without a word, while nourishing her most recent child at the breast.[23] It was up to her to prove her patience and submission to the will of God in the face of adversity, misery and daily cares, like the character in the 'Cottager's Chapter' who, unlike the lazy, impious and rebellious wife, prayed and sacrificed continuously. When there was no butter for lunch, 'she looked up to Christ, who is the bread of life'.[24] The worst sin a demanding wife could commit was to hold envy towards members of the privileged classes, that is to say, to harbour that sense of injustice which is the seed of social revolt. By continual self-sacrifice and by working miracles on meagre wages, she was supposed to help her husband tolerate injustice and exploitation; thus playing an essential part in maintaining the status quo.

We shall see later that the wife's ignorance in domestic matters was one of the most powerful arguments used by the opponents of work for women. As Engels[25] and W. R. Greg,[26] among others, noted, a working woman employed in a factory from the age of nine did not have the time to learn housekeeping. Long working hours also ruled out its practice.[27] Even after the institution of the ten-hour day in textile factories and successive adjustments of the time-table between 1850 and 1911, a working woman was out of the house from before six a.m. until nearly six p.m. It was the same in pottery and agriculture. The meals of Lancashire textile workers generally consisted of bread, bacon, treacle, tea, coffee, cheese, meal and potatoes. It is significant that the working-class wives who showed most competence around the house were those who had been servants.[28]

If middle-class women were a long way from feeling themselves the 'mothers of immortal souls' what about the working classes? According to the accounts of urban life by Gilbert, Greenwood and Engels, the most persistent problem was not child morality but child mortality. Amongst the disinherited it was not a question of saving the soul but the life of children threatened by under-nourishment, fevers and epidemics.[29] Mothers working were studied in detail by M. Hewitt. Apparently, one of the effects of their working was to encourage early marriage. Observers noticed that mothers under seventeen were not rare; and these very young women were particularly badly equipped to look after a house and children.[30] The statistics of the Fertility Commissions between 1851 and 1911 show that during the nineteenth century the fertility of women in cotton districts was lower than that in the mining and agricultural regions and that in families with mothers working the number of children was less. On the other hand in agricultural and mining areas married women worked and yet the fertility was higher than in the textile regions.[31] Attempts to account for this suffer even more from lack of information than with middle-class families; the Sadler Report of 1933–4 and the Fertility Commission of 1911 only give figures and the results of interviews for the beginning and end of the century.[32] The possible influence of birth-control propaganda cannot be ruled out. The 'diabolical handbills' of 1823 were aimed, primarily, at the working classes and circulated in the industrial North. On the other hand, Knowlton's work, *The Fruits of Philosophy*, was republished in 1834 as a sixpenny pamphlet and 42,000 copies were sold in the next forty years. An inquiry by the Manchester Statistical Society in 1835 showed that 600 copies of works on birth-control, including *The Fruits of Philosophy*, had been sold in the previous year in Manchester.[33]

But this slow infiltration of some birth-control propaganda did not stop motherhood from being a terrifying ordeal for most working-class women. Every account shows that many women continued working until the last moment, and began again as soon as possible. Before female labour was forbidden down the mines it was quite common to see wretched women in an advanced state of pregnancy harnessed to the coal waggons. 'The belt and the chain are worse when we are pregnant', wrote a witness. Another was said to have given birth to three or four children at work. Of her eight children, four were still-born.[34] Children barely even premature were born, dead or alive, in workshops and fields. Not until 1891 did an Act, 'The Factory and Workshop Act', forbid women's work during the four weeks preceding confinement. The reports of the commissions of inquiry and of factory and health inspectors and the observations of people like Engels and Gilbert all comment on high infant mortality. 'Infanticide is practised as extensively and as legally in England as it is on the banks of the Ganges',[35] wrote Disraeli. The mortality was generally caused by undernourishment, insalubriousness and overcrowding in the slums, both urban and rural.[36]

Contemporary and modern studies show that infant mortality was more severe in the sectors where women worked, for example in areas like Lancashire where the textile industry was concentrated, even if you allow for the exaggerations and distortions intended to influence opinion in favour of limiting the woman's working day or returning her to the home.[37] It was generally believed that infant mortality was due to the mother's absence, when the children were entrusted either to elder sisters, often not more than seven or eight years old, or to nurses who might be aged, infirm, and unscrupulous. Those who had not yet been weaned by their mother were fed too infrequently; even if quantity was sufficient, the milk that might or might not be contaminated with germs, or bread soaked in sugared water was not exactly nourishing.[38] Not only were children badly fed, but the high number of accidents, burns, falls and drownings testify to the lack of care.[39] Worse still, in order to calm or put the children to sleep, exhausted mothers and above all, nurses often used alcohol or laudanum-, morphine- or opium-based narcotics,[40] which could bring about convulsions.

Outside the factory population, it seems that the nursing profession was one of the few open to mothers seeking a paid occupation. Gilbert described the slave market where middle-class families recruited nurses for their children while the nurse's own offspring was entrusted to strange hands, perhaps to waste away and die. Mothers 'are kept solely as domestic animals, for the nourishment they yield'. The commentator compared the rich child to a young vampire sucking the blood of the poor man's son.[41]

In the mines, fields, factories, workshops, women, married or not, worked in inhumane conditions.[42] The philanthropic reaction, was to attempt to give her the domestic training – cooking, hygiene, child-rearing – that she lacked, and above all to shorten her hours of work. The traditional ideal was still very largely that of the woman in the home. There was few adherents of the opposite approach – planning the social organization to allow mothers to work. But there were signs of future change, the first crèche was founded in London in 1850 and was followed in the north of England by several others between 1864 and 1874.[43]

[4]

The Myth in the Novel

The contemporary feminine ideal was that of Wife and Mother. Her social position was one of subjection and humiliation. The resulting tension between ideal and reality is one aspect of the problem of realism in the Victorian novel. Given this context, what kind of image of her does fiction then present? It depends upon each writer's awareness of the contradiction between women's ideal role and their actual position in society. Thackeray for instance combines a keen sense of the social and psychological problem with the irrational cult of an ideal image. Before looking at the fate of the wife-mother, we shall first examine how the main aspects of the myth of woman are taken up by novelists.

The novels of Dickens are full of the mythic wife-mother, portrayed either in complete achievement or its opposite; both extremes being equally unrealistic, socially and psychologically. Fiercely caricatured or highly venerated, her function is to incarnate Good and Evil. As early as 1840, in *Sketches of Young Couples*, Dickens had become a conventional spokesman for Home and Family as sources of virtue and true happiness. Young couples must be convinced, he wrote, that '... in home, and all the English virtues which the love of home engenders, lies the only true source of domestic felicity ...' He went on to stress the unique position of daughters and mothers within this framework. Without enlarging on the role yet, of the wife, he specifies:

We have purposely excluded from consideration the couples in which the lady reigns paramount ... holding such cases to be of a very unnatural kind, and like hideous births and other monstrous deformities, only to be discreetly and sparingly exhibited.[1]

Such unnatural creatures appear in several novels with the traits of Mrs Jellyby or Mrs Pardiggle, the scourges and destroyers of man, child and humanity, everything a wife and mother ought not to be. John Butt and Kathleen Tillotson have identified Dickens's model for Mrs Jellyby – Mrs Caroline Chisholm, who in May 1850 had founded an organization to encourage emigration, The Family

Colonization Loan Society. Dickens supported her but at the same time was horrified by the way she neglected her home and children.[2] On 14 March 1850 he wrote to Miss Burdett-Coutts: 'I dream of Mrs Chisholm's housekeeping ... The dirty faces of her children are my continual companions ...'[3]

Dickens presents Mrs Jellyby and Mrs Pardiggle in much the same way as he does their counterparts, Miss Wisk in *Bleak House*, Mrs Pocket in *Great Expectations*, Mrs Bricks and Mrs Hominy in *Martin Chuzzlewit*. Mrs Jellyby is so preoccupied by the problem of English emigration to Africa, especially by coffee cultivation and the settlement of 200 families in the area of Borrioboola-Gha, that she has no time to look after her own. With obvious pleasure Dickens lingers comically over the description of an indeterminate number of children left to themselves and exposed to the most dreadful catastrophes. The unfortunate Peepy, never yet washed in his life, periodically disappears or gets his head stuck between iron railings;[4] and the eldest daughter spends all her time looking after the huge correspondence of a mother who totally neglects the daughter's physical and moral education. In the same way, Mrs Pocket, absorbed by her grandiose dreams, is incapable of attending to her six children, of holding a baby without the risk of its dashing its head against a table or harming its eyes with the nutcrackers.[5] As for the formidable Mrs Pardiggle, her five sons have become real wild beasts 'weazened and shrivelled',[6] sacrificed to their shrew of a mother, who drags them from one philanthropic meeting to another and forces them to give their entire pocket-money to diverse 'causes'. Mrs Jellyby's husband, a 'non-entity', does not benefit from any masculine prerogatives: his wife neglects all his needs.[7] Her criminal negligence drags the whole family into ruin. Mr Jellyby is threatened with bankruptcy: in his calvary he loses all marital illusions.[8] As for their home, Dickens delights in emphasizing its inhospitality: everything conspires against human beings in a place where you can freeze with cold, or suffocate with smoke; where meals are not properly cooked, the staircarpet is riddled with holes, and the staircase itself is an obstacle course; where the cupboards are filled with strange, threatening objects.[9] Finally – a distinctive trait in the child-wives and the anti-women – Mrs Jellyby and Mrs Pocket are incapable of superintending their servants properly. The Pockets' cook is found dead drunk in her kitchen; Caddy often complains about the chronic alcoholism among the servants that quickly succeed one another in their house.[10]

Using all the resources of his comic imagination, Dickens compares the neglect and exploitation of children and husband, and the
slovenliness of the home, with the 'Mission' to which these philanthropists are wedded. The effect is achieved through a series of
contrasts, which Dickens never tires of introducing in different
forms, within and between characters, but always illustrating the
same basic theme: interest in a distant and abstract 'Cause' and
indifference to immediate duties towards house, family and self. The
aim of his arbitrary contrast between public and private domain,
philanthropy and family, was to condemn the expenditure of time
and energy for the sake of the Cause (no matter what it was);
which, according to Dickens, invariably brings selfishness and moral
blindness in the family. His butts were the American lady-
philosophers who met on Mondays to discuss the philosophy of
crime, on Wednesdays to discuss the philosophy of the soul, and on
Fridays to discuss the philosophy of vegetables. 'Domestic drudgery
was far beneath the exalted range of these philosophers', says Mr
Bevan.[11]

The point was to convince the reader that any woman with a
philanthropic and political 'mission' is a monster, an unnatural
being. One can understand John Stuart Mill's irritation with the
crude means employed by Dickens to discredit feminism and
woman's autonomy.

That ... Dickens, whose last story, *Bleak House,* much the worst of
his things ... – has the vulgar impudence ... to ridicule rights of
women. It is done in the very vulgarest way – just the style in which
vulgar men used to ridicule 'learned ladies' as neglecting their children
and household etc.[12]

With regard to the *vulgarity* of the means, Mill could also have
cited Dickens's article, 'Sucking Pigs', in *Household Words* of
November 1851, where he rather crudely satirizes 'Bloomerism'
the person of Mrs Bellows, a rough sketch later filled out by Mrs
Pardiggle and Mrs Jellyby.[13] There he develops again his theme,
the contrast between woman's public and private activity, and
naturally exalts her influence within the latter sphere. 'Is not the
home voice of our Julia as the song of a bird, after considerable bow-
wowing out of doors'?[14] – it was almost like Paul of Tarsus who
forbade women to express themselves in public.

Parallel to the contrasts within characters, one can also discern a
series of contrasts with other figures, intended likewise to discredit

their philanthropic and social action. By continually comparing Mrs Pardiggle and Mrs Jellyby with Esther, Caddy and Ada, Dickens succeeds in consigning the one lot to outer darkness. Thus Caddy, a small ink-stained shadow, a child sacrificed by a bad mother, evolves beautifully into a wife and mother devoted to her husband and family. Exceptionally, *her* work outside the home receives absolution from Dickens because it is not independent and autonomous but a sacrifice born of love for her lame husband.[15]

In the same way, Dickens contrasts Mrs Pardiggle's policeman's philanthropy with the instinctive, modest and pragmatic generosity of Ada and Esther Summerson. Mrs Pardiggle's rigid authoritarian attitude, which consists of 'pouncing upon the poor, and applying benevolence to them like a strait-waistcoat',[16] and which naturally only arouses hostility and aggressiveness, is set against the spontaneous neighbourly love that Esther and Ada express through affectionate gestures, tears and pitying lamentation.[17] Moreover, that great-hearted man, Mr Cheerybles, has no female counterpart in Dickens's novels, analagous to the generous women of good works in *Coningsby*, *Yeast* and *Alton Locke*.[18]

Dickens's natural hostility towards all systems of thought and action, the Poor Laws in *Oliver Twist*, the utilitarian philosophy in *Hard Times*, became repulsion when a woman was inspired by principle. The vision of these 'committee-women' called forth a caricature in the *Punch Almanac* of 1853: the father, carrying a baby, and surrounded by eight children, clears a path in the office of a wife disappearing amidst piles of old papers, newspapers and petitions.[19]

Caddy Jellyby's and Louisa Bounderby's capacities to be wives and mothers themselves are nearly destroyed, by a bad mother in one case, and a rigid educational system in the other: they both start life under a handicap. Other heroines have a marvellous aptitude for their fairytale domestic mission. Even in the filthy jungle at the Jellybys' Esther can create a home with three gestures: she lights the fire, she tells the children stories, and she washes Peepy.[20] To know how to transform the most sordid interior into a home is, according to Dickens, the great female gift. The good fairy of the home is capable, at the wave of a wand, of accomplishing household miracles. Mrs Chirrup's talents in 'The Nice Little Couple' include 'mysteries of confectionery-making, pickling and preserving', even needlework, not to mention the art of carving poultry.[21] The syntax of the passage dealing with the carving of the goose expresses Mrs Chirrup's fairytale gift: the operation and the agent of the operation

6. 'The Parliamentary Female.' From the *Punch Book of Women's Rights*.
Father of the Family. 'Come, dear; we so seldom go out together now –
can't you take us all to the play to-night?'
Mistress of the House, and M.P. 'How you talk, Charles! Don't you see
that I am too busy. I have a committee to-morrow morning, and I have my
speech on the great crochet question to prepare for the evening.'

are omitted: the result alone is described, effect without immediate
cause, quasi-magical.[22] Mrs Chirrup is the domesticated woman *par
excellence*. The adjective 'little', referring to her, recurs eight times
in six lines.[23]

Ruth Pinch in *Martin Chuzzlewit* is her twin. Before adorning the
home of her husband Ruth was the perfect housekeeper for her
brother Tom: domestic tasks were carried out with every imagin-
able perfection and feminine grace. Ruth 'bustles out' to shop at
the baker's, the butcher's and the grocer's. Shopping, washing-up,
mending, cooking, all these operations follow one another in a sort
of graceful ballet, a poetry destined to bewitch reader and narrator.

Being a child and dancer, Ruth is never caught walking: she trots
about, springs forward, dances in and out of rooms, amidst laughter
and song. The preparation of the beefsteak pudding, that highlight
of English culinary art, is an entrancing story that takes not less
than three pages to tell. There are nine lines of text for her apron
and the way she puts it on.[24] During her domestic phase and after her

conversion, Bella Wilfer embodies the same idyllic image of the homely wife frenziedly absorbed by a thousand insignificant domestic tasks, which in Dickens's imagination take on an epic dimension.[25]

When George Eliot describes the domestic pursuits of Mrs Amos Barton, her ingenuity in meeting her tasks, and the courage daily demanded of a poor mother of six children, there is admiration but it is tinged with pity. The author praises a woman who knows how to make shoes and slippers look new, to salt bacon, to iron, to patch and mend eternally.[26] But the thankless nature of these harassing and endlessly repeated tasks is recognized too.

Why should the image of the good household fairy in her strictly domestic role have plunged Dickens into such ecstasy? Why celebrate with such lyrical fervour the small thankless and often sordid tasks of the home? The famous 'creative' function of woman in her domestic role, a mystification still rampant in our own time (however much it has been denounced by Lenin,[27] not to speak of Betty Friedan and others more recently)[28] – for Dickens took on the form of a magical force.

Only intense frustration and the consequent elaboration of phantasy can, it seems to me, explain the irrational, sentimental and dreamlike resonances of these imaginary creatures. The frustration could have two sources: on the one hand, the solitary childhood of the author, who as it happens was deprived of the warmth of a home and a mother in her domestic role;[29] and, on the other, Catherine Hogarth's like shortcomings. It appears that one of the causes of Dickens's and Catherine's incompatibility was her lack of practical skill. Catherine was as incapable of writing an address correctly as of seeing to the household duties; Dickens himself dealt with all the tradespeople and took all decisions about the family's various removals, while his sister-in-law, Georgina, looked after the house and the children. When we take into account that Dickens was at once extraordinarily busy, a stickler for order and organization and convinced that marriage consisted of 'a sweet and brightly coloured domesticity'[30] this second frustration must also have given an edge to the portrayal that came so easy to him.

A deeper meaning can also be found in the talents of the good home fairy. Significantly, the husband plays only a very small part in the vignettes of this heaven on earth. The person who bears the responsibility for the success of one exemplary couple is, without any doubt, Mrs Chirrup.[31] Similarly when Dickens describes the cold and soulless house of Louisa Bounderby, it is *her* domestic incapacity, linked as it is with her upbringing, which makes her home barren. That bare, graceless, uncomfortable house reveals no trace of a woman's presence. And this absence – of which Louisa is aware – betrays a more serious defect.[32] For the perfect housewife's domestic talents are the tangible manifestation of the moral essence, of the specific sacred mission of the wife-mother within and without the home. 'I want to be something so much worthier than the doll in the doll's house',[33] says Bella Wilfer in her idyllic little queendom. These words, at the time Bella uttered them, had a very specific meaning that did not herald the revolt of the suffragettes but, by contrasting the doll or child-wife to the 'helpmate' evoked the wife-guide's transcendental mission.

The cult of the wife-guide, collaborating with the man in his work, while serving him and inspiring him to seek the highest ends, is expressed in diverse female characters in the novels of Dickens, George Eliot, Mrs Gaskell and Charlotte Brontë. Esther Summerson in *Bleak House*, Little Dorrit, Lizzie Hexam in *Our Mutual Friend* and Florence Dombey belong to the group of sacrificed and altruistic women. But there is no better representation of Dickens's ideal than Bella Wilfer's evolution in *Our Mutual Friend*, and, on the other hand, the antithesis between Dora and Agnes in *David Copperfield*.

In the beginning Bella Wilfer is part of the cash nexus which forms the basic structure of the novel. Destined to marry a rich man, she spends her entire childhood behaving as a spoiled, capricious child. Far from sacrificing herself to her parents like the many virtuous girls mentioned earlier, Bella twists them round her little finger, behaves like a princess, and artlessly admits her calculation and ambition.[34] Her experience of the damage wrought by wealth on Mr Boffin and her budding love for John Rokesmith, change the spoiled, selfish child into an altruistic woman, devoted to husband and father, worthy of her title and function. Boffin's stratagem when he simulates a growing greed and dehumanization precipitates in her a genuine conversion. Unlike Dora, Bella is submitted by the author to a process of maturation.[35] In Dickens there is for once a serious attempt to create a more complex and varying person than Dora and Agnes. Within the family Bella's change of attitude marks the first important stage in her spiritual development. 'I mean to be cook today', she declares to her mother, and dressed in the uniform of white apron, pins, dimples, smiles, she decides to play the servant and prepare the meal.[36] Then the signs of a deep change begin to multiply. It is a sign of humility and maturing that she does not protest when she learns she has been the victim of a hoax.[37] In her very conception Bella Wilfer is the most complete female character in Dickens. Even in her negative part of the spoiled child, she shows herself capable of a candour and a freedom of opinion unknown to the general run of the novelists's heroines. Unlike them she is neither an angelic creature blushing in a stammer of confusion or a yelling virago; whether or not it was the influence of the woman generally regarded as his model, the actress Ellen Ternan, the fact remains that the character matures, the spoiled child becomes the devoted wife-mother, the doll becomes an adult.

In *David Copperfield*, conversely, the child-wife is incapable of growing up, of being the hero's helpmate, and all Dickens can do is to dismiss her and link David's fate to that of a guide and angel. The Dora-Agnes antithesis in the novel emphasizes the demands Dickens makes of the wife, as well as the real meaning of domestic virtues within the limits set by the needs of social ascent among the lower-middle class. The analysts of Dickens's manuscripts have underlined the importance of two points within this perspective. The first is Dickens's hesitation concerning the heroine. After examining the manuscript, John Butt and Kathleen Tillotson conclude that Agnes Wickfield was at all times cut out not only for the role of guardian angel, but also for David's wife. Dickens as he went along became more and more attached to Dora and was very reluctant to get rid of her. In May 1850, during the drafting of the fourteenth number, he wrote: 'Still undecided about Dora, but MUST decide today.'[38] The second point is that in the notebook for the first chapter David's mother is much more explicitly condemned than in the novel itself. 'Young mother. Tendency to weakness and vanity.'[39] In her earliest scenes Dora already manifests the faults that will lead the couple to failure. From the very beginning she is incapable of understanding or even accepting the essential facts of David's position – poverty, work, and need for efficient organization. 'I am a beggar' states David, after his aunt's ruin. 'How can you be such a silly thing ... telling such stories ... I'll make Jip bite you.' When David tries to make an impression on her by means of moralizing clichés, 'the crust well-earned', etc., she reacts peremptorily, like a spoiled child: 'I don't want to hear any more about crusts! ... And Jip must have a mutton-chop every day at twelve ...'[40] Faced with the unpleasant aspects of a young reporter's life – poverty and toil – she tries to escape with tears and tantrums. The child-wife is incapable of emerging from the dream world to face

7. 'Our Housekeeping.' Illustration by 'Phiz' from *David Copperfield*

reality. And David, in his own eyes, feels like a monster trampling down the frailties of the fairy kingdom.[41] When David and Dora marry, the couple are exposed to all the vicissitudes foreshadowed by Dora's reactions during their engagement. She is incapable of seeing to the varied domestic chores of a modest household, and organizing the servants. She is far from being equal to the role laid down so forthrightly by Mrs Beeton of commanding a regiment or running a business. When David tries, without conviction, to initiate her to the practical problems of purchasing a leg of mutton, or making a stew, Dora relies on others, the butcher or the cook, and delegates to them her own responsibilities as mistress of the house. Dora's attempts to instruct herself in the domestic arts meet with failure, for the tradesmen and servants take advantage of her inexperience and sell her bad lobster or hard meat at a ransom price.

The saddest tale is the servants'. It will be recalled that in the sordid dens of the philanthropic anti-women the servants were always ineffectual and drunk. With Dora and David the servant problem takes on the proportions of a permanent disaster. Their home is a parade-ground of servants running periodically from kitchen to pub, taking the household linen to the pawn-shop, nobbling clothes, watches and food, in short taking advantage of their employers in every possible way, or sometimes repenting in the gasps and stale smell of spirits. The result is twofold. First, the disorganization, disorder and waste in the home mean that David is often obliged to swallow poorly prepared food in haste, or do without. Overwhelmed by work, he does not receive from his wife the sustenance he needs and is constantly harassed by financial problems created by the boundless expenses of a household ruled by waste. Secondly, the wife's inability to play her part as the domestic mainstay, affects the circle of tradespeople and servants for whom the employers, in the paternalistic perspective of their time, felt responsible.

> Our want of system and management, involves not only ourselves ... but other people ... there is contagion in us ... we incur the serious responsibility of spoiling everyone who comes into our service ... unless we learn to do our duty to those whom we employ, they will never learn to do their duty to us.[42]

Here too the responsibility of a wife spreads far beyond the family nucleus. Failing in her example and duties to those beneath her, the very social hierarchy crumbles; the corruption reaches all those who come into contact with the nucleus of *chaos*. The worm eats into the fruit, then the entire tree.

The narrator-author did not fail to deliver himself of sinister warnings about the dangers facing a marriage threatened by 'unsuitability of mind and purpose'.[43] The parallel between Dora, the child-wife, and David's own mother is very clear. While the censorious judgement is firmer in the Notebook than in the finished work, the author portrays perfectly clearly Mrs Copperfield's irresponsibility, weakness, and what finally amounts to cowardice. The docility and the blindness of the Murdstones' victim are indeed responsible for her son's unhappy childhood. David's ironic questioning by Betsy Trotwood when he announces his marriage to Dora is likewise a prophesy. And the words of Betsy Trotwood: 'blind, blind, blind'; following David's confused and enthusiastic exclamations about Dora point unmistakably to his grievous lack of insight.

The Myth in the Novel

When married, David's reflections about his incompatibility with
Dora indeed confirm that hero and narrator consider his choice of
her not only an error of judgement but also, and this has a definite
meaning in the value-system of the novel, 'the first mistaken impulse
of an undisciplined heart'.[44] These very words were spoken by
Annie Strong for the first time about her adolescent affection for her
rascally cousin. The two couples are thus associated in the common
censure.

When David eventually gives up educating his pretty fairy, this
is a sign of a growing maturity. They both cut the house adrift and
take refuge in a childlike dreamworld peopled with affectionate
nicknames, guitars, songs, painted flowers, a world where Dora
herself appears as a statuette in Dresden porcelain, a fragile little
flower. All is done to define Dora as a decorative element, a useless
luxury and, within the limits of lower-middle-class life, even a
dangerous object. While the oncoming of self-awareness is a stage
in spiritual maturation, in the *Bildungsroman* tradition, one can also
read it as an analysis of the wife's role in a lower-middle-class
family. For what are these realities to which Dora cannot adapt, if
not the wife's duties within the laborious and needy existence of a
journalist-writer, of a lower-middle-class man on the make? The
child-wife is an intermediate category – and only possible in the
privileged classes – between the good and bad working woman of
The British Mothers' Magazine. Despite her charm, her innocence,
she is a threat to the status quo. What David preaches to Dora is
'worldly prudence', economy, wisdom, the ascetic organization of
the family for work and productivity. He speaks the language of the
middle class, not that of prodigal bohemianism. Dicken's biographers have of course compared Dora and Agnes to Kate Dickens
and Georgina Hogarth.[45] Such real-life data may help to define the
contrast which underlies the novel's design, but it only takes on its
full meaning in the light of the philosophy of womanhood held in
Victorian society. David's relations with Dora and Agnes must also
be set against other marriages in the novel: marrying for love or
convenience are contrasted, positively, with the mercenary union
envisaged by Uriah Heep.

The balance-sheet is drawn up by Dora herself. 'I was too
young ... I was not fit to be a wife.'[46] Conversely, Agnes, the
devoted daughter to her father, belongs with Esther Summerson and
Ada in *Bleak House*, Florence Dombey, Rachel and Sissy Jupe in
Hard Times, and Little Dorrit, all cut out for their proper mission.

David's first meeting with Agnes Wickfield defines her in her essence. Like Dora, Florence Dombey, Lizzie Hexam, she is at once there, all complete, made, but not to develop. She is presented straight away as the tutelary angel of the home when, armed with the required bunch of keys, she presides over the tea ceremony, works at her sewing, and makes music for her father and his guest. That inexpressible influence for quiet kindness and peace[47] already emanate from her, which also surround Rachel in *Hard Times*: Rachel only has to appear for a cold and sinister interior to become a Home filled with radiant warmth.[48] By just existing women of this type inspire the most noble conduct in the people around them: David is frantic with shame that Agnes has witnessed his drunken state. All Stephen Blackpool's revolt and hate founder in Rachel's presence. Agnes, Rachel, Esther, Florence and the others are all sacrifice and altruism for those around them: and father, lover, friends are graduated as guardian angels. And the weak sinners, David, Stephen, Esther Dombey, mutter forth thankful litanies to their purifying influence.[49] David too says and says too often, 'Agnes ... you are my good angel ... my good angel, always my good angel'.[50] He even entrusts Dora to her heavenly care. The role of Agnes and those like her is that of the wife in Mrs Ellis's work: in the midst of the bitter struggle to acquire success, and fame, that inexorably discourages and corrupts the combatants, the wife-mother, as the source of inspiration and moral strength, helps her man to resist temptation. Agnes is frozen into a statue whose imperious finger points the way ahead.[51] The novel ends with this image. These heavenly figures often conjure up light and radiance. The purity of Sissy and Florence lights up the shadows surrounding Louisa Gradgrind and Esther Dombey.[52]

Sources of light, fountains overflowing with love, objects of worship, these disembodied creatures are almost drained of all life. Esther Summerson in *Bleak House* is always blissfully grateful to her tutor, or steeped in kind actions towards Ada and Richard, towards the poor, towards her little maidservant Charley and her sinful mother. She carries sacrifice and gratitude to the point of wanting to marry and to love a tutor much older than herself. She is perhaps the most set, the most insipid, of Dickens's angelic women, a person with a narrative and didactic function robbed of life to bestow it upon the novel. This is due, according to W. J. Harvey, to her function as the 'moral signpost' of the novel: the character acts as lifeline and brake in the structure of a work threatened with disintegration by the author's runaway imagination. Esther has to be static, to accept her duty and her passive role as witness.[53]

This brings up Dickens's young sister-in-law, Mary Hogarth. The premature death of a woman he loved dearly could have been his unconscious starting-point. Dickens was also the stout defender of the transcendental theory of women, and it was from this point of view that he advised them to complete their education. On 26 February 1844, at an evening in a Mechanics' Institute, Dickens made a speech in favour of girls' schools. It was in the interest of women 'who are our best teachers, and whose lessons are oftenest heeded' to improve their minds. Their education, rightly understood, could only contribute to the further spiritualization of an already angelic nature: 'every ray that falls upon you at your own fireside, from any book or thought communicated within these walls, will raise you nearer to the angels in the eyes you care for most. (much cheering)'.[54] The acclamation shows to what extent public opinion approved.[55]

The modern reader needs to resign himself to seeing these women as purely symbolic creatures.[56] The heroines are desexualized. This is not only because they lack physical consistency. In Dickens's social universe – and this is true of other novelists of the time, especially Thackeray and Charlotte Brontë – there is an almost systematic confusion between different sorts of love: filial, fraternal, maternal, passionate. Agnes constantly takes on the figure of a sister for David; Dr Strong, who is much older than his young wife, plays the part of her father or even grandfather. Annie's attitude towards him is made up of tenderness and gratitude for his kindness, patience and experience. Perhaps the most irritating case is that of Esther Summerson and her tutor Jarndyce. Esther launches into a song of gratitude for Jarndyce's kindnesses[57] and confuses this with love. And to the very last moment she believes she ought to marry him. In fact, from the heroine's point of view (she is also the narrator), and in the unfolding of the plot, this union with her tutor which she foresees and in spite of a few qualms, desires, is much more credible than the wave of a wand by Jarndyce which makes Esther one with Allan Woodcourt. It is not easy to account for this peculiarity, even if it is at the heart of Victorian sensibility. But at any rate one point to make is that this particular mode of relations, operating in reality and in literature, suggests a defence mechanism in the face of passionate love, erected by those who, before Freud, knew nothing of the sexual and incestuous components of oedipal family links. The sublimation of passion was intended, perhaps, to desexualize not only woman, but, through her, men as well.

The worship of the wife-mother was not peculiar to Dickens: the same kind of thing is found (with variants of course) in the work of Mrs Gaskell, Anne and Charlotte Brontë and Thackeray. In Mrs Gaskell's story, *Lizzie Leigh* (1850), the wife goes to look for their daughter, a wandering and repentant sinner, and does so against her husband's wishes. The belief in a saving mission that she has to accomplish inspires her with the strength to defy her husband. In *Right and Last*, Margaret convinces her husband, a counterfeiter's son, to resist blackmail and face first the hostility of public opinion and then the poverty which follows the revelation of his father's identity. It is the disappearance of John Barton's wife which is held responsible for his isolation, bitterness, growing revolt, and finally for his crime. His wife had saved him, up to then. In *Wives and Daughters*, the wife of Squire Hamley inspires all around her by her kindness and gentleness. When she dies it is as if an angel had disappeared. In the same novel the young Molly Gibson displays her qualities of sacrifice, selflessness and a wife-mother's disinterested tenderness alike towards her father, the Hamley family, her mother-in-law, Mrs Gibson, and her half-sister Cynthia. But in this unlike the more bloodless heroines of Dickens, decisions required of virtue such as the acceptance of her father's remarriage are here taken in suffering and grief. 'We are not angels',[58] she says, if angelically. Molly's altruism is contrasted with Mrs Gibson's narrow-minded egoism, and her integrity with Cynthia's facile ethic. Molly, at important stages in her life, her father's remarriage, her thwarted love for Roger Hamley, is inspired by a sense of sacrifice, by forgetfulness of self and the imaginative capacity to feel for others. In this sense at least she belongs to the same species as in Dickens.

Margaret Hale, the heroine of *North and South*, is similar. She had been a daughter devoted to a weak mother and a father tested by life. Her apprenticeship to duty developed within the family. Given her mother's inability to face the difficulties of life and adapt to industrial civilization, Margaret feels she has to take over the responsibility when her parents emigrate from the south to the north of England. Only when her father is away on a short journey does Margaret realize the extent to which she has had to repress all her personal worries. To fill the emptiness of her existence she reacts by creating ever new obligations: visits to the tubercular working woman, Mary Higgins, teaching the Boucher children. She contrives in deadly earnest to make herself useful and to replace the 'natural duties' of a wife and mother by self-imposed ones. Margaret Hale's vocation is of a superior kind. The task of bringing about a reconciliation between the archaic agricultural South and the industrial North, and between the antagonistic classes of workers and employers, devolves on her by virtue of her intelligence and her high humanitarian and religious consciousness. She urges humility on the disgruntled worker Higgins, asking him to swallow his pride and be reconciled with his employer. She prevents him from drowning his sorrow in alcohol and brings him back to religion. On the other front, with the feminine weapons of sweetness and persuasion, she fights the authoritarian and even despotic attitudes of the manufacturer Thornton, and reminds him of higher things than profit, above all his responsibility towards his workers.[59] Finally, she provides him with a gift of the necessary funds to attempt an enlightened capitalistic policy. Thanks to her, he is humanized; thanks to her he discovers within himself a knightly and Christian inspiration. So Mrs Gaskell's heroine embodies the spirit of charity and philanthropy which, according to the Christian socialist outlook and to philanthropists like Shaftesbury and Carlyle, would reconcile social classes and humanize the brutal world of work. What more noble fate, what task more appropriate, to the potential wife-mother, than this almost cosmic reconciliation, in the age of capitalism, between the regions of England, between the antagonistic classes, between the past and the future?

Even in more realistic authors such as Anne Brontë and George Eliot, the same cult has an important place. In *The Tenant of Wildfell Hall* Mrs Huntingdon allows herself to be persecuted for a long time by an alcoholic husband, before resigning herself to fleeing the marital home in order to save her young son from corruption. At this period Anne Brontë and George Eliot are intoning canticles to the glory of the mother's noble mission. Simultaneously 'Shield, instructor, friend – she must guide him along the perilous path of youth, and train him to be God's servant.'[60]

In *Scenes of Clerical Life*, 'Amos Barton' and 'Janet's Repentance', motherhood is presented in an almost unbearably tearful style. In a paradox that surprised no one at that time, Mrs Amos Barton combined the blushing shyness of an adolescent girl with the majestic presence of a Madonna.[61] In Janet Dempster the author evokes 'the force of motherhood', the little children who would have prevented her from sinking into alcoholism, sleeping or kneeling around her.[62] The tone is more like the sentimental excesses of Thackeray and Dickens than the restrained lucidity of George Eliot's later insight. Charlotte Brontë, however, whose heroines are single for the greater part of their life created one or two wife-mothers who are variants of more interest on the stereotype. Her aesthetic success is less striking than her awareness of the acute contradictions in the female situation, which she was one of the few authors at the time to understand. Her attempts to resolve them in *Jane Eyre* and, above all, in *The Professor*, were not equally successful. Janet showed early on a reluctance to be indebted to Rochester for too many favours, to lose her name, to be kept by him. She is keen, for a time at least, to carry on with a job and earn her board and lodging.[63] She desired independence; she was puritanically hostile to the immoral notion of 'support', or marriage seen as a sort of legal prostitution. Then again, Jane rejects love without duty – the bigamous marriage to Rochester – and duty without love – marriage to the missionary priest, St John Rivers.

The Professor is an attempt, even if it failed, to create a new type of woman who manages to reconcile a job with the traditional virtues. Frances Henry, an orphan who first taught needlework at a school in Brussels, then became a lace-mender, finally obtained a post in a school in the same town, teaching geography, history, grammar and French composition at the rate of 1,200 francs a year for six hours' work a day. When she married another teacher, William Crimsworth, she continued working and their existence was more arduous than ever: they parted at eight in the morning and did not meet again until five in the evening. But soon, by dint of hard work and sacrifice, the teacher and the lace-mender, carried along and united by their common goal, were in a position to invest what little capital they had accumulated, to purchase and set up a school. As joint managers of the undertaking, they collaborated in its improvement, as anxious to raise the level of teaching as that of the school fees.[64] The enterprise succeeded. Their social and financial ascent followed. The accumulated capital allowed them to invest enough to stop working, to put money by for their son's inheritance and give considerable sums to charity. The wife's (limited) emancipation through associating in work with her husband was part of a conventional success story.

Frances Henry was as ambitious as her husband for professional and financial success; like Roxana and Moll Flanders she was a 'mulier economica'. Dissatisfied with her 1,200 francs a year (her husband earned 8,000) she decided to increase her earnings, convinced that a woman, like a man, ought to devote her time to an important profit-making activity. On the one hand, idle would not be ideal, an idle life spent waiting for her husband would be unbearably boring; on the other, she thought that mutual understanding could only be enhanced by common work and effort.[65] A modern conception of woman? The wife's emancipation in a fulfilled marriage? Not at all. The heroine, who has achieved financial and professional autonomy, continued to be the good fairy experienced in all the household arts. Much younger than Crimsworth – they are respectively nineteen and thirty – whom she continued to regard as her teacher, she respectfully called him 'Monsieur' even at the most intimate moments. A few hours after their wedding, their home had already become peace, warmth and order. And every evening the learned, severe and just headmistress disappeared and was transmuted into Frances Henry, the little lace-mender,[66] a humble and submissive wife, a tender mother: every husband's dream. Among other things this novel expresses the author's dissatisfaction with the idea of the traditional wife. But in Charlotte Brontë's vision, the new essential element in Frances Henry does not transform the traditional relationship between man-wife, and does not modify the psychology and role of the woman, which are regarded as unchangeable facts. The mythic image persists even within this new partnership.

Thackeray raises a particular problem. No other novelist of the period, to my knowledge, unites in the same work and sometimes in the same character two such contradictory tendencies – a literally ferocious criticism of the willing subjection of the wife and an unsparing adoration of the virginal figure of the wife-mother, especially in her aristocratic, British manifestation. His travels abroad, particularly in France and America, served only to confirm in his eyes the superiority of 'a high-bred English Lady'.[67] His criticism of the social and psychological position of women will be examined later. I will touch now on his 'model wives'.

Even in his early works he shows a strong tendency to idealize 'other sacred, defenceless creatures'. Thackeray, travelling all around London (Belgravia, Mayfair, Bloomsbury), found it peopled with ladies whose robes he liked to kiss or merchants' wives sewing buttons on to their waistcoats. In comparison with masculine sensuality, women had purity.[68]

His novels are teeming with idealized figures, all with the same sweetness and purity, who manage to communicate more or less directly with the Almighty. Amelia in *Vanity Fair*, who is not a shining example of intelligence or wit, asserts her superiority as a 'true lady' or 'real gentlewoman' through her submission, sweetness, and kindness.[69] In a letter dated July 1840, Thackeray was already stating his preference for 'this milk-and-water in women' and for their qualities of heart: 'a woman's heart is the most beautiful thing that God has created.'[70] Some years later it was this same kind of woman, 'an artless young virgin' knowing nothing of the world, that he said he would marry.[71]

In his penultimate novel, *The Adventures of Philip on his Way through the World*, he celebrated the happiness of the lowly home and the self-effacing and eternally sacrificed 'Little Sister' who dedicates herself body and soul to her seducer and his son.[72] Wives and others worthy of the names are made guides for husband and family. Laura Pendennis, for example, plays the role of a suavely feminine mentor to Arthur Pendennis, recalling him to his obligations towards his mother and standing between him and the temptations of a young man exposed to the corrupting influence of the town, in particular, the temptation to seduce Fanny Bolton. In *Pendennis* Arthur contrasts the dissolute and flighty life of ladies of the world with the purifying influence of 'good women' living in the country. 'In the country a woman has her household and her poor, her long calm days and long calm evenings.'[73] (The poor were like pets!) Laura herself analyses the way women are preserved from the corruption that overtakes men. Like Ruskin, she recognizes that the battle the man has to fight in order to win money, success and fame must equally make him hard, selfish and self-seeking. Author and heroes, enthusiastic worshippers of 'the dutiful woman', prostrate themselves before these representatives of the Beyond. Henry Esmond's first vision of Lady Castlewood is that of an inaccessible virgin: the child kneels before an apparition bathed in love, surrounded by a halo of light.[74] He later vows the same reverence a medieval knight has for his lady as he sees her kneeling before the holy books, still surrounded by a halo.[75] On the same note Arthur Pendennis implores Laura to show him the way: 'Teach me my duty. Pray for me that I may do it – pure heart'. Warrington 'groans out', 'Amen', and Arthur is lost in awful contemplation of 'a smile heavenly pure ... of love and purity'.[76] The devotion of man, that weak, selfish and materialistic creature, is addressed to mediators of salvation endowed with privileged communication with the other world, and with the power to build 'an invisible temple ... round them; their hearts can kneel down there'.[77] When Laura Bell, later Mrs Pendennis, summons religion, which constantly 'filled her heart and influenced all her behaviour', her husband can only stand respectfully at the entrance while 'this pure creature entered the Holy of Holies'.[78]

Worship of the ideal woman merged with worship of the mother, who takes the form of 'an angel transfigured and glorified with love ... the look of the sacred eyes beaming with an affection unutterable'.[79] The mother has an even greater role as mediator between frail humanity and the Creator. Short of vocabulary, Thackeray constantly uses Spanish Baroque images of the Madonna, 'Virgin mother with a bosom bleeding love', surrounded by her prostrated adorers.[80] The modern reader can hardly fail to be exasperated by these mystical raptures, but the contemporary public found Thackeray's female creations very uplifting.[81] Even Trollope, who rarely indulged in such sentimental frenzies, admired the qualities of feminity, sweetness and altruism in Laura Bell.[82] At the end of the century, however, critics began to be more severe. Charles Whibley, in his book on Thackeray in 1903, made use of the latest in technology when he described Helen and Laura as 'bottles of tears, reverberating phonographs of sobs'.[83] The only rebellious and prophetic voices – contemporary with Thackeray but unheard in England – were Flaubert's and Taine's. '*Mother-worship* is one of the things that will make future generations burst out laughing. Just as our respect for *love*.'[84]

The idealization and worship of 'good women', symptomatic of the author's over-involvement in his characters, certainly originate in Thackeray's emotional life. Except for his mother, the women he was involved with were of 'soft, simple, innocent and womanly' character.[85] Isabella Shawe, whom Thackeray married in 1836 when she was eighteen, was generally considered to be a small colourless woman lacking personality. In 1833 Thackeray confided to his mother his dream of petit-bourgeois wedded intimacy: to 'live in the little house in Albion Street, going to church regularly, rising early, and walking in the park with Mrs T. and the children'.[86] The first four years of their life together seemed to pass without shadow. The first clouds were Isabella's apathy when Thackeray could not persuade her to get up in the morning, and her apparent failure to understand she must not on any account disturb her husband's work.[87] It seems also that charm, innocence and kindness – all primordial qualities for Thackeray – could not totally compensate for their lack of common aims and interest.[88] Isabella began to show unequivocal symptoms of unbalance, which, after 1840, found expression in inexplicable fits 'of languor and depression ... and excessive lowness of spirits'.[89] After attempting suicide on 12 September 1840, Isabella, who had given birth to three children in four years, entered an asylum in 1841. Thackeray of course visited her regularly. In 1843 she entered a psychiatric establishment where she died in 1893, after fifty-three years of schizophrenia.[90] Among the causes of Isabella's illness the psychiatrist Stanley Cobb distinguished a hereditary factor, the excessive hold of a too possessive and authoritarian mother and, to trigger things off, a sudden change in her way of life within marriage, three successive pregnancies and the shock of the death of one of her children.

At an early age and after only four years of wedded life Thackeray was therefore a widower, yet still prisoner of an indissoluble, non-existent marriage. Even if Thackeray's letters do not often reveal it, his suffering and feeling of loss were not less acute.[91] He reacted in the usual way to the great emotional emptiness of single married life by devising a timetable to guard him from having to face himself for even one moment. He spent a great deal of time at receptions, paid visits of all kinds, and worked enormously hard. But he did not delude himself about his motives for his frantic activity.[92] His domestic failure was sadly evoked when, being reproached for portraying only saints or viragos and not 'a family, enjoying the genuine blessings of calm, domestic felicity', he replied: 'how can I describe that ... domestic calm? I have never seen it. I have lived all my life in Bohemia.'[93]

During Isabella's rapid deterioration, when Thackeray had to face the practical difficulties brought about by her growing incapacity, he was greatly helped by his mother. Thackeray, an only, coddled child, was yet sent to boarding-school at the age of six. His mother's love, her charm and strong personality,[94] may have increased his awareness of how cruel this precocious separation had been, and reinforced his passionate desire for an inaccessible and adorable being. G. N. Ray holds that Thackeray's 'remembrance of what his mother had been for him in youth fixed once for all his idea of womanhood', and that his early loss of a home due to his mother's remarriage and the educational methods of the period, created for ever in him 'this dichotomy between the warmth and trust of a happy home circle and the selfish indifference of the outside world'.[95] His letters clearly show how during his trials at boarding-school[96] he clung to the image of his mother for protection; when his home began to disintegrate his mother again saved him. The identification he had already made between wife and mother was reinforced by his family situation: his mother became – episodically in real life and in his phantasies – the mother of his children, that is to say a wife as well. In one letter Thackeray even grieved that his mother could not be 'mother, sister, wife' for him all at once, and expressed his jealousy and 'disappointed yearning'.[97]

With his wife's disappearance, and his mother all too present in her son's adult life, the third figure in the trinity was Jane Brookfield. Thackeray's unhappy passion for this wife of a vicar has been fully described by his biographers, as has its effect on the novel *Henry Esmond* (1851) at the time of their final break.[98] Jane Brookfield seems to have made an immediate impression on Thackeray at their earliest meetings. His love was kindled by Brookfield, who not having found in Jane the domestic wife of his dreams, often treated her coldly, even brutally.[99] An inaccessible wife, the mother of three children, the patient victim of a brutal husband, Jane, in Thackeray's imagination, took on more and more the traits of 'Mater Dolorosa with a heart bleeding with love'[100] and he innocently described his idol's perfections to her husband.[101] He seems to have decided almost deliberately to sublimate his love; and in his letters Jane remains a beloved and chastely venerated 'sister'.[102] When the break in her marriage came about, Thackeray held on to the categorical imperative of Duty, a word he kept repeating, duty especially towards Brookfield whom he held in high regard despite everything. The way he recalled the episode in 1853 might be seen as a regret for a passion that remained platonic, and for all his scruples: '(the devil) whispers me ... *a quoi bon* all this longing and yearning and disappointment ... a couple of lies and the whole thing might be remedied. Do you suppose other folks are so particular?'[103] At the moment of the break in 1851 he speaks with the anger of a man who feels he has been cheated.[104] All this reticence, this extraordinary mixture of friendship, love, desire, veneration and rancour towards a potential mistress reveals an emotional immaturity which was as much characteristic of the period as of him. Thackeray went so far as to explicitly to embody Mrs Brookfield, his mother and his daughters in a sort of redeeming Holy Trinity, intended to strengthen him on the road to grace and purity.[105]

His fate can be compared with that of George Eliot and G. H. Lewes, John Stuart Mill and Harriet Taylor, and even Dickens and Ellen Ternan, who were more defiant of Victorian conventions.[106] His personal frustrations helped to breed the contradictions inherent in his conception of the opposite sex and the doubts that underlay his attitude to life.

The life-stories of Dickens and Thackeray may have helped to reinforce their view of the transcendental woman. But they were not alone. Generally, the heroines of fiction corresponded more or less to the female idea sketched by contemporary moralists and philosophers, who were also but reflectors for society. Whether fairy or soul of the home, moral tutor or interceding angel, the wife-mother was a shield against the thousand perils thrown up by society. She lighted the family and with it all humanity along the path of duty. Sternness underpinned by sweetness would ensure to everyone reward according to the tenets of Christian and capitalist morality.

[5]

The Countervailing Criticism

The sharp criticism of the wife's position also found in the Victorian novel contrasts strikingly with her idealization. As the century went on, this tendency, which was already implicit in Jane Austen's ironic vision, often asserted itself in a more tragic mood, especially in Meredith, Hardy and George Moore. While the wife-mother appeared as victim to social, family and legal conventions, some writers were equally aware that both the educational system and her state of subjection generated a dialectic of master and slave. A few novelists, George Eliot and Emily Brontë in particular, managed to synthesize all these elements into a symbolic representation of woman's tragic destiny.

The marriage-market, a recurrent theme in Dickens's social criticism, was an aspect of the destiny of many heroines – Louisa in *Hard Times*, Dombey's first wife and Edith in *Dombey and Son*, Mercy Pecksniff in *Bleak House*, Bella Wilfer in *Our Mutual Friend*. Louisa is given to Bounderby although she has no taste for him whatever. In *Dombey and Son*, Dickens punished Dombey for taking for his wife 'a lady with no heart to give him'[1] out of pure self-interest: to 'represent' and to bring an heir into the world. The marriage of Dombey and Edith stems from the same motives. Edith, a beautiful and respectable young widow, but without resources, is given over by her mother to Dombey. They have nothing in common. Edith keenly feels the shame of being auctioned like an animal or a slave. This type of marriage of 'interest and convenience' was an everyday practice; it made of Edith a 'fallen woman' and exposed Louisa to a temptation which nothing in her family background or education had taught her to resist.

Trollope's attitude to the marriage-market was tinged by a sense of humour alien to the other novelists mentioned. Conservative by temperament, he observed that marriage was necessary – it was 'a woman's only career'.[2] A woman had to prove herself realistic and sensible enough to choose a materially and intellectually compatible partner. She must not end up an old maid.[3] In many a novel he denounces the intolerable and irresponsible pressure families, for material reasons, put upon young girls to force them into the arms of the first-comer. In the *Vicar of Bullhampton* Mary breaks with the wealthy and propertied Gilmore, despite his enviable social position, when she realizes that she does not love him,[4] and, undeterred by his poverty, rejoins the man of her life, Captain Marrable. *The Small House at Allington* is a marriage-market on a large scale. The matrimonial plans of the squire for his nieces are to unite possessions, money and lands. But after the attempts of the Courcey family to marry off a girl of nearly thirty have failed, she remains unmarried, poor and unhappy.

The author's sympathy goes out to men or women who, like Bell and Lily, dare to resist social and family pressure. In *Can You Forgive Her?* he studies one of these tragic marriages of convenience. Lady Glencora is forced to marry one very young man at a time when she is in love with another. Trollope is willing to admit that it is the family's duty to oppose a young girl's marrying a blackguard but he believed that it is unforgivable to force her to marry against her will.[5] Marriages contracted blindly and without love lead to disaster. Trollope saw such errors in a society governed by money as needing to be identified, analysed and fought, but decorously, without excessive indignation or melodramatic remonstrance. As in *The Kellys and O'Kellys* the characters are generally not traitors or victims, angels or demons. And even when the fate of the young people is decided for them rather than by them, Trollope seems to think they they have not been too hard done by.

A contemporary critic said that Thackeray's central purpose in *The Newcomes* was apparently to analyse 'that social disease, unhappy wedded life'.[6] From his *Punch* days on he had denounced the affliction of the marriage-market with a somewhat wearisome insistence, and criticized the plots and financial demands of families. 'I will sell you my beloved daughter, Blanche Stiffneck, for a hundred thousand pounds.' In the same article he invented the lover's ten commandments: 'Thou shalt not love without a lady's maid; thou shalt not marry without a coach and horses ... without a page in buttons and a French bonnet.'[7] He also cudgelled the Court Circulars and their ridiculous advice on dress for the 'mothers, daughters, aunts, grandmothers of England'[8] dear to Mrs Ellis. In *Sketches and Travels in London* he again denounced the exigencies of 'the gentility' and the consequent ill-assortment of couples.[9]

His protagonists are generally divided between idealists and cynics. Ignoring, if not the conventions, then at least the respective incomes of the parties, the former speak highly of love marriages. While Pendennis's uncle exhorts him to marry a rich woman who can promote his career, Colonel Newcome urges Clive to marry Ethel and praises the superiority of 'a happy home (over) the finest house in Mayfair'.[10] But the naïve and idealistic colonel is himself trampled on and broken. *The Virginians* is a hymn to those who marry for love without money: the happiness of Colonel Lambert and his wife, of George Warrington and Theo Lambert, who knew how to resist the pressures of a society pitted against prodigal sons, is contrasted with the broken lives of the previous novel, *The Newcomes*. In family conspiracies the mother often has the formidable role of go-between, as in *Dombey and Son* and *Our Mutual Friend*. This is not exactly a new theme in the English novel; it was there in the family of Clarissa Harlowe and, later, with Jane Austen, in the satiric figures of the match-making mothers, Mrs Bennett and Lady Catherine de Bourgh in *Pride and Prejudice*.

In his criticism of the marriage-market in a society ruled by money, Thackeray was at least being consistent. When he married Isabella Shawe, he was earning £400 a year as a journalist on the *Constitutional* and she was supposed to have an annual income of £100 payable quarterly. But his mother-in-law stopped paying after the first two instalments.[11] The details were taken up in *The Adventures of Philip on his Way through the World,* which dwelt upon the vicissitudes of Charlotte's small income which a cruel mother neglected to pay her.[12] In these novels disinterestedness and austerity are always justly rewarded by marital happiness. Thackeray himself remarked in 1859 that he could not objectively judge what some called 'early and imprudent marriages', and that he contemplated with a partial eye young people 'qui s'aiment'.[13] And yet when it was a question of what should happen to his own 'motherless' daughters, whose future rightly preoccupied him, his romanticism was notably attenuated: he deplored the 'romantic, visionary' ideas of the girls and begged them to renounce any idea of marriage with 'a penniless young clergyman with one lung'. He dreaded having in his charge a needy son-in-law incurably ill and demanding to boot.[14]

Pendennis, Henry Esmond and *The Newcomes* deal with the social customs which condemn couples to long suffering, and daughters, like Ethel in *The Newcomes* and Beatrix in *Henry Esmond* to the role of victim and martyr. Society considers women as commodities, tagged with title, beauty or wealth. Thackeray's allusions to this are never-ending.[15] There are two categories of victim: some, like Lady Clara and Rosey in *The Newcomes*, accept the laws of supply and demand from the start and put up no resistance to family and social pressures; the others, and the more interesting, are more or less conscious rebels who through revolt forge their own destruction. Becky Sharp, and above all Ethel Newcome and Beatrix Esmond, belong with the latter. They are at once the most vital of Thackeray's female characters, and the proofs of the way the marriage-market works. Their careers illustrate the range of Thackeray's outlook.

Beatrix and Ethel are like sisters in their behaviour and even in the language they use, although Ethel's portrait is more elaborate, and her role in *The Newcomes* much more important than Beatrix's in *Henry Esmond*.[16] Both women are keen to attract to climb the social ladder. Dazzling, beautiful, moody and selfish, Beatrix has been engaged three times. She has no illusions about herself; she ceaselessly contrasts her selfishness, her greed for flattery, diamonds and carriages with her mother's angelic disinterestedness.[17] She knows too that she is 'born to shine in great assemblies, to adorn palaces, and to command',[18] and must never think of marrying a man of slender means. Her cynical lucidity throws a dazzling light on that vast market in which she is one of the finest articles on sale: 'My face is my fortune, Who'll come? – Buy, buy, buy!'[19] Intended by her grandmother, Lady Kew, to marry Lord Kew, Ethel Newcome repulses Clive's advances for the sake of family plans she accepts as inevitable. 'Neither you nor I can alter our conditions.'[20] No more than Beatrix would she think of marrying a poor man. Surrounded, like her, by suitors, she aspires to blandishments and luxury. But the portrait becomes more complex than Beatrix's, for Thackeray makes clear that this solitary child deprived of warmth through the upper-middle-class or aristocratic way of life, is at once the more or less rebellious victim and ardent denouncer of the laws of the marriage-market. It is she who enunciates the credo of the young society girl: 'I believe in elder sons, and a home in town and a house in the country! ...', the law of the market-place. 'The Circassian beauties don't sell under so many thousand purses.'[21] Yet she denounces the baseness of girls who lend themselves to these underhand dealings[22] and causes a scandal by appearing at a family dinner wearing a green ticket from a sale of pictures marked 'sold',[23] while all the while accepting her family's arbitrary decisions. She rejects Kew's offer of marriage, an opportunity for a magnificent satire of the absurd idealization of women by men[24] but she resigns herself to not marrying Clive, thus condemning him and herself to lonely unhappiness.

This is where the fates of the two rebels diverge. Attracted by the romanticism and royal splendour, Beatrix tries her luck with a soap-opera Prince, an adventure that her virtuous family aborts. Thackeray then exiles her to France, prematurely aged by her 'débordements', 'to what a fate I disdain to tell'.[25] Beatrix turns up again in *The Virginians* in the shape of Madame la Baronne Bernstein, cast out by the American family.[26] Ethel, on the other hand, who takes on more and more the figure of heroine, walks the path of sanctity and renunciation: her contradictions are characteristic of Thackeray, torn on the one hand between a realistic instinct and the idea of revolt, and on the other hand by the concessions he has to make to Mrs Grundy. The requirements of the heroine's dignity lead Thackeray to make a false rebel of Ethel and finally, after she has been an ambitious and charming coquette, he turns her into a sort of incoherent saint. Once more, as in *Vanity Fair*, the author does not know which side he is on. Ethel, sacrificed by the families Thackeray denounces as tyrannical, Mammon-worshippers, is admitted into the community of ideal women, exemplifying self-sacrifice. The rest of her existence is spent as mother to her nephews who have been abandoned by Lady Clara and in various charitable works. The tenor of her remarks to Laura Pendennis and the vagueness in which the author leaves Clive's future after Rosey's death suggest a real conversion on Ethel's part.[27]

The wife's subjection, like the market which is fatal to the couple's happiness, is one of the essential social criticisms of these novelists. The theme is tackled very early by Thackeray in a review of George Sand's novel: *Indiana*.[28] The type of man often designated as a Turk or sultan wants a consenting slave: 'A humble, flattering, smiling, child-loving, tea-making ... (slave) who laughs at our jokes, ... coaxes and wheedles us in our humours.'[29] Law and custom combine to subject the wife to varying but uniformly humiliating uses, and to crush intelligent women whom the men then tend to scorn.[30] In *The Ravenswing* the wife appears as a being who adulates her husband, whatever his weaknesses: stupidity, vanity, infidelity, brutality, exploitation.[31] For 'these women were made for our comfort and delectation, gentlemen – with all the rest of the minor animals'.[32] Rendered submissive and hypocritical by the power of conspiracy, the wife becomes the dull flatterer of her lord and master: like Sir Pitt's second wife she keeps herself busy with endless and absurd tapestry-making, sewing, musical exercises, mere parades of her uselessness and bondage.[33]

Thackeray wrote *Henry Esmond* when he was suffering from the blow of the break with Jane and indignation at Brookfield's behaviour towards his wife. Critics were particularly struck by his portrait of the misunderstanding between the Castlewoods, and Thackeray, foreseeing with satisfaction Brookfield's rage on reading these lines, hoped he would treat his wife better in the future.[34] The resentment of Lord Castlewood was aroused in part by his acknowledgement of the real superiority of the woman whom society assigned to the role of 'slave and bedfellow'.[35] Hence his indifference, infidelity and even brutality.

In one sense the husband's tyranny was banal. But Thackeray, Anne Brontë and George Eliot took away the banality from the unlimited despotism 'of the Monarchs governing their own dominions at home',[36] unrestrained by any law. The theme of *The Memoirs of Barry Lyndon* is a brute's abuse of the husband's legal omnipotence. By persecuting Honoria and threatening her admirers, Barry Lyndon has compelled her to marry him. Having thus possessed himself legally of her fortune, he practically imprisons her in her home under the supervision of the servants. He lives largely on his wife's fortune and every time he needs her signature to sell or dispose of her possessions, he extorts it from her under threat. He keeps her captive by threatening his son – systematically corrupting the child, who at the age of five drinks and swears and abuses the vicar and the servants.[37] The author states that Lady Lyndon must remain alive, for if she were to die, her husband would become penniless, the heir to her fortune being the son of a first marriage.[38]

In that part of the plot of *The Newcomes* which concerns Lady Clara and Barnes, Thackeray deals with divorce among the aristocracy. The timid and fearful Lady Clara is compelled by her family to give up the beloved of her life, Jack Belsize, and is literally sold to Barnes Newcome, a notorious blackguard. Beaten, neglected and despised, Lady Clara finally leaves the family home with her former suitor, now Lord Highgate. The wealthy Barnes can avail himself of the procedure described earlier in Chapter 2: divorce or annulment of the marriage through a private Act of Parliament preceded by an action brought by the supposedly wronged husband against his wife's lover. Thackeray shows how the attenuating circumstances – desertion and cruelty by the husband – are not sufficient to strengthen the wife's case, even with the help of a lawyer.[39] The serjeant describes an imaginary family paradise, children prattling around their loving parents, the abandoned husband in his house deserted by the unworthy wife, and vehemently defends 'the rights of British husbands!'[40] This caricature of a court, this jury made up of 'respectable men and fathers of families themselves'[41] heavily penalizes Lord Highgate and awards generous damages to the allegedly thwarted husband. Thackeray was indignant at this travesty of justice and sketched a sinister portrait of the fate awaiting the divorced wife.

> She scarce dares to look out of the windows of her new home ... all the sisterhood of friendship is cut off from her ... She knows she has darkened the lot ... and the home of the man she loves the best.[42]

The author's indignation against those responsible for the marriage and his sympathy for the persecuted wife are coupled with reservations about her desertion. Contemplating this stage of the wretched existence of Lady Clara, Thackeray no longer denounces society's injustice,[43] and his interest in reforming the law is secondary.[44]

In *Hard Times* the injustice of divorce is approached from the point of view of the poor, and of the exploited man: Stephen Blackpool is too poor to consider divorce proceedings and to break with the outcast his wife has become. While she could, within the limits of the couple's common possessions, squander Stephen's, this fact of course worked more frequently against the wife.[45] In *Eliza Cook's Journal* this is mentioned in connection with the exploitation of Betsy Trotwood by her husband.[46]

In *The Tenant of Wildfell Hall* Anne Brontë tells of the bondage of a woman whose married life is made a mockery by her brute of a husband. Like other contemporary protests, the novel criticizes not the husband's privilege within the framework of the marriage laws, but the abuse of his powers. The heroine married Huntingdon. He is riddled with debts, and his lands mortgaged. She decides to devote the whole of her income to paying off what he owes. 'For all I have will be his, and all he has will be mine',[47] she states naïvely. Only through her uncle's foresight does she hold on to a tiny income which her husband cannot touch.[48] Like Lady Stanley, Helen Huntingdon is left more and more to herself, away in the country, while her husband leads a gay life in London for three or four months a year, feasting, drinking, gambling. Helen, a paragon of virtue, does not disapprove of her husband's 'healthy' pleasures like hunting. But she revolts against his chronic alcoholism (inspired by

Branwell Brontë),[49] his brutality, and, worse of all, his attempts to corrupt the child. At the end of her tether because of his insults, carousing and infidelities, she secretly leaves the conjugal home, and has to pass herself off as a widow under a false name. Such a portrait of a vicious husband's baseness and a virtuous wife's tribulations was too frank for contemporary critics: they accused the author of 'a morbid love of the coarse, if not of the brutal'.[50] In 1903 one critic, exasperated by the exhibitionistic saintliness of Mrs Huntingdon, indicts her for her severe and reproachful attitude and makes her responsible for her husband's bad ways.[51]

'Janet's Repentance' in *Scenes of Clerical Life* brings something new on to the scene. Her very first fictional work shows George Eliot's original treatment of female characters: the novelty is Janet's alcoholism which though reactive (defence against a brutal and alcoholic husband's tyranny) removes her somewhat from the stereotype of the wife-mother. Janet drinks because her husband neglects and brutalizes her. She is not strong enough to resist and is only vaguely aware of the protection the law might give her if she could prove her life in danger from her husband.[52] George Eliot does not let her have the most effective weapon against despair, a mother's love, or professional training. She is incapable of supporting herself. Janet's life is not idealized before her conversion: her alcoholism, for example, is obvious from the expression in her eyes.[53] George Eliot's correspondence and biography reveal that her publisher John Blackwood, while regretting that 'the poor wife's sufferings should have driven her to so unsentimental a resource as beer', all the same admitted the character's authenticity. But he asked George Eliot to soften the portrait as much as possible.[54] As she already had toned down her models considerably, as well as the village of Milby and Janet's martyrdom, she was not happy about accepting this advice.[55] All the same she did. G. S. Haight quotes passages from the manuscript which George Eliot suppressed in the printed version: 'not more than half a dozen married ladies were . . . observed to become less sure of their equilibrium as the day advanced'.[56] The portrait of Milby and the Dempster couple in the published version represents a compromise between the prescriptions of the epoch and the realism of George Eliot, often affirmed in her critical articles in the *Westminster Review*.

The victim of the marriage-market and of the laws governing marriage and divorce is thus a recurring figure especially in middle- and upper-middle-class and aristocratic circles. At a time when numerous contemporary documents denounced the even more cruel enslavement of women in the lower classes and the widespread practice of wife-beating, their lot was only rarely discussed in fiction. Dickens and Mrs Gaskell were the exceptions. In *Bleak House* several working-class women suffer bad treatment at the hands of their husbands. One who sports a black eye is married to a mason drunk three days a week. Another awaits in terror the return home of the one she calls 'my master', who thrashes her soundly.[57] Later on in the novel, Allan Woodcourt finds a poor woman in the hovel of 'Tom-All-Alone' and guesses that her wound is the doing of her husband.[58] In *Mary Barton* and *North and South* Elizabeth Gaskell evokes the misery of the slums. A suffering mother gives her shrivelled breast to a two-year-old child to allay his hunger. After her husband's death she courageously takes on responsibility for the welfare of the whole family and earns by baby-farming and needlework.

The wife-mother was conditioned by her dependence. Once more it was Thackeray and George Eliot who went furthest in critical analysis. Systematic dependence produced a slave mentality. Thackeray never tired of making the point, in the form of direct commentary, or through plot and dialogue. The slave constantly breaks out in simulated adulation of her lord and master. Hypocrisy and dissimulation become character traits, and often the instrument of survival and domination.[59] Even the best among them, hypocrites despite themselves,[60] smile at the husband's most jejune jokes and appease his anger with sweet words. A cynical diatribe by Barry Lyndon even points to something like female masochism, which heralds the psychology of a later time.[61] In Mrs Ellis's female strategy the first rule is to do nothing that might cast aspersions on male dignity (read authority and virility) and to give way on the little things in order to gain on the large.[62] (Women's magazines today put across an identical message.) Thus the wife comes across as both victim and accomplice in the Master/Slave relationship.

Cunning is a striking feature of Becky Sharp, but also of Lady Maria in *The Virginians*, who tries to catch the young Harry Warrington by deceiving him about her age. Thackeray is divided between indignation and admiration at a woman's power of dissemblance when disappointed in her dearest and most secret hopes.[63] Affectation and duplicity characterize Blanche Amory, who knows how to induce male admiration by feigning charm, tender sentimentality and various accomplishments. She succeeds in captivating Arthur Pendennis. He is dazzled by her exquisite sensibility (above all when she sings '*Mes Larmes*') and her parlour talents.[64] The narrator's hostility towards this heartless hypocritical creature is plainly expressed when he describes her 'ogles' and the shaming nature of all her feelings: enthusiasm, love, hate, etc.[65] Though she loses two suitors, Harry Foker and Arthur Pendennis, who are disgusted by her duplicity, she, like Beatrice, finds a husband in France, the ever-open land of deliverance for Englishwomen of doubtful morality. Madame la Comtesse de Montmorency becomes a Parisian adventuress.[66]

The enslavement of women forced them to use cunning in order to survive. But for Thackeray that was not all. Possessiveness and jealousy also betrayed their deep insecurity. Despite her admiration for *Henry Esmond* which she read three times (she detested *Vanity Fair*), Harriet Martineau criticized the female characters of the novel and felt certain that Thackeray had never known 'women of excellent capacity and cultivation'.[67] Rachel Castlewood is indeed the martyred and at the same time abusive wife we described earlier. In her we find the characteristics of a Virgin Mary figure: abnegation, spirit of sacrifice, etc.; but the stereotype comes and goes. She is at once diminished and enhanced through the contrast with Beatrix. Beatrix and her mother are a multifaceted couple: Beatrix, worldly, flighty, ambitious and selfish; Rachel, altruistic, disinterested, devout. Weak and conformist, Rachel accepts the constraints of marriage while Beatrix revolts unsuccessfully against the conventions and alienation of women. There is no doubt that the first of these contrasts dominates. But Thackeray suggests that Rachel, who is intellectually and morally superior to her husband, crushes him with her virtues of nobility, purity, lack of passion. 'She neither sins nor forgives.'[68] Her possessiveness and jealousy weigh not only on her husband but also on Harry when he shows interest in a young village girl. Her possessiveness for the male sex, makes her into her daughter's rival, despite herself. That she fights with all her force against this jealousy, and against her growing passion for Harry, is only one of the contradictions in the character and one of Thackeray's ambiguities. For her as for the other female figures he alternates between irrational enthusiasm and unforbearing lucidity.[69]

Rachel Castlewood's most interesting feature is precisely what shocked contemporaries most: the evolution of maternal feelings, complemented by Harry's filial ones, into heterosexual love. The incestuous connotations were for once clearly suggested. George Eliot, Mary Russell Mitford and Mrs Jameson were indignant.[70] Particularly denounced were the heroine's ambiguous sentiments. A *Times* critic went so far as to deprive Harry and Rachel of their heroic dignity.[71] At any rate the whole makes sense in terms of Thackeray's own life. The early episodes in the novel, notably the filial relationship between Harry and Rachel, are coloured by the writer's childhood. Later in the novel his complicated relationships – both amorous and sublimated – with Jane Brookfield are superimposed on the first scheme.[72] Thackeray has familiarized us with this type of sublimation in his own relations; his feelings towards Jane Brookfield, 'my mistress, my sister' and his mother were latent with incest. For a long time Rachel claims and sincerely believed she loves Harry like a son, and Harry Rachel like a mother. In *Pendennis*, Arthur's relationship with his mother (possessive mother and son aggressive towards mother's suitor) also suggests the same oedipal fixation.

The clearest denunciation of maternal possessiveness is also to be found in *Pendennis*. The worship of Helen, that 'all-absorbing mother' for her son, is condemned by Thackeray as being harmful to young Arthur's development. In the first volume she spends all her small savings on repayment of this gently born youth's debts for champagne, cigars, clothes. Her maternal selfishness accepts that Laura too should sacrifice her savings. She becomes parsimonious at home in order to maintain her son in luxury. This type of pandering and Helen Pendennis's illusions about his talents make it more difficult for Arthur to face the world.[73] The Helen who behaves like this is partly inspired by Thackeray's memory of his mother, but the two women differ on one essential point: Mrs Carmichael-Smyth was a cultivated and refined woman, endowed with a strong personality, whereas Helen, 'a rather provincial prude'[74] is conspicuous for platitudes, like the one about the 'evils of premature engagements'.[75]

It is the love of Pendennis and Fanny Bolton that reveals in Helen and Laura all the pettiness and snobbery of middle-class wife-mothers. Their arrival at Arthur's bedside, till then devotedly cared for by Fanny, is like that of avenging Furies. 'The widow whose face had been hopelessly cruel and ruthless ... pale and solemn' brushes Fanny aside. Armed with watch and bible she takes possession again of the house, and removes all traces of the girl's presence.[76] Female sadism is provoked by Fanny's state of slavery.

Intuitively he perceives the part the women play as guardians of the status quo.[77]

Jane Brookfield's reaction was just as petty as that of the novel's characters. '[I] cannot help being sorry you dignify the Fanny Bolton fancy with the name of "love", – it seems degrading the word to apply it to the "dear little girl who drops her H's".' This shows that Thackeray's satire was not exaggerated.[78]

Putting on show the cruelty and snobbery of these two 'pure' women does not prevent Thackeray from justifying their ostracism of Fanny. 'My mother would have acted in just such a way if I had run away with a naughty woman – that is I hope she would.'[79] Thus the attitude of the writer towards his two wife-mothers, in turn venerated and despised, leaves the reader with a feeling of unease. Thackeray was too much inhibited by the Victorian ethic and hesitant about the liberties he could take with it. According to Lady Ritchie, Thackeray once said revealingly that he did not love Laura and that if he created such characterless or wicked women it was because that was his experience of them.[80]

Amelia in *Vanity Fair* is also revealing. If Amelia has given rise to many contradictory commentaries, it is because Thackeray's conception of the character and his ambivalence towards the only person who, along with Dobbin, finds favour in his eyes,[81] calls his realism into question. Amelia is a foil to Becky: each of the two characters is unimaginable without the other.[82] Amelia, a coddled and protected child, is completely disarmed when, alone in the world, she tries to provide for herself and her son. The ironic enumeration of her talents, recalling Miss Matty's (*Cranford*) in analogous circumstances, is also a condemnation of the education of young middle-class girls.[83] Amelia is the complete victim: victim of the marriage-market, of her father's ruin and the hostility of her in-laws, of her blind love for a husband unworthy of such devotion. When he leaves for the war and is killed she nearly loses her reason. Thackeray observes with a critical eye this impotence in the face of the trials inflicted by life. He implies that the transference to young Georgy of the excessive adoration of the missing husband is as harmful as Becky's coldness towards *her* son.

We know that Thackeray's preference was for good, kind, generous women, towards the qualities of the heart rather than the mind. Only love, according to him, could save society from the sinister coldness of human relations that hold sway in *Vanity Fair*.[84] And it is the superiority of heart over intelligence which is the major theme of the Becky-Amelia opposition. 'Some are made to scheme, and some to love.'[85] The argument is often explicitly in Amelia's favour: 'kind, weak and tender woman ... so pure ... so meek and humble that she could not but needs be a *true lady*'.[86]

Enamoured of submissive femininity, of the domestic ideal in the Biedermeier style,[87] Thackeray shows the effect of education in the 'German chapters' of *Vanity Fair*. The Germans of the Duchy where Becky took refuge still read *Werther* and consider Goethe's *Elective Affinities* 'an edifying moral book'.[88] Goethe's novel, which describes two pairs of noble characters falling in love with each other, is implicitly contrasted with the mediocre evangelical literature on which Amelia was nurtured. In the novel these edifying tracts have titles such as 'The Washerwomen of Finchley Common', 'A Voice from the Flames', 'A Trumpet Warning from Jericho', 'The Fleshpots Broken', or 'The Converted Cannibal'.[89] The heroines of *Don Juan* and *Fidelio*, which Amelia hears at the Cologne Opera, are worlds away from her: Elvira conjures up tragic passion, Donna Anna heroism and Fidelio is the romantic heroine triumphing over tyranny at the risk of her life. Amelia's mixed feelings after hearing *Don Juan* – ecstatic joy and guilt – emphasize the narrowness of her puritan background.[90] 'She has been domineered over by vulgar intellects. It is the lot of many a woman',[91] states the author. On the whole contemporary reactions were clearly favourable to Amelia, with some reservations from Thackeray's mother and Jane Brookfield.[92]

While Thackeray's female characters are generally ambiguous one category of them is not. Mothers-in-law are villains. The first of these viragos appeared in one of the *Yellowplush Stories*, 'Miss Shum's Husband'. The most notable ones are Rosey's mother in *The Newcomes* – Mrs Mackenzie, 'Campaigner' – and Mrs Baynes in *The Adventures of Philip* ... These shrews are clearly derived from Isabella Thackeray's mother, Mrs Shawe. From the time of their engagement in 1836, Mrs Shawe, a possessive authoritarian lady, had attempted to keep her daughter from the impecunious young journalist. The details and the ensuing three-day quarrel between the fiancés are transposed in chapters twenty-four to twenty-eight of *The Adventures of Philip* ...[93] Later on, when Isabella fell ill, it appears that Mrs Shawe proved consistently selfish. Thackeray was very bitter about her.[94] Like Clive Newcome, he had to suffer in silence for fear of reprisals against his wife. Relations hardly ever improved between them. Thackeray, after informing his mother-in-law that he had entrusted Isabella to Doctor Pugin at Chaillot, admitted his unwillingness to see her again.[95] Mrs Mackenzie, the grimacing and intriguing old campaigner of *The Newcomes*,[96] tyrannizes daughter, son-in-law and servants, and even the son-in-law's venerable father. Not the least of her crimes is to have annihilated the personality of her daughter, and made of her a doll without will or identity. Rosie dies of a broken heart and inability to adapt to the difficulties of life, also from lack of love; for her gentleness, her passivity and her songs do not compensate for the deep incompatibility between her and Clive.[97] The other caricature of mother and mother-in-law is Mrs Baynes in *The Adventures of Philip* ... Like Mrs Shawe, Mrs Baynes ceases to pay the annual income of £100 due to her daughter Charlotte. She persecutes her by submitting Philip to wounding remarks about his poverty.[98]

All modern critics of Thackeray, and Taine before them, have noted his hesitations, his perpetual compromises, particularly with female characters. With Laura Bell, Amelia and Mrs Pendennis or Rachel Esmond it is true[99] that there is a clash between the actions of the heroines as the author represents them and the commentaries of the narrator. 'He creates ninnies, then kneels before them', wrote Taine.[100] Thackeray could not refrain from analysing pitilessly and clearsightedly what made his characters tick; the artist, in short, was honest and faithful to his observations. But the man or the 'Victorian gentleman', the novelist and the magazine editor in whom somehow the public person and the moralist were dominant, adapted his tastes and judgements to the conventions of the era. According to the code then in force, Amelia, Laura Bell, Helen Pendennis, and Rachel Esmond had to form part of the favourable constellation in the structure of the novels. At once rebellious and conformist, but more conformist than rebellious in his private and public life, and simultaneously, a detached and committed commentator, the author inevitably stumbled and floundered. Perhaps because of these recurring compromises, F. R. Leavis seems to have considered him as no more than a creator of plot and incident, and a dull one at that.[101]

In the works of Mrs Gaskell we find another kind of female mentality. She worried little about the dependent status of woman. The working middle-class wife – like herself – does not appear in her novels. On the other hand, parallel to the idealized wife-mothers, she created a woman who was narrow-minded, lacking in generosity and breadth, and therefore unable to perceive the highest forms of life and the spiritual torments of noble souls. Margaret Hale's mother in *North and South* is one of these 'small-minded characters',[102] at once incapable of facing the difficulties of a re-adaptation to a new mode of life, and of understanding, even intuitively, the scruples and inner debates of her husband which led to his resignation from orders. In the same way, the wife of the worker Boucher, incapable of understanding her husband's inner tortures, reacts pettily to his suicide. With her and Mrs Hale, the tragedy provokes panic and selfish laments against a stroke of fate that, in their narcissism, they imagine to be directed specially against themselves.

The most successful of these characters is Doctor Gibson's second wife in *Wives and Daughters*. She succeeds in capturing the attention of the doctor who is in search for a devoted wife capable both of helping a country doctor and acting as mother to his daughter Molly. Mrs Gibson is neither, and his error causes unhappiness for him and his daughter. The ex-governess wants to marry only in order to be kept in comfort and freed from the burden of earning a living. Mrs Gibson is depicted in the novel by means of a series of contrasts between her and Molly and her daughter Cynthia. She is above all narcissistic. While Molly constantly puts her father's comfort before her own both in everyday matters and when great decisions have to be made, and understands the meaning of his calling, Mrs Gibson only knows how to use the people surrounding her for her own interest. She does not miss an occasion to extort things from her husband: dresses, money for her daughter, baubles and knick-knacks, a footman. She engages in Machiavellian manoeuvres to marry off her daughter Cynthia. In relation to Doctor Gibson, Molly and even Cynthia, Mrs Gibson embodies selfishness against altruism, superficiality and pettiness against depth and generosity, hypocrisy against sincerity.

Emily Brontë's *Wuthering Heights* is quite another matter. Given its essentially symbolic nature, this novel totally transcends its era. If anything, Emily Brontë's imaginary universe, the unredeemed Old Testament world, the paroxysms of passion, hate and love that devour the characters, conjure up the later climate of Hardy, or the earlier Romantic period.

The essentially *other* nature of this novel was revealed, paradoxically, by Charlotte Brontë's naïve comments in the preface to the second edition of the novel in 1850. She was trying to present the work to the public, but was naturally embarrassed by the monstrous Heathcliff. She tried to justify the novel by seeking 'good' characters in it, and thought she had found one in Nelly Dean, 'a specimen of true benevolence and homely fidelity', and another in Edgar Linton, as 'example of constancy and tenderness'.[103] Though Charlotte was mistaken about the complex significance that Nelly Dean and Edgar Linton had for the author, whose values were foreign to her, G. H. Lewes showed an astonishing understanding for that time, when he admired in Cathy the coexistence of affection for Edgar Linton and passion for Heathcliff,[104] and the 'truth' of the work. In fact most contemporary critics were, to say the least, surprised by this novel.[105]

The two most interesting female characters are Cathy Earnshaw and Isabella Linton. The whole novel may appear to oppose Nature to Culture as two antagonistic worlds symbolized in Wuthering Heights and Thrushcross Grange. The heroines pass from one to the other through marriage: from Nature to Culture for Cathy, and Culture to Nature for Isabella, both journeys ending with death. Cathy grows up at Wuthering Heights with Heathcliff in an intimacy of spontaneity and revolt. Despite Heathcliff's tyranny, they flower in complete freedom, escaping to the moors or hiding in a corner of the house. Very early in the novel, as she notes in her diary, Cathy takes part in the revolt against family and religious authority.

When little by little Cathy enters the 'civilized' world of Thrushcross Grange, she accepts for a time that she must bend to the rules of a society governed by the laws of alliances between assets, properties and families. The stages of Cathy's 'taming', the change of a natural, spontaneous, wild creature into a socialized, almost stable being are perfectly clear in the novel. After her first five weeks' stay in Thrushcross Grange Cathy returns transformed, at least superficially, in behaviour and clothing.

... instead of a wild, hatless little savage jumping into the house, and rushing to squeeze us all breathless, there lighted from a handsome black pony a very dignified person with brown ringlets falling from the cover of a feathered beaver.[106]

The paraphernalia of a young Victorian girl continues the job of separation, coming between her and the inhabitants of Wuthering Heights like a screen. She moves away from the dogs in case they dirty her, puts her arm delicately round Nelly, who is covered with flour; she embraces Heathcliff, however, but reproaches him for his dirtiness and entertains fears that he might have spoiled her dress.[107]

In Balthus's illustration to this scene, she is indeed a 'little savage'.[108] When later on she agrees to marry Edgar she obeys materialistic and narcissistic considerations, hardly different from those of Beatrix Esmond or Ethel Newcome; Edgar Linton is handsome, young, rich, in love with her. But by denying momentarily within herself her passion for Heathcliff, by abandoning him and Nature, of which she is an organic part, Cathy brings about her own destruction. Torn from the elemental and violent world of Wuthering Heights, she suffocates in the civilized frame and debilitating order of Thrushcross Grange. Cathy's love for her foster-brother Heathcliff, with its incestuous connotations, is total. 'My love for Linton is like the foliage in the woods: time will change it ... my love for Heathcliff resembles the eternal rocks beneath ... Nelly, I *am* Heathcliff.'[109] It is also communication with all nature.[110] Each possesses the world through the other. Without the other, the world ceases to exist. 'If all else perished and *he* remained, I should still continue to be; and if else remained and he were annihilated, the Universe would turn to a mighty stranger.'[111]

Cathy dies at Thrushcross Grange, exiled from her very substance, from Heathcliff and the whole world. When she ignores Nelly's prudent protests she opens the window despite the cold, and tries to rejoin the moor and Heathcliff, to become one with them.[112] As usual Nelly Dean wants to enclose her in the iron collar of prudence and a morality at once constraining and worldly; was she not indignant when Cathy admitted in all innocence that she coveted Edgar's wealth and position, without renouncing her love for Heathcliff? Cathy marries Linton in part, she says, to help Heathcliff escape from his brother. If it is true, as J. Blondel thinks, that, through the presence of Mrs Dean, Emily Brontë wants to retain 'tacitly acknowledged moral notions'[113] in the novel, this morality, made out of cowardice and compromise, is rudely put to the test; Nelly Dean's remarks on the 'duties you undertake in marrying' and Cathy's lack of principles[114] appear flat and abstract beside the symbolic and poetic power of Cathy's language, the dialectic of leaf and rock, moon and lightning, frost and fire.

Isabella Linton is destroyed by the opposite process. While Cathy dies from sequestration and suffocation, Isabella succumbs to the sudden exposure to brutality and inhumanity in a world not governed by the complex and indirect modes of communication prevailing in civilization and culture. Cloistered in a rarified and hypercivilized milieu, Isabella sees Heathcliff through a screen of illusions, like a novel hero within the novel.[115] Fed on Romantic literature, she falls in love with a chimera, despite Cathy's brutal warnings, 'he'd crush you, like a sparrow's egg'[116] and Heathcliff's cynical candour.[117] Such is the breadth of her misapprehension that when she arrives at Wuthering Heights, her new home, she asks for the servant. Here too Nelly Dean intervenes by way of respect for social convention and humane behaviour, and claims for Isabella the symbols of order Heathcliff repudiates: comfort and service.[118]

Heathcliff's victory does not only consist in the cruel sufferings he inflicts on her. He succeeds in reducing the 'lady' formed in the mill of the conventions of a Christian society to a pagan thirst for vengeance: 'I'd rather he suffered *less*, if I might cause his sufferings ... if I may take an eye for an eye, a tooth for a tooth, for every current of agony, return a wrench, reduce him to my level.'[119] Is that not the perfect antithesis of the Victorian female ideal, of the model of the wife-mother? Woman, who is generally seen as being entrusted with the highest mission, here becomes an instrument of hatred and vengeance. Isabella is restored to the geographical and psychological universe of the Old Testament and the jungle where brutal elemental instinctive forces rage without restraint and humanity, and rejoins the animal and primitive world of savages, like the children in *Lord of the Flies*, before escaping from it, mortally wounded.

Thus the two women succumb to a similar phenomenon: brutal transplantation from their origins. Cathy is in some sort punished for having considered marriage an expedient, and for betraying Heathcliff, namely a part of herself. Isabella, a weak and defenceless creature, is guilty of having seen reality through the distorting prism of her romantic imagination. This world, in contrast to that of all our other novelists, is without compromise. Passions provoke confrontations that can only be deadly. The destructive role of Heathcliff is difficult to bear, even for the modern reader, even though Emily Brontë succeeds in not making a monster of him. Indeed this arbitrarily dispossessed creature uses the same weapons as his adversaries: cruelty, humiliation and the appropriation of his enemies' lands through marriage. One understands the reasons for his quest for vengeance.[120] Like Caliban, like the furies in Genet's *Maids*, like Fanon's colonized man, Heathcliff must resort to terrorist methods, swifter and more cynical perhaps than those of his enemies, but not more immoral, when for example, he uses women as an object of exchange to reconquer the land and person of his oppressors. In so doing, he also destroys the 'middle-class values' that truly appear in the novel as the superstructure of the mode of exploitation represented by the Lintons, Nelly Dean and Lockwood.

Sylvia's Lovers, one of Mrs Gaskell's richest novels, appeared a little later in February 1863. It belongs to her last creative period. Despite the complicated plot with countless sentimental and historical meanderings, the author created an unstereotyped wife character whose complexity bears some resemblance to George Eliot's heroines.[121]

Sylvia is not seen as an ideal woman, nor as her husband's prey, nor as a fallen woman. Her story is only that of a victim of circumstances: her father's unjust execution and the disappearance of the man she loved. Pressured by her mother, by her father's death, and Philip Hepburn's sentimental blackmail, and persuaded of the death at sea of her lover Kinraid, Sylvia resigns herself to marrying her cousin, Philip. She agrees to this marriage of convenience as a result of her despair, her sense of filial duty and her impotence before life's difficulties. The petulant, passionate girl becomes an indifferent and sad wife, a creature of duty and resignation.[122] The author presents a convincing portrait of the tragedy of a loveless marriage. An exemplary mothe r and wife, a devoted and obedient daughter, Sylvia seems to want to compensate for the absence of love by increased scruples. But all Philip's tenderness, and her straining her will to breaking point, could not compensate for her lack of love and passion.[123] The contrast between Sylvia's sexual attraction for Kinraid and the physical quasi-repulsion she feels for Philip is more than hinted at, despite the author's discomfort with this kind of problem.[124] Furthermore, such an instinctive and spontaneous creature is languishing in the closeness of the rural setting. Avid for space and freedom, she has trouble accepting the social constraints and all the symbols of a life 'of respectability and prosperity'.[125] The only moments of happiness are those she spends alone with her child, dreaming by the sea. When Kinraid returns from captivity and wants to marry her, Sylvia chooses the way of duty and fidelity to her husband. But she cannot forgive him his lie until the moment when, influenced by Philip's heroic expiation and softened by life, she loves him at last.

This wife's character does not seem artificial. The husband, the wife and the lover are the creatures of fortune. Sylvia's guilt, if guilt there be, resides in her lack of love and charity: she is incapable of forgiving Philip (who acts out of love and a desire to protect her from a reputedly unfaithful lover). The author's suggestion is that maturity and generosity are only acquired at the price of exceptional suffering.

Wives are at the centre of George Eliot's fictional world. Marriage with a superior or mediocre man is generally seen as a significant moment within the two dimensions, selfish narcissisms or search for the absolute – the two forces that drive George Eliot's heroines. A criticism of education underlies not only Mrs Transome in *Felix Holt the Radical*, Romola and Dorothea Brooke, but all her heroines. It is because she hungers for escape and not for intellectual discipline that Maggie Tulliver in *The Mill on the Floss* would sometimes like to have read 'all Scott's novels and all Byron's poems'.[126] Dorothea Brooke's lack of education and culture is also denounced as a further cause of illusion. Nearly all George Eliot's heroines, generally exceptionally gifted, suffer from a vocational vacuum which makes them less lucid and more vulnerable in their sentimental lives. Deprived of the means of fulfilling high and noble aspirations in their quest for the ideal, they are tossed about at the mercy of circumstance. Male influences hold sway over them. In the words of Virginia Woolf:

> Each has the deep feminine passion for goodness ... but ... she no longer knows to whom to pray. In learning they seek their goal, in the ordinary tasks of womanhood, in the wider service of their kind. They do not find what they seek and we cannot wonder.[127]

While woman's tragedy is harped on throughout the novels, this awareness never leads to militant feminism. George Eliot, however, thought highly of the pioneers of the 'Cause', Barbara Bodichon, Bessie Rayner-Parkes, Mrs Cornwallis. In February 1852, she wrote: 'Miss Parkes is a(n) ... ardent, honest creature, and I hope we shall be good friends'.[128] In 1853 she announced that she was going to meet Mrs Cornwallis, concerning two articles about the wife's legal position.[129] In 1854 she expressed the wish to read B. R. Parkes's pamphlet, *Remarks on the Education of Girls*.[130] In 1856 she circulated Barbara Bodichon's Petition demanding married women's right to their earnings[131] and she believed in the salutary effect of such a measure on 'the position and character of women'.[132] In 1858 she congratulated B. R. Parkes on writing the first in a series of articles on female labour in *The English Woman's Journal*.[133] She encouraged university education for women and made a gift of

£100 for Girton College.[134] All these acts witness to her interest in the feminist cause. That she was not a leader of the movement can be explained in many ways: total absorption in intellectual work – criticism, then novel writing – her private life whose marginal nature made her suffer all her life, even in the late phase of the celebrated evenings at the Priory. And finally, her attitude inclined her more, as Edith Simcox observed, 'towards enthusiasm for the discharge of duties than for the assertion of rights'.[135] Numerous studies have analysed the components of George Eliot's lay morality, built of stoicism, resignation, and an ethical altruism which places a higher value on acceptance than on revolt. The apologia for duty is in some senses the antithesis of the feminist revolt. Christian morality saturates the work of the woman who valued 'religion in so far as it was a metaphor for conduct'.[136]

Mrs Transome in *Felix Holt the Radical* (1866) has been the subject of mutually contradictory appreciations by Henry James and F. R. Leavis.[137] A mother and adulterous wife, presented by the author 'with the weight of time behind her'[138] she has nothing of the stereotyped sinner about her. Through Mrs Transome, George Eliot delivers herself of a devastating criticism of the education of a young girl drawn from the gentry. She has read Chateaubriand in secret and admits that 'these stories of illicit passion' give her forbidden pleasure. She claims to share the conventional view of the immorality of 'these dangerous French writers'.[139] Apart from this reading, the 'accomplishments' earlier taught to her, riding, smatterings of music and water-colouring, have withered with her, 'as valueless as old-fashioned stucco ornaments'.[140] Deprived of artistic and intellectual resources, she suffers the physical and moral sclerosis of a premature ageing, without ever having been enriched by maturity.

No emotionally rich family life compensates for the intellectual wasteland. Wife, mother, mistress, in all these roles Mrs Transome's existence is one long frustration. Even in the innocent eyes of Esther Lyon, Mr Transome seems a very strange being, come from another world, miles away from his wife. As for the neighbours, they feel sorry for her being bound to a feeble-minded partner only interested in entomology. But it is the disappointment caused by her relations with her son that brings the frustrated wife the most cruel suffering, and is one of the most important themes in the novel. It matters little that the son – a banker – is revealed as a hard creature, devoid of tenderness and humanity, concerned above all with his career, his wealth, his social ascent. What George Eliot underlines is the universal nature of the suffering of mothers, of disappointed hopes, and the gulf between illusion and reality. In the time immediately following Harold's return to the family home his mother is suddenly overwhelmed by the awareness of the failure of a whole life. Her son was the subject of immense aspirations before his conception, before his birth, during his years of absence, the subject of heart-rendering decision, and the moment of their long-awaited meetings has 'no ecstasy, no gladness'. George Eliot describes with a rare lucidity the maternity 'without generosity' of a woman who only knows how to be a mother: the idyll of the first years, when the child is in a state of emotional and physical dependence, then the painful distancing of growth and adolescence. 'The mother's ... raptures had lasted but a short time.' This 'expansion of the animal existence', this biological mutation occurring in motherhood,[141] is ephemeral. When the child grows up and goes away 'there are wide spaces of their time which are not filled with praying for their boys, reading old letters'.[142] An argument *pro domo* perhaps, but also a satire on the worship of motherhood, and awareness of a psychological and social problem that is still not resolved today. In 'Janet's Repentance', the tragedy of the mother's fate had already been raised, a search whose object was indefinitely postponed until the moment of truth when the aged woman fingered the vanity of her useless quest. Her last hope was the grave.[143] Mrs Transome's suffering is indeed 'that sorrow of aged women'.[144] 'A woman has never seen the worst till she is old',[145] she says to her chambermaid. Nor does her sinister affair with a businessman bring any compensation. There too she plumbs the human depths of baseness as a result of Fermyn's selfishness. And her suffering culminates in the moment when her son learns the truth: not only his mother's 'sin', but his consanguinity, the identity of his father, his worst enemy.

Esther Lyon is the other face of woman's destiny in the novel. Younger, more independent, she has not been subjected to a rigorous intellectual discipline, and her life could flow by in a narcissistic dream of luxury and status. In other circumstances she would easily become a Mrs Transome or even a Hattie. But as the daughter of a vicar of slender means, belonging to another generation, she gives lessons; work in this case confers freedom in the choice of husband. Above all she is fortunate enough to meet the 'didactic hero'[146] needed by positive characters to teach them a broader vision. Felix

Holt, indeed, offers her both 'love and salvation'.[147] Esther is one of the rare George Eliot heroines to be saved by marriage, to fulfil her highest aspirations in union with an exceptional being, happier in that than Maggie, Hetty Sorel, Mrs Transome, Romola and Dorothea Brooke. 'I am weak. My husband must be greater and nobler than I am.'[148] It is true she is capable of a moral progress whose stages are marked by successive renunciations: sacrifice for her adoptive father, abandonment of her inheritance and the life of luxury Harold Transome would offer her, to share poverty and the risks of a 'radical's' existence. The self acquires a wider dimension, little by little includes the others, her father, Mrs Transome. The stony road leads her to happiness.

Even though the shadow of adultery weighs on the plot and atmosphere of the novel, Mrs Transome cannot be encompassed within the narrow limits of the 'impure woman'. And she cannot be studied as one any more than Anna Karenina or Emma Bovary. Her tragedy is that of the ageing and solitude of a mother whose milieu, the landed gentry, has deprived her of all personal resources and the capacity for adaptation. The world of the Transome parents is transcended by the 'young' generation: the hard and grasping businessman, Harold Transome, the young progressive idealist, Felix Holt, and Esther, better armed by her adoptive father for a life of struggle in a society in transition. *Felix Holt the Radical* was enthusiastically received by the contemporary press. The few reservations concerned the Transome episode.[149] The publisher, John Blackwood, was hanging on the plot, anxious to know what 'Mrs Transome has done'. Frederick Harrison admitted with regret that he was shocked by Harold asking his mother, 'who is my father?' But the tragedy of the novel moved him to the point where he 'can think of nothing else'.[150]

'Renunciation', for George Eliot, is the essence of virtue; and it is the chief moral reality implied by her whole outlook.[151] In *Romola* renunciation characterizes the stages of the heroine's development: with Dinah Morris, Maggie Tulliver, Dorothea Brooke, she belongs to those whom Henry James called 'that group of magnificently generous women'.[152] Her evolution is a journey that removes her from Florence, then brings her back, and which leads a generous but still limited soul to an identity that is raised to the dimensions of humanity after the stages marked by the different men who stand out in her existence: her husband, her father, and Savanorola. In turn daughter, wife, then disciple, her devotion to these three people only offers temporary objectives in her quest for the absolute; she finds her reason for existence in sacrifice to the community, the poor of Florence and the victims of Tito, his mistress Tessa and their children.

Romola first appears in the familiar figure of the devoted daughter: she collaborates in the works of a blind and scholarly father. Isolated as a result of her hyper-intellectual education and the shared existence of an invalid, she falls in love with the first man who presents himself: the young Tito Melema. George Eliot implies that her mistaking his character is to be explained by a lack of experience inherent in her education and idealism. As she gets to know Tito better, she experiences one disillusion after another. Right from the start of their relationship, George Eliot indicates, Tito is crushed by the moral superiority he senses in Romola, and is blinded by the halo round her head. He would have preferred her less noble and more human.[153] And it is precisely caressing, animal, grace he looks for in Tessa, to flee the rigorous and demanding morality of his wife.[154]

On her father's death Savanarola reveals another obligation to her: Florence and suffering humanity. Bitterly deceived by a husband whose baseness she is forced to acknowledge, she receives Savanarola's message at the very moment when she is completely vulnerable. 'There is no compensation for the woman who feels that the chief relation of her life has been no more than a mistake. She has lost her crown.'[155] However, she feels she must continue to fulfil her wifely obligations despite her change of feelings. (Casaubon dies very opportunely in *Middlemarch*, and spares Dorothea this dilemma.) But she now has a cause worthy of her aspirations. Smitten with renunciation and with the absolute, Romola finds vocation and duty in the salvation of Florence and its people. Yet her intellectual upbringing and critical mind quickly help her discern in Savanarola's activity ambitious political motives, a narrow fanaticism that her whole nature rejects. She leaves Florence for the first time, to flee Tito, and the second time to escape Savanarola's hold: this time, alone and lost, having abandoned the vision 'of any great purpose, any end of existence which could ennoble endurance'.[156] But even torn by doubts about the activities of Savanarola and his disciples, she awakens to a larger and nobler mission than devotion to a father and husband: 'an enthusiasm of sympathy with the general life'. 'Florence had had need of her.'[157] From now on, Romola transcends the conflicts and disappointments concerning individuals among whom she sought vainly 'the didactic hero', and discovers her own vocation. Romola's pilgrimage from the self to humanity involves an idealization to which contemporaries were not indifferent. Whether the heroine appears to the rough peasants in the village decimated by the plague as The Blessed Lady,[158] or as a Sister of Charity when she helps the poor of Florence,[159] she arrives at the end of her spiritual journey as an incarnation of the Madonna. The author seemed perplexed and almost angry at this aspect of her character; it seemed to catch her off-guard. As Miss Hennell wrote to her in 1863: 'I say Romola is pure idealism – very, very beautiful – because she lies so outside ... *above* my own experience ... She must be worshipped as ... a saint ... therefore I feel that in Romola you have painted a goddess, and not a woman.'[160]

Conscious of the idealization, George Eliot willingly admitted she did not know how to solve all the difficulties inherent in such a character and in a historical novel whose documentation sometimes swamped the author.[161] In this respect it is interesting to note the reaction of critic in the *Westminster Review* who saw Romola not as a heroine of the fifteenth century but of the nineteenth.[162] Romola is a product of her era, indeed, and one of those who substitute for the constraints of religion the imperatives of an even more demanding morality, systematically distrustful of any impulse and instinct. F. R. Leavis notes that Romola is singularly like her author and, like her, is characterized by 'intellectual power, emancipation, inherent piety, and hunger for exaltation'.[163] She could only have been conceived by the woman who wrote à propos *Jane Eyre*: 'all self-sacrifice is good – but one would like it to be in a somewhat nobler cause than that of a diabolical law which chains a man soul and body to a putrefying carcase.'[164]

Romola, the heroine of duty and obligations, is contrasted at once with Tito, a flexible, even invertebrate nature (belonging to the group of Hetty and Rosamond Vincy and others), evasive, charming, and finally criminal, because it is the easier way; and with Tessa, a naïve soul, who has no other ambition than happiness with husband and children. George Eliot associates her constantly with symbols of innocence and play, kid goats and little children. While Romola the heroine always appears as prompting moral Guide the character is however, more modern than the wives of Elizabeth Gaskell and Charlotte Brontë. When Romola realizes that a weak husband or a fanatical master is preventing her from fulfilling her noble aspirations, she goes her way alone. The heroines of Charlotte

Brontë, like those of George Eliot, are seeking a superior being on the intellectual and physical plane. But when they find the venerated master they abdicate once and for all, except on the moral plane, where they show the way. But George Eliot renounces this simplified picture: contradictions and conflicts between the two creatures, between two vocations, are carried through to their tragic end; there is the search for identity on the part of a woman superior morally and intellectually to her husband, and there are the centuries of dependence ('the ancient consciousness of woman'),[165] on the person society considers her 'natural' master. Romola and Dorothea Brooke do find freedom and fulfilment but, as Virginia Woolf has written, at the price of compromise and tragedy.

SINGLE
AND
WORKING WOMEN

[6]

From the Woman's Sphere
to the
Practice of a Profession

From the seventeenth century onwards the evolution towards a capitalist mode of production was deeply affecting woman's role in society. The industrial revolution and capitalist concentration broke up the family productive unit within which women had played an important part. The decline in home industry and increasing specialization meant among other consequences that female labour began to be devalued,[1] and this became increasingly so during the first part of the nineteenth century. In the struggle to survive, women found themselves in the following dilemma: to work for starvation wages in dying sectors of the economy or to depend financially on a family to which they could not easily make a financial contribution. The latter solution was increasingly approved by a society which prescribed for a woman in the home an ornamental, metaphysical and morally inspiring role.

Unmarried women found themselves in an impasse, which after being economic became social. In three stages of the development of the word and concept, 'spinster', the emphasis changes from a legal and economic reality to a value judgement.[2] Originally 'spinster' designated the trade of spinning-girl, and then the civil status of an unmarried woman. The pejorative connotation of the term ('poor spinster') was heard for the first time only in 1719. Barbara Bodichon had traced this development, from which she drew a logical conclusion: the work of the spinster being henceforth done by machines, 'we must find fresh work'.[3] Thus a specific professional problem, resulting from economic and social upheavals, led on a cultural level to a lack of respect for the unmarried woman. Having lost her role and dignity as producer, and deprived of the new transcendent function of wife and mother, she became almost an outcast. It was this absolute division between a positive and negative role for woman, this social condemnation of the old maid, which the reformers and pioneers of women's work made every effort to attenuate, if not abolish.

Paradoxically, the spinster or 'feme sole' was favoured by the

8. 'VIRGO – Unmatched enjoyment.' Caricature by George Cruikshank from *The Comic Almanack*

law over the married woman. For in the eighteenth and then the nineteenth century the concepts on which women's legal position was based were still those of patriarchal Roman law which vested legal existence only in the head of the family.[4] The feme sole on the other hand could acquire possessions and dispose of them freely, rules which changed the moment engagement or a promise of marriage intervened; she could no longer dispose of anything belonging to her without the agreement of her future husband.[5] As owner of her goods and chattels, the feme sole was recognized as being fit to be bound by a contract, to incur responsibilities for her debts, to sue and be sued. In short her legal position was from every point of view identical to that of a man. It was not the same for public and political rights. For these purposes all women, married or not, were at that time treated as minors. They could not be members of liberal professions, nor were they admitted to universities to take degrees. It was necessary to wait for the Education Act of 1870 and the end of the nineteenth century for the bastions of the liberal professions and the universities to be progressively thrown down, under pressure from the feminist pioneers. Only in 1918 and 1920 were women enfranchised.

'One great ... cry rises from a suffering multitude of women, saying, "We want work",'[6] wrote Barbara Bodichon in 1857. All the testimonies, reports of commissions of inquiry, censuses and contemporary or modern studies indicate the numerical importance of women who had to work for a living and the insufficient opportunities offered to them.

In the middle classes the old maid led a withdrawn, melancholic, embarrassed existence. A contemporary saw her as a sad shadow who, having renounced all personal existence, consoled, listened, helped, and resigned herself to living through others and then effaced herself more and more, as if to excuse her existence. 'Single woman! Is there not something plaintive in the two words standing together?'[7] exclaimed the author of *Our Single Women*. Still young, or relatively young, doomed to a materially difficult existence, the languishing spinster pined away[8] during the degrading wait for a husband expected to provide her with board, lodging and a purpose in life thrown in.

As for the millions of women who had come down in the world or were of humble origin and worked for starvation wages, the lack of opportunities and the depreciation of female labour on the work market, precipitated them 'into workhouse graves'. They were 'forced downwards to the paths of hell', and there was 'destruction of bodies, of consciences, of souls'.[9] The role that devolved on to women, the social and ideological pressures that weighed on them to keep them in the state of minors dependent on men, devoted to marriage and the 'female sphere', stood in the way of their practising a profession and acquiring the necessary education. In the middle of the century more and more attention was drawn to these 'redundant women' who were becoming more and more numerous, and had to earn a living.[10] Asked in 1849 by one of the editors of *Household Words* to write an article about women's work, Harriet Martineau accused Dickens of being one of those who 'ignored the fact that nineteen-twentieths of the women of England earn their bread ...'[11] The 1851 census showed that three-quarters of unmarried women worked, or lived on their own earnings.[12] In 1855 Anna Jameson took up the estimates of the census indicating that there was an excess of half a million women over men – 104 women to 100 men. A third of the women over twenty-one were independent workers, as Miss Martineau pointed out in 1865.[13]

These statistics served the cause of female labour. Anna Jameson was in agreement with Barbara Bodichon and later with Josephine

Butler in recognizing as dogma the view that the woman's place was in the home. As these writers constantly emphasized, the principles of education which aimed to make girls the ornament and soul of the family rested on a falsification of the facts. And the disparity sensed by a still larger public between the necessity to work and the possibilities offered rendered a 'lady's' education increasingly absurd and also helped to undermine the prejudices against female labour.[14] Harriet Martineau remarked that in England, as compared with America, adversity forced millions of women to prove their capacity.[15] In her case, her family's brutal ruin meant liberation, the occasion for shaking off the yoke of 'respectability' imposed on a middle-class girl, in short living instead of vegetating.

In a very short time, my two sisters at home and I began to feel the blessing of a wholly new freedom. I who had been obliged to write before breakfast, or in some private way, had henceforth liberty to do my own work in my own way; for we had lost our gentility.[16]

But Miss Martineau was unusual. All occupations requiring solid training and instruction, in other words all the liberal professions, were closed to the middle-class girl. According to the existing law, she had no right to any public post except that of queen. The jobs which fitted more or less the traditional view of woman's nature remained those in the home or the work of governess in someone else's family. In the absence of sound instruction and pedagogic training, this occupation which combined the 'female' characteristics of mother and servant allowed a girl to get some financial benefit from her middle-class education, however deficient it might be, however rudimentary her French and her 'accomplishments'. Nursing and of course domestic service, with all the well-known difficulties, were also open to her. These activities in different degrees fulfilled the needs considered as part of 'female nature': altruism, spirit of sacrifice and so on. They could be pursued where woman was supposed to confine herself: in the home, be it her own or not.

We need not linger over the position of women of letters, any more than that of servants, for these two types of activity in different social classes had a traditional character and did not undergo any important changes at the beginning of the Victorian era. At that time the career of letters was open only to a minority of those with talent who could manage with the scanty education provided for the majority of girls. The end of the previous century had already seen the rise of the woman's novel. At a time when the novel was still considered an inferior genre critics readily related the low level of women's education to their infatuation for fiction.[17] And with a few exceptions, female literary production at this earlier time conveyed through its mediocrity, its paralysing concern with propriety and its didacticism, the limitations of the woman's world. While Fanny Burney had noticed and even mentioned the loose women in certain areas or public gardens of London, moral rigour and obsession with middle-class respectability eventually restrained the researches of the lady novelists.[18] (Julia Kavanagh contrasted this conformist trend with the Romantic and rebellious individualism of Madame de Staël.)

When the laws of propriety were observed moralists considered that the occupation of author was compatible with woman's obligations and virtues. A writer in the *British and Foreign Review* remarks for instance that the female author was becoming a more widespread phenomenon, and need not cease being a good wife, mother and sister.[19] The author of an article on women artists was even more explicit: '(this profession) demands no sacrifice of maiden modesty, or of matronly reserve, or unseemly licence.'[20] And, geographically, the place of work could coincide with the Home which the woman was supposed constantly to adorn with her presence. Elizabeth Barrett, immobilized by an autocratic father and her fragile health, wrote in complete tranquillity. Harriet Martineau succeeded in evading family supervision even before going to settle in London; she began her literary apprenticeship at home, writing 'tales' and notices of books sent her by publishers.[21] Finally, what can one say about the scrupulous conscientiousness with which Charlotte, Anne and Emily Brontë pursued domestic tasks despite their literary activity?

The profession of letters could be pursued in a relatively sheltered realm that did not altogether exclude infrequent contacts with the outside world seen by the Victorians as a permanent threat to woman's purity. But it often assumed a clandestine aspect, a revealing sign of the taboos weighing on any female activity. Authors quite often thought it expedient to write under a borrowed identity. With the Brontë sisters and George Eliot the decision to take a pen-name was motivated by a clear awareness that a literary work signed by a woman would be judged by criteria irrelevant to the quality of the work. Charlotte Brontë wrote in the introduction to the 1850 edition of *Wuthering Heights* and *Agnes Grey*: '... without at the time suspecting that our mode of writing and thinking was not what is called "feminine"—we had a vague impression that authoresses are liable to be looked on with prejudice.'[22] Nine years later George Eliot gave similar reasons when she decided to take a pseudonym for her novels, even though she had established a reputation as a thinker and critic under her own name. 'The object of anonymity', she wrote, 'was to get the book judged on its own merits, and not prejudged as the work of a woman.'[23] Though she was secluded, and knew nothing of literary life and feuds, of the sophisticated atmosphere in which the critics operated, Charlotte Brontë had good reasons for taking precautions after her exchange of letters with Robert Southey concerning her vocation as a writer. Replying in March 1837 to a letter and poems she had sent him, Southey, while recognizing her talent, warned her against the perils of literature.

Literature cannot be the business of a woman's life, and it ought not to be. The more she is engaged in her proper duties the less leisure she will have for it, even as an accomplishment and a recreation.[24]

He advised her to cultivate her gift for the purpose of moral improvement. And it was in this spirit that Charlotte thanked him and followed his advice, making every effort, she said,

attentively to observe all the duties a woman ought to fulfil, (and) to feel deeply interested in them. I don't always succeed, for sometimes when I'm teaching or sewing I would rather be reading or writing; but I try to deny myself.[25]

When, some years later, she resolved the dilemma, and became a writer, her work was the victim of the usual prejudices. What a disappointment when G. H. Lewes, after discussing realism in the novel, the tastes of customers of the circulating libraries as judged by publishers,[26] and the merits of Jane Austen, devoted six pages of a review of *Shirley* in the *Edinburgh Review* to the characteristics of women and women's literature.[27] The blow was all the harder as she had a high regard for Lewes's judgement and had had long and fruitful exchanges with him concerning strictly literary problems. She gave a cry from the heart a little later in a letter to him: 'I wished critics would judge me as an *author*, not as a woman.'[28] The tone is just as bitter in a later letter where she flared up against the prejudices displayed towards women and the absurd demand that females should be 'grateful'.[29] In these circumstances it was not surprising that when suspicions were hardening about her identity, she should violently repudiate the authorship of her books.[30]

But for copyright reasons pseudonyms were an inefficient weapon, and other complications generally forced authors to reveal their identity. Thus in 1848 Anne and Charlotte Brontë went to London to present themselves at the office of Smith and Elder in order to prove who they really were. In the same way, George Eliot, faced with the threat of a fraud being organized around the presumed author of her novels, had to reveal her identity in *The Times*.[31]

Despite prejudices and difficulties, the profession of letters was opened more widely to women from 1840, to such an extent that in 1859 W. R. Greg saw hardly any difference between it and the notoriously over-crowded sectors of governesses and dressmakers.[32] George Eliot also was of the opinion that too many women lacking in talent were trying their hand at literary creation.[33] In fact *The Cambridge Bibliography of English Literature* gives a list for that period of 40 lady novelists, with around 400 novels between them.[34]

The most common profession for young middle-class girls seeking a livelihood was that of governess or tutoress. In 1850 there were officially reckoned to be 21,000 such, which was probably a conservative estimate.[35] An article in *Eliza Cook's Journal* stated that the number of applicants for each advertised situation was increasing daily, 'notwithstanding the acknowledged severe labours (and) the most slender pittances. Why should so many young women', wondered the writer, 'be eager to exchange the home and the family in which they have been brought up, for the household of the stranger, where they assume no higher position than that of a hired servant.'[36] To answer this question one must consider the conditions of supply and demand. Demand was conditioned by the deplorable standards of the schools for girls and by the increasingly pronounced interest in middle-class education in industrial and commercial circles. Thus governesses and tutoresses invaded the families of tradesmen, farmers, and the lower-middle class,[37] for whom increasing spare time and the acquisition of 'accomplishments' to fill this well-bred idleness were the specifically female contribution to the conquest of social prestige.

The supply was more than ample, given the few openings for girls, the inadequacy of their education, the demands of middle-class respectability. It was not respectable to work with one's hands, or in commerce, which implied the manipulation of money. One recalls the dilemma of Miss Matty in *Cranford*, and Elizabeth Gaskell's remark that she had numerous governesses among her friends, but no daughters of tradespeople. So there was hardly anything left save the profession of teacher in its least professional form. Despite the

9. 'The Scholastic Hen and Her Chickens.' Caricature by George Cruikshank from *The Comic Almanack*. Miss Thimblebee loquitur: 'Turn you heads the other way my dears, for there are two horridly handsome Officers coming.'

low standards prevailing in girls' schools, more than amateur talents were required for a post. (When Charlotte Brontë thought of taking on Miss Wooler's school with her sisters they decided to complete their education in a school on the continent, especially to improve their knowledge of French, German and Italian.) 'They say schools in England are so numerous, competition so great that without some such step towards attaining superiority, we shall probably have a very hard struggle and fail in the end.'[38] On the other hand, anyone whom another governess had inculcated with the rudiments of French, music, painting, reading, writing, good manners, elegant deportment, in short a middle-class or aristocratic education, could plunge into this arena. Thus, as Anna Jameson and others pointed out, it was not so much a question of choice as of double necessity: the necessity of having a profession, and of this particular one being the '*only* means by which a woman not born in the servile classes *can* earn the means of subsistence'.[39]

Girls became governesses without pedagogic training or solid foundations, impelled by necessity and the belief that educative gifts (as F. D. Maurice said) emanated 'from the Spirit of God himself'.[40] 'Many young women ... governess(es) in private families cannot write a correct note.' 'What do they know? ... Nothing',[41] remarked a contemporary. Harriet Martineau spoke of 'the astonishing ignorance ... of the bad health, bad manners, bad temper ... of reduced ladies driven to obtain a maintenance'.[42] 'Pretence of education', or depths of ignorance, the reality was constantly attested by the testimony of commissions of inquiry.[43]

Florence Nightingale's conflict with her family and friends about her aptitude for teaching revealed the extent to which low expectation was taken for granted. Nothing appeared more ridiculous to them than the discouragement she felt at her own ineffectualness. 'I had had no education myself', she wrote, '... and when I began to try (to teach) I was disgusted with my utter impotence ... this nobody could understand ... they had never wanted instruction, why should I?'[44]

Their professional incompetence exposed governesses to exploitation against which they were helpless, and going to teach in a family always seemed a dreadful prospect. 'I *hate* and *abhor* the very thoughts of governess-ship',[45] wrote Charlotte Brontë. When in her early years Harriet Martineau decided to work in London, she hoped her young sister would avoid 'the cold dark sphere of governessing'.[46] The difficulties of this bogus profession were psychological and material. Salaries were miserable in themselves, and especially in view of what the governess was supposed to teach. An advertisement appearing in *The Times* in 1843 offered an annual salary of £12 to a 'morning' governess 'of ladylike manners, capable of imparting a sound English education with French, music and singing, dancing and drawing, unassisted by masters'.[47] Under the heading of 'White Slaves', Barbara Bodichon quoted

a letter to the *Times* by an applicant for a post of governess: I at last obtained an interview with the lady, and learnt that the duties of the governess would consist in educating and taking the entire charge of the children, seven in number, two being quite babies, to perform for them all the menial offices of a nurse, make and mend their clothes; to teach at least three accomplishments, and 'fill up the leisure hours of an evening by playing to company'.

For these combined duties the munificent sum of 10 (pounds) per annum was offered! I ascertained for a fact that the two domestic servants in the same family were paid respectively £12 and 10 [pounds].[48]

111

Examples of this kind are legion. The author of an article in *Eliza Cook's Journal* spoke of 'paltry remuneration ... generally below that of the cook and butler, and not above that of the housekeeper, footman and lady's maid'.[49] The average was between £20 and £30 but could, as we have seen, drop to as low as £10. So if one considers that the cost of keeping a child for a year in a Bath boarding school was as much as £70 or 80,[50] families – above all large families – saved a lot of money by hiring a governess. Badly paid, suffering from hunger and cold, the governess found herself burdened with diverse and ill-defined tasks, many of which ought to have been the province of nurse or chambermaid rather than hers.

Bad material conditions were not the only problem. The frequency of mental disorders was attested on all sides. 'Alas', said *Eliza Cook's Journal*, 'governesses constitute the largest clan of tenants in our lunatic asylums.'[51] When she visited a Bedlam with Lord Shaftesbury in 1844, Lady Eastlake noticed 'eight women – looking like governesses or tradesmen's daughters – reading, playing and drawing'.[52] Florence Nightingale had also observed the mental and physical frailty of governesses. On the subject of the 'Institution for the Care of Sick Gentlewomen in Distressed Circumstances' which she had begun to reorganize in 1853, she wrote:

The patients ... were chiefly governesses and the cases ... almost invariably hysteria or cancer ... I think the deep feeling I have of the miserable position of educated women in England was gained while there (or rather of half-educated women).[53]

There were all kinds of psychological pressures: nervous tension and anxiety created by their inexperience and the deficiencies in their education,[54] being a stranger in a family, the indifference if not the contempt of the employers, the impossibility of being alone, all of which Charlotte Brontë felt strongly.[55] The twofold hostility of employers and servants was notorious. The unqualified, badly paid governess occupied an ambiguous and ill-defined no-woman's-land between the two. The frontier between governess and other employees was not as clear as the one between masters and servants. E. Rigby commented on her psychological isolation. Being taboo, she was uninteresting to most men, who were forbidden to pay her the kind of attention usually reserved for the female sex. Most women were bored by her, or worse, feeling that she was a living reproach to them. And the servants detested her because despite being a subordinate like them she was in many ways their superior. Not even her pupils could be her friends. E. Rigby saw no possibility of improvement. The isolation appeared to her to be the only way to keep the necessary distance from the other actors on the household stage. A self-respecting governess would disdain to accept the familiarity that would abolish isolation.[56]

Many protests on behalf of governesses were registered, demanding reasonable salaries, and ridiculing those who drew up long lists of the intellectual and moral perfections expected of them (in *Punch*, *Fraser's Magazine* and other periodicals).[57] Anna Jameson wrote a small handbook of conduct for the use of the mother and the governess of her children.[58] She tackled all aspects of the question, material and psychological, advising the mother to treat the governess as a human being, and the governess to display pliability and discretion.

The current of opinion in favour of the protection of governesses took form in a friendly society founded in 1843. At first, the main aim of 'The Governesses' Benevolent Institution', was strictly philanthropic: to grant aid to aged governesses with no resources, or to those who were unemployed; and to encourage them to save. In 1844 a home was founded where they could temporarily stay and put their name down free of charge on an employment register. There was such a flood of applications that the society's funds were immediately exhausted. In 1847, for example, there were ninety candidates for four £75 annuities. Of the ninety, seven enjoyed an income of from £46 to £14 a year; the others were totally destitute. The following year the number of thirty-two annuities still proved insufficient.[59] But the figures published after a few years, proved the success of the operation: £180,000 accumulated in Government securities by the members of the society, 100 annuities granted to aged governesses, 3,000 women temporarily lodged in the Home, and 14,000 governesses supplied with a post through the registration office.[60]

However, to organize charity and mutual aid was to attack the effects, not the causes of an evil that derived from lack of training and schooling, and from the absence of official qualifications to enable them to practise this profession with a minimum of professional security. Even those in favour of the thesis of 'the natural aptitudes of the woman' – of which one was supposed to be education – recognized the urgent need for the development of these talents. In 1848, on the initiative of F. D. Maurice, Charles Kingsley and Tennyson, and under the patronage of the Queen, Queen's College opened in London, intended primarily for governesses, but open equally to any adolescent girl over twelve.[61] Bedford College was founded the following year. In the level and choice of subjects taught Queen's College resembled secondary schools; but the system of lectures and marking corresponded more to that of higher education. In 1864, recalling the relatively recent creation of these two establishments and the opposition they aroused, Harriet Martineau proclaimed the irreversibility of progress in woman's education. 'The briars and brambles are cleared away from the woman's avenue to the temple of knowledge. Now they have only to knock and it will be opened to them.'[62] From that date secondary and higher education for women developed rapidly, notably under the influence of Emily Davies and Frances Buss. The decisive year was 1867–8, the date of the report of the 'Commission of Enquiry on Schools' which officially noted the deficiency of the educational establishments available and declared itself in favour of the principle of higher education for women.[63]

More even than education, any activity that provided moral, physical or material help to suffering creatures, the poor, the ill, was considered to be the particular refuge of women. 'Women have always been visitors among the poor; for the last half-century they have been active managers of schools and parochial societies ...'[64] wrote F. R. Parkes, the pioneer of female education. According to B. Harrison, slumming had long been a way for women in England to come out of the home into the world.[65] There is no shortage of high-society ladies devoting themselves to good works: Lady Stanley of Alderley, Mrs Gladstone, Lady Frederick Cavendish, and above all Baroness Burdett-Coutts, whose money and good intentions were channelled by Dickens into his centres of interest, homes for reclaimed girls and 'ragged schools'.[66] A Christian and aristocratic tradition of philanthropy was taken up by middle-class evangelists obsessed by the moral progress of individual and society, and on this basis the advocates of work for women, towards the middle of the century elaborated a theory of 'the legitimate sphere of Christian women'.[67]

In two lectures in 1855 and 1856 Anna Jameson built up and illustrated the theory of the 'communion of work'. Her theory immediately became authoritative, for it simultaneously satisfied received ideas about 'the faculties which belong characteristically to each sex',[68] and the innovating, humanitarian inclinations of those who wanted to find a solution to a critical social problem. Anna Jameson wrote:

> Domestic life, the acknowledged foundation of all social life, has settled by a natural law the work of the man and the work of the woman. The man governs, sustains and defends the family; the woman cherishes, regulates, purifies it.

The communion of work between man and wife consisted in widening their respective roles to encompass society at large, seen now as one vast family.[69] Thus any activity deriving from woman's specific role of mother, exercising an ennobling and purifying influence in the natural framework of her family, alleviating suffering and sacrificing herself to others, was recognized as legitimate.

This conception of the woman as 'helpmate' to society justified an activity that could simultaneously improve vast backward sectors: education, health, poverty, and provide solutions for the acute problem of 'superfluous' women. It had the tone of 'self-help', and belonged to the cult of work and individual effort. It echoed the diatribes of Mrs Ellis and others against women's idleness and the poetic rehabilitation of women's work by A. H. Clough in his narrative poem, *The Bothie of Taber-na-Vuolich*.[70] At the same time the doctrine of 'equality in difference',[71] still aimed at maintaining the superiority of the dominant or oppressor group, did not cut across the dogma of male superiority, and thus left intact the foundations of patriarchal society.

Since, according to F. D. Maurice, sacrifice was part of the woman's role and calling,[72] and since, in the words of Harriet Martineau, 'every female infant born into the world is a nurse by nature',[73] she was advised to act and train in the sphere where there was a crying need: hospitals, workhouses, psychiatric asylums. The philanthropists were of the opinion that 'there are many abodes of misery in all our towns and parishes in which our English ladies may do incalculable good ...'[74] and they looked favourably on the creation of a female staff. Needless to say it should be auxiliary.

Nursing in the 1840s was as disorganized and professionally non-existent as private teaching, but underwent like the latter some important changes,[75] and shifted fairly quickly from charity to profession. Recruitment was hybrid and brought together women from different backgrounds and vocations. The most ancient tradition was that of Catholic nursing orders like the nuns of the principal hospitals of London and Paris, the sisters of Saint-Vincent de Paul, the Beguine nuns and so on. The Protestant nursing orders were more recent: the first was the House of the Deaconesses of Kaiserwerth on the Rhine, where Florence Nightingale began her apprenticeship; a similar community, the Protestant Sisters of Charity, took root in England on Mrs Fry's initiative. Despite the name, the sisters did not belong to an order, and they received medical training. In 1857, ninety nurses had been trained in Elizabeth Fry's institute.[76] Parallel to this, an Anglican charitable order, Miss Sellon's, was set up on Pusey's instigation, more or less inspired by the French order of the Visitation of Our Lady. The Anglican church's first important nursing order was Saint John's House, founded in 1848.

When Sidney Herbert entrusted Florence Nightingale in 1854 with the task of organizing the nurses in the military hospitals of Scutari, she chose thirty-eight people out of the numerous applicants. Twenty-four of them belonged to religious orders, predominantly Anglo-Catholic.[77] No doubt at that time the Sisters of Charity offered unique guarantees of competence and devotion. When the scandal of the hospitals of Scutari broke at the beginning of the Crimean War, the War Correspondent of *The Times* who disclosed what hell the wounded were living in, noted the superiority of the sanitary organization of the French army, whose excellence he attributed partly to the Sisters of Charity.[78] Among the nuns recruited by Florence Nightingale, some, like the Sellonites who had looked after the victims of a cholera epidemic in 1853 in the slums of Plymouth and Devonport, had demonstrated their experience and outstanding efficiency. There were many who, like a *Times* reader in October 1854[79] and Anna Jameson in her 1855 lectures, deplored the rarity of nursing orders in England. On the other hand, the easily explicable professional competence of the Sisters of Charity provided arguments for the advocates of the absolute superiority of women's voluntary work 'by right divine'.[80] But the religious training also had its drawbacks and sometimes made the sisters more heedful of the salvation of the soul than of hygiene and healing the body. Florence Nightingale ironically described the devoted women, more at ease in a heaven than in a hospital, flying around the sick like angels without hands, assuaging their souls but neglecting their bodies.[81]

The nurses who formed the majority of the hospital staffs, and whom families sometimes also engaged, were very different from these 'angels without hands'. They were women from the labouring

10. 'How to Get Rid of an Old Woman.' Caricature by George Cruikshank
from *The Comic Almanack*

class without education, often as devoid of common sense as of self-sacrifice. These Mrs Gamps, sometimes coarse, brutal and alcoholic, made no small contribution to the chaos reigning in the hospitals: the lack of hygiene which resulted in repulsive dirt, indifference if not brutality towards the patients, deficiency and incompetence in care. A local paper published testimonies about the county hospital of Lincoln: fits of rage by the nurses and acts of violence on the patients; furthermore, '... the nurses were constantly in the habit of eating the food of the patients, and also of drinking their wine.' This state of affairs was not surprising, said a witness, as '... they hired nurses from the streets – persons employed during the day, and engaged to nurse at night – who, instead of attending to their duties, fell asleep.'[82]

One day a dead-drunk prostitute was nursed by Florence Nightingale. In her days of glory she had made five guineas a week as a nursing lady.[83] In the workhouse infirmaries medical care was administered by alcoholics, often part-time prostitutes.[84] Mrs Jameson described the horror of a workhouse room where the sick women were in the hands of human wrecks, outcasts, old, invalid, wooden-legged, one-eyed, who extorted money from patients in exchange for the slightest attention.[85] For though these Sarah Gamps were not trained, or inspired by the devotion of the nuns, or equal to their task, it must not be forgotten that their working conditions were scandalous. With no room or bedroom of their own at the hospital, they slept in the wards with the patients, men or women. In a letter of 1854 Florence Nightingale described the wooden cages placed on the landing which served for the nurses' bedrooms.[86] The low social level of the recruitment and the purely material considerations which motivated acceptance became very noticeable at the time of the organization of the small contingent that was to go to Scutari. For the most part the candidates belonged to the humblest classes: maids-of-all-work, paupers seeking employment, attracted by the marvellous earnings (12 to 14 shillings a week, plus board and lodging, a salary which after three months could rise to 18/- and after a year to 20/-) compared with the average weekly wage of 7 to 10 shillings[87] which was normal in London hospitals.

Despite the strict sorting of applications it was impossible to eliminate completely the professional 'vices': and in her reports on her nurses in the Crimea, Florence Nightingale commented on the 'sobriety' and 'propriety' of each one. She spoke of a Mrs Davey: 'she is good-hearted, kind and clever and has a tender conscience –

she has struggled hard and generally with success against her one besetting sin, intemperance'. A Mrs Nesbitt is: 'active, useful, clever ... but (suffers) from the long established habits of intemperance and what this always brings in its train'.[88]

Along with the nursing sisters and the Sarah Gamps one must also mention the ladies and girls of good family who followed Elizabeth Fry's tradition in helping the sick. A philanthropic tradition, aristocratic and paternalistic, has already been mentioned. Florence Nightingale's first experience was of this kind. Her mother, who later fiercely opposed her professional projects, encouraged her daughters to visit the local poor in the village of Holloway. The role of woman of good works could indeed be part of the moral education of a young 'lady'. The talents of sick-nurse were also valued. Through them girls were supposed to manifest their selflessness and devotion, preferably at the beside of a member of the family. But when it came to integrating these experiences into a profession which implied an apprenticeship, the entire contemporary ideology about the weaker sex stood in the way. Nothing indeed had prepared the young lady to face the rough common crowd of nurses and patients, and the poor of all kinds, among whom alcoholism, prostitution, obscene language and general promiscuity were common. Furthermore, she was suddenly exposed to a physical hell containing the most repulsive aspects of the human body in sickness, during operations and treatment; also to a mixed world enforcing close contact with the other sex. Think of Florence Nightingale's first experience in the Middlesex Hospital during the cholera epidemic of 1854,[89] or Agnes Jones's in Liverpool ten years later.[90]

The sudden penetration by women into the hospital world was a perilous business. The women were without training but often all too conscious of their social superiority, driven by good intentions that were sometimes suspect, and rarely equal to the job. Unused to discipline, accustomed to command, they risked provoking a ferment of disintegration in the circumstances Florence Nightingale found herself in when she arrived in the Crimea. In the official letter making her responsible for organizing the nurses Sidney Herbert wrote:

I receive numbers of offers from ladies to go out, but they are ladies who have no conception of what a hospital is or of the nature of its duties; ... and they would either recoil from the work or be entirely useless, and consequently – what is worse – entirely in the way. Nor would these ladies probably ever understand the necessity especially in a military hospital, of strict obedience to the rule.[91]

Sidney Herbert had prophesied clearly. During the journey out as well as in the hospitals the lady-nurses refused to be too closely associated with the 'paid nurses', to travel with them, to share the same rooms. Later on many of them used their ranks as an excuse to be served by the hired nurses, to whom they also left all their ward tasks.[92] In one of her reports Florence Nightingale appraised a Mrs Lawfield, engaged in October 1854: 'sobriety, honesty, propriety, irreproachable, too much of a fine lady to be a good nurse'.[93] It was already a success to have fitted them all out in the same ugly uniform: tweed dress and grey woollen jacket, white bonnet, short cape, and a shawl marked 'Scutari Hospital' in red letters.[94] It was characteristic that F. D. Maurice, in his lectures addressed to ladies of good society intending to take up social welfare, exhorted them not to have contempt for the alcoholic, incompetent and immoral 'paid nurses'. It was on these creatures as well as on the sick that the purifying influence of 'the better and more noble elements of their own sex'[95] could have an effect, the examples being these benevolent hospital visitors in 'the love and service of God' whom no salary, according to Anna Jameson, could remunerate for 'force of character ... humility ... great enthusiasm'.[96]

Such, in broad outline, was the state of the profession around 1840, before Florence Nightingale inaugurated a new style of nurse in a reformed if not renovated hospital system.[97] Thanks to her work, the gulf between paid personnel, incapable and often unscrupulous, and a religious tradition of nursing sisters would be progressively filled by a professional sector.

The first nursing school was opened on 24 June 1860, with fifteen pupils – the Nightingale School of Nursing, subsidized by the Nightingale Fund, raised after the Crimean War. The probationers had to have one year of training before receiving regular employment in hospitals. The first students resided in a specially built wing of St Thomas's Hospital. Florence Nightingale's views on medical teaching and sanitary problems were characterized by a search for efficiency, based on hospital organization and staff-training. Thus an 1869 text entitled 'Method of Improving the Nursing Service of Hospitals' made demands that today are a matter of course: rest during the day for night-nurses, modern equipment like hot and cold water in the whole hospital, lifts and other improvements intended to benefit the staff and improve their output.

While technical training was indispensable, discipline and morality were also essential. Florence Nightingale did not see hospitals as a refuge for disappointed lovers or reclaimed girls;[98] only the irreproachable could be enrolled as probationers.[99] Conscious of the necessity for many of the women to earn their living, she deemed it good policy – in order to recruit worthwhile individuals and offer openings to women of over twenty-five – not only to offer a fair remuneration but to pay the nurses during their year of obligatory studies. Florence Nightingale hoped to reduce social class differences through the common denominator of professional competence. All the probationary nurses of St Thomas's Hospital were subject to supervision and a draconian regime, in training and discipline. The monthly report on the pupils was divided into two parts. The first concerning conduct comprised five sections: punctuality, quietness, sense of responsibility, etc. The second comprised fourteen: bandaging, application of leeches, enemas, assistance at operations, washing the sick, etc.[100] The rigour of this training can be explained by the fact that Florence Nightingale knew she was working for the sake of posterity. These nurses whom she intended to support the hospital services, rather than to fill private posts, were to raise the general level of care and constitute the kernel of a new style of hospital staff, trained, competent, professional, who would progressively replace unqualified and amateur staff. Thus a profession for women arose, in which Florence Nightingale introduced in 1860, for the first time, new professional criteria, embracing teaching, training, hospital practice and a fair wage.

More generally, while it is true that nearly all the reformers believed in women's peculiar aptitudes centred on her ordinary family role, one can within that separate out two points of view. The more traditional was represented by Anna Jameson and the Lecturers to *Ladies on Practical Subjects*, and only stipulated social welfare activities for women. The other, which did not assert itself until the end of the 60s, was represented in the work edited by Josephine Butler, *Woman's Work and Woman's Culture*, in 1869. This went over some of the same ground covered by F. R. Parkes, Barbara Bodichon and Harriet Martineau. On customary limitations, by affirming the sanctity of work for *all*, demanding that women should be able to try their hand and prove themselves in all spheres. Among the liberal professions the anti-feminists succeeded in excluding women totally from medical and legal studies until 1876. As F. D. Maurice, himself a pioneer of education for women, had asserted in 1855: 'Englishmen would not have women surgeons or physicians; they find they must have them as *nurses.*[101] But the position was clearly improving elsewhere. At the prompting of Barbara Bodichon and F. R. Parkes and encouraged by George Eliot and Harriet Martineau, the *Englishwoman's Journal*, which began to appear in 1857, and the Association for the Promotion of Employment of Women contributed to the provision of more varied openings, in hairdressing, telegraphy and watch-making.[102]

Workshop, Mine and Factory

'After all that has been written, sung and said of women, one has the perception that neither in prose nor in verse has she ever appeared as *the labourer*',[1] wrote Anna Jameson in 1848. Her comment was doubtless inspired by the recently published reports of the commissions of inquiry on women's and children's employment 'in trades and manufactures', in agriculture (1843) and the mines (1842). An excellent article in *Eliza Cook's Journal* drew the contrast between the classes.

In polished society ... it has become customary to regard her as an agreeable toy to be flattered and caressed or neglected and despised as the caprice of the opposite sex might dictate ... there has been much exaggerated homage – much outward adulation, and little real respect ... in the poverty-stricken homes of the lower classes, woman is ordinarily the greatest sufferer. She has to endure the drudgery of the field and the factory, and to perform as she best may, the duties which devolve on the wife and mother.[2]

Of working women's trades, the best known to the public was that of the distressed needlewoman, generally associated with the governess. Accurate assessment is not easy in this 'domestic industry' because it is extremely difficult to distinguish dressmakers in workshops from the countless women doing more or less well-paid needlework at home.[3] The 1841 census counted 159,101 women over twenty 'in dressmaking and its allied occupations', the 1851 one, 388,302, in this ill-defined category including seamstresses of all kinds, stay-makers, milliners, glovers and shoemakers.[4]

The most complete source of information on the conditions of life and work of seamstresses is the 1843 report of the Children's Employment Commission. It showed that apprentices got their board and lodging for two or three years from their employers and were paid a sum varying from £50 to £60 a year. The working day, between twelve and thirteen hours on average, was considerably longer during the two London 'seasons', from April to

August, and again from October to December, when it could be as much as twenty hours a day, the average, however, being eighteen.[5] The workers toiled in tiny workshops that were dark, overheated or freezing, and airless; they crammed themselves into appalling cells at night, like the eighteen girls in one room with one window, or the five girls sharing an attic bed.[6] In peak periods meal-breaks were irregular and reduced to a minimum: ten minutes for breakfast, fifteen to twenty for tea. Dinner was often delayed until the end of the working day; and the food was insufficient and unwholesome. Undernourished, overworked, unhealthy, this mode of life exposed a seamstress to all kinds of illnesses, from swollen ankles and asthma to tuberculosis, blindness or spinal curvatures. Of the 669 patients in the North London Ophthalmic Institution, 81 were needlewomen.[7]

The average wage of a needlewoman in a workshop was from 1 to $1\frac{1}{2}$ shillings a day and an average of $5\frac{1}{2}$ shillings a week, with the extremes at 2 shillings and ten shillings. She was paid for overtime. The most wretched of these sewing jobs was undoubtedly that of the slop-worker: the needlewoman working at home. The report of the Children's Employment Commission revealed their miserable salaries: some earning less than $1\frac{1}{2}$ shillings a day, and sometimes only sixpence. Tenpence was paid for a dozen striped cotton shirts, $2\frac{1}{2}$ shillings for those of a higher quality.[8] These pitiful wages and the unbelievable poverty of the workers, illustrated by Thomas Hood's poem, *The Song of the Shirt* (which appeared in the Christmas number of *Punch*, 1843, just when the report on children's labour came out), were the consequence of non-professional, individual labour at home[9] competing with even cheaper manpower from the workhouses,[10] and threatened by growing industrialization and mechanization. Harriet Martineau described an establishment in London where seventy sewing-machines each did the work of fifteen pairs of hands.[11] The unmitigated wretchedness of the needlewoman was evidenced during a meeting of slop-workers held on 3 December 1849 which brought together slop-sellers, trouser-makers and seamstresses of all kinds. Four or five only of these unfortunates had underwear, 508 had borrowed clothes for the occasion; 151 had never slept in a bed; five only had earned more than five shillings the previous week.

After these revelations an Association for the Aid and Benefit of Milliners and Dressmakers was formed in 1843, under the presidency of Lord Ashley. This was the first attempt to organize and protect the profession. The Association asked employers to suppress Sunday work, to respect the twelve-hour day, and to pay a minimum weekly wage of 9 shillings.[12] It also opened a kind of employment office which placed seamstresses in establishments that undertook to respect the 'reduced' hours, and supplied these with extra staff during peak periods so as not to overwork the employees. The Association insisted on medical supervision, encouraged the workshop owners to use 'simple and cheap modes of ventilation', a model of which could be examined at the Association's headquarters, and finally, like the Association of Governesses, urged its members to save.[13]

But the sweating persisted despite the progress of industrialization, and continued to escape the spreading factory controls. The death of a seamstress described by the entire English press in June 1863, the circumstances of which were explained by Marx in *Das Kapital*,[14] bore witness to it. Attention was drawn to the accident for the first time in a letter to *The Times* of 17 June, signed 'a tired dressmaker'. She described a big West End sweat-shop, run as Marx said ironically 'by a lady with the pleasant name of Elise' and 'better conducted', according to the correspondent than other, similar establishments. In 1863 the twenty-eight workers of this well-reputed house worked in one room, from 6.30 a.m. until 11 in the evening, and more in peak periods. They slept two to a bed in an unventilated room, divided into cells, each containing two beds. The inquest and autopsy established that the victim, Mary-Anne Walkley, aged twenty, who had worked $26\frac{1}{2}$ hours non-stop, had probably succumbed to an attack of apoplexy caused by overwork and lack of ventilation. The press, roused to indignation, cried 'Our white slaves',[15] 'Egyptian bondage', 'the horrors of a slave ship'.[16] Replying to protestations of innocence on the part of Madame Elise's husband who told inquirers that he 'did all he could for the comfort and health of his young people', *The Times* leader-writer substantiated the charge: the cell, seven cubic feet shared by four people, represented an air-space insufficient for a single adult. Through letters to the press, articles, questions in the House, an outraged public opinion demanded different forms of protection for these 'weak and defenceless women', recourse to Her Most Gracious Majesty, but also inspection of workshops, regulation of sanitary conditions, and working hours. *The Times* leader-writer denied he was infringing the principle of 'general freedom of trade …

11. 'The Haunted Lady, or "The Ghost" in the Looking-glass' from *Punch* 1863.
Madame la Modiste: 'We would not have disappointed your Ladyship, at any sacrifice, and the robe is finished *à merveille.*'
Mary-Anne Walkley, seamstress, died that year from overwork in an ill-ventilated room.

For the protection of those who cannot protect themselves is always admitted as an exception.'[17]

As in other crafts, conditions in dressmaking did eventually improve. But the female working population, already large in the 1830s, grew unabated. The 1841 census gave an approximate number of 115,000 female workers of all ages for the cotton industry. In 1851, 143,624 women over twenty worked in the cotton mills and 385,000 adult women in the whole textile industry (cotton, wool, silk, linen, lace, straw, muslin, calico, etc.).[18] In a speech in Parliament on 15 March 1844, Lord Ashley, quoting from Factory Sub-Inspector Baker's report, demonstrated the continuing advancement of female labour: in one region for example, out of a total effective increase of 6,040 workers between 1838 and 1843, there were 783 men compared with 5,225 women of any age.[19] This state of affairs was due, in the first place, to the progress of mechanization. Power-looms, which were easier to handle, and which were progressively replacing hand-looms, could be operated by women and children. Engels explained that, when throstle spindles were introduced, the work mainly consisted of piecing broken threads, a delicate job requiring the agility of a small hand, rather than brute force.[20] Furthermore, the more docile women, who were less capable of organizing resistance to exploitation, were in certain regions more in demand than men. Whether cause or effect, wages were relatively low in this sector of textiles.[21] Finally, after the 1833 law limiting children's working hours, children were progressively replaced by women.

Women worked in atrocious conditions for more than twelve hours a day in the mills. In the spinning-mills, the temperature varied from 30° to 35°C or more; in the carding workshops the air was full of fluff which entered the lungs; ventilation was non-existent; the noise deafening. The linen-mills, where spinners learned the loom from the age of eleven, used the technique of wet spinning. Water flowed from the spindles, soaking the clothes of the workers, who were barefoot in the water, and saturated the atmosphere with steam.[22] On 15 March 1844, putting forward an amendment in favour of the ten-hour day, and using data from the reports of factory inspectors, Lord Ashley explained in a speech that a piecer standing up all day walked nineteen to thirty miles a day, to which hardship was added that of turning to the left and the right and leaning over the machine and straightening up 4,000 to 5,000 times a day.[23]

Meals were gulped down, the food often being covered in fluff. The few badly observed security regulations did not prevent workers from having limbs caught up in the machines.[24] Also, many workers succumbed to occupational diseases such as vitamin deficiency, exhaustion, blindness, ulcers, asthma and tuberculosis, diseases more serious and more frequent, said Lord Ashley, in the textile industry than in the rest of industry and agriculture.[25]

The twelve-hour working day for employees under eighteen, which was ordained in 1833, was not without effect on the work of adults. In the forties night work was exceptional, and the twelve-hour day fairly generally applied. But factory inspectors were still able to quote many cases of fourteen- and fifteen-hour days, particularly in silk and lace factories, which did not come within the prohibitions of the 1833 Act. In his 1843 report R. J. Saunders observed that in many Yorkshire factories girls of less than eighteen worked more than fourteen hours a day, and sometimes all night. It should be noted that, to put this situation right, Saunders proposed that the age-limit of 'protected women' should be raised to twenty-one, not that the work of adults should be regulated.[26]

Wages were generally low, although they varied greatly from one region to another. In 1834, a factory inspector's report gave the following figures for the Lancashire spinning-mills: the weekly wage of a female worker between 16 and 56 varied from around 7 to 10 shillings, that of a man of the same age from 10 to 22 shillings.[27] Women's wages were in general much lower than men's and, as stated earlier, this, in addition to the docility of female workers, encouraged employers to recruit them.[28]

The inquiries of the Commissioners, at first limited to children's work in factories and mines, finally included women. The first report on children's employment in mines appeared in May 1842. Two large abundantly illustrated volumes revealed the abominable working conditions. According to the 1851 census, 6,337 women over the age of twenty were working in the mines,[29] concentrated in the less heavily industralized regions, that is to say East Scotland and South Wales.[30] The inquirers stated that women and children were doing the hardest tasks in unimaginable conditions. Deep down in the mines men, women and children worked entirely or half naked. Bent double, in water up to their knees, the women carried heavy loads. Usually little girls of six or seven went down first and came up last, operating the doors for ventilation, and to allow the corves to pass through. Clothed only in old trousers and a shirt, women pushed the corves along the gallery rails. But in seams that were too narrow an antique and inhuman method was used: a harnessed woman on all fours – with a belt and chain that passed between her legs – drew along a sort of sledge over considerable distances in the sloping galleries. Workers questioned by the commissioners spoke of a working day that went from 4 a.m. to 4 or 5 p.m., sometimes without interruption, or with an hour off for a meal. Returning home after such a day, a woman was often too tired even to wash.[31] In some unprofitable shafts the owners judged it more economical to have women carry heavy baskets of coal rather than lay rails or buy pit ponies.[32] Only a few women were involved in mining compared with, say, the textile industry, but the horrible work, which reduced woman – imagined by some to be a creature of grace and purity – to the condition of a slave or animal, had a powerful effect on public opinion.

To understand the changes that came about, one must set the cause of protection for women at work in its historical and political context. On the one hand there was a confrontation between two rival classes, the industrial and commercial middle class and the landed aristocracy, and between two opposed philosophies, liberal utilitarianism and Christian philanthropy. On the other hand, there was a general evolution of new social laws. In an age characterized simultaneously by a philanthropic reformism of romantic Tory inspiration and the Whig dogma of absolute liberalism in commerce and industry it was for the protection of women and children that the growing intervention of the State was most noticeable.

Opposing these regulations was the powerful body of new manu-facturers (formed around the Manchester School and the Anti-Corn-Law League), inspired by a philosophical tradition inherited from Bentham and Mill, but still embodying the basic economic doctrines of Adam Smith.[33] Even if we no longer identify Bentham's philosophy with laissez-faire and with absolute hostility to any form of state intervention, one can still see that these principles underlay the activities of the Anti-Corn-Law League and of the textile manu-facturers as well as the parliamentary and extra-parliamentary agitation intended to hinder state protection of workers.

The enemies of industrial legislation were often contradictory.[34] John Bright, manufacturer and Whig Member of Parliament, a man known for his concern for the wellbeing of his workers and tormented, it seems, by the sufferings of the working classes, systematically intervened in the Commons against all legislation limiting the working day of adults.[35] In the same way, the economist Roebuck, who professed to be horrified by the spectacle of women and children in cotton-mills in 1838, voted against the Factory Bill of 1844 and for a long time opposed State intervention in industry.[36] Roebuck, Mill, the *Westminster Review*,[37] were opposed, in differing degrees to any measure that would hinder the free functioning of industry and commerce and would protect any one category of workers. Theoretically, even women were free and adult, and could therefore protect themselves.

To many contemporaries the laissez-faire school appeared to be supported by the facts, the enemies of women's labour in factories being suspected of exaggerating its horror. Admittedly, conditions were very variable. Even within one factory, for example, the weaving rooms, of a moderate temperature and suitably ventilated, were more bearable than the carding rooms, which were saturated with fluff, or the hot and humid spinning rooms. And the policy of employers towards workers was not everywhere identical, as several had reformist and philanthropic tendencies. The existence of an enlightened and paternalistic group of employers (like Mrs Gaskell's friend, the Lancashire industrialist Samuel Greg, who offered his workers singing, guitar, flute and drawing lessons,[38] or like John Bright and Henry Ashworth, who were concerned with the cleanliness and ventilation of workshops[39]) was widely used to support laissez-faire theories; and the health and wellbeing of the workers, illustrated by medical testimonies and comparisons with other trades, was a recurrent theme in the Commons, most notably expressed by Roebuck on 3 May 1844 in the debate about the length of the working day.[40]

There certainly seems to have been a tendency to exaggerate the number of married women in the mills. In 1844 John Bright concurred with Inspector Leonard Horner in placing the proportion of married women working in nine Lancashire spinning-mills at 27%. The laissez-faire adherents also pointed out that demoralization, prostitution and disintegration of the family were as widespread in the more traditional sectors of female employment that were outside the scope of the commissions of inquiry,[41] such as domestic service, agriculture and small-scale industries such as lace-making and dyeing. They also warned about the threat of unemployment among women in the mining regions following the ban on female labour in the mines, or, more hypocritically, pleaded for a woman's right to choose her job,[42] and even respect for the indefeasible rights of mothers which would be violated by state regulation of children's labour.[43] They stirred up, too, the spectre of a plot fomented by textile workers to limit their own working day to ten hours, while continuing to draw a salary for twelve behind a screen of agitation. Behind the arguments were the capitalist necessity for profit and the fear of financial loss that would follow from a reduction of working hours, and the expenses entailed by reorganizing work in the interests of safety. These purely economic considerations, often masked by an affirmation of the sacrosanct liberty of the individual, were disclosed in all their crudeness on the occasion of the 1842 Act concerning employment of women and children in the mines.

Lord Ashley, who had achieved massive support in the House of Commons for his Bill to forbid the employment of women and young people in the mines, and to strengthen safety regulations, met unexpected opposition in the House of Lords. The millionaire colliery-owner Lord Londonderry explained that in unprofitable mines where the seams were too narrow for coal to be carried by horses, and where women were employed for this purpose, mine owners would be ruined if forced to employ men at a higher salary for the same work. To close the mines, on the other hand, would deprive women and their families of their means of subsistence.

Theoreticians came to the help of manufacturers. The economist Nassau Senior demonstrated that the entire net profit of the manufacturers was made in the eleventh hour of work. Furthermore, cotton-work, easy as it was, could be done for 13–16 hours a day: 'The work is merely that of watching the machinery and piecing the threads that break ... I have seen the girls ... standing with their arms folded during the whole time that I stayed in the room – others sewing a handkerchief or sitting down.'[44] And the employers did not give up. In 1855 in Manchester the manufacturers formed a National Association of Factory Occupiers. The pretext was the interpretation of a clause in the 1844 Act in the fencing of machines; in fact many factories did not obey the regulations and the number of accidents remained just as high. But it does seem that the aim of this association of powerful directors, with 250,000 workers employed between them, was to amend if not repeal the 1844 Act, and in particular to limit the powers of the factory inspectors.[45] Harriet Martineau sided against the legislators in a violent pamphlet entitled *Factory Legislation. A Warning against Meddling Legislation*,[46] written in 1855, but Dickens, in *Household Words* as well as his novels, was hostile to the manufacturers' point of view, and derided their association which he called 'The National Association for the Protection of the Right to Mangle Operatives'.[47]

There was a sudden change in opinion around 1860. In 1861 the President of the Economic Section of the British Association expressed satisfaction at the results of the 1844 Act – which had been so fiercely fought by his kind – an Act which 'has cleared away a mass of depravity and discontent, has placed the manufacturing enterprise of the country on a safe basis'.[48] The factory inspectors found that the shorter working day was generally not prejudicial to profitability. And Roebuck, Cobden and other champions of liberalism converted to State control of working hours.

The counter-pressures for protection of the work force were of diverse origin and inspiration. They seem to have come on the one hand from an aristocratic paternalistic movement, full of nostalgia for a lost feudal order (like the Young England group),[49] and from the workers themselves on the other. In 1833 the first important Act had limited the working day and forbidden nightwork for all those under eighteen, and instituted factory inspect.[50] This Act, which had been the first step towards controlling female labour, and then all labour, was due to the efforts of well-known philanthropists of the time. Robert Owen was the first to act energetically, at several levels: he reformed work conditions in his factory, tried to convince the textile manufacturers of the advantages the reforms would bring, and finally, brought pressure on parliament. The cause was taken up by two Tories, Michael Sadler and Richard Oastler. Their method, apart from using the press (Richard Oastler's letters on 'Yorkshire Slavery' began to appear in the *Leeds Mercury* in 1840) and classical parliamentary agitation, was to create government commissions to inquire into work conditions. The first of the classic reports appeared in 1832, and was drawn up by the Select Committee on Factory Children's Labour, known as Sadler's Committee. A succession of reports between 1831 and 1876 studied the work force elsewhere: in industry, public health, agriculture, workhouses, theatres.[51]

The same methods were used by the most active and representative of the protectors of widow and orphan, Lord Ashley (later Earl of Shaftesbury). Labour legislation was only one of many social causes to which he devoted himself: the lot of chimney-sweeps, conditions in lunatic asylums, public health, 'ragged schools'. There was nothing of the egalitarian or socialist in him. When he said he represented the workers it was from a totally paternalistic point of view. Hostile to trade unionism, agitation, and all profound social transformations, he declared:

> There should be a careful abstinence from all approach to questions of wages and capital; that the labour of children and young persons should alone be touched; that there should be no strikes, no intimidation, and no strong language against their employers, either within or without the walls of parliament.[52]

Lord Ashley's most resounding success was the publication, in 1842, of the report on children's labour in the mines, adorned with illustrations and woodcuts and aimed at parliamentarians without the

12. 'The Coster-Girl' from Mayhew, *London Labour and the London Poor*, 1862

time to read the details. One week later he presented the draft of a Bill, put forward on 7 June, in a two-hour speech that moved his audience to tears. The new Mine Act (10 August 1842) came into force six months after getting on to the Statute Book, with its ban on women's and girls' employment underground, and its authorization for the apprenticeship of children only after the age of eleven.[53] It was a first step; there were further Acts to regulate the employment of women in industry. The 1844 Act replaced the fourteen- to sixteen-hour day by a maximum day of twelve hours for women and all those under eighteen, and banned night work.[54] It extended to women of all ages the provisions that, by the terms of the 1833 Act, only concerned 'young persons'. The 1844 Act also strengthened safety regulations and the powers of factory inspectors.[55] Three years later, in 1847, the ten-hour day was finally enforced (for women and under-eighteens). Later, in 1850 and 53, this was specified to be between in the morning and 7 at night, in order to suppress night-shifts.[56]

Thus the regulation of the working day and conditions which had begun in 1833 with protection for the under-eighteens, had then been extended in 1844, 1847, 1850 and 1853 to another group of workers, women. Indeed, the 1844 Act did not change the provisions of the 1833 Act on working hours, but included women in the definition of 'young persons'. Women were again treated as minors.

On the workers' side, there is no doubt that the agitation for the ten-hour day which began in 1825, encouraged in the beginning (1830) by Richard Oastler's articles in the *Leeds Mercury*, really aimed at the standardization of work for *all*. This fact emerges from the policy of the Short Time Committees, the workers' support for Michael Sadler, who was the Tory candidate for Aldeburgh in Yorkshire in the 1831 elections and who pledged support for the ten-hour day, from resolutions drawn up at electoral meetings and from testimonies before the Sadler Committee.[57] In fact, given the large and growing number of women employed in factories, any restriction on their working day had repercussions on the operation of the factory and obliged manufacturers to replace women by men, just as they had replaced children by women between 1833 and 1844. In Yorkshire the 1847 Act caused great rejoicing which indicates that in working-class eyes these measures affected everyone. And yet, under the 1847 Act, while the working day of women and young people was limited to ten hours, that of men over eighteen extended from 5.30 in the morning to 6.30 at night.[58] Furthermore, it became obvious to workers and inspectors that in 1849 the employers could easily get round the law by the shift system. The 1850 Act, which instituted a 'normal' day for women and children in a factory functioning from 6 in the morning to 6 at night was a great step forward; but the workers clamoured even more insistently for a limitation on the actual working hours of the factory itself, both to prevent the manufacturers from getting round the ten-hour law, and to establish an overall limitation on the working day.[59]

It is thus plain enough why public opinion was so long divided on this issue. There was a growing demand for female labour, especially once young children were removed from the factories. Women were a good substitute for children because they were considered almost equally docile. It was therefore in the self-interest of manufacturers to employ women without any hindrance, and, as always, the arguments of self-interest could be dressed in the clothes of altruism. The doctrine of laissez-faire blessed the selfish for the good they did to others. On the other side of the question were the paternalists who wanted to protect the weak, and the male workers who wanted to protect themselves from woman's competition and to see general regulations follow on the control of the hours of their rivals. The great quarrel was therefore between laissez-faire and intervention. But in addition there were other quarrels just as fundamental about women and especially about their 'proper' sphere. Was it at home, uncontrolled except by a powerful code, or at work, controlled by a fatherly State?

Those, like Lord Ashley, who tried to introduce legislation that specifically protected one category of women, appealed to Members of Parliament's humanitarian sentiments, but also to their conception of what women were supposed to be and do. Two spokesmen representing very different strands of opinion, Ashley in his Commons speech of 7 June 1842, and Engels in *The Condition of the Working Classes in England in 1844*, saw women's factory work as a factor in 'the dissolution of family ties' and in social disintegration.[60] The inquiries of factory inspectors and other testimonies revealed the problems created by married workers and mothers of families who worked like their husbands, or who even kept the family when the husband was unemployed (see Chapter 3, page 47ff.).

All female factory workers, whether married or not, were considered to be in a pitiable moral state. The Sadler Report and other inquiries, as well as Peter Gaskell's work, noted the working woman's 'immorality', attested by the higher number of illegitimate children, widespread promiscuity, prostitution, alcoholism, delinquency etc. But there was nothing to prove that women's 'demoralization' was more marked in industry than among servants or agricultural workers.[61] In one of his letters to Inspector Horner about his model factory Samuel Greg considered for example that mixed contacts in the place of work encouraged early marriage. He recognized however that such close contact between the sexes also posed a problem where it did not lead to marriage, and while endeavouring to reform and humanize the working conditions of his factory, he too tried as much as possible to separate men and women. Michael Sadler tried to use the results of his inquiry to isolate the specific effects of work and factory on the morality of young female workers. Promiscuity and precocious sexual development were encouraged by the rudimentary amenities in the factory and the terrible conditions of work: absence of changing-rooms, overheated workshops where workers wore hardly any clothes, the exhaustion and thirst which induced a need for stimulants,[62] and the general degradation as a result of overwork. Doubtless it was these symptoms taken as a whole that Lord Ashley called the 'demoralization' of the woman in his speech of 7 June 1847.

They know nothing that they ought to know ... they are rendered unfit for the duties of women by overwork, and become utterly demoralized. In the male the moral effects of the system are very sad, but in the female they are infinitely worse, not alone upon themselves, but upon their families, upon society, and ... upon the country itself. It is bad enough if you corrupt the man, but if you corrupt the woman, you poison the waters of life at the very fountain.[63]

This distinction between corruption in the two sexes is interesting for the light it throws on the beliefs prevalent among the philanthropic reformers, which in this echo those of the novelists and moralists. For it was not so much the physical and psychological consequences of overwork that determined the hostility of the legislator to female labour in factories as the moral danger of paid employment outside the home, bringing about more independence for women. Factories interfered with her exclusive devotion to the family. Engels and others deplored that as a result of endemic unemployment there was occasionally present a 'reversal of the normal division of labour within the family. The wife is the breadwinner while her husband stays at home to look after the children and to do the cleaning and cooking.'[64] Women then become the sole support, their husbands 'being virtually turned into eunuchs'.

Engels, Peter Gaskell and the factory inspectors were indignant at seeing men idle and women and children not. The phenomenon, although not all that common, was sufficiently shocking to contemporary sensibility,[65] and made enough of an impression, at least qualitatively, to be one of the grounds for Lord Ashley's campaign.[66] Engels was concerned about the reversal of traditional roles. His investigation of this extreme situation prompted him to consider the traditional relations between man and woman in marriage[67] and the role of money in these relations.

Factory work in normal circumstances by married or unmarried women, even when they were not the only breadwinners in the family all the same brought about a change in the traditional family structure (between spouses and between parents and children) by reason of their financial independence and absence from home. It is clear from the tenor and very terms of their comments on this subject that Members of Parliament and even Engels (whose attitude later underwent a change, in *Origin of the Family*) strongly objected to the alteration both of the traditional patriarchal structure of the family and of its most solid support: the concept of 'female nature' and the difference between the attributes and roles of the two sexes. The arguments of Engels, Peter Gaskell,[68] and Members of Parliament, in favour of limiting the working day of women rested essentially on the allegedly 'natural' role of the woman in the home. The Earl of Devon spoke of 'those domestic duties which it should be the desire of the legislature to encourage'.[69] Lord Ashley cited the evidence of Sir Charles Shaw, ex-chief of police in Manchester. 'Women by being employed in a factory, lose the station ordained them by Providence, and become similar to the female followers of an army, wearing the garb of women, but actuated by the worst passions of men.'[70]

The form of argument was always the same: women's employment 'disturbs the order of nature'.[71] It was in the name of this very nature that Lord Ashley disapproved of inhuman work for women, if not for men. He was also shocked to see women workers form clubs and associations where they 'meet together to drink, sing and smoke' and 'gradually (acquire) all those privileges which are held to be the proper portion of the male sex'.[72] The term 'privilege' is significant here as a notion underlying this whole controversy. Protection of women, yes, but also defence of the respective 'spheres' and privileges of each sex. Thus those who supported woman's protection at work, invoking an irrefutable argument against the laissez-faire school of thought and its alleged 'freedom of the adult', argued from the premiss that the law did not consider a woman and particularly a married woman as a responsible adult, but a minor. 'Did they decide and judge for themselves?', asked Sir J. Graham. 'So far as married women were concerned, the law held distinctly the reverse ... and to the female sex generally many of the rights of freedom are denied.'[73]

Sir Robert Peel also subscribed to this point of view. That did not prevent him from also defending the thesis that all should be allowed 'the power of determining for themselves what shall be the extent of the work and the nature of the labour to which they shall devote themselves'.[74] But in this whole movement one cannot exaggerate the importance of the traditional belief in the female vocation to ornament and inspire the man's home.[75] Harriet Martineau, for example, was nicely divided between feminism which gave her a new perspective and her sympathy for the principles of laissez-faire and utilitarian philosophy. Hostility to any state interference led her to oppose even the most moderate measures of labour regulation. She put her faith in education, as did W. R. Greg. Greg thought that a worker who had given some thought to the matter, and who was married to a sensible, economical housewife, would manage happily on a small budget and hate to see his children work.[76] Harriet Martineau also seemed to think that married women's problems would vanish in those evening classes where workers learned to cook and keep accounts.[77] Indefensible though this appears, Mrs Martineau at least did not share the commonest current prejudices. She saw the worker's material independence for women and men – in good conditions – as enhancing maturity, autonomy and sense of responsibility.

J. D. Milne had a remarkably open and enlightened approach for the times. In his study of woman's labour from the 1851 census he came to the conclusion that it was not realistic or even desirable to abolish female labour in industry, given all the factors which in an industrial society push in this direction. In a dialectical perspective he suggested that the solution was not to condemn the principle of female labour in the name of 'woman's nature', but to turn on their head the circumstances which turned this work into a commodity of such low value. What were the causes? The excessive demand and inadequate supply of work restricting women to servile or subordinate jobs; an untrained, unspecialized work force; the lack of opportunity for professional or financial advancement which led to

13. 'View of a Dust Yard' from Mayhew, *London Labour and the London Poor*, 1862

apathy and mediocrity; discrimination in employment and wages; the absence of trade-union organization.[78]

Much other evidence led to the same conclusion. A letter, for example, from the working women of Tormoden, replied to a suggestion in the *Examiner* for eliminating women from the factories. It is an ironic and unillusioned commentary and an excellent epitome of the new conditions of women's work: the disappearance of the hand-loom and of work at home, replaced by the power-loom and factory work, the large number of women obliged to earn their living, the small number of openings in domestic service and dressmaking, saturated and unenviable jobs.[79] Better than any theoretical argument, this testimony bought to light the anachronistic position of reformers who wanted purely and simply to send women back home, either out of a sincere belief in woman's family vocation, or through fear of competition.

Given the indisputable fact that out of six million women aged over twenty half were in industry and more than a third earned their living,[80] the only road to follow was the organization of work by means of labour legislation, of general and domestic education of workers, and the diversification of careers open to women of all classes. Current conceptions of the role of the two sexes still influenced middle-class reformers, with their traditionalist beliefs, throughout, but their awareness of social facts, led them to recognize the need for education and training in those activities recognized as being legitimate. The introduction and practice of proper training, even if only in medical care and education, was bound to extend to more and more professions. This was the first step in an irreversible development and a basis upon which feminism could develop. Its political nature was not to take long to assert itself.

Given the state of the labour market 'protection' of the female work force, even in the name of an anachronistic traditional notion of the woman in the home, undeniably marked social progress. It also led to protection for other categories of workers. Thus on every level factual change preceded theoretical questioning; pragmatic legislators and reformers participated in an evolution that would eventually change not just what women did but the idea of what they were.

[8]

Charles Dickens's Anti-Woman

The typical single women in Dickens's novels are not only those whose official status is single, widow, or divorcee. Betsy Trotwood, for example, is married, Mrs Gamp has been, Miss La Creevy is going to be. But these women are not *only* defined in their capacity as wife, mother or sister. A certain amount of autonomy is essential to them. Their position in society is different from a wife-mother's or a girl's. It can include a job. Conversely, in Dickens's world a single woman cannot be defined in terms of a job alone. A few months or years spent working as a governess may mark the early stages of some heroines' lives before they are called upon to fulfil themselves as wife-mothers: one thinks of Kate Nickleby, Madeline Bray in *Nicholas Nickleby*, Ruth Pinch in *Martin Chuzzlewit*, Esther Summerson in *Bleak House,* and Agnes Wickfield in *David Copperfield*. In the predicament of the wife-mother, the misfortunes of young middle-class women in straitened circumstances are meaningful as a test inflicted on the heroine before her family apotheosis. As with marriage, there are grounds for wondering if woman's celibacy appears in Dickens's work as an essence, or as one human condition among others, although with a particular social and psychological component. Dickens's single women can fall into caricatures and symbolic figures. In the first category the best represented are school-mistresses and governesses.

In *Great Expectations*, Biddy and Pip attend a village school run by a ghost-like character who is never identified other than by the words: Mr Wopsle's great-aunt. We only know she is a 'ridiculous old woman of limited means and unlimited infirmity', that her pupils learn nothing but eat apples and tickle each others' backs with straw.[1] The obvious deficiencies in the teaching, the confused and superficial nature of the knowledge inculcated, and lack of training on the part of the teachers, are suggested by the comic tone applied to the Ladies' Seminary in *The Old Curiosity Shop*. The widow Wackles has the good fortune to have voluntary teachers at her disposal in her unmarried daughters, who teach unusual and varied subjects – 'English grammar, composition, geography, and the use of dumb-bells ... writing, arithmetic, dancing, music and general fascination'.[2]

In *Our Mutual Friend*, Miss Peecher the school-mistress, hopelessly consumed with love for Bradley Headstone, is the very image of the small school-teacher enclosed in the small world of a small school near a small garden. She has doubtless had some instruction, perhaps even a little training. But this exceptional fact only provides Dickens with a pretext for satire:

She could write a little essay on any subject, exactly a slate long, beginning at the left-hand top of one side and ending at the right-hand bottom of the other, and the essay should be strictly according to rule.[3]

It would be useless to look for any conception of a profession. The rare psychological and sociological references contribute to the outline of the ridiculous couple of the teacher and her probationer pupil, whose meagre knowledge serves only to reduce science, geography and literature to nonsense.

Mrs Pichpin, head of an 'infantine Boarding-house of a very select description' attended by the young Paul Dombey, is characterized in a little more detail. She is a 'marvellous ill-favoured, ill-conditioned old lady, a stooping figure, with a mottled face like bad marble, a hook nose, and a hard grey eye'.[4] She wears dark bleak colours. The old hag's teaching principles are summarized in a lapidary formula: 'give them everything that they didn't like, and nothing that they did.' 'The Castle of this ogress' is as grim as the dame herself; the ventilation is unsatisfactory, the house reverberates with the sound of the wind, and it is adorned by cacti resembling hairy serpents. By means of the very objects surrounding her Dickens conveys the hostility mingled with fascination felt by young Paul for this bogey. As for Miss Blimper, the daughter of the head of Brighton School, she would be a fairly traditional teacher caricature (thin, dried up, with short hair and glasses), had Dickens not endowed her with a macabre love for dead languages and a ferocious hostility towards living ones. The educational information one can glean from these grotesque figures is secondary, and integrated into the design of the caricature.

In *Martin Chuzzlewit* Dickens describes the governess's calvary: before meeting the man of her dreams whose home she will adorn Ruth Pinch only ventures into work for a short trial. In a few scenes Dickens presents the governess's impossible position in the *nouveau riche* family of a copper manufacturer: her isolation, the servants' condescending hostility, the scorn and distrust of her employers and pupils, and the pin-pricks of the whole household. But the humanitarian pleading in this novel is also part of a pleading against a social class that Dickens execrated, the race of Dombeys and Bounderbys, the new magnates of industrial England, devoid of culture, heart and tradition, and not part of a general reflection on the problem of female labour.

We know that in education as in other social institutions Dickens's satiric creations – schoolmasters, flogging fathers, reform schools – were generally inspired by existing abuses. Gathering together the scattered data about girls' schools and school-mistresses in the novels, the overall picture of the conditions of life and work, of the material, professional and psychological deficiencies of the schools and staff does not contradict that of other contemporary writers.[5] Dickens participated in reform campaigns: he published stories of exploited governesses in *Household Words*, and exerted himself in favour of the admission of women to Royal Academy Schools.[6] But despite his contacts with the problems, his teachers are inspired more by the widespread myth of the cantankerous schoolmistress, the nagging and frustrated spinster, than by real, living individuals.

Miss Tox in *Dombey and Son* is an indistinct, faded and drab silhouette, recalling the melancholy figure of the 'OLD MAID', as described by D. Greenwell, 'of smooth braided silvery hair, and soft speech and eye ... ever serene and cheerful ... listening, consoling, cheering, at all times ready to take up a little of existence at second hand'.[7]

Here Dickens has created a type of the old maid who is a victim of her own uncomeliness, who, lonely and affectionate, tries desperately to integrate into a family; ignominiously chased out of the Dombey household, she lowers her social pretensions and devotes herself to the Toodle family. Such rare insights into the solitude of a single woman without any particular vocation and in search of a family identity are, however, lost in the mass of ridiculous, delightful details that Dickens could not stop himself from attaching to her. Her 'stupendously aquiline' nose decorates an angular silhouette bristling with incongruously embattled objects: artificial flowers that look like weeds, capes, boas, muffs 'not at all sleek, small bags with snaps to them, that went off like little pistols when they were shut up'.[8]

In *The Old Curiosity Shop* Miss Sally Brass is presented as 'a lady of thirty-five, of a gaunt and bony figure and a resolute bearing', who since earliest childhood has devoted herself exclusively to the office of her brother, a solicitor. She is a classical type of old maid, plain-featured and grumpy; for her defects and lack of femininity she compensates by a disproportionate and ridiculous professional passion – 'The law had been her nurse'. Dickens specifies the pettiest aspects of the profession; 'accomplishments ... of a masculine and strictly legal kind'[9] consisting primarily in copying documents and filling in forms. He isolates the most insignificant aspects of this work and reduces Miss Brass to a single dimension, the absurd and exclusive taste for accumulating old papers, a monstrous excrescence which has swallowed up grace, feminity and sweetness, all the attributes of his positive female character.

The character of Miss Murdstone in *David Copperfield* is constructed with the help of images which, through their colour, form and movement suggest hardness and separateness even before the reader is told about her role as one of David's mother's jailers. Miss Murdstone 'brought with her two uncompromising hard black boxes, with her initials on the lids in hard brass nails ... a hard steel purse ... in a very jail of a bag ... shut up like a bite'.[10]

Her panoply is at once completed by the bunch of keys she confiscates from Mrs Copperfield. This one-dimensional character is presented right from the start as she remains. Frozen in her jailor's metallic space, she undergoes no transformation. When David finds Miss Murdstone again several years later 'her cold stiff fingers ... the little fetters on her wrists and round her neck'[11] immediately remind him of the fetters over a prison door, and the bag with a steel clasp seems to bite, as in the past. Prison-warder, guard-dog, so many images imposing themselves on the reader's imagination, irreparably associate Miss Murdstone with an archetype of Evil, and play their part in the structure of contrasts where the Good are always opposed to the Wicked, the Copperfields and Peggotty to the Murdstones, Wickfield to Uriah Heep.

Mr Bounderby's governess and housekeeper, Mrs Sparsit, in *Hard Times*, plays a comparable part, achieved by the same effect. Dickens slides rapidly over her past and the reasons that have incited her to seek work; Mrs Sparsit is a widow who was very briefly married to a man fifteen years her junior dead at the age of twenty-four; from the start the author alienates sympathy from her by this ill-assorted marriage. Then Mrs Sparsit is presented once and for all in her role of Louisa's spy; past master in the art of the double game, she lies in wait like a wild animal stalking its prey. Needlework, which symbolizes the femininity of so many pure girls and mothers, is here the expression of her evil essence. When she pierces a piece of lace with scissors she reminds the reader of a falcon tearing out the eyes of a small bird. The grotesque image is again evoked through an antagonistic mechanism of psychological or social investigation: Mrs Sparsit's behaviour, like Miss Murdstone's and others', is never submitted to examination, never develops, and is never presented in everyday language.

Among the women with a profession are Madame Mantalini, owner of the sweatshop where Kate Nickleby works, Miss Knag, the forewoman, and of course Mrs Gamp in *Martin Chuzzlewit* Dickens gives some precise data on work in the shop; the workers have a twelve-hour day and extra hours during the season, in a badly lit and ventilated workshop,[12] for a weekly wage of five to seven shillings. But he does not stop at the sociological aspects of this exploitation, and presents Madame Mantalini as the victim of a libertine husband, irresponsible and extravagant, whom she is more or less obliged to keep, while he has free rein of everything belonging to her. Miss Knag is a shrew, jealous of Kate, and she abuses her authority. Her profession is only one of the means by which she manifests her cantankerous and authoritarian nature, immunizing her – unlike Kate who is sweet and gentle – to the hard work in the shop. Once more there is neither psychology nor an attempt to study one particular female condition.

Among the women Dickens associates with a profession, Mrs Gamp is certainly the most memorable creation, and the best worked out. In principle a nurse, she is supposed equally to look after the sick, the new born and corpses; she takes 18 pence a day from working people, and 3s. 6d. a day from 'gentle folks'. But again the rare details of her profession are lost in the abundance of picturesque and ridiculous notations.[13] Dickens once more uses the device of a series of contrasts. There is first of all the contrast between the solid sensual egoism of Mrs Gamp – for whom 'A shilling's-worth of gin and water ... a little bit of pickled salmon with a nice little sprig of fennel, and a sprinkling of white pepper ... new bread ... with jest a little pat of fresh butter, and a morsel of cheese',[14] are all that makes life worth living – and the abnegation expected of a nurse. These implicit demands are contrasted with the deliberate brutality, even sadism of Mrs Gamp and her imaginary acolyte,

Mrs Prig. Mrs Gamp has, for example, very special therapeutic techniques to make her patient swallow his medicine: she presses on his trachea. To calm an old man she takes him by the collar and shakes him a dozen or two times, 'that exercise being considered by the Prig school of nursing (who are very numerous among professional ladies) as ... highly beneficial to the performance of the nervous system'.[15]

Sarah Gamp also manifests a macabre love for corpses. Dickens is not afraid to endow his greedy, selfish and ignorant nurse with necrophiliac sadism. The supreme ecstasy for her consists in devouring her salmon at the bedside of a dying man while placing his limbs in the position of a corpse: 'he'd make a lovely corpse'.[16] The character belongs rather to the infernal regions of Bosch or Brueghel than to everyday reality.

Dickens was obviously inspired by the 'paid nurses' described earlier, who still formed the majority of the medical staff in families and hospitals in 1843–4, the year *Martin Chuzzlewit* came out, and before Florence Nightingale's reforms. By making Sarah Gamp and her double, Mrs Prig, comic brutes, and by attributing their acts to an evil nature, Dickens avoided putting a social and psychological problem before his readers. In the series of contrasts that characterize the structure of Dicken's novels, Mrs Gamp the alcoholic shrew, is not contrasted with the professionally trained nurse representing the future, but with the woman of works inspired by Providence who comforts through her miraculously beneficent influence.

Like other characters of Dickens, these single women are caricatures, obtained by blowing up an occupation or dominant trait to which the entire personality is reduced: '... Gamp is my name and Gamp my nater.'[17] Thus Sarah Gamp is defined as an essence. The very name of Miss Brass and her gestures define her as law become woman. In the more elaborate caricatures dialogue and gestures, images and accessories serve to express the unique dimension. In Dickens's manichaean vision these caricatures, the negations of femininity, are evil-minded creatures. But he presents also some single women who are conceived with real sympathy.

Miss La Creevy in *Nicholas Nickleby* 'was a mincing young lady of fifty'.[18] She rents a flat from the Nickleby family and ekes out (her meagre) income by painting portraits. Situated socially as an 'unprotected female', she is however satisfied with her position; and her solitude is represented by Dickens not as a closing in on herself but as proof of personal resources; Miss La Creevy remains good, generous, sentimental even. Thus she manifests qualities too remarkable not to be noticed, and Tom Linklater, a bachelor of fifty, asks her to share his life. This marriage is part of the final idyll where all the good people find themselves rewarded. Miss La Creevy, despite her fifty years and a few quirks, was too richly endowed with the qualities of a good wife to remain unmarried in the novel's imaginary world.

Betsy Trotwood is another sympathetic unmarried figure. She is revealed as an admirable adoptive mother, who is in fact a victim wife whose maternal gifts lie fallow. In the course of the novel, Betsy Trotwood undergoes a development as spectacular as Bella Wilfer in *Our Mutual Friend* and Caddy Jellyby in *Bleak House*. She is shown at first as an eccentric type, enclosed in behaviour patterns, manias that are not purely grotesque inventions but reveal a denial of certain traumatic aspects of life. It is true that the comic retains its hold: the aversion to donkeys, the taste for extravagant accoutrements, and the often very eccentric behaviour. But Betsy is also the person who has decided that David would be a girl and who, for long years, prescribed as his imaginary model his sister Betsy Trotwood. Thus for a time she only accepts the male sex in the form of an innocent and an orphan both entirely dependent on her for their subsistence. Little by little there emerges from rigid behaviour patterns a personality at once strong, tender and generous, which overcomes the neurosis created by her disastrous marriage.

Betsy Trotwood is one of Dickens's most complete female characters. She is capable of victoriously opposing the perfidious Murdstone clan, of losing her money without batting an eyelid, all the while keeping secret the role her friend Mr Wickfield might have played in her ruin; of maintaining in secret a black sheep of a husband; of playing, vis-à-vis David, the role of the most devoted mother, psychologically and materially, and withdrawing discreetly when he reaches manhood. Unlike the simplified figures who abound in Dickens, Betsy is a character with several dimensions. At once motherly and independent, she develops from an eccentric spinster to an unselfish mother. But are not these realized maternal gifts all signs of the good wife-mother, since Betsy Trotwood is revealed as the discreet and consenting victim of an unscrupulous libertine, a human wreck whom she will help until the day of his death? Certainly she is part of a system of relations in the centre of which the hero is caught between the good and the bad. In this sense, the novel can be interpreted as a tale whose good fairy is Betsy

Trotwood, though it must be borne in mind that such an interpretation does not take her psychological development into account, and therefore throws light on only one aspect of a character who for once is multi-dimensional.[19]

These 'false spinsters' who, although endowed by accident with all the moral attributes of the wife and mother, cannot set up a 'normal' home, bring to mind Dickens's sister-in-law, Georgina Hogarth. 'Since 1842, Georgina had devoted herself to the care of the children, teaching each in succession to read and write',[20] Edgar Johnson writes: Kate Dickens only remotely took part in the administration of the house and the education of the children, and remained to one side of her husband's intellectual and creative life. More and more dissatisfied with Kate's deficiencies and his marital life, Dickens drew nearer to Georgina who was capable of organizing the house, watching over the material and moral wellbeing of the children and of Dickens himself, and giving him understanding and intellectual sympathy. She even took the family on holiday to Broadstairs while Kate, pregnant with her ninth child, stayed in London. Georgina was also equal to playing the part of hostess. 'She is the active spirit of the house, and the children dote on her',[21] wrote Dickens. Thus Georgina, a spinster, played the role of wife and mother, without any of the accompanying social privileges. The painter Augustus Egg had asked her to marry him, but she refused; the part Dickens played in her decision remains obscure. In September 1853 in a letter to Miss Burdett-Coutts he wondered 'whether it is, or is not a pity that she is all she is to me and mine'. In an obscure passage of another letter, he seems also to allude to a declaration of love from Georgina. 'I have left the matter where it was; trusting to its wearing itself out, on her part, in due course.'[22] Did Georgina voluntarily sacrifice herself to Dickens and his children? was she carried away by admiration or love for him? Much later she questioned the wisdom of her choice: had her life been 'all a mistake – and a waste?' Dickens too wondered about it when she reached the age of thirty-three. 'I doubt if she will ever marry ... I don't know whether to be glad of it or sorry for it.'[23]

The separation of Dickens and his wife after the Ellen Ternan scandal drew him closer to his sister-in-law, since Georgina decided to remain at his side despite the Hogarth family's hostility and the inevitable questioning about her relationship with her brother-in-law. Her margin of choice was narrow. She had not been trained for anything. She was also too attached to Dickens to abandon him and join his accusers.[24] She became more and more indispensable to him, watched over his health, his diet and the smallest details of his comfort, for example sending him books and papers, or an umbrella and linen. Mistress of the house at Gad's Hill, she seems to have been proud of her role, despite the rumours.[25]

It was said for example that she was mother of three of his children. Annie Fields noted in her journal: 'Poor Miss Hogarth spends her life hoping to comfort and care for him ... I never felt more keenly her anomalous and unnatural position in the household. Not one mentioned her name.'[26] After Dickens's death, Georgina looked after the children who were not already married, served as a link between them, and settled the details of his will. In short she found the opportunity to realize to the full her qualities of mother of a family. All the members of Dickens's family seem to have loved and respected her.

Betsy Trotwood, the most positive of Dickens's single females, had overcome the failure of her marriage. Miss Wade in *Little Dorrit*, Rosa Dartle in *David Copperfield*, and Miss Havisham in *Great Expectations* are all more or less deeply marked by the emotional humiliations that destroyed the germs of kindness and humanity in them. They are symbolic figures in whom all comic elements have disappeared. Miss Wade, who teaches rebellion to Tattycoram, is a 'self tormentor', and a rather imprecisely drawn figure. She constantly manifests a hatred for humanity which appears gratuitous to the reader until he is familiar with this orphan's long past of suffering and humiliation. Materially and emotionally exploited, Miss Wade constantly takes vengeance on humanity. Motivated by bitterness and hatred, she attempts, like Miss Havisham with Estella, to make of Tattycoram an accomplice in her desire for vengeance. Miss Wade is undoubtedly a victim, but Dickens makes her a melodramatic one: 'the anger ... flashed out of her dark eyes ... quivered in her nostrils, and fired the very breath she exhaled ...'[27] Ten years after *Dombey and Son* this is a less elaborate version of Edith Dombey, a victim indeed, but whose female essence is irreparably damaged.

The inspiration for Rosa Dartle in *David Copperfield*, was drawn from Mrs Brown, ex-governess, and intimate friend of Miss Burdett-Coutts. In his letters Dickens alludes to the taste for contradiction and the extreme susceptibility of the woman he called the 'general-objector'.[28] Rosa Dartle, an orphan like Miss Wade, had always been in the subordinate position of 'companion'. Physically unimpressive, small, dark and not much to look at, 'she was a little dilapidated – like a house – with having been so long to let'.[29] Her most striking feature, a scar across her lips, fades or reddens according to her emotions, and fascinates her interlocutor. Rosa Dartle's drama, her love for Steerforth and the cruel way he trifles with her are gradually revealed to David. Dickens makes her a theatrical personage, characterized by excessive attitudes; her behaviour is now mock-humble, punctuated by protestations of ignorance, and betraying a sharp aggression, now paroxystic, her rage directed not only against her tormentor Steerforth, but for no apparent reason against Emily. Are the fury and physical cruelty unleashed on Emily purely the violence of a character out of a melodrama? 'I would have her whipped! ... I would have her branded on the face, drest in rags, and cast out in the streets to starve.'[30] Or is Rosa trampling savagely on the image of what she might have become, had she not endured the humiliations of her position in the Steerforth family? She insults the poor girl at leisure in a melodramatic scene that is fabricated and over-long. 'The resolute and unrelenting hatred of her tone, its cold stern sharpness ... the flashing black eyes ... the passion-wasted figure ... the scar ... quivered and throbbing as she spoke ... contemptuous laugh.'[31] The victim of Steerforth, and of social and family circumstances: 'I descended ... into a doll, a trifle for the occupation of an idle hour, to be dropped, and taken up ... I have been a mere disfigured piece of furniture between you both',[32] Rosa Dartle, physically and morally disfigured, is nothing more than a monstrous puppet.

With Miss Havisham Dickens created a symbolic implausible figure who yet exercises a powerful hold on the imagination. She reigns in Satis House where time stopped on her wedding-day at 9.20, the time when she learnt that the adventurer she idolized had abandoned her. Clothed in rich fabrics, satin, lace, and a white veil over her white hair, Miss Havisham is henceforth nothing but a ghost in whom the married woman survives alongside the old maid. When Pip sees her for the first time, the bride in her wedding-dress is a wax skeleton with black eyes.[33] In the dark room with closed windows and drawn curtains, theatre of the promise of glory and of her ruin, she has withdrawn from the land of the living; teeming, destructive nature has taken possession of the objects abandoned by men; the flowers are yellow and faded, spiders and mice are settled in the cake, on the still laid table. Having lost their significance, the marriage emblems, harbingers of a new life, have become symbols of death.

Just as the parasitic animals feed on the rotting waste and relics, so Estella is a monstrous excrescence born from what life Miss Havisham has left: her hatred for men and her desire for vengeance. Having committed symbolic suicide, she devotes her disfigured humanity to shaping Estella into an unfeeling monster intended to avenge her by inspiring blind and devouring passion in the stronger sex. Estella, for whose frigidity and indifference Dickens would have drawn on Ellen Ternan,[34] is less a woman than a symbolic projection of Miss Havisham – whose corpse Pip saw rocking behind her – made to destroy feelings and the 'Christmas philosophy'. Like Edith Dombey and Louisa Gradgrind, Miss Havisham manifests the destructive power of money to which her fiancé's machinations have sacrificed her. In her turn she uses it to detach Pip from the simple world of Joe Gargery's forge and inspire in him the wish for a more refined life; she succeeds in destroying the innocence of a child who is henceforth obsessed by ambition to rise in society. The forsaken lover, who tries through Estella to make an active principle out of death and destruction, commits a crime against life for which she is punished by the cruelty of her relationship with Estella herself. Her first tragic error was to give a universal dimension to a particular failure and to an idea of mad, passionate love that Dickens wants to caricature. 'I'll tell you ... what real love is. It is blind devotion, unquestioning self-humiliation, utter submission ... giving up your whole heart and soul to the smiter ...'[35]

Victim of a double error of judgement, both in her idea of love and in her attribution of one man's perfidy to the entire sex, Miss Havisham, the purest symbol of death in life, embodies the tragic echo of a betrayed and solitary woman.

The single women in Dickens's novels, however varied they may be, pathetic or grotesque caricatures, symbolic figures, have like his wife-mothers one common characteristic: they explain neither the particularity nor the complexity of human beings, nor the specific problems of a particular condition or profession. Single life and its psychological happenings and the sociological problem of women's labour do not interest Dickens. The representative of a socio-professional category, 'the paid nurse', becomes a grotesque archetype of the sadist, and, mutilating her, he relegated her to the anti-woman already described. These puppets and symbols, whose life is exclusively derived from the author's imagination and lies outside any psychological and social references in Dickens's imaginary universe, show the reverse of the myth of the virgin.

9

Revolt and Duty in the Brontës

The majority of Anne Brontë's heroines, and more particularly Charlotte's, after being alone and independent for a time, end by marrying. They nevertheless have their place in this section, because Charlotte endows them with strength enough to struggle with the psychological and social problems of being single women, that is idle young girls, old maids or exploited governesses. Even though the predicament is dealt with incompletely, the types of character she portrays (unlike those of Dickens) bear the stamp of genuine personal experience.

The heroines of *Jane Eyre* and *Villette* were seen by contemporary critics as familiar characters as well as interesting social cases. It was with reference to *Jane Eyre*, *Vanity Fair* and the 1847 Report of the Governesses' Benevolent Institution that Lady Eastlake (Elizabeth Rigby) wrote on behalf of governesses:

> Jane Eyre is not precisely the mouthpiece one would select to plead the cause of governesses, (who are) not only entitled to our gratitude and respect by (their) position, but ... by the circumstances which reduced them to it.[1]

While criticizing the spirit of revolt which, she found, ran through the work, she used it as a pretext to draw public attention to the exploitation of governesses and to advertise the recently founded friendly society. A review of *Villette* in 1853 appreciated the new kind of novel that presented women, apprentices, dressmakers and governesses as coming to grips with the most difficult daily tasks.[2]

For several years the Brontë sisters had suffered the same experience of the majority of the heroines of Charlotte and Anne. Anne was only nineteen when, in 1839, she took her first post with a Mrs Ingham at Blake Hall, Mirfield. Charlotte was successively pupil and teacher at the Wooler school for young ladies in Roe Head, governess in two families, then pupil and teacher at the Héger boarding school in Brussels. As she wrote to Emily on 2 July 1835, it was 'necessity' which dispersed the family, and 'Duty' that obliged her to accept a teaching post at Roe Head, so that Emily would not have to pay school fees. The money thus available could be used for Branwell's education at the Royal Academy.[3] But neither the prospect of teaching in 1835 nor the experience of a year at Roe Head trying to handle gifted but recalcitrant students were pleasant for her. For Emily, teaching in 1837 in 'a large school ... near Halifax ... from six in the morning until near eleven at night', 'this is slavery'.[4] Charlotte's stories about her life in the Sedgewick family in Stonegappe in 1839, then with the John Whites in 1841, emphasized her inability to adapt to being a stranger in a family and governess to boisterous children. According to a cousin of the Sedgewicks she lacked any teaching gift and was constantly depressed.[5] At the Whites she complained of overwork and indicated her meagre emolument; theoretically £20 a year, but in fact £16 for they kept back £4 for her laundry.[6] But the psychological disadvantages affected her more: she mentions

The miseries of a reserved wretch like me, thrown at once into the midst of a large family – proud as peacocks and wealthy as Jews – pampered, spoiled and turbulent children, whom I was expected instantly to amuse as well as instruct.[7]

It was unutterably painful for her to live among strangers with whom she could not communicate in depth.[8] In her biography Mrs Gaskell noted that, like her sisters, Charlotte lacked any taste for young children and natural aptitude to teach them. They would certainly have been more successful with older children, were it not for their own inadequate education. To fill these gaps Charlotte and Emily decided to complete their education in Brussels, in the Héger school. At twenty-six Charlotte found herself on school benches again, very satisfied, it seems, with this step back into *statu pupillari*. The following year, 1842, M. Héger proposed that she teach English, in return for which she would continue to learn French and German, and receive her board and lodging.[9] On her second stay she would receive a salary of £16 a year to be the supervisor of the top class and give English lessons. She herself had to pay for German lessons. While the life of a governess had only brought her torment and humiliation, she seems to have derived real satisfaction from a profession for which she must have felt better and better qualified; only her sense of duty to her father made her reluctantly refuse a post of first governess in a large Manchester boarding-school with a salary of £100 a year, a position that would have enabled her to expend her unemployed energies and recover from the sentimental trials of Brussels.[10]

However little gifted Charlotte Brontë was for teaching, however painful the conditions of the work may have been, it must have been even more intolerable for someone who felt she was sacrificing the best of herself, her writer's vocation. As early as 1836, the time of Roe Head, and when she began to teach, she was aware of destroying the imaginary or creative life in her. As Winifred Gérin states in connection with unpublished extracts of the 'Roe Head Journal', the conflict between moral conscience and creative need which was already asserting itself, persuaded her to ask Southey's advice in December the same year. Southey's verdict, which she accepted,[11] perhaps put a temporary end to her uncertainties, but seems to have increased her mental torments. After her stay in Brussels she seriously considered founding a school with her sisters. At this time she still reckoned that a literary career was out of the question.[12]

The experiences of the three sisters as governesses appears in an almost unvarnished state in Anne's novel *Agnes Grey*. This may be due to her lack of literary originality and the fact that she was a governess longer than her sisters.[13] This novel recounts the adventures of a governess in two families. The tale lacks intensity, warmth and emotion. The detached tone is like that of a fragment of a private journal in which she is dryly recounting the events of her sisters' and Branwell's life.[14] While contemporaries reproached *Agnes Grey* for an excess of colour,[15] Charlotte on the contrary thought ' "Agnes Grey" should please such critics as Mr. Lewes, for it is "true" and "unexaggerated" enough.'[16] The novel is the banal story of a vicar's daughter who loses what little she owns at sea. In order to help the family, but also prompted by curiosity and desire for independence, and full of youthful illusions, the heroine decides to become a governess, to 'train the tender plants, and watch their buds unfolding day by day!'[17] Her illusions are brutally destroyed in her first job. Her employer is a rich merchant retired from business who 'could not be prevailed upon to give a greater salary than twenty-five pounds to the instructess of his children'. The governess has nothing but obligations. She has to educate and discipline naughty children without having the right to punish them : her only weapon against the whole family's scorn is patience. She goes home and looks for another post. Discouraged by unsuitable advertisements she has one appear setting out *her* talents : 'Music, Song, Drawing, French, Latin and German'. She is offered a position at £50 a year and two months' holiday. As in *Villette*, the image of the poor, honest, cultivated, plain governess contrasts with that of the pretty young girl of good family, hare-brained and conventional, incapable of deep feeling and true culture. Treated as a stranger and inferior by parents, children and servants, the governess spends all her energy trying to teach these elegant and superficial creatures absurd drawing-room talents and a gloss of culture, while she herself remains hidden in humble obscurity. The main interest of this inventory of the problems raised by a profession without standards and qualifications is documentary: the heroine's personality, a not excessively critical presence, is only silhouetted against this background; she records the injustice done her in nostalgic images, even clichés: the glow-worm, the book-worm, doomed to solitude and obscurity.[18] In vain does the reader look for the note of revolt, the affirmation of self, the lyrical dimension of Charlotte's governesses.

Charlotte's attack is more fundamental. In *Shirley* Mrs Prior, who refrains from harbouring feelings of envy and insubordination towards her superiors, yet complains of the isolation of a governess. The author puts in her mouth the very words of an article by E. Rigby in *The Quarterly Review*.[19] 'The gentlemen regarded me as a "tabooed woman" ... the ladies too made it plain that they thought me a "bore". The servants "detested me".'[20] Her state appears to her as 'sedentary, solitary, confined, joyless, toilsome'. Jane Eyre does not linger over the material and moral conditions of a situation that is essential to the Jane-Rochester intrigue. We know that she is pleasing to Mr Thornfield, that she is completely free in her work, that her relations with her pupil Adele are good even though, as a fierce Anglo-Saxon, she deplores Adele's French coquetry and frivolity. Mr Rochester has enough books in his library for her teaching needs. Finally, one of the reasons that prompted her to accept the job is the prospect of a salary double the one she received at Lowood, £30 a year instead of £15.[21] These particulars are sufficient to place Jane socially and to set the scene. She manifests little interest in teaching; forming the mind and tastes of the little Adele brings her no particular satisfaction, any more than teaching country folk, of whom she speaks in the condescending tone of a missionary among the natives. As soon as the possibility is open to her, she does not hesitate to give up the hard task of teacher, from which she drew only moral satisfaction: a sense of duty accomplished and pride at having faced up to an additional ordeal.

In *Villette*, Charlotte's last novel, the significance of work for the heroine Lucy Snowe, and the head of the boarding-school Madame Beck, is more emphasized. Without forgetting that her perception of the characters, of the educational system and the total emotional tonality of the work can only be understood in the context of the Brussels trauma, we may say that it is work that provides Madame Beck, a sour and disagreeable person, with a positive dimension. Despite Lucy-Charlotte's *a posteriori* reproval of a 'papist' system of education founded on mistrust and reciprocal spying, and with no confidence in human nature, and despite Madame Beck reflecting the ambiguity of Charlotte's feelings towards Madame Héger, a certain admiration emerges for her efficiency and energy. For though her strange methods are derived from the principles of Jesuit education, professionally Madame Beck succeeds. The pupils are well treated and in good health. She knows how to get the best out of the teachers. Madame Beck forces Lucy to go beyond her limits and to emerge from her voluntary blinkers by entrusting her with the second division where she has to tackle haughty and insolent girls from noble families. Thus it is work which provides Madame Beck with the opportunity to prove her gifts for organization and leadership.

For Lucy Snowe, on the other hand, 'work had neither charm nor hold on my interest'[22] even though she prefers by far to give lessons than be a governess.[23] This preference – Charlotte's too – makes her refuse a post of governess with M. de Bassompierre and a salary three times higher, as she is loath to be a 'bright lady's shadow'. The monotony, regularity and discipline of work alleviate anxiety and calm her fragile nerves. During the holidays, left to solitude and idleness, she collapses, a prey to depression. Regular occupation can act as a powerful tranquillizer, and despite her boredom, gives her a kind of peace. Her colleagues dream of a lover or, like the 'Parisian', respecting neither law nor religion, give themselves up to the low sensual pleasures of dress, perfume and cosmetics. But Lucy Snowe, like Jane Eyre, a protestant puritanical Englishwoman, derives her pleasure from the ordeal overcome, from self-control, from the victory of will over instinct.[24] Thus we can hardly speak of Lucy Snowe's 'professional' satisfaction: besides, when she describes the success of the little school that M. Paul gave her to keep her busy whilst she was away, she does not take personal credit for it.

The secret of my success did not lie so much in myself, in any endowment, any power of mine, as in a new state of circumstances, a wonderfully changed life ... The spring which moved my energies lay far away beyond seas, in an Indian isle.[25]

Charlotte Brontë's novels also pose the problem of unmarried women in fairly specific terms, through characters of traditional and unemployed old maids and girls who, conscious of the anachronism of their condition and the unlikelihood of their getting married, want to find a new way. The problem of redundant women which preoccupied her contemporaries confronted Charlotte personally, as someone who, given the marriage-market and her own isolation, had few chances of finding a partner. Her reaction to the Reverend Henry Nussey's proposal of marriage in 1839 was characteristic: conscious that 'romantic and eccentric' she would not be suitable for him, she proudly took the risk of never marrying and sketched a meaningful portrait of the wife who would suit him. 'The character should not be too marked, ardent and original, her temper should be mild, her piety undoubted, her spirits even and cheerful, and her *personal attractions* sufficient to please your eyes.'[26]

The theme of the calmness, pliability and tranquillity necessary for a wife often recurred in her letters. Like Harriet Martineau[27] her temperament did not dispose her towards marriage, any more than her physique or her social position.[28] Thus in imaginary compensation she contrasted in her novels the conventional heiress – pretty, rich and superficial – with the poor teacher, whose romantic soul, depth and originality would seduce equally exceptional men. When she violently denied the rumour that she would be getting engaged to M. Héger, she added, 'it is an imbecility which I reject with contempt – for women who have neither fortune nor beauty – to make marriage the principal object of their wishes and hopes.'[29]

Aware of all the things that predisposed her to spinsterhood, Charlotte defended and rehabilitated spinsters, fighting what she called the 'stigma of an old maid'.[30] She wrote to Miss Wooler, headmistress of the school she attended in 1831 (where she made the acquaintance of a charitable old maid, the inspiration behind Miss Ainsley in *Shirley*):

There is no more respectable character on this earth than an unmarried woman who makes her own way through life quietly, perseveringly – without support of husband or brother, and who having attained the age of 45 or upwards – retains in her possession a well-regulated mind ... fortitude to support inevitable pains, sympathy with the suffering of others ...[31]

In *Shirley* Caroline Helstone, despairing of ever getting married, decides to study the life of the old maids in her immediate surroundings and to reflect on the condition threatening her. The most typical, to the point of caricature, is undoubtedly Hortense Moore. At thirty-five, she already has fads, especially in the way of clothing, of which Caroline tries in vain to relieve her. Her flaws of character are more serious. With a finical conception of teaching and female education, she teaches Caroline French (Belgian) with the same disorganized mind and obsession with detail she uses to tidy up drawers; in her teacher's role as in her personal habits, she is grumpy and unpleasant. As retrograde as the most narrow-minded of the women-haters in the novel, she would like to destroy in her pupil the smallest leaning towards initiative or originality. Hortense Moore seems a desperate case and, despite all her efforts Caroline cannot find anything positive in her. On the other hand, when she decides to interest herself in Miss Mann, the latter reveals unsuspected virtue beneath a forbidding appearance. Her Medusa-like gaze, the monotonous voice, the acid comments on her neighbour are only superficial, not 'deeper than the angel-sweetness of hundreds of beauties'.[32] She is a good woman who has fought and suffered for her neighbour, and Caroline discovers her stiffness is a defence built up against ingratitude and the stigma of spinsterhood. The other old maid, Miss Ainsley, also conceals beneath her ridiculous straight-laced exterior an immense generosity and universal kindness.

So Caroline discovers that unmarried women are real victims of society. They often have a more useful function than many wives and mothers; and it is the stupid ostracism practised against them that contributes to their common embitterment. They are the by-product, the waste, of an archaic ideal of woman, that dooms her only to be a wife-mother. Caroline, Charlotte's mouthpiece, comes to see single women as a sacrificed class, 'like the houseless and unemployed poor' for whom a fabricated ideal of life has been made up wholly, in the shape of sacrifice to others, to hide the fact that they are *a priori* deprived of a reason for living. Society says to old maids

Your place is to do good to others, to be helpful whenever help is wanted ... a very convenient doctrine for the people who hold it ... is there not a terrible hollowness, mockery, want, craving, in that existence which is given away to others, for want of something of your own to bestow it on? ... Does virtue lie in abnegation of self?[33]

Like Barbara Bodichon, Caroline denounces society and the prejudices that deprive women of a useful and absorbing field of activity. The educational system, founded on an erroneous idea of woman's nature and role, is responsible, in her eyes, for so-called 'female' faults; namely the inordinately powerful emotions, the moral and physical depressions, the duplicity needed to catch a husband. In a tone too passionate not to give the author away, Caroline makes a genuine appeal to the fathers, brothers, men of England, to persuade them to treat their daughters and sisters as adults capable of playing a part in society. In a review of the novel, G. H. Lewes noted that Caroline sometimes talks like Charlotte Brontë and not like a vicar's niece, especially in the long tirade on the position of woman which he compares to a page of Harriet Martineau.[34] Jane Eyre sometimes has a similar tone when she demands a field of action for women and rebels against an outdated conception of female psychology. She climbs to the top of the castle tower and gives free reign to her feeling of confinement.

Then I longed for a power of vision which might overpass that limit; which might reach the busy world, towns, regions full of life ... I desired more of practical experience ... more of intercourse with my kind ...

Then the protestation becomes more general.

Millions are condemned to a stiller doom than mine, and millions are in silent revolt against their lot ... women are supposed to be very calm generally: but women feel just as men feel; they need exercise for their faculties.[35]

Jane is not satisfied 'with making puddings, knitting stockings',[36] noted a critic who attributed her dissatisfaction to an ambition out-of-place in a woman.

In *Villette* the conventional image of the ideal woman, a virtuous angel confined to her home, and reduced to the role of fiancée, wife and mother, preferably completely ignorant, is satirized in the exaggerated tastes of Paul Emmanuel, for whom a ' "woman of intellect" ... was a sort of "lusus natursae", a luckless accident.'[37] In a choice Victorian vignette Paul Emmanuel and Lucy are described during a visit to the museum in 1842, in front of pictures which have been tracked down in the catalogue of a Brussels exhibition.[38] Paul tears Lucy away while she is examining Cleopatra critically, in order to make her meditate on *The Life of a Woman*.

The first picture represented a 'Jeune Fille', coming out of a church-door, a missal in her hand, her dress very Prim, her eyes cast down ...

The second, a 'Mariée' ... kneeling at a prie-dieu ... The third, a 'Jeune Mère' hanging disconsolate over a clayeye and puffy baby ... These ... 'Angels' were grim and grey as burglars, and cold and vapid as ghosts.[39]

Through her explicit demand for a sphere of activity for women outside the home, through the satire – rare, it is true – of the female ideal of Angel, Charlotte Brontë takes her place in a perspective of protest, if not feminist, at least feminizing, which brings her somewhere near the company of R. F. Parkes, Anna Jameson and Barbara Bodichon.

Jane Eyre and Caroline Helston refuse to remain cloistered in the family sanctuary. Caroline revolts against the altruistic mission prescribed for those who have renounced conjugal bliss, the life of sacrifice for which society shows no gratitude. The claim only concerns the young woman whose marital destiny has not yet been fulfilled, or the spinster whose family deprivation is confirmed, namely the alternative to what is still deemed woman's natural destiny. It is in the same perspective that, for her part, Charlotte envisaged professional activity, and not as an essential fulfilment of herself. From Roe Head to Brussels teaching for her was strictly an economic necessity, imposed upon her by her family situation. Consequently, for Caroline Helstone and Lucy Graham, work more and more often fulfilled the double function of distraction and victory over self. At Roe Head, at the Héger boarding-school and above all after Brussels,[40] literary work (to which in any case she did not have the leisure to devote herself) was above all intended to calm the morbid ruminations of a person with powerful depressive tendencies, to attenuate the sufferings caused by love, and, in her own words, to fill her solitude. 'Lonely as I am – how should I be if Providence had never given me courage to adopt a career? ... I wish every woman in England had also a hope and motive. Alas there are many old maids who have neither.'[41]

In 1848 she wrote even more plainly that work was a woman's only recourse when she is deprived of her natural vocation by the lack of 'a little family to rear and educate and a household to conduct'. When Charlotte reluctantly agreed to express a general opinion on the problem of women's work, she confined herself to stating what was wrong without putting forward solutions.

The market for female labour is quite overstocked; but where or how could another be opened? ... the professions now filled only by men should be open to women also; but are not their present occupants

and candidates more than numerous enough to answer every demand?
Is there any room for female lawyers, female doctors, female engravers,
for more female artists, more authoresses? One can see where the evil
lies, but who can point out the remedy? ... She (the single woman)
must do what she can ... bear ... work ... (and) when patience has
done its utmost and industry its best, whether in the case of women or
operatives ... and pain and want triumph, the sufferer is free, is
entitled, at last to send up to Heaven any piercing cry for relief, if by
that cry she can hope to obtain succour ...[42]

She barely recognized the right of complaint for the victims of social
injustice. Her conception of work as a mere compensation for those
who felt they had missed their family vocation considerably irritated
her feminist friend, Mary Taylor.

... this first duty, this great necessity you seem to think that some
women may indulge in – if they give up marriage and don't make
themselves too disagreeable to the other sex. You are a coward and a
traitor. A woman who works is by that alone better than one who
does not.[43]

Charlotte Brontë adopted the same tone in her rare comments on
feminism. In 1850 she mentioned an article from the *Westminster
Review* entitled 'Woman's Mission', whose feminist message on the
whole she approved. She rejoiced that 'men begin to regard the
position of women in another light' but added that woman can only
modify certain minimal aspects of their position.[44] In a letter of
20 September 1851 to Mrs Gaskell she mentioned H. Taylor's article
on female emancipation which she thought was written by John
Stuart Mill. She approved of its common sense position, which
aimed at countering anti-feminist arguments: 'if there be a natural
unfitness in women for men's employment, there is no need to make
laws on the subject; leave all careers open; let them try; ...' but her
opinion of the style of the author whom she sees as a militant feminist
reveals anti-feminist prejudices.

When I first read the paper, I thought it was the work of a powerful-
minded, clear-headed woman, who had a hard, jealous heart, and
nerves of bend leather; a woman who longed for power and had never
felt affection.[45]

She was much more favourable to the article when she corrected her
'mistake' and attributed it to Mill.

Her passivity before feminist problems was symptomatic of a
more general attitude different from Mary Taylor's, brought up

unlike Charlotte in a radical and evangelical family tradition.[46] In *Jane Eyre* Mary Taylor deplored the absence of protest and the acceptance of the established order though its literary qualities she otherwise admired.[47] She contrasted Charlotte with Emily and Anne who, she felt, addressed themselves more to the great number of respectable readers whom it was proper to instruct and enlighten. Mary Taylor had discerned the reality of Charlotte's philosophy behind the appearances of revolt. Besides, when the latter compared herself to Mrs Gaskell and Harriet Beecher Stowe, she regretfully recognized that 'books handling the topics of the day ... book for its moral ... a philanthropic scheme' were not in her sphere,[48] that critical reflection on political and social events and institutions played no part in her poetic and imaginative life, even though in *Shirley* she described the context of Luddite incidents which she had carefully documented.[49] Already 'reactionary' at fifteen,[50] Charlotte Brontë remained conservative all her life. She harboured a fervent admiration for Wellington, the hero of her youth, defended the established church and felt only hostility towards revolutions in general and the French revolution in particular.[51]

In the context of the class system the behaviour of her characters confirms her horror of 'disorder' and any questioning of the social hierarchy. Despite their lucid independence and awareness of isolation, Lucy Snowe and Jane Eyre accept what is and unlike Julien Sorel in *Le Rouge et le Noir* do not revolt against those responsible for their exploitation. Eugene Forcade, a critic of the *Revue des deux Mondes*, could not find words enough to praise such resignation: '... what charmed me above all was that the author did not think for one moment to fulminate apocalyptically against society'.[52] This was a long way from the contemporary comment of Elizabeth Rigby who saw *Jane Eyre* as 'a murmuring against the comforts of the rich and against the privations of the poor ... the tone of mind and thought which has overthrown authority and violated every code human and divine abroad, and fostered Chartism and rebellion at home'.[53] Thus *Jane Eyre* was generally well received, and the first edition rapidly went out of print. Only some were shocked by the 'unregenerate and undisciplined' heroine.[54]

In their independence perhaps lay the originality of Jane Eyre, Lucy Snowe, and Shirley. Alone in the world, the heroine has to find her identity outside the family context, in material and psychological isolation. Lucy Snowe, an orphan, accepts a post with the good Miss Marchmont; after her death she is alone once more, with fifteen pounds, even more isolated than when she arrived in London. Solitude and poverty are the lot of a girl whose condition is perceived and constantly exploited by everyone.[55] Was Charlotte thinking of her own adventures or of the 'unprotected female', the heroine of a *Punch* serial, to whom she alluded in 1850?[56] Jane Eyre too, placed in a family that treats her like an inferior alien, very quickly learns to rely on her own resources. Alone, she advertises for a job. Alone, she arrives at Thornfield; alone, she leaves. It is this independence, energy, the habit of relying on one's own resources, both to subsist and to appreciate a situation, all characteristics that were hardly 'feminine', which shocked some contemporaries. The heroine who must constantly fight, to whom nothing has been given from birth, asserts her superiority by her struggle.

The class theme is always present in *Jane Eyre* and *Villette*: the positive characters being constantly contrasted with the rich heiresses, Blanche Ingram and Ginevra Fanshaw. The heroine sees them as young, pretty, rich, and with the exception of Pauline de Bassompierre and Shirley, as selfish, mindless and conventional, incapable of a deep feeling or genuine behaviour. One of Lucy Snowe's roles in *Villette* is precisely to dig down to the truth in the female characters and in particular those who are socially and materially privileged. Concerned above all with authenticity, the heroines scorn the 'female ruses' girls of good families use to attain their ends in a world where women must act like slaves in order to avoid being treated as though they were. Concessions to refinement can be among the weapons of the feeble creatures scorned by the Brontë heroines; and the latters' frankness is sometimes at the expense of good manners. When her 'master' asks Jane is she finds him handsome, she quietly replies in the negative, not without realizing that her reply ought to have been 'conventionally vague and polite'.[57] Her behaviour towards a being who is at once her 'superior' and a member of the male sex is far from conforming to the usual custom. Here too authenticity wins over convention. She does not deny the reality of her love, confesses it even before Rochester himself, and listens attentively to the tales of his past. In short she refuses to play the roles that a certain class would like to assign to her – modesty and shyness towards a suitor, humility towards employers; just as Shirley refuses to be an attentive and submissive pupil. It is the denial of these conventions, the frankness of feeling and language that aroused in some critics either amused astonishment or severity and the accusation of coarseness. As one wrote:

> Love in a kitchen ... is a favourite subject of the author of 'Jane Eyre' ... Rochester and little Jane herself had a sneaking regard for brass candlesticks and copper kettles and oftener carried on their courtship in the scullery than in the drawing-room ...[58]

Others, notably Kingsley[59] and G. H. Lewes, were shocked by the 'Yorkshire Roughness', the 'vulgarity' of Shirley and her behaviour towards her tutor.[60]

Their morality has the same air of autonomy. Charlotte's heroines go their own way, uncorrupted and incorruptible, recognizing no outside authority. Lucy Snowe scorns the papist hypocrisy and intriguing of Madame Beck and some of her colleagues. Effortlessly, she remains the strict and righteous Protestant whom Paul Emmanuel admires. Secure in her moral judgement, Jane trusts only herself and refuses the right of age, experience and even religious vocation to guide her in the way of duty.

By their authenticity, inner independence and originality Charlotte Brontë's heroines are distinctly removed from the traditional idea of woman and the contemporary conception of 'the female sphere'. What is the effect on human relations and love relations in particular?

Virginia Woolf compared Charlotte Brontë to Thomas Hardy in respect of 'the power of his personality and the narrowness of his vision'. Contrasting her with Tolstoy and Jane Austen, whose characters she found infinitely more complex, she called her 'self-centred and self-limited'.[61] One of Charlotte's closest collaborators, George Smith, considered that her mind lacked the breadth of genius.[62] And indeed, as soon as it is a question of love, the intellectual and emotional horizon of the heroine is conspicuously narrowed down. Once the chosen one, sufficiently original and liberated from convention to appreciate the riches hidden within the simple governess, the teacher or the haughty heiress, appears on the scene, we witness these creatures finding at last in love a reason for living. After the disclosure of her feelings for her teacher Lucy Snowe sees in Paul Emmanuel a totally different person.[63] The rest of the world ceases to interest her and her work no longer has any meaning, save to carry out his will. Totally absorbed by her passion, the heroine becomes a passive subject of his desires, very different from Emily's heroines when they are similarly swept away. The proud Shirley is transformed in the same way – she who formerly administered her realm with authority, challenged the prejudices of blinkered priests, shocked the neighbours and G. H. Lewes by her independence and scorn for the decencies. Once in love with Louis Moore, the 'panther' is tamed and after a brief struggle yields completely, and defeat is the realization of her deepest desire:

... did I not say I prefer a *master*? ... one whose control my impatient temper must acknowledge. A man whose approbation can reward – whose displeasure punish me. A man I shall feel it impossible not to love, and very possible to fear.[64]

In an article on *Villette* in the *Daily News* Harriet Martineau complained that love and passion were the characters' only preoccupations.

All the female characters ... are full of one thing, or are regarded by the reader in the light of that one thought – love ... so incessant is the writer's tendency to describe the need of being loved ... It is not thus in real life. There are substantial, heartfelt interests for women of all ages, and under ordinary circumstances, quite apart from love.[65]

Indeed a love that makes a single individual the centre of her universe and forces her to renounce independence removes Jane's dissatisfaction, cures Lucy's nervous depressions and puts an end to Shirley's reformist inclinations. We cannot be surprised that Harriet Martineau and Mary Taylor, champions of female independence, saw themselves challenged both by the role of love in the evolution of Charlotte's heroines and above all by the way passion was lived. For, from one novel to the next, we find the same relationship between the couple: submission and respect towards the loved man, apparently justified by the difference in age and the master-pupil relationship. Lucy kisses Paul Emmanuel's hand and calls him 'sir'. For a long time Jane Eyre, like Frances Henry in *The Professor*, continues to say 'sir' to Rochester. To a certain extent in *Villette* and *The Professor* the theme of intellectual equality of man and woman plays a part in the relationship of the couple. It is Frances Henri's intelligence that first attracts W. Crimsworth. In *Villette* Paul Emmanuel develops from a caricature of anti-feminism to someone who recognizes Lucy Snowe's moral and intellectual autonomy. But in these two novels, when satisfied with a certain degree of self-expression the heroine is happy to abdicate totally before a superior personality.[66] Thanks to the exaltation of love, the desire for freedom and action yields to a deeper need, that of placing one's destiny in the hands of a stronger creature within the conventional marital framework.

The men characters are shaped to fit. They are deliberately endowed by the author with what she takes to be specifically male attributes,[67] at least for one inhabiting Charlotte Brontë's psychological universe. Paul Emmanuel, Louis Moore and Rochester share an exotic and mysterious dimension, rough appearance and behaviour, a certain lack of social polish that shock and attract their matches. Dark, fascinatingly ugly, they are forces of nature irradiating authority and power. Their physique does not correspond to the canons of classical beauty, but expresses – through the intensity of their gaze, the asymmetry of their features, the expression of their torment[68] – the virile strength and impassioned temperament to which the heroines aspire. From her earliest contact with Rochester Jane felt she was in the presence of a 'master'. She is seduced by the Byronic character of the rootless traveller in search of peace of mind and his ideal partner. 'I sought my ideal of a woman amongst English ladies, French countesses, Italian signoras, and German gräfinnen',[69] says Rochester – Don Juan.

In this romantic yearning to be lost in love, it is tempting to see an imaginative compensation for a sentimental life where passion was a short unhappy spurt. When Charlotte rejected Henry Nussey's proposal in 1839, she wrote: 'If I ever marry, it must be in that light of adoration that I will regard my husband.'[70] But in 1840, even before her unhappy love for M. Héger, she saw passion as a dangerous force that women in particular must beware of, for reciprocal ardour is a rare thing. 'God help her, if she is left to love passionately and alone.'[71] Geraldine Jewsbury had also observed that woman's education predisposed her to a monstrous and fatal exacerbation of the life of feelings.[72] Charlotte even went so far as to write to Ellen Nussey: '... "une grande *passion*" is "*une* grande *folie*" ... mediocrity in all things is wisdom.'[73] Her pathetic, roughhewn passion for M. Héger sadly confirmed her intuitions. Rectifying in her biography the image Mrs Gaskell, anxious not to wrong her heroine's memory, gave of Charlotte's relations with M. Héger, Winifred Gérin presents this episode as the unique and devastating experience in Charlotte Brontë's life.[74] The torments of this platonic passion poisoned not only her second year in Brussels, but also the years after her return to England, at least until 1845.[75] The few remaining letters, of those she wrote to M. Héger, tell clearly enough the intensity of her feelings and her despair that they were not reciprocated and that she could not master her passion.

I have done everything ... I have denied myself absolutely the pleasure of speaking about you ... but I have been able to conquer neither my regrets nor my impatience. That, indeed, is humiliating – to be unable to control one's own thoughts ... To write to an ex-assistant-governess ... but for me it is life. Your last letter was stay and prop to me – nourishment to me for half a year...[76]

Winifred Gérin has been able to distinguish between fact and fiction in Paul Emmanuel, the hero of the novel, who is based on M. Héger. In general the novelist is faithful to her original, in his unusual appearance: 'his heavy black moustache and his black hair', his fits of gaiety, and his real kindness. Elsewhere she describes his irritability and sees him as a 'little black ugly being' and compares him to an 'insane tom-cat ... a delirious hyena'.[77] But this demanding master subjugated her, just as Paul Emmanuel, Rochester and the Professor subjugated her heroines.

With Arthur Nicholls, whom Charlotte married a few months before her death, it is a long way from the world of passion and fascinating Byronic figures. She spoke of him for the first time in 1845 as a 'respectable young man'.[78] Then in 1847 and 1851 she was irritated by his role of bashful lover. 'I cannot for my life see those interesting germs of goodness in him *you* discovered; his narrowness of mind always strikes me chiefly.'[79] In 1853, he proposed to her, which considerably upset the Reverend Brontë. Despite her indignation at the injustice and violence of the paternal opposition, Charlotte, terrified by her father's condition, which seemed to portend a stroke, yielded and promised to show poor Nicholls the door the next day.[80] Charlotte may have taken pity on him and said to herself she was possibly losing what was the most precious thing in life, 'genuine attachment', but she did not dare oppose her father's will. His possessiveness was only equalled by the passivity of his daughter who, however, recognized more than just simple hostility towards Nicholls; that is, 'vehement antipathy to the bare thought of anyone thinking of me as a wife'.[81]

The father's possessive jealousy takes on quite another cast if it is true that he feared the dangers of pregnancy for her fragile health.[82] Whatever his motives, the Reverend Patrick Brontë gradually gave in as it became clear that the marriage would deprive him of neither his assistant nor his daughter. She was decisively influenced by knowing that her union would not deprive her father of her presence and that he would be looked after in his old age, with the help and affection of his son-in-law.[83] The creator of solitary heroines, without family attachments, was herself very strongly anchored to Haworth. For her father, she sacrificed a job, journeys, another stay in Brussels, and perhaps any husband without the advantages of Arthur Nicholls. Marriage for Charlotte was a solution that reconciled happily 'the demands of both feeling and duty'. The decision once taken, 'her happiness', she wrote, 'is of the soberest order'. She valued the affectionate nature, the conscientiousness and the principles of Nicholls.[84] Marital life accentuated the intellectual and imaginative disparity of these two beings but brought home to Charlotte the precious feeling of being constantly desired and a full life that never left her any time to think.[85] This fulfilment of marital happiness – that time did not put to the test, it must be said – confirmed Thackeray's ironic judgement on the author of *Villette*. 'I can read a great deal of her life as I fancy her in her book, and see that rather than have fame, rather than any other earthly good or … heavenly one she wants some Tomkins … to love her and be in love with.'[86] In any case the marriage satisfied her need for submission to the masculine authority of a husband as well as a father. After her marriage she felt great satisfaction in leaving initiatives and decisions to her husband, – as Mrs Gaskell observed.[87] Having once been ravaged by passion, in life Charlotte finally reconciled herself to an ordinary marriage. Her passion took its revenge in her imaginative life.

In her novels Charlotte's heroines do not find their identity in submission alone. In *Shirley* Robert Helstone, the man dedicated to action and greed for power in a world where money and power reign, asks Caroline to intercede for him in her prayers. Caroline, a pure and contemplative creature, sheltered from the defilements of the world, intervenes for sinners, and like Kingsley's ideal wife,[88] pleads the cause of the oppressed to Helstone. At the height of their conflict, Rochester sees in Jane Eyre his good angel and the best of himself, and a spectacular reversal of roles ocurs: the poor, solitary teacher, distinguished neither by beauty nor intelligence, refuses to be morally dominated by the one she considers her 'master' in age, experience and authority. At the end of a desperate contest, it is the woman who affirms her moral superiority and imposes her values on the proud Byronic hero. The heroine who refuses to yield to temptation gains friends, fortune, strength and health. The poor hero, alone and frail, sees his love purified, despite himself, by Jane who imposes on him her own morality and vision of the world. The last scene is a veritable conversion of Rochester, of the sinner confessing his sin: 'I did wrong; I would have sullied my innocent flower.' Deprived of strength and pride he humiliates himself before his creator. 'I humbly entreat my redeemer to give me strength to lead henceforth a purer life ...'[89] In Rochester's conversion and salvation, Jane recognizes herself as the humble instrument of divine providence. Thus the solitary heroine, yearning for freedom and action, ends by playing the role prescribed for woman in family and society, that of moral Guide and Angel of the Home. What remains of the alleged 'anarchy of passion'[90] since passion is sublimated into spiritualized love? What remains of the feminist protest, since the heroine fulfils herself in a dutiful union of laws and sacraments, consecrated by marriage and maternity?

Some contemporary critics were pleased to record the heroine's observance of the conventional moral code. An article on *Villette*, which noted the originality of the authoress's new heroines, expressed satisfaction that the tone of the novel opposed that of

The American woman's rights advocates ... It is a good sign that here at all events ... our best thinkers and most eloquent writers point to the development of the tender and domestic side of woman's nature as that which gives the surest promise of happiness and usefulness.[91]

A critic in the *Revue des deux Mondes* was astonished at the attacks on *Shirley*, since marriage itself was not questioned.

In England there is no novel where marriage has been treated with irreverence or bitterness ... In France ... [the novelist] enters into the very marriage, and tears away the mystery ... violates its sanctity ... and aggravates the corruption of manners ...[92]

The critic had probably not read Thackeray's novels, nor *The Tenant of Wildfell Hall*, but he at any rate appreciated the part that marriage played for Charlotte Brontë's heroines.[93]

This imaginary world, of impassioned women seeking a virile and ferocious master, of an inequality where the master-pupil relationship prevails and blossoms into marriage, derives from a vision whose intensity cannot be denied, but which betrays the emotional immaturity of the author. Charlotte's fixation on her father was consolidated and justified by the death of her mother and all the other Brontë children, and in this perspective Charlotte's stay in Brussels and her satisfaction in being a pupil can indeed appear as 'a

prolonging of the novitiate, always welcome to passive characters'.[94] Even though such an analysis underestimates other biographical and social factors there is no denying the importance of
her relationship with her father, which determined her whole life,
the repeated master-pupil relations in the novels, the circumstances
of her marriage and the chronic nostalgia for an authoritarian,
paternal and virile figure.

F. E. Ratchford's and Winifred Gérin's study of the genesis of
the novels, starting with the heroes of the 'Angria Cycle', shows
among other things the Romantic influence on the collective work of
the Brontës. Their adolescent reading of the 'Annuals', of Byron and
their interest in the work of the engraver John Martin were integrated into the world of Angria. It also echoes the great feats of
Wellington whose hold over Charlotte has already been noted.[95]
The Duke of Zamorna, 'personification of the Napoleonic-Byronic
ideal', constructed out of the heroes of Byron, of Milton's Satan and
Branwell Brontë, physically and morally colours the character of
Rochester, and in a more subdued way, the other male figures:
W. Crimsworth, Paul Emmanuel and Louis Moore.[96] The emo-
tional world of the novels remained that of Angria. As F. E.
Ratchford observed, 'She modified, re-shaped, and adapted in conformity with her two adult experiences – teaching and study in
Brussels – but she *created* practically nothing.'[97] One adaptation
concerns the behaviour of women faced with passion and masculine
desire. The female characters in the early works, Caroline Vernon
and others, yielded to the ardour of Zamorna.[98] Influenced by
Byronic romanticism or the freedom of adolescent fantasies, sensuality asserted itself in Angria as never again in Charlotte Brontë's
novels. Henceforth the heroines learn to listen to the voice of Duty,
to fear the traps set by instinct, and therefore to obey the common
code. Thus the combination of romantic elements (though attenuated compared with the Angria Cycle) and Victorian Calvinist
asceticism confirms the theory of an incomplete emotional development which is bound to reproduce the patterns of adolescence.[99] The
poverty of Charlotte's sexual life and the schematic nature of love
relations in her novels can be seen as a particular case of a phenomenon already noted in the first part of this book: the emotional
configuration typical of the Victorian era in general, analysed by
P. Cominos in his remarkable study.[100] As Virginia Woolf suggested in *Three Guineas*, the moral conventions which established
the submission of children to the family as an absolute duty fortified

oedipal fixations in the individual, hindering his normal emotional development and liberation from his family.

The psychological deficiency of the male characters, the adolescent nature of personal relations, the contrast between the heroine's abdication in the field of action and her role of moral and metaphysical authority, form part of a vision of the world that is marked by a demand for obedience to laws or duty. The pattern deserves closer examination. In *Jane Eyre*, the 'happy end' which reconciles the imperatives of passion and respectability is obtained after intense suffering by the heroine.[101] A genuine moral and physical martyrdom is inflicted by Jane on her idol in her hope for salvation, in the course of which Jane constantly follows a morality that appears foreign to the twentieth-century reader precisely because of its pronounced disproportion between ends and means. Tyrannic duty permeates the novel's atmosphere and Charlotte was understandably horrified when the work was accused of being 'godless' and 'pernicious'.[102] Kathleen Tillotson considers the end envisaged by Jane, her resistance to bigamy or free union, to be in no way inspired by a sense of social propriety.[103] However, some of Jane's reactions, especially when she listens to the tales of Rochester's affairs, seem to be dictated by a banal and false modesty: her dread of undergoing the same fate as his mistresses – if she agrees to share his life without the sanction of marriage[104] – and her ostentatious recoil from certain affectionate gestures of Rochester's because they are no longer 'permitted' at the very moment when she is overwhelmed by their mutual love.[105] She completely internalizes the convention that cohabiting, even with the man she loves above all, henceforth would make her a fallen woman, cursed by society. Her reticence is breached for a moment when Rochester emphasizes the conventional and arbitrary nature of the institution of marriage and reproaches her for taking these considerations into account. At this stage of the conflict, when Rochester resorts to arguments that reach home, her resistance takes on a transcendental dimension. The intense religious motive of her conduct comes to the fore: 'I will keep the law given by God; sanctioned by man'.[106] Thus in the eyes of both the author and the heroine God's law is identical to the laws of society, and the conventional morality which Jane accepts blindly, to George Eliot's regret,[107] is of divine origin. This philosophy, which rules out any possibility of genuine revolt, is that of a Calvinism which has accepted the fundamentals of the social order and is obsessed by the idea of sin. David Cecil has stressed the Manichaean nature of Charlotte Brontë's fictional world, the stage for an 'eternal battle between sin and virtue'.[108] In this world of predestination Charlotte associated, for example, the character of Beatrix Esmond with Evil. 'Beatrix cannot be an honest woman and a good man's wife. She "tries" and she *cannot*. Proud, beautiful, and sullied, she was born what she becomes, a king's mistress.'[109]

It is true that by not yielding to the fascination of the life of sacrifice, prescribed by the ascetic and inspired figure of Saint-John Rivers, by refusing to obey a missionary call, Jane does symbolically set aside the most austere and fanatical solution. The ideal she obeys often recalls the clergyman's: 'I advise you to live sinless; and I wish you to die tranquil.'[110] Thus Jane, a judge, takes leave of Rochester. In her moral choices she constantly associates evil with easy virtue, with the pleasures of the flesh, with enjoyment of a lazy life with her love in the sunny South of France. Good is identified with a life of austerity and sacrifice, with the deprivations of a school-mistress in the icy north of England, with the trials demanding character, with the exaltation of duty and, after all these tribulations, a withdrawn existence with a blind, one-armed man. And Jane wonders

which is better? – To have surrendered to temptation; listened to passion; made no painful effort – no struggle; – but to have sunk down in the silken snare; fallen asleep on the flowers covering it; wakened in a southern clime, amongst the luxuries of a pleasure-villa ... Whether it is better, I ask, to be a slave in a fool's paradise at Marseilles – fevered with delusive bliss ... or to be a village school-mistress, free and honest, in a breezy mountain nook in the healthy heart of England?[111]

This counterpoint of languid Mediterranean and bracing England of guilty pleasure and redeeming effort expressed a chauvinistic puritanism that could hardly belong to any other period.

The same type of austerity manifests itself in many details of Lucy Snowe's behaviour, in the symbolism of everything French in the Bronteian dialectic of virtue and sin. Little Adele, who demonstrates a reprehensible leaning for dress and frivolity, is the daughter of the French dancer who lived with Rochester and was then unfaithful to him. When Jane finally decides to take Adele's education in hand, she is careful that 'a sound English education corrected in a great measure her French defects'.[112] Lucy Snowe's French colleagues in *Villette* are sybaritic hypocrites and frivolous. In *The Professor* we find the same commiseration towards girls who have not had the privilege of a solidly protestant English education. France cannot escape its associations of moral laxity, guilty pleasures and sin.

The strictness which shows no interest in the causes or effects of action, but respects duty for duty's sake and advances the ideal of unconditional obedience and an obsession with sin, are part of what Matthew Arnold called the 'Hebraic attitude of conduct and obedience',[113] which he contrasted with the critical and intellectual Hellenic attitude. Matthew Arnold accused Hebraism of being a reducing and sterilizing influence in the life of the mind and feelings. Blondel has also pointed out the powerful influence of religion and Methodist morality.[114] The family's Calvinism derived solely from Miss Branwell, Charlotte's aunt – the Reverend Brontë for his part did not embrace the doctrines of predestination – and, for a long time, all her life perhaps, the novelist experienced the conflict bebetween election through grace and the need for Christ's perfection to gain salvation for the soul.[115]

Whatever its nuances, Wesleyan Protestantism inspired Charlotte with an ascetic spirit, with scorn for the flesh, for beauty and for pleasure, all considered as obstacles to moral progress. It dictated to her the mystic exaltation corrected by punctilious moral discipline[116] in which her heroines, and above all Jane Eyre, live. The nature of the sacrifice, its advantages and inconveniences for the individuals concerned are neither evaluated nor examined; nothing counts except self-control and obedience. Thus Jane reaches the point of conforming completely to current conventional morality, expecially about the absurd impossibility of divorce, an abuse that far from criticizing she uses as a salutary test-case of moral progress.

The dogma of obedience to duty was a rule of life that Charlotte did not hesitate to prescribe for others.[117] Even when she was deeply depressed and thought only of escaping from the memory-laden bounds of Haworth, anxiety for her father prevented her from accepting the desired invitation.[118] In 1846 she was already expressing her desire to leave the place where her life was flowing by, unused. 'When I am free to leave home I shall neither be able to find place nor employment – ... but whenever I consult my Conscience it affirms that I am doing right in staying at home',[119] she wrote after her father's cataract operation. She almost sacrificed her writer's vocation to the conventional notion of woman's duty when she accepted Southey's judgement on the incompatibility between literature and 'the business of a woman's life'. The tyranny of her moral conscience asserted itself once more when in 1851, at the age of thirty-five, she refused the pleasures of an invitation to London ('I don't deserve to go'), and then a trip on the Rhine with George Smith.[120]

Charlotte Brontë's life thus appears as a perpetual combat between duty and inclination. Conforming at once to the precepts of her Methodist education and to the conventional wisdom and morality she had rarely called into question in her novels as in her life she made duty triumph. In her heroines Romantic impulses are fused with the Victorian female ideal. They simultaneously refuse to conform to the conventional model of the girl and to liberate themselves from the myth of the Angel of the Home. 'Conventionality is not morality', Charlotte Brontë wrote in the preface to the second edition of *Jane Eyre* in 1848. Yet all conflicts are in the end resolved by obedience to the prescription of chastity and monogamy. Does the melodramatic and artificial ending of *Jane Eyre* have any other aim than to reconcile passion and social convention? Such compromise was quite excluded from the world of Emily Brontë, where good and evil, revolt and order, Romanticism and Victorianism confront each other without hope of respite or synthesis. Driven to love and hate by destructive violence and romantic paroxysms, the characters live by their own original system of values, what George Bataille called a hypermorality.[121]

Charlotte's heroines are all alike. Their life unfolds beneath the same sign, their destiny is marked by the same vicissitudes, the same joys, always within a strictly limited world. The contradictions that tear them apart and which they triumphantly overcome are those which beset their creator: delayed emotional (as opposed to intellectual) maturity and desire for material independence acquired through work coupled with the quest for psychological dependence; conflict between the need for personal realization and the ideal of duty and domesticity prescribed by society; conflict between the thirst for passion and the absolute and the need for stability and integration. All these contradictions were inherent in the position of Victorian woman and consequently insoluble on the individual level. Does not the aesthetic unease felt by the reader at the destiny of her heroines come from the fact that Charlotte Brontë wanted at all costs to resolve the contradictions – marriage and *l'amour fou*, permanence and passion, duty and happiness – in an improbably reconciled world, instead of carrying them to their logical and tragic end, as do Flaubert, Tolstoy and her sister?

10

A More Realistic Portrayal by Elizabeth Gaskell, Trollope and Disraeli

Dickens's single women, pathetic, grotesque or monstrous, have a complex and distant relationship with the real world. Their negative function in the structure of the novel is intended to enhance the ideal image of the wife-mother. Charlotte Brontë's heroines, very like their author, express the contradictions within a woman with artistic and professional aspirations, contradictions artificially resolved in an attempt at reconciliation, where the author produces a conventional happy ending and conforms with current feminine ideology. For all that she states the predicament of the single woman in terms close to those used by the pioneers of women's work.

With Elizabeth Gaskell, Trollope and Disraeli we approach novelists endowed with a less powerful imagination, more open to everyday life and social problems. It is true that their awareness of outstanding social changes and their effects on the position of women varies considerably. Trollope studied a milieu that was relatively stable, at least in the provinces. Elizabeth Gaskell and Disraeli were horrified, and fascinated, by the condition of the workers. But these novelists in different ways, and according to their personal viewpoints and sensibilities, do try to place the individual within her social group.

Among the female characters of Elizabeth Gaskell's novels, many are spinsters and old maids, or women and girls who fit into society through professional work. Dickens presents his unmarried characters as manifestations of an eternal and immutable essence and, like the mothers and wives, embodying an archetype. The reasons Mrs Gaskell's spinsters have not married are to do with the girl's role in the family structure, the importance of money in the marriage-market and the rigidity of the class system. Miss Matty, for example, yields to the pressures of a family who considered her lover to be socially inferior. Miss Galindo, daughter of a vicar, is an heiress: when a less rich lover proposes, her family persuades her he is only interested in her money.[1] As for Miss Matty's sister, for

Susan Dixon in *Half a Lifetime Ago*, and Ellinor in *A Dark Night's Work*, their chances of having their own home are destroyed by their sacrifices for a member of the family. Susan Dixon is abandoned by her lover because, bound by the vow she made to her mother on her death-bed to look after her idiot brother, she refuses to put him into an asylum. She sets duty first. Ellinor too renounces both lover and marriage, in order not to betray the secret of her father who has unintentionally killed his partner in a quarrel. Thus family pressures or the daughter's womanly 'dutifulness' are responsible for the unhappy spinsterhood of these devoted creatures, who always pay for their choice with the death of their hopes and a brutal passage from youth to maturity. Ellinor ages in one night. Miss Galindo's heart is broken.[2] In contrast to Charlotte Brontë's heroines, Mrs Gaskell's spinsters, even the youngest who are capable of reconversion, never criticize the injustice and absurdity of the fate which is the lot of old maids. Once the most difficult sacrifice is accepted – renunciation of the condition of a wife-mother – a life of abnegation and altruism follows naturally. Marsh explains how, excluded from 'woman's natural work', she decides to look around 'for the odd jobs God leaves in the world for such as old maids to do'.[3]

Alice Wilson, in *Mary Barton*, gathers medicinal herbs in the fields, makes up little bouquets for ill neighbours and confesses to find happiness in a life constantly devoted to others. Miss Galindo executes fine embroidery that sells badly because it is old-fashioned. She is always prepared to visit the sick. She even goes so far as to employ a sickly, blind, deaf, hunchbacked or tubercular person, for whom she acts as nurse and maid.[4] In the same way, Ellinor's sacrifice to her fiancé is the renunciation of any personal life and satisfaction. This process seems to be considered normal: once marriage has been ruled out the only fulfilment for the ageing single woman is to devote herself to her neighbours, the poor, or her family.

But such a deviation of woman's faculties is bound to cause damage to the individual. These old maids are cut off from the sources of life. They have been frozen into small idiosyncrasies and habits that give a tiny rhythm to their abnormally calm lives. Phoebe and Dorothy Browning in *Wives and Daughters* go to bed at nine o'clock in order not to exhaust the charms of cribbage which they play from five o'clock, for Winter is very monotonous at Hollingford.[5] In *Cranford* some ladies spend hours exchanging methods for washing lace.

Your ladyship knows that such lace must never be starched or ironed. Some people wash it in sugar and water; and some in coffee ... but I myself have a very good receipt for washing it in milk.[6]

In this quiet life which is neither enlivened nor troubled by family hubbub, a trifle like buying a hat or a length of cloth (see *Cranford*) or going to a party becomes an event. The Misses Browning would have been heartbroken if they had not been invited to the annual Charity Ball, although they are past the dancing age.[7] 'I do like hearing of a love-affair ...' murmurs Miss Phoebe.[8] Inquisitive, scandal-mongering, or simply seeking out the romantic, Mrs Gaskell's old maids try to fill the gap in their love lives by lingering over those of others, and inventing them if necessary. Thus for a girl like Molly Gibson, whose reputation is the most precious and fragile thing she has and who is suspected of having a relationship with Mr Preston, the old maid can constitute a danger by becoming the persecutor.[9] Spinsters, like those of *Cranford*, have the tacit authority to legislate on the conduct of members of the community and consign them to public opprobrium. Respectability and excessive respect for convention and social hierarchy are the essential possession of old maids. Egalitarian or feminist demands cannot be expected of them. Miss Galindo does not begrudge My Lady Ludlow anything, not even working for her steward; it is on the contrary a favour done for her by Her Ladyship with whom she has a feudal relationship that makes her later revolt all the more spectacular. The visit of the Misses Browning to the castle of Lord and Lady Cumnor is an event in their life and young Lady Harriet's sudden visit to them a real revolution.[10]

Defending social propriety the Misses Browning imagine London as the capital of vice whence no girl can emerge intact, and they watch Cynthia for signs of deterioration.[11] Their reactions compounded of provincial narrow-mindedness recall, *mutatis mutandis*, the fantasy of sin and perdition evoked by the South of France in Jane Eyre's imagination. Austerity is accompanied by an attitude to marriage like to that of the old maids of Cranford. 'If they must be married, let them ... go through the affair with dignity and propriety.'[12] In *Cranford* Miss Matty and her sister betrayed the same revulsion towards the outward signs of love and procreation. Miss Matty's maid is forbidden to have lovers. In this world without men it is tempting to see sexual frustration on every hand.[13] Fanatical observances of good manners (eating peas with a fork, not sucking oranges in public) and obsessive fear of burglars can be symptoms of frustration; but they are also rules for living that an isolated and persecuted group observes in its own defence, through giving a high status to its very deprivations. The single state, gentility and the middle class are intimately linked; the aristocrat, Lady Glenmire, marries Higgins, a country doctor, who smells of medicines and dines or rather 'sups' on bread and cheese; Betty the maid has a lover, then a husband, then a child. Everything happens as if the old maid totally internalizes the conventions to which she sacrifices herself, fabricates new ones and brings this yoke down heavily on those around her. Psychologically impoverished, she hides fanatically behind the rampart of custom, hierarchy and the existing social order.

Mrs Gaskell has also a few pairs of unmarried sisters who protect themselves against solitude by creating an emotional world like that of a heterosexual couple. 'I've always wanted to see the kind of *ménage* of such people',[14] said Lady Harriet about the Misses Browning. These ménages always comprise a masculine element, embodying authority, and a feminine element, submissive and dependent. Miss Matty is dominated by her elder sister, to the point of finding herself ruined through following the advice of the one supposed to have greater experience of the world. There is the same dependence in Phoebe Browning towards Dorothy. In *Mr. Harrisson's Confessions* there are a couple of old maids, the Misses Tomkinson, thirty-five and fifty-five respectively. The younger is 'petted and caressed and cared for' by the elder, who encourages and organizes the capture of a young doctor for her sister. The elder sister is rather hard and 'masculine-looking', the younger sweet and sentimental.[15] Relationships of dependency similar to those of a family or a marriage are recreated. One may even see in the 'female' element a prolonged nostalgia for marriage, a desire for maternity and an emotional immaturity characteristic of Victorian girls and women. This nostalgia obsesses Miss Matty in her dreams. Miss Benson in *Ruth*, who only agrees to take in Ruth and her son under the authority of her brother and with the greatest distaste, becomes attached to the child as to a son. With Miss Galindo, this instinct materializes despite all obstacles when she takes charge of the illegitimate daughter of her ex-fiancé. When, not knowing what to do with the girl, she braves My Lady's hostility and brings her into her own house this provokes a break in relations with her noble patroness. By receiving and getting accepted her lover's illegitimate child, who will make a respectable marriage with the vicar, Miss Galindo has in this genteel world achieved a small revolution.

Miss Matty and Miss Galindo deserve some attention: old maids, they emerge from the tight and narrow limits of their milieu and low income, and, in the one case, through a reversal of fortune, in the other through good-heartedness, enter professional employment. After losing her capital Miss Matty thinks of reducing her living standards 'to quietly exist upon what would remain after paying the rent'.[16] It goes without saying that she is unfit for any job, even that of governess; in the end she is persuaded to open a little tea-shop. Miss Matty, who prefers deprivation to the initiative and effort demanded by a job, and passivity to action, regretfully submits. At first only the fact that she will not be too exposed to male contacts, gentlemen rarely coming in to buy tea, encourages her. The activity later enriches her life and allows her to escape from the stifling sisterhood of the respectable old maids of Cranford for the infinitely more lively contacts with village ladies, Martha, Jem and their children.

To be of service Miss Galindo agrees to fulfil the functions of clerk to Lady Ludlow's steward. Still living in a world of innocence, like Miss Matty with her youthful memories, she naïvely thinks that her beautifully moulded handwriting and literary ambitions have prepared her fittingly. Having equipped herself with a pair of desk sleeves she honourably performs her secretarial work, but not in a way to protect her from the misogynous prejudices of Mr Stewart Horner. She therefore decides to live down her sex by doing her work 'as ship-shape as a masculine male-clerk'.[17] Which for her means not making any mistakes in spelling or arithmetic, putting her pen behind her ear, whistling and even proffering one or two swear-words. Beyond a good story, does not Elizabeth Gaskell suggest that Miss Galindo, like Miss Matty, has experienced something that has helped her emerge from the narrow sexual world of old maids and adolescent dreams where so many women linger? For Miss Galindo the source of life, that is to say of change, is certainly her brief experience of work and her adoptive motherhood – the consequence of her aborted passion for Mark. Maternal instinct will give her the strength to revolt against the feudal world of Lady Ludlow and to scorn conventions.

The spinster characters with private means, however limited, have an assured subsistence without having to resort to regular professional work. But in Elizabeth Gaskell's novels, as in those of other Victorian novelists, we do find spinsters of another type – often temporarily in that state and not necessarily touched with the irreversible psychological changes that hallmark the old maid. Alone in life or supporting a family they must have paid employment. Elizabeth Gaskell was convinced of the need for solid training prior to a woman's useful employment. When she sought a school for her elder daughter she was shocked by the amateurism rife in educational establishments, the majority of which did not profit from the academic resources offered by the new Queen's College.[18] Like Dickens and Charlotte Brontë, Elizabeth Gaskell criticized the idleness of 'do-nothing ladies' who, like the daughters of the factory manager Carson in *Mary Barton*, make music and embroidery to pass the time. We feel the same censure at work against the bone-idle Mrs Gibson in *Wives and Daughters*, and Margaret Hale's cousins in *North and South*. Elizabeth Gaskell, also influenced by the Puritan middle-class ethic, believed in the intrinsic and redeeming value of work. She was morally on the side of those who, like Miss Galindo, Margaret Hale, and Molly Gibson, strove for useful employment, and those who like Mary Barton, Ruth and Bessy Higgins, must earn their living by the sweat of their brows.

Among the major writers of the first half of the Victorian era Elizabeth Gaskell is certainly the only one to have dealt fairly fully with female labour. Although she explores the professions of governess and school-teacher less deeply than Charlotte Brontë, she is also interested in jobs that are not just the overcrowded fief of middle-class girls come down in the world but done by working women – nurses, dressmakers, factory workers – and generally ignored in novels of the period. This interest is obviously linked with her own personal circumstances, her marriage to the minister William Gaskell which banished her from Knutsford to Manchester. We know of her hesitation between town and country, North and South, which not only produced different protagonists but also represented two different ages in the history of England. All the same, her life in Manchester, her experience, visual at least, of the slums of a great industrial town, her local philanthropic activities and those of her husband,[19] her contacts with circles involved in the controversies over free trade, the recent Chartist revolt, her gifts of observation and sympathy with the 'wretched of the earth' and the misery all around her, all this contributed to widening her interest in female occupations well beyond the conventional.

Although she had no personal experience as a governess Elizabeth Gaskell, like most middle-class ladies, could draw on people
she knew intimately. 'My dearest friends, all through my life, have
been governesses, either past, present or future',[20] she wrote to
Caroline Norton. She was probably thinking of her two sisters-in-
law, of the Brontë sisters and countless contemporaries like Harriet
Martineau and Mrs Jameson. How are they portrayed? Ruth, in the
novel of the same name, works for a time as a governess with the
Bradshaws before being ignominiously thrown out of the family the
day the illegitimacy of her child is discovered. Later, she thinks
nostalgically about the happy time when she taught writing and
arithmetic to two young girls who treated her more as older sister
than as teacher. With her pupils she shared the family lunch, then
went home at four o'clock. Unlike Jane Eyre and other governesses
or teachers of the Brontës and Dickens, Ruth enjoys excellent conditions of work. She lives away from her employer's house and has
fixed hours of work. She is thus less exposed to the ostracism of the
household. The author's purpose in this work is not to expose but
to make the reader understand the plight of the unmarried mother.
For her heroine any place she can find herself in society, however
thankless, is an occasion to redeem herself; she obviously does not
emphasize the drawbacks of her trade. Work for Ruth has a deep
and urgent meaning as a symbol of reintegration and a method of
providing with dignity for her own and her son's maintenance.

Miss Monro, in *A Dark Night's Work*, has been a governess and
teacher. We see her in two relatively satisfying jobs. At Mr
Wilkins's she enjoys relative freedom, and there is good understanding between her, her employer and her pupil. When Mr
Wilkins dies without leaving her the annual pension that he had
led her to expect, she gives lessons to the children of canons and
other clerics in a cathedral city, preferring to be employed by
clerics rather than businessmen. The only aspects of the profession
emphasized are the positive ones which in these conditions combine
peace and independence for a woman. What a difference between the
quietude of these two posts and the calvary endured by Anne and
above all Charlotte Brontë!

In *Wives and Daughters* Mrs Gibson, the doctor's wife, had been
in turn schoolmistress and governess before her marriage. Of her
years as a teacher she only recalls the boredom and poverty. Mrs
Gaskell glosses over teaching conditions; at most we learn that her
little school is barely profitable and only just allows Mrs Gibson to

cover her expenses: rent, taxes, laundry, salaries. This work is for her slavery, entirely coloured by her life's ambition – marriage envisaged as one long holiday. Unlike the heroines of Charlotte Brontë she appreciates the social preferment represented by a post of governess in a rich family, which enables her to escape from the squalor of her old furniture and the stews shared with pupils to the aristocratic luxury of castle, rose-garden, snacks served on porcelain.[21] In the main Mrs Gaskell does not throw any light on the other side of a governess's position: the poor wages, the material and psychological exploitation. The social criticism is muted by the very conception of Mrs Gibson's character, her narcissism, her laziness, her dreams of grandeur and idleness. The obscure Miss Eyre, engaged by the doctor to attend to his daughter and two assistants awakens our sympathy more strongly. Despite being persecuted by Betty, the old family servant, she resolves on keeping her post and conscientiously does the work prescribed by her employer: to teach Molly sewing, reading, writing and arithmetic.[22] On excellent terms with Molly and her father Miss Eyre has no reason to complain of her fate. Daughter of ruined tradespeople, she is the typical old maid (though only thirty-five), devoted to her employer and his family. Mrs Gaskell does not describe what she does in detail. She lingers over the psychological drawbacks rather than the material conditions, when, for example, she attributes part of the reason for Cynthia's instability to her being separated from her mother,[23] introducing the favourite argument of those who oppose female labour – its disturbing effects on family life. The dark side of the life of the governess is illustrated by Cynthia's remarks when, despairing of everything, she envisages that like her mother she will have to 'go out as a governess'. Such a prospect for a young middle-class girl is a last resort, meaning a dull alienated life. For Ruth, Mrs Gibson, Miss Eyre and Miss Monro, all 'superfluous women', the job is just a hard option among very limited possibilities.

In the gamut of occupations filled by Ruth on her long road from Sin to Redemption, the profession of nursing has an important place. Can one speak of 'profession' when Ruth, rejected by all, her 'sin' discovered, sees it as the last resort? Much more than a profession, and a living on the side, her role offers her a possibility of redemption, along with an opportunity for altruism. Probably inspired by Florence Nightingale's experience of the Middlesex Hospital during a cholera epidemic,[24] Elizabeth Gaskell has Ruth die of typhoid, earning for herself the certainty of salvation and eternal life. In the letter where she describes Florence Nightingale's hospital experience the novelist gives picturesque and concrete details. In the novel she does not come to grips with the sordid reality of the profession in all its aspects: salary, training, conditions of work. She dwells rather on the importance of refined gestures, of the proper tone of voice, behaviour and religion, in short on the standard components of the female influence.[25]

Despite her different orientation, Florence Nightingale appreciated *Ruth* as a literary work. She expressly approved of Mrs Gaskell for not making 'Ruth start at once as a hospital nurse, but arrive at it after much *other* nursing that came first'.[26] When her daughter Meta contemplated taking up the profession Mrs Gaskell was ready to encourage her and advised her not to wait to acquire experience. She promised to help her arrange to visit hospitals but she had reservations about the seriousness of her vocation: 'it is not everyone who can be Miss Nightingale'.[27] Ruth's experience, and the way Elizabeth Gaskell spoke of this job for her daughter, 'a nurse's life of devotion', shows that while understanding the need for preparation she saw the nursing profession as a vocation demanding talent, sacrifice, love for one's neighbours, in short a cluster of moral qualities, rather than as a trade as such requiring technical knowledge and specific competence. She depicted the nurse as the lay charity sister of Anna Jameson and of those who contributed to the *Lectures to Ladies* ... The idea of training is secondary, if not non-existent.

Anna Jameson had written in 1846 that in literature women had never appeared as *the labourer*. She does assume this role however in some of Mrs Gaskell's novels. Among the favourable comments on the realism of her vision of the industrial world in *Mary Barton*, Samuel Bamford, the author of *Passages from the Life of a Radical*, drew particular attention to the heroine: '... of John Bartons, I have known hundreds, ... whilst of his daughter Mary, who has ever seen a group of our Lancashire factory girls ... and could not have counted Mary?'[28] Ruth, before her 'fall', and Mary Barton, are for a time apprenticed as seamstresses. Mrs Gaskell is more generous with details of the worshop than of the hospital. Ruth and her companions work uninterruptedly all week, often till two in the morning, beginning again at eight. They have half an hour's break for a standing snack of beer, cheese and bread. Nothing is organized for the workers on Sundays when, in as much moral and material solitude as Ruth, they risk yielding to a temptation they will pay for all their life. Mary Barton chooses this employment because it appears to her and her father more 'respectable' and less arduous than the factory workers'. The apprentice has to work without pay for two years. After that she will have the right to two meals a day and a derisory payment every three months, the amount of which Mrs Gaskell does not reveal. For two whole years she brings her meals to the workshop. In summer the working day begins at six in the morning and does not end at a fixed time. In *Mary Barton* the criticism of the apprentice's working conditions, salary, hours, and lack of hygiene, is more accurate than that of *Libbie Marsh's Three Eras*. But despite all those who accused the author of injustice towards employers,[29] Mrs Gaskell proves astonishingly indulgent towards the owner of the workshop.[30] The misfortunes of Margaret, who loses her sight doing miserably paid needlework at home, arouse no protest. Margaret's Christian resignation during this 'trial' serves to emphasize the weak side of Mary's personality which as much as the evil influence of the workshop exposes her to temptation. *North and South*, a later and better balanced book, puts forward sounder arguments. The protest against working conditions becomes more pointed. Bessy Higgins, a worker in a textile factory, dies of a tuberculosis brought about by constantly absorbing fluff.[31] But such instances are rare.

Except in *North and South* Mrs Gaskell tends to gloss over the material and sanitary aspects of women's employment; and her vision of working life is a long way from the horror that was generally rife. On the other hand, her portrayal of the damage undergone by working women occupies a disproportionate amount of space. Her arguments against women's work came under two headings: the risk to virtue and the damage done to family life, particularly for married women. These themes are developed in *Mary Barton*. John Barton asserts that a working woman is exposed to promiscuity and the sexual dominion of her male superiors. He goes further and makes the material and financial independence Esther acquires through her work the cause of her moral degradation. This is more than a verbal charge: in the plot itself work in factory and sweatshop is made responsible for the 'fall' or temptation of Ruth, Esther and Mary. But as contemporaries, notably Maria Edgeworth, had already noted, the demonstration was not convincing. None of the three is sufficiently immersed in her social context. 'Esther ... might be ... in every town of the Empire as well as Manchester.'[32] The 'temptation' Mary undergoes is all the more insidious because the family is reduced to its male element. Her mother dies in labour and her aunt Esther, formerly a worker, flees with her lover and then becomes a prostitute.

From all this it is clear that Mrs Gaskell was convinced that the place of mother and daughter was in the home. Like the political opponents of female employment, Mrs Gaskell meant to prove that the destruction of the home was aggravated by the incompetence at home of workers like Mrs Wilson in *Mary Barton*, who has been in a factory from the age of five,[33] like Bessy Higgins and her younger sister in *North and South*.[34] One can see that her objections, the danger of immorality and the dissolution of the family bond, are based on a conventional notion of the woman's realm.[35] It would however be unjust to play down her growing awareness of industrial problems. In *Mary Barton* the exhaustion of the apprentices, Margaret's blindness, Mrs Wilson's accident due to insufficient protection from the machines; and in *Ruth*, the overwork, hunger and cold were minimized and only vaguely touched on. In *North and South*, however, the real problems of inhuman working conditions in factories are stoutly faced and not obscured by the supposed moral dangers of this kind of life. At the same time the reader senses the irreversibility of the industrial phenomenon and the participation of women in it. Indeed, when the heroine Margaret Hale seeks a servant she observes a growing disaffection in this northern region for the 'profession' that is traditional, and now considered degrading. Like Harriet Martineau and J. W. Kaye, Elizabeth Gaskell saw that young working women were attracted by 'the better wages and greater independence of working in a mill'.[36]

Mrs Gaskell's hostility to women working in factories had humanitarian and moral motives. Her view corresponded to that of Shaftesbury and the whole philanthropic attitude which was founded on belief in the woman's 'nature'. All the same she did not support protective legislation. Such a stand would have clearly been difficult to maintain in Manchester, the headquarters of free-trade and laisser-faire industrialists and economists.

In what one can call Disraeli's propaganda novels the subject of female labour has a relatively important place, reflecting the preoccupations of a politician. In *Coningsby* and above all in *Sybil or the Two Nations*[37] there is a striking diversity of female characters – some created by fantasy, others directly derived from the Blue Books and from personal observation.

In *Coningsby* the problem of the employment of young girls in factories is briefly described as it figures in the romantic imagination of Coningsby, a young aristocrat, who is travelling around to find out for himself what the state of England is. He goes to the 'great city', which is none other than Manchester, where he is amazed at the industrial progress, especially the gas-light in his bedroom,[38] and the poetry of machines and factories.

Does not the spindle sing like a merry girl at her work, and the steam-engine roar in jolly chorus, like a strong artisan handling his lusty tools, and gaining a fair day's wages for a fair day's toil?

The young aristocrat discovering the miracle of mechanization and progress imagines a charming scene in which grace combines with ardour for work. The idyllic evocation is complete.

... a thousand or fifteen hundred girls may be observed in their coral necklaces, working like Penelope in the day-time; some pert, some graceful and jocund, some absorbed in their occupation.[39]

The picture of industrial life is less poetic in *Sybil*. It seems to be directly inspired by Disraeli's reading of the parliamentary reports, whose influence however he did not acknowledge.[40] The similarity between the small town of Willenhall where R. H. Horne studied working conditions and the metal town of Wodgate in *Sybil* has been noted before.[41] Apparently Disraeli sometimes borrowed not only themes – which after all are constant in studies of industrial life, the reports of commissions of inquiry and factory inspectors, and parliamentary speeches – but the very images, details and phrases of Horne's report.[42] In particular he describes the destitute Wodgate apprentice wounded by his employer with a file and 'a stunted and meagre girl, with a back like a grasshopper; a deformity occasioned by the displacement of the bladebone, and prevalent among the girls of Wodgate from the cramping posture of their usual toil'.

The description of the emergence from the mine in *Sybil*[43] is also much the same as in the pages from the previously cited Commission report on children's employment in mines.[44] Like the members of the Commission Disraeli was shocked by the clothing, the same for men and women and the crude language coming from what ought to be the pure lips of present or future mothers. But, he observes, how can we expect anything else from creatures reduced to the condition of slaves and beasts of burden? He describes in detail the system of harnessing women to carts, the interminable working hours, the slavery of children who open and close the trap doors for the corves and in order to ventilate the galleries.

When Disraeli described this 'second nation', the responsibility for which he wanted to persuade industrialists and aristocrats to assume, he was as resolutely hostile to degrading work for men as for women. As for married women, he seems in *Sybil* to share the widely held opposition to the employment of wives and mothers, as voiced by the chartist Walter Gerard. He took up again the arguments of Ashley, Engels and others against the demoralization of the home, and even the 'infanticides' perpetrated by the kind of mothers and nurses who would give the children opiate sedatives to stop them yowling.[45] These pages show how the 'industrial hell' struck the imagination of the author, along with other paternalistic and philanthropic members of Young England. Disraeli generally supported the efforts of Lord Ashley to secure labour legislation, notably in May 1844 and the ten-hour Bill.[46]

Some female characters in *Sybil* contrast strikingly with those described by Mrs Gaskell in her novels and Lord Ashley in his speeches. Disraeli – it is all the more surprising, given that he idealized women, and seems to have believed wholeheartedly in a specifically female nature and influence – sketches portraits of young emancipated working women, rare at this period. Most observers bewailed the reversal of male and female roles and the loosening of family links caused by female employment in factories. By contrast, Disraeli's portrait traces their integration into a restored context and mode of life. The girls do not appear as passive and exploited victims or creatures lost through vice but as relatively stable creatures who had adapted to a new mode of production and a profound transformation of the family structure. In the new society that Disraeli points to it is the parents who are sacrificed for their incapacity to adapt to industrial society. Ashley deplored these changes instead of understanding them – the insubordination of the young earners who no longer recognized parental authority, the disobedience of the wife for the same reasons, the acquisition by girls of 'those privileges which are held to be the proper portion of the male sex', such as forming clubs and associations.[47] Ashley thought that by suppressing women's work things would return to tradition and the submission of the wife and children to the head of the family. Disraeli on the other hand draws attention to the conflicts separating the generations and the artisan's impasse in the age of machines. 'Why did you not go to the machine years ago like other men, and so get used to them?', says the dying mother to her weaver husband who works twelve hours a day at his trade for a penny an hour to feed an ill wife and three children. 'I should have been supplanted ... by a girl or a woman',[48] retorts the husband.

Disraeli and the Young England movement exalted the role of the artisan in a humane society where the aristocracy would watch over the wellbeing of the lowly. But the artisan in *Sybil* no longer has a place in the new capitalist society. He has lost his creative role. The worker's function is to watch over machines which enslave him. Disraeli certainly does not condemn the younger generation. The brief portrait of Harriet who abandoned her poor family dependent on her salary shows a degree of sympathy on the part of the author. These young workers have acquired an independence that Disraeli does not identify with the immorality which the majority of legislators feared and criticized. There is a certain freakishness in their clothing, but also order and propriety. The workers have left their families. Yet they live together in a pleasant room and have friends for tea. Harriet's friend is 'a pretty demure girl' who speaks in a virginal and hesitant tone.[49] Mick, a young worker, himself already married or at least living with someone, brings them to the 'Temple of the muses', a large café, to eat sausages and drink. In this vignette of daily life, Disraeli takes care to point out that this unusual freedom is perfectly innocent.'If I was a lady' says one of them, 'I would never drink anything except fresh milk from a cow.'[50] And Harriet loves tea above all; but these drinks are too dear for their purse. In these mixed outings of a new kind the girls prove their intellectual maturity by deliberately intervening in political discussions. When Mick speaks of the ten-hour Act and the ban on work before the age of sixteen, Caroline intervenes to propose the age of fifteen. She stands up too against the closing of the Temple on Sunday evenings. Harriet delivers slogans that none of the major novelists of the period would have ever put in a woman's mouth: 'As for the rights of labour ... the people goes for nothing with the machinery.'[51] One cannot imagine Mary Barton or even the workers in *North and South* making such remarks in such places. The role of chorus is played by the widow Corey who comments on the events in the name of previous generations: the young girl's decisiveness and initiative and the family responsibilities of a very young man astonish her.

I think the world is turned upside downward in these parts. A brat like Mick Radley to live in a two-pair, with a wife and family ... and this girl asks me to take a dish of tea with her and keeps house! Fathers and mothers goes for nothing ... 'Tis the children gets the wages.[52]

It seems that Disraeli wanted implicitly to show that from a psychological as well as material point of view these young men and women show a new maturity that justifies their emancipation. He sketches the portrait of a young generation of working men and women, independent, stable and adapted to a new society. Even though these are only hints, the tone and perspective are very different from those of the novelists examined earlier and from the views of so representative a figure as Lord Ashley. In the general perspective of Disraeli's trilogy – of a Tory romanticism full of nostalgia for a return to the middle ages, of a hatred for contemporary utilitarian and liberal tendencies – these relatively modern views are remarkable.

The state of the spinster is described in fiction in general therefore, to different degrees, as a deprived one. Whether in Dickens with his caricatures in his vision of a manichaean world, or in Mrs Gaskell, Charlotte Brontë and Trollope who, more realistic and less imaginatively powerful, interest themselves in psychological and social aspects, the unmarried woman always appears as unfulfilled. The old maid occupies a secondary place in these fictional universes. When these women become heroines, spinsterhood and work prove to be only a trial period crowned by marriage, without which any woman's life is considered a failure.

How is one to evaluate this fictional image in the context of the social problem sketched at the beginning of this section, over-population among women obliged to provide for themselves? Among the major novelists only Charlotte Brontë (in *Villette* and parts of *Jane Eyre*) delivers, out of her personal experience, an attack on the psychological bondage in which society maintains young women by assigning them, against all the evidence to the contrary, to the single destiny of wife and mother, and refusing them any other opening for self-fulfilment. The tone and content of these pages are those of the protests of Barbara Bodichon, Harriet Martineau and Anna Jameson. But Charlotte Brontë's case is considerably weakened by the deep aspirations of women who only find their true identity in the ecstasies of love but within the conventional frame. To teach, to write even, never seems anything but a means of filling the void, of using up unemployed energy, of soothing metaphysical and sentimental anguish, or of proving moral strength. As with the majority of reformers work in Charlotte's eyes appeared indispensable only for redundant women, for the young and for old maids who for different reasons could not realize their female vocation. Where the ultimate self-realization is fusion rather than creation the demand for independence and work is secondary.

The portrayal of work, in the rare trades open to women, is considerably toned down. Governesses, nurses and working women are there but their being workers is never one of their essential dimensions. On the whole the novels pass over exploitation in the rare overcrowded and underpaid trades accessible to middle-class girls without professional qualifications. Traditional reformers, as we have seen, tried to get acceptance for the idea of specifically female employment linked to a family vocation. But within the small kingdom of the lady of Christian works and of charitable nursing the need for technical and professional training began to be recognized. However there was no reforming tendency of this kind in characters like Mrs Gamp, Ruth or Jane Eyre. The novels remain well within the timid demands of the pioneers of women's work, who from 1840 established Queen's College and Florence Nightingale's nursing school. Still less did the novel echo advanced opinion on the professional equality of men and women (F. R. Parkes), the dignity of paid work (Barbara Bodichon and Harriet Martineau), freedom of thought and action in an independent existence outside the confines of the family.[53] Nor is there any of Elizabeth Browning's ironic questioning of a specifically female vocation for carrying lint and caring for the sick.[54] And the literary convention of the 'happy end' came to be added to the traditionalist views of the 'feminine sphere' to allow marriage to triumph as every heroine's destiny.

The woman worker, as such, is even more rarely present. In the novels of Mrs Gaskell, Kingsley, Dickens and Disraeli, she appears as an occasional idealized silhouette (except, as we have shown, in a few pages of Disraeli). Of all the authors Mrs Gaskell does most with her but stays well away from the horrible reality of the work women and apprentices had to carry out. She is also preoccupied with the consequences of employment on the morality of women and the stability of the family group. Her criticism of woman's work, like that of the legislators and philanthropists, was inspired primarily by humanitarian protest sometimes linked with opposition to the economic individualism in industrial civilization; and secondly by a belief in woman's vocation which was destined to flower in the first instance in the family.

This is not surprising. A middle-class novelist writing for middle-class readers necessarily had few contacts with working-class people. The two nations were foreign to each other, communicating only in relations of production or within the limits of philanthropy. But the abyss separating the two visions of the world was nowhere as deep as in the conception of woman. The physical and moral decay which was thought the female worker's condition was the very negation of the ideal dreamed of by novelists. These females from the other nation, in their mines, factories and workshops, were too inimical to the myth to figure outside the reports of parliamentary Commissions. The vision of woman alone and at work had at that time still not been separated from the idealization of her marital and family function.

3

FALLEN WOMEN

11

The Great Social Evil

The absence of contemporary statistical studies on prostitution has often been noted.[1] Yet there exists a considerable amount of literature with the characteristically vivid titles of the period: 'The Great Sin of Great Cities', 'The Great Social Evil', 'London's Curse'. The anonymous tracts distributed by the philanthropic organizations concerned with the welfare of the 'nymphs of the *pavé*'[2] and the evidence and figures from the reports of the commissions of inquiry about other sections of the population – which appeared before Josephine Butler's campaign – provide a fair amount of information of varying degrees of plausibility.

The notion of 'impure woman', lost girl, unmarried mother and adulterous wife could not be thoroughly dealt with in inquiries and reports. Furthermore, the evidence of working-class behaviour was often distorted by moral prejudice.[3] All the same, a look at prostitution, centred on known facts, and bearing in mind the attitudes of the people concerned and of the investigators towards 'sin', seduction and the suggested philanthropic cures, can help clarify certain aspects of the sinning woman in the novel. Some recent studies by P. Cominos, B. Harrison, Stephen Marcus and Keith Thomas have notably advanced research on this subject.

Contemporary works on prostitution[4] for the most part use the same sources: the annual reports of The Society for the Suppression of Vice and of The London Society for the Protection of Young Females and the Prevention of Juvenile Prostitution (with James Beard Talbot as a secretary and founder), and the statistics and reports of the Metropolitan Police. The authors frequently quoted each other. Greenwood quotes Acton, Acton quotes Greg. Engels quoted P. Gaskell, Greg quotes Mayhew.

Women of the town, women of doubtful reputation, nymphs of the pavé, prima donna, women of pleasure, fallen women – to list only a few phrases in the terminology hints at the intensity of this clandestine life. But when one looks for numbers contemporary estimates do not always coincide. The variations are due to the

14 .'The Great Social Evil' from *Punch* 1857.
Time: Midnight. A sketch not a Hundred Miles from the Haymarket.
Bella: 'Ah! Fanny! How long have you been gay?'

statistics sometimes referring to London and the City, sometimes
only to the West End.[5]

The number of brothels in London is equally subject to variation, though all sources agree there were many.[6] Mayhew claimed
that accurate figures were impossible to come by because these
establishments, shutting in one place, opened again elsewhere, the
authorities only keeping a distant eye on them.[7] In Parliament, in
1842, Lord Ashley put forward the following figures for Manchester: 309 brothels to 111 'lately suppressed', 163 'brothels
where prostitutes are kept', 223 'houses of ill-fame where prosti-

tutes resort', and finally 763 street-walkers.[8] The works of Mayhew, Greenwood and Marcus, and *My Secret Life*[9] and *Doings in London*[10] can be consulted for similar details. In the present framework the main interest of these books lies in their confirmation of the proliferation of 'vice' on the London streets. The houses of 'ill-repute' were never far away. They were all over the place, in the neighbourhood of churches, chapels and courts, Parliament and the Law Courts, schools, 'squares and respectable streets'.[11] In 1857 William Acton mentioned a protest by the citizens of St James's to the Home Secretary, Sir George Grey, against the Regent Street prostitutes and their clients who obstructed the pavements from the early afternoon and exposed decent females to obscene gestures and language. Further on he describes the congestion caused in the evening when people were leaving the theatres in the Haymarket.

> The prostitutes and their followers are in possession. The corruptible are wedged in with corruption; and youth and virtue are with difficulty extricated from the melée.[12]

To avoid the mixing, Acton suggested traffic regulations on the pavements during the half-hour following the end of plays. The same year the author of a letter to *The Times* announced the opening of a House of Refuge in the same district,

> the chief centre of all the well-dressed fallen women in London ... attracted hither by the large dancing saloons ... and by the fashionable character of the principle streets ... Piccadilly, Saint James' Street, Pall Mall, Haymarket.[13]

As a *Lancet* author wrote flamboyantly, no one could honestly claim to be without knowledge of the existence of prostitution, not even the 'pure matron'.

> There flourish at the West-end gorgeous houses where passers-by see only the painted face of Jezebel look out of the windows from which sight Virtue averts her face and blushes ... the children of Cornelia inquire concerning the 'beautiful lady'...[14]

James Greenwood confirmed the aggressive presence of these 'brazen-faced women, blazoned in tawdry finery, and curled and painted' in the numerous shady bars in the Haymarket and in music-halls where respectable people went with their families.[15] Whether in bars, music-halls or streets in the centre of London, so-called 'pure' women and women of doubtful morals were in constant proximity. Greenwood relates the mistake of a policeman, 'an overzealous blockhead', 'charging' a respectable mother who had missed her train ...[16]

In the course of his 'researches after concentrated prostitution' one of Acton's most interesting pages concerns the Argyll Rooms and Cremorne Gardens.[17] The former, which operated between 1849 and 1878 in Great Windmill Street was a kind of 'gay casino'[18] where people came to mingle with the demi-mondaines and dance till dawn.[19] Walter, the unknown author of *My Secret Life*, called such places 'the resort of the handsomest and best-dressed gay women'.[20] But Taine was overwhelmed by the 'impression of misfortune and degradation' that emerged from this debauched place where a braided and white-tied usher went and fetched women for the dancers.[21] In Cremorne Gardens in Chelsea galas, 'village feasts', fireworks and concerts were laid on. Fought by the local religious sects, notably the Baptists, the garden closed its doors in 1877. Before it did so, after 10 in the evening, wrote Acton, 'old age and innocence' retired, leaving the place to dancers, men of the upper and middle class and *'prostituées plus ou moins prononcées'*.[22]

While 'women of pleasure' abounded in the smart areas of great cities this was even more so in the poor quarters. In 1840, Flora Tristan, the French feminist and socialist, observed in her *Promenades dans Londres* that prostitution was ubiquitous. In the suburbs she met 'swarms of prostitutes with shameless bearing, staring lubriciously'.[23] In the slums she came up against lost souls of the kind described by Emile Montégut: 'a miserable creature lying on the steps, dead drunk, a glass in one hand and a bottle in the other'.[24] Around St Giles 'missionaries' observed the decay of these 'nymphs of the *pavé*' who from being *'belles* of Regent-Street walk' were reduced to the condition of destitutes.[25] This quarter of wretched vice had struck Louis Enault, the author of a work on London illustrated by Gustave Doré.

St Giles is on top of Oxford Street, of Piccadilly where gold flows as between the shores of the Pactolus ... big half-naked girls gaze at you provocatively and fiercely ... And now their hideous features, object of horror and disgust, bear the trace of all their depravity and degradation.

Doré's magnificent illustrations bring to life women and little girls in the streets and in the inns.[26]

When the pioneers of social inquiry asked about the prostitutes, the reply was unanimous. They came from the common people and worked in industry or as artisans. We saw earlier that dressmaking and its countless ramifications[27] employed an unqualified labour force at starvation wages. Prostitution was rife among them as the commissioners of inquiry into female employment observed.[28] With the help of police reports Mayhew had sought and classified in order of importance the trades pursued by prostitutes who had been arrested in the decade 1850–60.[29] Hatters and trimmers came first, followed by laundresses and servants equally, then 'shoemakers'. Mayhew divided 'disorderly' prostitutes into four categories: the first consisted of those workers already mentioned, and the second, servants who, according to M. Ryan's estimates, formed a third of all prostitutes.[30] The immorality prevalent among them was due, according to him, to their hatred for their work,[31] and to conditions particularly favourable to seduction. Rare were the servants endowed with Pamela's ability to turn an affair into marriage.

Maid-servants in good families have an opportunity of copying their mistress's way of dressing and making themselves attractive to men of a higher class ... Flattered by the attention of the eldest son ... or some friend of his ... the pretty lady's maid will often yield to soft solicitation. Vanity is at the bottom of all this ... The housemaids flirt with the footmen, the housekeeper with the butler, the cooks with the coachmen, and so on.

An anecdote of the author of *Dives and Lazarus*,[32] the adventures of an 'obscure medical man in a low neighbourhood', corroborates this evidence. The young woman, a housemaid in a gentleman's family, is seduced by a footman and, pregnant, is thrown out.[33] From the other side of the fence, the author of *My Secret Life* described the experience of the 'consumer'. Servants initiated young gentlemen sexually and derived a certain pride from this function, which offended no one. That the young woman was dismissed when her crime was discovered appeared unfortunate but perfectly normal.[34] After all, servants are fair game. In this context the analysis of W. R. Greg, who stated that being a servant was a suitable calling for a woman, is remarkable. In an article entitled 'Why are women redundant?', he explained how in his eyes the advantages of this profession largely compensated for the few inconveniences. 'They are fully and usefully employed; they discharge a most important and indispensable function in social life.'[35]

But prostitution was not confined to dressmaking and domestic service. It was one of the ills of industrial society and figured in all the reports of the commissions of inquiry into working life (metallurgy, mines, textiles, etc.), in an article by W. R. Greg on juvenile and female employment and, more famously, in the work of Friedrich Engels.[36] In his indictment of capitalist exploitation, *The Condition of the Working Classes in England in 1844*, he charged industrialization with being the instrument of 'social murder'.[37] Engels painted a truthful portrait of the atrocious living and working conditions of the proletariat. Prostitution and promiscuity are mentioned in every discussion of the slums of the great industrial centres, London, Manchester and Birmingham.[38] In the urban hell of Engels moral and sexual decay is one of the normal consequences of a chronic state of misery, hunger, cold and exhaustion.

Though prostitution was seen essentially as linked to industrialization this was not to say there was any pristine idyllic purity in the countryside. W. R. Greg drew on the 'Report on the Employment of Women and Children in Agriculture' which noted the fact of immorality in rural areas.[39] The author of *Dives and Lazarus* blamed the 'infamous (poor) laws' which forced the two sexes to live together in the worst and most wretched conditions.[40] And Walter in *My Secret Life* tells how he raped two young peasant girls working in the fields in front of their indifferent foreman.[41]

As to the causes of urban or rural prostitution, starvation wages were, before anything else, responsible, in the opinion of Mayhew[42] and the investigators of the commissions of inquiry.[43] Greg wrote of those 'for whom there is no fall ... for they stood already on the lowest level of existence'.[44] Prostitution was just a source of supplementary income in all the underpaid jobs mentioned earlier, or the only source when the individual had no other trade. Before becoming a prostitute Julia Desmond had tried to earn her bread respectably; she saw no other alternative to the 'white slave trade' than death or the pavement.[45]

In the course of his many excursions Walter observed countless times that many young women prostituted themselves for food for their families or themselves, and that typically they were peasant girls earning at best ninepence a day, or else were like 'Kitty', the fifteen-year-old daughter of a housekeeper, who with her illicit earnings embellished her ordinary fare with 'sausages, meat-pies and pastries'.[46] One unemployed young milliner questioned by Mayhew went on the streets to feed her docker father who, being ill, could not work.[47] He gives many examples of workers selling themselves to feed a child.

Among the worst effects of penury were the frightful living conditions – even worse in town than country. Greg quoted extracts from the 'General Sanitary Report' of 1842. In Hull the inspector saw a fifty-year-old mother share the bed of her twenty-one-year-old son, and the room with a lodger. In a Liverpool cellar a mother and her adult daughter slept in the same bed. A young Hull girl became a prostitute after sharing a bed with her sister and brother-in-law.[48] During visits in May 1856 the doctor, William Gilbert, found a courtyard on Holborn Hill, 230 feet by 10 feet, inhabited by 130 men, 203 women and 315 children. A *Times* editorial on 16 May 1853 described such misery and insisted on the promiscuity to which cohabitation gave rise.

> There they live, or rather rot, 70 or 100 in one small light-roomed house, 20 in a room, all ages and sexes in actual contact; and destitute as they are of proper clothes, preferring to lie in heaps for the warmth's sake.

Thus, in general, social inquirers treated prostitution and promiscuity as social problems. 'In poor neighbourhoods', wrote William Gilbert of the local practitioners, 'poverty is the parent of vice'.[49] It must not, however, be supposed that these writers were indifferent about female sin. Though aware of the sociological aspects they did not stop thinking in categories of sin or notions such as 'the unbridled indulgence of animal desire'.[50] W. R. Greg was not the only one to use Paulinian conceptions about female nature. Even Mayhew, the most modern of the writers in his sexual attitudes, put in second and third place among the probable causes of a girl's 'fall', 'Natural levity and the example around them ... love of dress and display coupled with the desire for a sweetheart.'[51] In contrast to what he calls accidental causes due to circumstances, Tait mentioned vanity and pride as two of the natural causes driving women to deck themselves out in finery.[52]

But feminine nature did not only consist of frivolity and aspiration for a higher position. The desire for abnegation was often seen as a specifically feminine trait that could incite the lost ewe to sacrifice her virtue. Here is a female type in Mayhew who reminds one of Marguerite Gauthier in *La Dame aux Camelias*:

> The love of woman is usually pure and elevated. But when she devotes her affections to a man who realizes her ideal, she does not hesitate to sacrifice all she holds dear, for his gratification, ignoring her own interest and her own inclination.[53]

W. R. Greg does not go as far as Mayhew but his portrait is just as full of pathos: 'There is in the warm fond heart of woman a strange and sublime unselfishness, which men too commonly discover only to profit by, – a positive love of self-sacrifice.'[54]

In view of this warm heart the seducer was always condemned, as Walter was.[55] Walter considers the majority of his conquests as cattle, as a means towards one single end, his pleasure or his curiosity. He usually deals with women of the lower orders, professional prostitutes, servants, peasants, workers, and affirms his complete feeling of superiority towards them as a gentleman, whose rank and money confer power. He explicitly and implicitly considers the somewhat brutal attentions he visits on them as an honour.[56] Walter's behaviour illustrates admirably the fact that woman's virginity was the property of her family, then of her husband, and if she had neither she was defenceless.[57] This attitude, rooted in antiquity, persisted in the middle of the nineteenth century though it was totally opposed by moralists and novelists in their mission of society's superego. Like Mrs Gaskell and Dickens, Ryan, Mayhew and Greg violently denounced male impunity and the world's judgement which, without punishing the guilty, makes the victim an outcast.

> The divine law, however, equally condemns both sexes; ... the heartless seducer is, however, received into society, while not only odium and disgrace, but disease, destitution, and misery, fall upon his innocent victim.[58]

Like the novelists, these writers are all of the opinion that the unfortunate girls 'are more sinned against than sinning'.[59]

The masculine 'depravity' encouraging prostitution was, in Acton's eyes, imputable not only to the unbridled sensuality of the average man, who must undergo 'moral and physical training'[60] but also to what he called 'the anti-matrimonial tendencies of modern middle-class society'. An editorial in *The Times* on 5 May 1857, observed that there was a clear decrease in the number of marriages between 1853 and 1856 (from 164,520 to 159,183).[61] This phenomenon was again described and discussed in a letter to *The Times* of 7 May 1857 signed 'Theophrastus', entitled 'The other side of the picture'.[62]

In a society where the criteria of respectability and the external signs of wealth were taking on more and more importance, young people were faced with strong social pressure to delay marriage until their standard of living was as high as their parents'. Prostitution was seen by Theophrastus and William Acton as the dark side of the marriage system in a commercial society where nothing counted more than

a Belgravian house ... a footman in splendid uniform, and at least a brougham ... But there is a reverse to the canvas, and that a very dark one. How has the bridegroom been living since he attained his manhood?[63]

There followed a description of the temptations and their sad consequences.

The investigators indicted society and the seducer and protested against the double standard. And, like their predecessor Parent-Duchatelet, Acton and Ryan, as doctors, were horror-stricken by the ravages of syphilis throughout the whole population, including children.[64] The desire to prevent the disease from spreading, given agreement with Greg's contention that prostitution was an indestructible evil of modern times,[65] encouraged the two doctors to advocate measures of sanitary control for prostitutes. They could refer to France as a precedent. In 1864, 1866 and 1869 the Contagious Diseases Acts instituted compulsory medical checks in garrison towns and ports. Every known or suspected prostitute had to submit to a periodical medical examination, on pain of up to three months' imprisonment.

The double standard and opposition to it were present together. Novelists and investigators affirmed the male responsibility for immorality. Acton, Greg and J. Greenwood demanded heavy penalties for the seducer, 'deserter', the agents of prostitution, pimps, etc. But at the same time, as Josephine Butler noticed, legal control, clamoured for by the very people who emphasized masculine responsibility in a way institutionalized prostitution and also the double standard. For control of prostitution through the female partners discriminated against the female sex as such even while it recognized the continued exploitation of working women by all the Walters of society. It was a recognition that the prostitute fulfilled the essential social function of guardian of the home. This fact was acknowledged by the historian W. E. H. Lecky,[66] and by the poet Barbier.

> Allons, mes soeurs, marchons la nuit comme le jour,
> A toute heure, à tout prix, il faut faire l'amour,
> Il le faut, ici-bas le destin nous a faites
> Pour garder le ménage et les femmes hônnetes. (Lazare)

Mayhew and Acton were at least led by their research to observe facts and behaviour that did not tally with the novelists' treatment of the 'sinful woman'. Remorse, for example, and a sense of guilt did not necessarily accompany sin. The evidence gathered by Mayhew and Ryan from several prostitutes reveals many different feelings, ranging from more or less acute remorse to satisfaction with an easy life, via indifference and the fatalism of those who have no choice. Mayhew insists more than once on the false ideas that were circulating.

It is a vulgar error, and a popular delusion, that the life of a prostitute is as revolting to herself, as it appears to the moralist sternly lamenting over the condition of the fallen; but, on the contrary, investigation and sedulous scrutiny lead us to a very different conclusion. Authors gifted with vivid imaginations love to portray the misery that is brought upon an innocent and confiding girl by the perfidy and desertion of her seducer.[67]

Ryan mentions the typical case of Martha Bull, a young victim of the white slave trade quoted during the trial of a brothel-keeper in the Middlesex Adjourned Sessions on 13 July 1838. Her resigned indifference[68] characterizes several of the testimonies collected by Mayhew as well as the experiences of Walter. Mayhew questioned one named Ellen: 'I certainly think it is wrong to live as I am doing. I often think of it in secret, and cry over it, but what can I do?'[69] The majority of women questioned understood the advantages of a life that was easier than that of a servant or worker.

I don't leave off this sort of life because I'm in a manner used to it, and what could I do if I did? ... I don't think much of my way of life. You folks as has honour, and character, and feelings, and such, can't understand how all that's been beaten out of people like me. I don't feel *I'm used to it...* I get enough money to keep me in victuals and drink, and it's the drink mostly that keeps me going ...[70]

Mayhew sees in this tale a summary of the 'philosophy of sinning' and states that nothing in her earlier life had taught her anything else.

Mayhew also wrote of 'kept mistresses ... prima donnas or those who live in a superior style'. One of them told of her wandering life and her seduction. After living in London with four different men, of whom she quickly tired, she set up with a male 'friend' who adored her. 'What do I think will become of me? What an absurd question. I could marry tomorrow if I liked.'[71]

And yet the British public continued to cherish its alleged moral superiority, as witnessed by an interesting letter to *The Times*. The author contrasts prostitutes of English origin with their French colleagues. The former, he wrote,

have generally had in childhood at least a semblance of religious training; our race is, besides, in itself perhaps more moral than any other in the world; whereas the French women – at least those who frequent the streets of London – seem perfectly unconscious that they are doing anything wrong. They follow this profession as they would follow any other.[72]

Instead of the extremities described by novelists, of the eternal marital happiness of pure women or solitude and punishment for the damned, in reality there was an abundance of half-way houses. 'Prostitution is a transitory state, through which an untold number of British women are ever on their passage',[73] insisted Acton. One of the most interesting findings of this kind of inquiry was that the rehabilitation of the former prostitute in society – most often through marriage – was frequent. Another error dear to novelists was vanishing according to Mayhew – 'The foolish idea ... which still lingers in the minds of both men and women that the harlot's progress is short and rapid, and that there is no possible advance, moral or physical.'[74] On the other hand, in an article on female employment, J. W. Kaye held, and with proof to substantiate it, that a little pity and compassion was often sufficient to reclaim lost girls.[75] Mayhew's interviews proved, too, that fallen women married more often than allowed by mother and wife, novelist and moralist. As a woman questioned by Mayhew remarked, not without black humour:

We may now and then die of consumption; but the other day a lady friend of mine met a gentleman at Sam's and yesterday morning they were married at St George's, Hanover Square ... It is very true this is an unusual case; but we often marry, and well too; why shouldn't we, we are pretty, we dress well, we can talk and insinuate ourselves into the hearts of men by appealing to their passions and their senses.[76]

While Acton, Mayhew and Greg did not go so far as to question the prevailing code they seem to have realized that it was inapplicable below a certain level of welfare and culture. Mayhew, for example, did not hide his impatience with the middle-class novelists who interpreted reality through the prism of the prejudice which had taught them to consider the poor as barbarians;[77] and William Acton, without renouncing his convictions about the absence of physical desire in a normal woman, or the 'poetical or theoretical appreciation of female virtue', recognized that the majority of the population was indifferent to 'those laws of society and religion by

15. The gilded night house of Kate Hamilton, queen of London's night-life, from Mayhew, *London Labour and the London Poor*, 1862

which they are supposed to be swayed'.[78] Walter, too, observed that chastity did not exist among the young in the poorest classes and that among them promiscuity was rife after the age of fourteen.[79] Thus commentators shared at least a doubt about, if not a challenge to, the universality of the middle-class moral code. For Engels, the propensity of the workers, reduced by capitalism to sexual promiscuity, was a meaningful form of revolt, the class struggle a negation of the oppressors' system of values.[80]

Yet at a time when charity was at its most popular, it would be astonishing if philanthropy had not tackled 'the great social evil'.

I appeal ... to every virtuous, to every moral person ... to lend a helping hand against the destroyer, against the wicked. I appeal to Christians, parents, brothers, and sisters and all virtuous and good men to co-operate with those who are strenuously endeavouring to control and diminish licentiousness ...[81]

wrote J. B. Talbot, the secretary of the London Society for the Protection of Young Females and Prevention of Juvenile Prostitution.

There were numerous organizations and individuals employed in researching, reforming and improving the 'nymphs of the *pavé*'.[82] The two main ones, described by Mayhew and Ryan, were Talbot's – mentioned above – and the 'Midnight Meeting Movement'.[83] Mayhew also listed nineteen homes in London, with eloquent names: 'British Penitent Female Refuge', 'Home for Penitent Females', 'London Female Penitentiary', etc.[84] Dickens's discreetly named Urania Cottage is not on Mayhew's list.

There were all kinds of homes. One, announced in a letter to *The Times*, was 'The Saint-James's Refuge and Home for Penitents', intended for 'fallen women of a superior grade'.[85] 'The House of Mercy' at Brewer near Windsor, was founded on 19 June 1849 by an Anglican vicar's widow. It numbered among its trustees the Lord Bishop of Oxford and the Right Honourable W. E. Gladstone, and was meant to be the first of many.[86] Anonymous tracts publicized and appealed for funds for a 'Female Temporary Home' (founded in 1852) with preventive and curative aims.[87] The tract described the Home's activity, the results obtained, and published extracts from the letters of its collaborators and respondents. Lieutenant Blackmore, R.N. Superintendent of the Home, went through the streets of the great metropolis at night, distributing tracts to the unfortunate women who had strayed from the path of female virtue to persuade them to accept a refuge far from the life of dishonour. These 'missionaries' were not the only ones to take it upon themselves to 'seek the lost sheep in the desert'. Not happy with contributing large sums to the homes Gladstone wandered the streets of London at night, armed with a stick, and suggested to prostitutes that they come to his house to rest and recover, so that he could urge them to change their lives. His courage and ingenuousness – he did nothing to hide his activities – were the cause of some misadventures, calumnies and threats of blackmail.[88]

Another important figure in this branch of philanthropy was Charles Dickens, who among his numerous charitable activities such as Ragged Schools and penitentiary reform closely collaborated with Angela Burdett-Coutts on the creation and administration of Urania Cottage.[89] Dickens's correspondence with Miss Burdett-Coutts provides information about the organization of the home and about his ideas for helping and redeeming the prostitutes. The home at Shepherd's Bush, sheltered thirteen girls and two female supervisors.[90] For recruitment purposes Dickens suggested opening a consulting room near the Magdalene Hospital, to clear up all kinds of misconceptions, for example, the widespread belief that emigration and transportation were the same thing. He considered it essential to present virtue to prostitutes in an attractive light, and to avoid any pressure. 'I mean nothing but kindness to you', he wrote in the prospectus – An Appeal to Fallen Women, 'I write as if you were my sister'.[91] He does not seem to have imposed any particular conditions on admission. At Brewer, on the other hand, future inmates had to undertake to provide a certificate guaranteeing their good health, both physical and mental, to obey the rules, to repent, and with rare exceptions to pay a sum of £5.[92]

The letters to Miss Burdett-Coutts abound with practical suggestions for the home's internal organization. Dickens anticipated that two distinct services would be needed. In one the newcomers would be put to the test. The other would be aftercare. Discipline would have to be enforced by means of 'Captain Macconochie's system', a strict and complicated system of pluses and minuses, which moreover did not have Miss Burdett-Coutts's approval.[93] Dickens supervised all the details with extraordinary thoroughness, whether the interior decoration of the Home, or the clothing of the inmates whom he did not want all to be dressed alike. Despite his human concern for reform by persuasion, many of his reclaimed women showed insubordination: temporary or permanent flight,[94] petty theft or often bad conduct.[95]

It was certainly Dickens's aim that at the end of their re-education the reclaimed girls would return to society and lead a normal life. But the rehabilitation was so hedged around that Dickens's philanthropic practice resembled his literary treatment of the 'sinful woman' or the fate assigned to Martha and Emily. His prime intention was that the boarders should emigrate on leaving Urania. His outlook on their destination was completely imperial: it was a question of rendering the 'greatest service to the existing male population, whether expatriated from England or born there'.[96] Thus from the start marriage was subordinated to the cause of peopling the British Empire. This long-term culmination was to follow a long process of repentance and redemption. Reintegration of 'fallen women', if you like, but very conditional; and it does not appear that Dickens ever imagined his 'fallen sisters' might become 'fully fledged' women. On this details of the home's organization are revealing. While Dickens decided not to enforce uniforms, he insisted all the same that they dress like 'respectable plain servants'.[97] His understanding of the psychology of 'fallen women' was based on his permanent conviction that he was dealing with the strange and peculiar temperaments[98] of lost and errant souls. Many a passage in his famous appeal could be drawn from an episode in the career of Emily, Martha or Nancy.[99] His fallen women, stereotyped and melodramatic, are consistent for a man who saw himself as the censor of public morality, obliged to clear ne'er do wells off the streets of London. Having ascertained that swearing in public was indeed an offence according to a new decree, with a repugnantly clear conscience he had a seventeen-year-old boy arrested, put on trial and imprisoned. The police were unwilling but he pushed them.[100]

According to contemporary sources this kind of philanthropy, or 'rescue work' in the stock phrase, seems to have had appreciable results. An article in the *Quarterly Review* in 1848 noted the final redemption of two thirds of the inmates of a Magdalene Hospital.[101] The author of the pamphlet, *London by Moonlight*, gave a list of those entering and leaving a home between August 1852 and December 1853, with their original background and trade and situation on leaving. Out of 107 leavers, four had emigrated, thirty-three had a job, nine had rejoined their families, two worked as dressmakers, six were living with friends, one was dead, seventeen had left the home of their own choice, one had been dismissed for bad conduct, and nineteen were still in the home.[102] Mayhew made a similar list from figures provided by the 'Midnight Meeting Movement',[103] and Ryan gave some results provided by 'The Society for the Suppression of Vice'.[104] Brewer generally kept the boarders for two years, and always found them a job on leaving; but a large number married.[105] Finally, Dickens gave a report on Urania Cottage in an anonymous article in *Household Words* in 1853. Out of fifty-seven boarders thirty had been established in Australia and elsewhere, seven had married in England; of the rest, seven had voluntarily left the Home, ten had been dismissed, three had again fallen on the way to Australia. Dickens put the success rate at fifty per cent.[106]

All these efforts, individual or collective, were the precursors of the Great Crusade: the political and feminist philanthropic movement led by Josephine Butler. Her campaign, which began in 1869, had to fight the Contagious Diseases Acts (1864–1868). After her heroic campaign, supported at a distance by Harriet Martineau, Florence Nightingale and John Stuart Mill, by illustrious foreigners like Mazzini and Victor Hugo,[107] and by a good part of the working classes, the decrees were temporarily repealed in 1883 and definitely in 1886.

12

Dickens's Sinners

The most typical 'impure women' in Dickens's novels are, in chronological order, Nancy in *Oliver Twist* (1837–9); Esther Dombey and Alice Marwood in *Dombey and Son* (1846–7); Emily and Martha Endell in *David Copperfield* (1849–50); Lady Dedlock in *Bleak House* (1852–3). To this group can be added Rosa Dartle in *David Copperfield* and Louisa Bounderby in *Hard Times*, even though they are drawn less fully.

Oliver Twist is the book most affected by the literary fashion of the 30s, the Newgate novel. As main characters Dickens chose wrongdoers living outside the law in the London underworld, under constant threat of prison (Newgate) and the gibbet (Tyburn). Although it contained themes already in vogue in the eighteenth-century novel (for example in *Jonathan Wild* and *Moll Flanders*) and also gothic elements, the Newgate novel was clearly linked with the 'Age of Reform'.[1]

Oliver Twist deals with topical themes of the 1830s familiar to the author in his capacity of parliamentary journalist from 1832 to 1836: the abuse of penalties like deportation and capital punishment and reforms of the penal code between 1833 and 1837.[2] Dickens was interested in the psychology of young deliquents, in the irrational and tireless attachment of the prostitute to her pimp, as is evident in some of the *Sketches by Boz*, in particular 'The Hospital Patient' where the badly beaten young girl refusing to accuse her assailant may be the origin of Nancy.[3] Nancy had a particular significance anyhow. 'I hope to do great things with Nancy', Dickens wrote on 3 November 1837. And in the preface to the third edition of *Oliver Twist* (1841), instead of just asserting the likelihood of Sykes behaving the way he does, he states much more categorically: 'Useless to discuss whether the conduct and character of the girl (are) probable or improbable ... it is true'.[4] In the preface to the 1867 'Charles Dickens' edition IT IS TRUE is in capital letters.

In the same 1841 preface Dickens laid down for himself the task of describing the life of crime in its sordid reality, stripped of the picturesqueness given it by a certain literary fashion. But while wanting to be a social critic, he also wanted to spare the feelings of the reader. Determined to educate his reading public, he refused 'to abate one hole in the Dodger's coat, or one scrap of curl-paper in Nancy's dishevelled hair'.[5] But some lines later on he describes the concessions he makes to decency: an expurgated vocabulary and sordidness and vice suggested rather than proved 'elaborately in words and deeds'.

How is Nancy portrayed in the context of the Newgate novel as up-dated and reshaped by Dickens? Soon after the novel had appeared, Thackeray was indignant about Nancy's unreality compared with the female types he himself had observed in the underworld.

Boz, who knows life well, knows that his Miss Nancy is the most unreal fantastical personage possible; no more like a thief's mistress than one of Gessner's shepherdesses resembles a real country wench. He dare not tell the truth concerning such young ladies.[6]

The same year, Thackeray, for whom a few contradictions on the problem of realism or the subjects proper for a novelist to tackle didn't matter, deplored that all London was interested in Dickens's 'set of ruffians whose occupations are thievery, murder and prostitution ... the street-walker may be a very virtuous person ... but it is better to leave (her) alone.'[7] Since then, criticism has emphasized that nothing in Nancy's character made explicit or even suggested the business of a prostitute. While Dickens finally did use the word in the 1841 preface,[8] it does not appear in the novel nor does he make any allusion to it there. The only hint at her 'profession' are her protests of guilt and perhaps the angelic Rose Maylie's instinctive reaction to move away from Nancy for a moment.[9]

Nancy has also been reproached for speaking with inappropriate propriety, at once grammatical and controlled. Her roughest expression in a fit of rage or drunkenness is: 'never say die'.[10] On these two points – the occupation and language of Nancy – we note a reticence which is not only verbal[11] but which reveals the dead-end in which the Victorian novelist found himself. Nothing in her behaviour or her colleagues' suggests the promiscuity which was rife in the underworld and among the common people.[12]

In the first thirty-nine chapters Nancy lives in the capital's underworld. While it is true that Dickens does not clearly characterize her as a prostitute he does attempt to place her, psychologically and socially, among the thieves of London. Nancy appears in Oliver's world first as a vague and slovenly silhouette, and then decked out in a 'red gown, green boots, and yellow curl-papers'[13] agreeing without too much reluctance to kidnap Oliver. At first she is a passive and indifferent accomplice. Later she is revealed as having a moral conscience. Finally, after an inner conflict manifested through gestures and melodramatic expressions she decides to risk her life and save Oliver from downfall while at the same time devotedly caring for Sykes. Then she makes the decisive move, actually and symbolically, through her journey from the underworld to the respectable world inhabited by Rose Maylie. To do this Nancy has to go through all the circles of hell: she has to escape from her accomplices and brave the scorn of flunkeys towards the common people and fallen women.[14] Till now she has been a victim, deserving sympathy to the extent that without regard for personal safety she took the risk of facing the wrath of her accomplices. On the other hand she was placed as if ready for the change – her clothes, her fits of temper, the outburst of pity for the child, the attachment to her lover. Suddenly, in the fortieth chapter, Dickens the puritan preacher intervenes on the stage where the forces of evil are fighting it out.[15] Nancy is no longer sketched as a particular character in a given situation but in abstract terms: 'there was something of the woman's original nature left in her still ... miserable companion of thieves ... fallen outcast of low haunts.' Finally she delivers the expiatory tirade of a Magdalen in a melodrama: 'I am the infamous creature ...'[16] Thus there is an uncertainty in the author's attitude: she accuses herself of the worst sins, then implicitly recognizes, a few images later, that she is the victim of circumstance.

A major shift in perspective and style occurs. The preacher takes the place of the observer of manners and sees the two characters, Nancy and Rose Maylie face to face, as ontologically antagonistic principles. The result of Nancy's tribulations is an ineluctable advance towards physical death and a calvary of redemption. What restrains her from escaping a life she abhors is her attachment to Sykes, which appears as a fairly natural feeling: 'I cannot leave him now! I could not be his death',[17] But a moment later she herself suggests that these chains she cannot break are perhaps the punishment heaven has inflicted for her sins. Her love for a criminal which is seen as the instrument of the sinner's punishment is rhetorically described. In the scene by the dark and sinister Thames in a deserted and hostile city where Nancy reveals the machinations of Monks, the setting and her nightmarish presentiments conjure up the death

being prepared within her.[18] She refuses to flee, voluntarily sacrificing herself to expiate her sins. After the murder scene the last
station of calvary is reached when the author presents the reader
with a crucifixion or 'melodramatic curtain'.[19] Nancy dies on her
knees, raising high Rose Maylie's white handkerchief, the symbol of
a possible redemption she finds in death, and of the actions of the
agent of Good in this world of darkness. The break that occurs in
the fortieth chapter when Nancy's psychological and social dimensions disappear in the moral perspective of the conflict of good and
evil within her, is marked by a melodramatic style, long tirades,
gestures and expressions translating extreme feelings, sharp suffering and remorse. Nancy cries, falls to her knees, weeps, twists her
hands. It is a gothic atmosphere of danger and sinister conspiracy;
a transparent attempt to create pathos, to excite horror, indignation
and pity; a confrontation between clear-cut human types, hero and
traitor, angel and fallen woman.[20]

Oliver Twist is the novel of Dickens that has most often been
adapted for the stage.[21] Episodes such as the confrontation with Rose
Maylie in the fortieth chapter when Nancy, a shadow on the run,
hastens towards the black waters of the Thames, and finally her
death, seem to have been written for acting. We know that
Dickens, despite the violent reactions this scene provoked in the
audience and himself,[22] refused to drop it from his repertoire of
dramatic readings. Contemporary accounts describe him in the part
of Nancy, alternating between terror and supplication.[23]

Through theatrical techniques which expressed modes of sensibility very close to his own Dickens created the figure of a repentant
sinner out of a girl from the underworld. He is inciting society to
tender a helping hand to these victims, while he burdens his character with the weight of guilt which, at that time, was the price of sex
outside marriage. This produced inextricable contradictions: the
sinning woman appears both as a victim of circumstances and as a
criminal, prey to remorse whose only resolution is the more or less
voluntary sacrifice of her life.

From the point of view of social criticism three other novels,
Dombey and Son, *Bleak House* and *Hard Times* can be seen as forming
one group, making a similar condemnation of industrial and commercial society. H. House has noted that the atmosphere of *Dombey
and Son* is that of England in full development, prey to the fever of
money and railways. The attitude of the characters towards wealth

has changed, as well as the way money operates. The rich are no longer, like Mr Pickwick, Mr Brownlow (*Oliver Twist*) or the Cheeryble brothers (*Nicholas Nickleby*), adepts of the Christmas philosophy of Christian charity and bounteous gifts.[24] Money here and in *Great Expectations* has become the reificatory force of capitalist society, invading every sphere of public and private life. House places this transition in Dickens's philosophy at around the time *Dombey and Son* was written.[25]

From the first page, Dombey is presented not as an individual but as the embodiment of his company's image, taking on the cosmic dimension of a force imposing its rhythm on the whole earth. 'The earth was made for Dombey and Son to trade in, and the sun and moon were made to give them light. Rivers and seas were formed to float their ships.'[26] What more striking images could be found to express the conquests of world markets by British commerce? In what passes for his private life Dombey applies the same rules of conduct as in business. Young Paul's birth is an event that concerns the future of the company. Dombey's two marriages are also harnessed to commercial success.[27] Other human begins are objects that are or will be possessed.[28] The business ethic has annihilated feeling, even family feeling.

The world of *Hard Times* is similar. In a society dehumanized by 'utilitarian' principles money and commerce reign as in *Dombey and Son*, if in a more abstract form. The critique of radical doctrines was aimed at the most rudimentary and least philosophical version of utilitarianism, that of the economists and industrialists of the Manchester School.[29] It reflected the prejudices of a rather ignorant conservative.[30] In the world of the Bounderbys and Gradgrinds, marital and family love and all the values Dickens praised to the sky are non-existent. This is the backcloth against which Louisa's childhood unfolds, fed with facts, statistics, numbers, deprived of love, feelings, of the 'graces of the soul'.[31] She is bartered to Bounderby for the brother's security, like Edith to Dombey, and like Edith, hovers on the edge of adultery.

The death of feeling, the solitude of human beings in a world of implacable materialism, such is the society of *Bleak House* and, in particular, the aristocratic circles in which Lady Dedlock moves. The law courts that consume so many lives are the centre of a corrupted world drowned in one Protean cloud: London fogs, the deadly miasmas of the slums of 'Toms'-all-alone', and the humid mists of Lincolnshire where Sir Leicester and Lady Dedlock live.

Lady Dedlock's splendour and the wretchedness of 'Toms'-all-alone' are part of a single totality that Dickens welds more or less artificially together as his plot meanders on.

The 'two nations' in *Bleak House* communicate in a deadly osmosis, the highest spheres being contaminated by the epidemic that ravages the rest.[32] Lady Dedlock is the product of a parasitic aristocracy; Louisa Gradgrind of a society where only facts matter, and the objective of making men into 'reasoning animals';[33] Edith Grangers and Alice Marwood of a world where the Victorian ideal of the home, the sanctuary of the wife-mother, cannot hold together against the impurity of work and business. Their tragic destiny, adultery real and fancied, and marriage caricatured as legalized prostitution, illustrates the operation of the marriage-market in a capitalist society. Edith's marriage is a business to be handled between her mother, Mrs Skewton, and Mr Dombey who is in search of a new wife to perform a social and reproductive role. Its object is the alliance of wealth and blood. 'She had beauty, blood and talent, and Dombey had fortune: and what more could any couple have?' states Major Bagstock.[34]

Dickens conceived Edith's character in these terms: 'Daughter who has been put through her paces, before countless marrying men, like a horse for sale'.[35] In a letter of 10 March 1847, Edith's silhouette is sketched.

About thirty – not a day more – handsome ... well-dressed, – showy – and desirable ... Goes about with an old mother who rouges and who lives upon the reputation of a diamond necklace and her family. Wants a husband. Flies at none but high game, and couldn't marry anybody not rich.[36]

The whole character is there, firmly fixed once and for all in her physiological and psychological dimensions.

The role of mother as go-between in these dealings is a crucial one. Mrs Skewton is a ferocious caricature of the mediating mother moved by love of lucre and sordid calculation. Her feigned admiration for Edith dupes no one. Mrs Skewton's greed is completely symmetrical with Good Mrs Brown's, whose rapacity is more squalid. She steals clothes, collects rabbit-skins, bones, ribbons and so on. At the two extremities of the social scale two unworthy mothers use their daughters as merchandize. Each of them has committed the worst possible crime – the destruction of the generous spontaneity of childhood. Deprived of love and happiness the two children become the objects of commercial transaction. In *Hard Times*, also, Louisa Gradgrind marries Bounderby without love, to please her father and brother. As with Edith, there is no question of uniting her life with the man she loves. She is forced into an act of legal prostitution aimed at procuring certain advantages for her family.

The parallelism between the two pairs of mother-daughters, Edith and Mrs Skewton, Alice Marwood and Good Mrs Brown, is emphasized variously. Chapter titles (27: 'Deeper Shadows', 34: 'Another Mother and Daughter'); the arrangement of meetings between Good Mrs Brown and Edith and between the two couples in Brighton (chapter 40); the secret link via Carker who has achieved Alice's ruin and is preparing to do the same with Edith; finally, direct comment: 'Wretched marriage don't come of such things, in our degree. Only wretchedness and ruin.'[37] This parallel focuses on the complex role and career of the impure woman, adulteress or prostitute in society. Dickens shows clearly that the destruction of sentimental values happens more or less overtly, more or less sordidly, at every level of society. The corruption that strikes women affects the very sources of good feeling.

There is one particularly interesting parallel between Alice and Edith. The proletarian Alice Marwood is seduced, then accused of a mysterious unspecified crime, and condemned to deportation. Seduced and, by implication only, prostituted, she sinks to the depths of moral decay in sordid poverty unrelieved by any family tenderness. Alice and her mother remain as poor as ever. Could this be because no writer might suggest an even purely material reward for prostitution?[38] Obeying the same laws, and following an analogous pattern, Edith's fall takes place to the rhythms of a slower ritual. There is no doubt that Dickens foresaw the character's final fall. 'Daughter ... like a horse for sale. Proud and weary of her degradation ...', he wrote in the notes for instalment no. 7. Butt and Tillotson point out that Dickens was corresponding with Miss Burdett-Coutts at this time, about the 'Home for Fallen Women'.[39] In his description of Edith Dickens writes significantly: 'Quite a lady in appearance, with something of a proud indifference about her, suggestive of a spark of the Devil within' (see note 36). We know that Dickens had decided on Edith's adultery with Carker and that a reader's objection made him change his plan.[40] Edith's destiny as an impure woman and, in fact or in intention, an adulterous wife is determined in advance. From a childhood without love she passes through two loveless marriages to the point where she decides to take her revenge on Dombey by fleeing the conjugal home with Carker. She is less and less obedient to the clauses of the contractual relationship. There is no longer any emotional link between the couple. Edith constantly drapes herself in the few attitudes that the author assigns to her: pride, arrogance, frigidity. From respectable iciness the Dombeys' relationship sinks into intense hatred. At last Dombey reminds her of the terms of the contract. She refuses to observe them. She asks for a separation.[41]

Though barely sketched, the relations of Louisa and Bounderby are marked by the same coldness, the same neutrality, in an atmosphere from which all feeling, even anger and resentment, is absent. The couple's bleak life continues in a home without the chilly display of wealth of Dombey's house, but just as icy and impersonal, just as lacking in what Dickens thought of as feminine presence.[42]

While Alice and Edith move towards their predictable fates, the psychology is the stereotype of the *femme fatale*. Instalment no. 7 is taken up again the first time Edith appears. 'The proud beauty of the daughter, her graceful figure ... expressed in all her elegant form, from head to foot, the same supreme disregard of everything and everybody.'[43] From this point on, whether she is playing the piano or the harp, or is present, silent, at her mother's odious manoeuvres during Dombey's dinners, Dickens always portrays her with the same features.[44] Frigidity, pride and boredom mark the behaviour of many of his impure women: Lady Dedlock in *Bleak House*; Estella before her sinister secret begins to show in the signs of suffering,[45] and even Louisa. 'She was so constrained and yet so careless; so reserved, and yet so watchful; so cold and proud.'[46]

The indifferent arrogance with which the impure woman protects herself against the insults and pity of the world, alternates with fits of rage and remorse. These paroxysmal states always manifest themselves in the same way through signs of intense emotional palpitations, change of face-colour, convulsive clenching of the fists, tears, intent and wild flashing of the eyes.[47] One recognizes again the heroine of melodrama when Edith blasts the unspeakable Carker from her full height with 'the sparkling in her eyes';[48] and when, on the point of eternal perdition, and suddenly confronted with the Angel, Florence, she shivers and tries to disappear: 'shuddering through all her form, and crouching down against the wall, (she) crawled by her like some lower animal, sprang up, and fled away'.[49] One of the most theatrical and artificial procedures is the sudden

16. 'Edith and Florence, on the Staircase.' Illustration by 'Phiz' from
Dombey and Son

succession of contrary feelings. Lady Dedlock passes from intense remorse, from paroxysms of humility, to pride and then despair, all in a few moments;[50] Edith, from tenderness to fury.[51]

The melodrama is plastically fixed in the illustrations by the theatrical poses of Edith and Alice which are almost identical in their outbursts of feeling. Her scene with Carker shows Edith's noble bearing, hairstyle, diadem, the pose of a Tragedy Queen.[52] Alice's expression is as incensed, and her gestures as expressive, but she has the unkempt hair of a girl from the lower orders.[53] Several episodes in the novel, the dinner at the Dombeys, Edith's flight when surprised by Florence, the trial of strength with Carker, could be staged almost unchanged. The final scene between Carker and Edith, for example, has particularly struck Mario Praz[54] and Edmund Wilson – the doors well-placed for exits and entrances, the suspense created by the presence of servants, the obligatory tirades, the pretentious language, the reversal of roles,[55] and gestures like breast-beating. When Kathleen Tillotson defines this recourse to melodrama as a method of getting the sinful woman accepted in the framework of family readings,[56] isn't she saying in substance that this mingling of genres conveys the anxiety at a taboo subject and the inability to treat sensuality and sexuality in their psychological complexity? The author translates and simplifies them through a popular theatrical device whose conventional vocabulary could be easily decoded by the reader. In melodrama the sinful woman becomes a character both familiar and completely foreign to daily life, and therefore harmless.

Another technique is the use of counterpoint in the narrative and symbolic structure of the novel: the opposition of Edith and Florence, Lady Dedlock and Esther, Louisa and Sissy, the confrontation between impure woman and angel. Florence's angelic function has been pointed out many times; it is obvious that she belongs with Nell, Agnes and Rose Maylie. From her earliest childhood she is a creature of love, sacrifice and purity. The function of this spiritual principle -- mediating salvation – in a withered materialistic society corrupted by money is suggested in the semi-allegorical frontispiece to the first edition of *Dombey and Son* in which Florence, sitting next to Paul, occupies a central position. Above her an angel raises his arm towards a celestial choir. Florence is depicted by two death-beds and with Edith.[57] The effect of her purity on Edith is manifest from their first contact: Edith, proud and detached, senses in Florence an essence so different from herself and her surroundings that she displays unusual hesitation, and then an outburst of tenderness even more unwonted. In contact with Florence, 'her manner was so subdued and gentle'.[58]

The innocence of the angelic creatures, Florence, Esther Summerson, Rose Maylie, gives rise to a sort of inner conversion, which comes out in frantic fits of humility and crying, and in imploring postures. The revelation of transcendence breaks down defences, bringing about confessions of impotence, a sense of sin, and remorse. Before Dombey's inflexibility awakens in Edith a desire for vengeance she weeps in Florence's lap. Louisa devotes herself in all humility to the gentle Sissy.[59] The proud and haughty Lady Dedlock, who, unlike Louisa and Edith, fell into sin before her marriage, is provoked into an outburst of humility and self-accusation by Esther's innocence. 'O my child ... I am your wicked and unhappy mother! O try to forgive me!'[60]

Short-lived repentance does not lead to salvation or change the course of events. The antagonists react in conventional terms and with conventional gestures. Their individual identity disappears and they are just the mouthpiece of the moralist. The result is always artificial and often clumsy. After a bombastic description of Edith the narrator abandons all psychological coherence, and depicts the moral battle through his characters, haranguing them and the readers. 'Was this the woman whom Florence ... Oh, Edith! It were well to die, indeed, at such a time! Better and happier far, perhaps, to die so, Edith, than to live ...!'[61] Instead of direct comment, value judgements are often made through association of images – between sinner and darkness, angel and light.[62] The sinner is often associated with psychological and physical shadow. 'I must travel my dark road alone', says Lady Dedlock to her daughter. Shadows assert themselves in her fate to such an extent that the three illustrations by Phiz where she figures – in flight in the storm and snow, on the road, and dead in the cemetery – are all three equally dark even through the last is entitled 'The morning'.[63] Louisa's flight and her meeting with Harthouse take place on a rainy windy evening.[64]

Louisa Bounderby, Alice Marwood, Edith Dombey and Lady Dedlock, women of industrial society as impure as the Newgate prostitute, are stereotypes based on a contradiction. These victims of society's values appear as doomed sinners marked by an inexpiable sin: real or symbolic death is the only fate they can hope for. Lady Dedlock expires on her lover's tomb. 'When you leave me in this dark room, think that you have left me in the grave',[65] says

Edith to Florence. As for Louisa, Dickens indicates clearly that she has lost the female privilege of the gift of life: marriage and maternity. At best she can share in Sissy's happiness.[66]

In *Dombey and Son*, *Hard Times* and *Bleak House*, the impure woman is part of a critique of society. From a realistic point of view Edith and Alice and even Nancy are only the victims or the by-products of a world where the innocent and the good are condemned. Given the author's manichean view of the world, they also embody the forces of sin, 'a spark of the Devil'.[67] In *David Copperfield*, with Emily, we find seduction reflecting older social relations. The theme of seduction is generally set in the social class system of a feudal society (the theme of Mozart's *Don Giovanni*, and Mozart's and Beaumarchais' *Figaro*) where the nobleman reigns over his serfs and in particular, the virtue of his female subjects. While in industrial society, the dynamic of class changes, the continuing inequality still allows the aristocratic seduction of young girls of modest origin. But the process is lived and judged according to different norms. Whereas in the relatively cheerful, licentious world of Fielding and Beaumarchais, noblemen and maids, aristocrats and peasant women could come together without drama in generally implicit acceptance, the social upheavals of the industrial revolution made this impossible any longer. On the one hand, as in *The Vicar of Wakefield*, the seduction of a young girl is a tragedy for her and dishonour for the group. On the other hand, as in *Pamela*, the servant who forces the master to marry her brings off a victory both real and symbolic: a woman of the people, she forces the aristocrat both to admit her morality and to give her official entry to a higher class. In Victorian England seduction was accompanied by the guilt marking any sexual and emotional behaviour not consecrated by marriage and family. In the Victorian novel, seduction is a tragic theme challenging not only all the sexual taboos but also those governing the separation of the classes.

The social dimension of Emily's fall in *David Copperfield* is complex and includes both the traditional and contemporary aspects. Emily's family, her cherished uncle Mr Peggotty and a cousin are humble folk typical of Dickens. They live modestly in the picturesque and cosy setting of a converted fishing-boat. Through David's words, Dickens traces an idyllic portrait of this mini-paradise of order and propriety. Gathered together by the fire, the orphans, Ham and Emily, Mr Peggotty smoking his pipe, and Mrs Gummidge with her knitting, form a portrait of domestic Christian intimacy emphasized by the bible, the religious prints and the teapot. Though Emily is an orphan she has not been deprived of a warm and serene background. She divides her days between her school and her dressmaking apprenticeship.[68] But although her life is perhaps too easy and coddled for an orphan, the daughter of a fisherman, and in spite of her polished speech,[69] Emily is strongly aware that she is no lady.

In contrast Dickens places the seducer, Steerforth, in the upper-middle class. The intimacy corresponding to the geographical constriction of the Peggottys' boat is contrasted with the luxury and space but also the coldness of a huge abode marked by the solemnity of the residents and the furnishings.[70] While in *Dombey and Son*, the seducer, Carker, belongs to the new class of businessmen possessed by the taste for money and power, and obliged to work for a living, Steerforth is a privileged idler who awakens in David and others ambivalent feelings. As a result of David's benevolent and naïve vision we recognize among Steerforth's varied talents, his charm,[71] his nobility and his freedom, the signs of high birth and wealth. Moreover, Dickens endows him with pride and scorn towards the lowly, feelings which caricature the aristocracy.[72] 'The seducer ... up to *Dombey*, is a crude class symbol',[73] as Angus Wilson has written, and illustrates an anachronistic power which revolted Dickens. Indeed Dickens seems to measure out accurately both charm and arrogance to make Steerforth a perfect symbol of the top-drawer seducer.

Embodying the confrontation between two worlds, the seduction of women is felt as a class problem by all the protagonists. From her very first contact with David, Dickens puts into Emily's mouth a desire, childish certainly, to better her condition, to become a lady; which at this stage signifies fine clothes for her uncle and protection from the perils of the sea, the security which is the privilege of the rich.[74] When she flees with Steerforth, moved by love or by the desire to rise in society (the strictness of the seduction pattern does not permit the author to say which) she swears never to return if he has not made her a lady: that is to say a wife, and a woman of his own social rank. The double meaning of 'to make her a lady' is applied literally. How does Emily's circle react? Mr Omer feels that the desire to rise in society is a great danger, and a weakness on Emily's part.[75] But once the seduction has taken place, the perspective changes. That Steerforth is a criminal does not prevent Mr Peggotty from doing everything in his power to make him marry

Emily, to achieve for her social integration. And while the Steerforth group has nothing but scorn for the family of fishermen, scorn
which develops into hatred at the threat of his marrying beneath him,
the Peggottys, indirectly through David's tales, and directly, remain
subjugated by Steerforth.[76] In the eyes of Littimore, that odious
caricature of a servant, though Emily may well behave as a lady,
and prove gifted in foreign languages, her association with Steerforth has not for one moment removed her from her class. Littimore
deems himself more than an advantageous match for Emily, given
her origin and her 'fall'.

In the eyes of humble folk, small tradesmen like Mr Omer, or a
young bourgeois like David, wanting to become a lady signifies
being seduced, accepting illegitimate and irreparable passion, in
other words resigning oneself to destruction. This David expresses
in another way when he points out that Emily would have had the
right to the joys of maternity 'had she been a poor man's wife'.[77]
Dickens stresses the fact that Emily has the education and distinction of a woman of higher rank; and that the qualities of heart of the
lowly are unequalled. Nevertheless the gulf between the classes can
only be crossed at the price of ruin for the woman, and dishonour for
her group.

Dickens, being interested in the psychology and redemption of
prostitutes, also gave the theme of seduction contemporary re-
sonance, an echo of his activity in the 'Home for Homeless Women'.[78]
In *David Copperfield*, outside the family circle people lack the most
elementary compassion for the seduced girl. By exaggeration of this
scorn, even hate (Rosa Dartle), Dickens wanted to awaken pity.[79]
That this intention was close to his heart is proved by a letter where
he expressed the hope of seeing Emily's character immortalize his
memory.[80] Other aspects of Emily's adventures must have reminded
contemporaries of ever-present dangers such as the risk for the
seduced and rejected girl of sinking for ever into 'the sin of great
cities'. This danger is accurately described and Martha's terrible
experience serves to save Emily from complete degradation. In the
same way emigration offered as the solution for the prostitute's
recuperation or symbolic death was realistic enough. This fate had
the advantage of reconciling the imperatives of respectability and
charity with those of colonial expansion, as happened with the
inmates of Urania Cottage.[81]

These few elements that place Emily in her time are not sufficient
to make a psychologically coherent character of her, or of Martha

for that matter. As Mario Praz notes, the sinner has lost the poetic halo the romantics gave her but she has not in return acquired realistic dimensions.[82] Seduction illustrates the control and ascendancy of one class over another. The nobleman can still in all impunity possess a woman of lower rank. Only poetic justice condemns him to perish in a way appropriate to the circumstances, shipwreck in *David Copperfield*, Carker run over by a train in *Dombey and Son*.

The image of the impure woman has hardly deepened then since Nancy.[83] With Emily, Dickens had the following problem to solve: how to make her a creature near enough to the female ideal to awaken the public's compassion and, at the same time, suggest traits that expose her to the danger of falling into the trap of seduction. Emily is, therefore, presented to the reader as a subtle mixture of goodness and weakness. Her goodness is shown by her love for her people, but her behaviour also augurs ill for the future: coquetry towards David and Ham, and in particular a diffuse dissatisfaction and instability which disturbs the spectators of the drama.[84] Obviously associated with general agitation so unbecoming to a young fiancée is her desire to become a lady. Dickens thus suggests a traditional aspect of woman's nature, frivolity, coquetry, dissatisfaction with her condition, a taste for unwonted refinement difficult to get in a village.

Emily's inner conflicts before, during and after the crisis are ignored. Once more psychologist and writer of manners stand down before the moralist with his classic tale of temptation, fall, punishment and repentance of the sinner. Emily's temptation and fall are described pathetically and absurdly in the letter she leaves for her family. Here are the stereotyped feelings of the sinner condemned to the torments of hell: grief, sense of her own worthlessness, remorse,[85] the ephemeral joys of a wandering life in a Mediterranean country.[86] According to the tales of Littimer Emily after growing tormented leaves her lover fairly quickly. Then comes punishment and the dawn of a new life of atoning for her sin.[87] She is only saved from total degradation by Martha, who brings her back to her people. Repentance and redemption are linked to the return to the cradle, to the warmth and purity of the home of which Nancy, Edith Dombey, Louisa Bounderby were deprived, and the memory of which saves Kate in *Nicholas Nickleby* from the dangers of the great city.

Despite her family's forgiveness, it is out of the question that Emily might return to a normal life in her village and marry her fiancé. For her it must be emigration to Australia and a solitary life of good works and devotion. The refusal of marriage, which might appear astonishing[88] since Martha does marry, is perhaps evidence of moral superiority and degree of repentance. But it does not fit with the redemption of the sinner – for Dickens to a certain extent encouraged the return of the girls in Urania Cottage to a 'normal' life of marriage and maternity,[89] but only once they were in Australia ...

The melodrama comes from the parallelism with Martha. In the counterpoint of these two lives Martha warns of the fate awaiting any girl taking the first step to the abyss: prostitution. Mr Peggotty and Martha try to save Emily from a danger so frightful it cannot be clearly described. Prostitution is the probable outcome of seduction and of society's ostracism of the sinner. When Dickens insisted, in the version of *David Copperfield* adapted for the stage under the title of *Little Emily* and played for the first time on 9 October 1869, that Mr Peggotty's feelings of pity for Martha should not be suppressed,[90] he surely wanted to persuade the audience that the two destinies were dangerously similar.

Martha appears as a shadow dogging Emily's steps at several decisive stages in her decline. The first apparition takes place when Emily removes her arm from Ham's and gives it blushingly to Steerforth. This scene appears charming to the naïve David. But as Nemesis, a 'black shadow', Martha crosses the stage and has all the distinctive signs of the fallen woman: 'she was lightly dressed, looked bold, and haggard, and flaunting, and poor'.[91] Her second appearance comes after the scene with Miss Mowcher, who pronounces the fatal word 'elopement'.[92] At this moment the kinship between Martha and Emily is melodramatically emphasized and their identical fate pointedly announced. They were at school together. 'I was once like you', says Martha. By a stroke of dramatic irony the uncle cannot bear to see them next to each other, the fallen and the innocent. After this scene Emily delivers herself of a great tirade of self-accusations, the very words of which herald both her fall and the tenor of the letter she leaves her uncle.[93] Finally, Martha appears in the famous chapter as a wandering shade on the bank of the Thames, amidst a host of symbols associated with death: prison, ruins, rusty boilers, a grave yard of machines, barges stranded in mud.[94] Her frantic expressions and gestures, her weeping and clenched fists, all express with the usual rhetoric the soul-states of the melodramatic sinner: her desire for expiation and death, her

17. 'Martha.' Illustration by 'Phiz' from *David Copperfield*

sense of her own downfall.[95] After this funereal scene although she has redeemed herself by saving Emily from the white slave trade, one is astonished to learn she is getting married, admittedly only in Australia where, as Peggotty makes clear, women are rare![96]

The same effect is probably aimed at by the prediction which is more or less naturally realized: for example David's premonitory vision of Emily's fate which was not in the first draft of the book.[97] In this passage Emily expresses her desire to be a lady and to David's consternation makes a mad leap on to a plank jutting out over the sea. Emily's lack of awareness and this useless danger are a sinister omen. The narrator tells himself that the little girl's flirtation with death as she danced over the abyss was nothing in comparison to the fate awaiting her.[98]

Emily, the stereotype of the seduced girl, and Martha, the stereotype of the prostitute, exist by virtue of a myth of female purity and by virtue of Dickens's desire, as philanthropist and reformer, to present to the public, without offence, a social problem in bowdlerized form as he had done previously in *Oliver Twist*. In a letter to Miss Burdett-Coutts he explained the difficulties facing the novelist who wants to inform and move without shocking;[99] but he had no qualms about the result.

Dickens's impure women, whether actual or potential adulteress, seduced girl or prostitute, all appear as variants on the character of the repentant sinner and belong, in situation, conception and style to melodrama. Among the stock seducers, in Dickens and others, are numerous figures of rural England – squires, peers, landed proprietors – like Steerforth, Arthur in *Adam Bede* and Bellingham in *Ruth*. In a play written after these novels, Watts Phillips's *Lost in London* (1867), the seduction has been modernized for industrial England and the seducer is a mine-owner.[100] Seduction or not, the story is generally as follows: girl returns home, tortured by remorse, after being taken away freely or by force, aspiring like Emily to rediscover the idyllic setting of her village and family. The idealization of village, of country innocence, of the goodness of the poor is often present.[101] While melodrama often allowed the victim miraculously to preserve her virtue, or the seducer to marry there and then the girl he has dishonoured, the unfolding became more pessimistic after 1860. In *East Lynne* adapted from Mrs H. Wood's novel and in *Lost in London*, the Old Testament law prevails: 'the wages of sin is death', and the sinner is condemned.[102]

Melodrama stages characters moved by elemental and extreme feelings in a world where good and evil confront each other without nuance.[103] If the impure woman in Dickens's novels regularly borrows the gestures, attitudes and language of the sinful woman it is because melodrama is the genre that best expresses a manichaean and anti-intellectual vision of the world. It was precisely these conventional situations, this division between traitor and hero, the confrontation between vice and virtue, the world of imaginary contrasts, which Bernard Shaw later wanted to expel from the theatre by restoring truth, complexity and the confusion of real life to the stage. But melodrama, which was the dominant form of popular entertainment, was at the same time the essential modality of all life and thought in nineteenth-century Britain.[104] Thus the impure woman could easily become a melodramatic sinner in the eyes of a sensibility that saw the world in terms as clearcut as Dickens did.

The fallen women of Dickens's novels, psychologically non-existent, have social and metaphysical significance. They illustrate and express what Dickens condemns in society: the role of money and commercial values in the industrial and mercantile era, the dryness of economic pseudo-science, the brutality of manners in the underworld, the surviving power of the aristocrat to fascinate. In the Victorian world, in novels aimed at a vast public and family reading in cheap instalments and by means of circulating libraries, the impure woman could not be the subject of a realistic treatment with enough complexity to do justice to the psychology of it, as was done for Anna Karenina or Emma Bovary, or even to do justice to the social problem as in the naturalistic novel of France and, later in the century, of England. The impure woman in Dickens's novels is therefore left with this significance that is above all moral and metaphysical.

13

Vanity Fair – The Siren and the Ladder

The register of melodramatic 'impure women' is suited to a fabricated world where the complex aspects of everyday life are replaced by simple and clearcut values, a world where traitors fall and virtue triumphs. Dickens's fallen women are the reverse of the contemporary ideal. Thackeray, Elizabeth Gaskell and George Eliot all move away from such absolute confrontations. Impure women there are but in context: for Mrs Gaskell, in a dehumanized industrial society, for George Eliot (Hetty Sorrel in *Adam Bede*) in a protestant peasantry within a feudal structure. For Thackeray in *Vanity Fair* the context is a range from the middle class to metropolitan aristocrats.

In his earlier work (reviews, tales, parodies and satiric sketches, most of them written under pseudonyms: Yellowplush, Fitz-boodle, Michael Angelo Titmarsh, and others, for *Fraser's Magazine*, *Punch*, the *Morning Chronicle*), Thackeray was already displaying a marked interest in the social behaviour of the individual within a group – snobbery, conformity and the desire to rise socially. When in critical articles[1] and his parody *Catherine*, he declared war on the Newgate novel, he condemned the conventions of contemporary fiction – heroic, romantic and pretentious – in the name of truth. He reproached Ainsworth for investing 'the low ruffians of the *Newgate Calendar* and their profligate companions with all the interest and the graces of romance'.[2] In *Jack Sheppard* the concern for psychological and social truth inspired him as much as the desire for effectiveness. At the same time, as early as 1840, seven years before his famous letter to Mark Lemon on the responsibility of the novelist,[3] Thackeray was showing his moral propriety in the choice of subject, thus foreshadowing the censorship exercised by himself as the director of the *Cornhill Magazine* some twenty years later over stories, which he judged to be improper, by Elizabeth Browning and Anthony Trollope.[4] He thought it unfortunate that Dickens, in *Oliver Twist*, should get the 'whole London public' interested in the doings and gestures of rogues who indulged in theft, murder and prostitution. Since it was impossible to tell the whole truth about them, it was preferable, he thought, not to tackle them at all.[5] Long before *Vanity Fair* the critic's demands for realism were tempered by an awareness of his responsibilities and the conventions that had to be observed for the sake of his readers.

After the early stages of his work on this book, Thackeray dropped the journalistic title, 'Pen and Pencil Sketches of English Society' for a more ambitious one borrowed from Bunyan. Its discovery gave him immense satisfaction.[6] But just as important and more shocking for the contemporary public was the choice of subtitle, 'A novel without a hero', which demonstrated his determination to distinguish himself clearly from the novelists he parodied in 'Punch's Prize Novelists' (Bulwer-Lytton, Disraeli, Lever, G. P. R. James, Mrs Gore), the very year he began to write *Vanity Fair*.[7] To make quite clear his intention of depriving the reader of a hero Thackeray kept his distance from the characters with whom male and female readers could be tempted to identify, namely Amelia[8] and Major Dobbin. He even drew up a list of what Dobbin needed to meet the obligations of a fictional hero.[9] By suppressing both hero and heroine the author was repudiating the absolutes of clearly defined and recognizable values.[10] Satisfied, uneasy or indignant, contemporaries were aware of the novelty of the undertaking. Mrs Proctor wrote to Abraham Hayward: 'The characters are neither angels nor devils, but living breathing people.'[11] Hayward appreciated the absence of a traitor, the natural style, the frankness, but also the perfect propriety of this work 'of a gentleman ... (who) ... never ... insists ... upon ... the horrors of the Eugene Sue School'.[12] On the other hand, Elizabeth Rigby in her famous article in the *Quarterly Review*, confessed to being dismayed by the pessimistic vision of Thackeray, even though she regretfully conceded his veracity. Rarely was nostalgia for the edifying novel, for precepts of conduct, more clearly expressed. 'With few exceptions, the personages are too like our every-day selves and neighbours to draw any distinct moral from. We cannot see our way clearly.'[13] Other critics found the book positively repugnant. Forster, for example, speaks of 'the atmosphere ... overloaded with these exhalations of human folly and wickedness'.[14] Bell, in *Fraser's*, criticized its 'foul atmosphere'.[15] Elizabeth Barrett Browning saw in it nothing but unhealthy cruelty and Harriet Martineau felt repulsion at it.[16] In 1880 Trollope explained what could have shocked and even overwhelmed the reader of *Vanity Fair*, that is to say its reversal of the usual relations between hero and virtue. More importance was granted to the vicious, to the absurd, than to the good and noble: if heroes there are, Becky Sharp and Rawdon Crawley are they.[17]

Readers were as deliberately deprived of the tribulations of hero and heroine before marriage, of a sentimental love story ending with altar and wedding-bells. Here too Thackeray deliberately challenged a convention and expressed his intention of exploring the 'marriage country' and verifying it 'all were green and pleasant there: and wife and husband had nothing but to link each other's arms together and wander gently down towards old age in happy and perfect fruition.'[18] Likewise, in the denouement Thackeray avoided the poetic justice favoured by the public by leaving Becky in relative prosperity instead of throwing her from the top of the Tarpaean rock. A similar fate unites Becky and Amelia in disenchanted maturity and in old age.[19] By different means Thackeray refused to yield to the average reader's taste. To his mother, for example, who found Amelia selfish, he replied:

> Don't you see how odious all the people are in the book (with exception of Dobbin) ... What I want is to make a set of people living together without God in the world ... greedy pompous mean perfectly self-satisfied.[20]

Before deciding if the idea of 'impure woman' makes sense at all in this corrupted world sketched by the author one needs to consider the setting. Two centuries earlier, this was how Bunyan described *Vanity Fair*:

> Therefore at this fair are all such merchandise sold as houses, lands, trades, places, honours, preferments, titles, countries, kingdoms, lusts, pleasures ... whores, bawds, wives, husbands, children, masters, servants, lives, blood, bodies, souls, silver, gold. ...[21]

In Thackeray's version the worship of Mammon has killed love. In 'the debatable land between the middle classes and the aristocracy'[22] everything is for sale. Money allows the bourgeois to obtain the mode of life and education of the aristocracy, if not for himself, then at least for his heirs. All classes of society implacably tread on each other in order to reach the summit. Young Osborne's father is only a tradesman, but because he can call himself a gentleman and travel in his own coach he scorns the grocer's son, Dobbin. Mrs Sedley thinks that her son Jos would come down in the world if he married the daughter of an artist. He has to remind her that she herself was the daughter of a grocer when she married Mr Sedley, the stock-broker.[23] The most striking seeker after status is Osborne senior, a rich tradesman in tallow and, as he defines himself proudly, a 'British Merchant'. His money allows him to pay for the education of his children (the best teachers for George and his sisters), contacts with the nobility (in the army),[24] and connections with the world of finance (one of George's sisters marries the banker Bullock). In the third generation, old Osborne's fortune procures a gentleman's entire apparatus for his grandson – elegance, amusement, education, horse and carriage – not forgetting arrogance.

Individuals and clans confront each other in a pitiless struggle. All the Christian values, charity, loyalty, altruism, gratitude, are sacrificed to ambition. Old Osborne has no qualms about breaking his promises about the marriage of George and Amelia and denying any obligation towards Sedley who helped him when he was starting out. He drives Amelia and her parents to misery in order to appropriate the heir who will perpetuate the progress of the Osborne family.

Marriage is only an essential transaction. Sons and daughters are sold by families or at least exchanged for advantages of fortune or rank, and exceptionally, also for beauty and intelligence. Unless, like the unfortunate Lady Gaunt, the woman is bought for the single purpose of reproduction.[25]

While the bourgeois tries to raise himself to the level of the aristocrat by every means in his power, the latter shows himself unworthy of his privilege. Old Sir Pitt Crawley, far from being the refined creature Becky imagined in her dreams of grandeur, is a slovenly and foul-mouthed old man, as greedy as he is sordid. Is it not scandalous, suggests Thackeray, that a creature as contemptible as he should be among the highest in the land?[26] The younger son, Rawdon, is a typical representative of an idle aristocracy. He leads a happy life, plays and carouses, is always in debt.

Generally speaking, with the exception of old Sir Pitt who, with one foot in the grave, proposes to Becky, the aristocrats jealously guard their wealth in order to prevent its falling into the hands of strangers. While the three brothers flatter their aunt, Miss Crawley, in order to get their hands on her inheritance of £70,000, she disinherits Rawdon when he commits the misalliance of marrying Becky, to whom, nevertheless, she takes a fancy. The higher aristocracy is no better. Thackeray finds no true nobility in the Marquis of Styne, peer of the realm, on familiar terms with the monarch, but an inhuman cynic.

Vanity Fair shows that those who have privilege are in general even more contemptible than those who use every means to acquire it. In this world money and the lack of it, are equally corrupting. Real wealth excites greed and engenders enmity even within a single family. Those with average wealth make every effort to get more. Poverty corrupts at the bottom.

Like the other 'puppets' in *Vanity Fair*, Becky is accurately placed in society. She is the only important figure not to come from a lower-middle-class, commercial or aristocratic background. Her childhood was psychologically and materially insecure, her future is precarious. She was deprived of her mother at an early age and we know what emotional significance for Thackeray was attached to that. Her father leads the traditional life of the artist: easy-going, gay, irresponsible and dissolute. Becky is unique in *Vanity Fair*. The protective clan has disappeared, and so there is no family trying to climb the social ladder. Plunged early on into the adult world of money, work and strife Becky was responsible for herself. Thackeray shows her isolated from her contemporaries, by her early maturity – the product of her precocious experience – which makes the artificially protected infantile world of Miss Pinkerton's Academy unbearable to her. She experiences exploitation early on when the headmistress tries to make use of her musical talents without payment. Attacked, she defends herself, as she had to as a child against her father's creditors. Having to battle not only for a place in the sun, but for survival, she is presented as an outsider. Her life as it struck numerous contemporary critics, seemed to explain if not justify her lack of scruples. 'Becky is the shrewd, venturesome, resourceful woman created by her misfortune ... the artist's daughter born in an attic, raised by daubers ...' wrote a critic in the *Revue des Deux Mondes*.[27] Even Elizabeth Rigby admitted that 'the Soho *ateliers* were not the best nurseries for a moral training'.

Becky's essential otherness was quietly stated by the same critic: 'You are not one of us, and there is an end to our sympathies and censures.'[28] Conditioned by her childhood, Becky sees her relationship with society as a power struggle. Having learned early that prestige and power are based on the wealth of 'that Creole' or the high birth of the 'earl's granddaughter' Becky sets about putting the lesson into effect.

The first fundamental step is of course marriage. In a world where women may only aspire professionally to despised subordination, Becky's sole chance to rise in society is to make a good match.

She tackles the first man she meets on leaving school, Jos Sedley, and unsuccessfully tries to seduce him. Rawdon Crawley, her second quarry, combines high birth with hopes of wealth. Thackeray implies that it is the general hypocrisy that makes Becky a schemer: she is neither more nor less one than the majority of girls whose one objective is marriage. But Becky, alone in the world, has to do the dirty work generally done by mothers or families,[29] and her tactics are similar to those of a mother, Mrs Bute Crawley for example. The difference lies in the distribution of roles. Combining the two functions of selling and being sold, and the initiative required for this effort, have something unusual and shocking about them which both Becky and the narrator emphasize.

When Becky lays siege to the Crawleys her position as an 'unprotected orphan' is once more stressed. 'I am alone in the world ... I have nothing to look for but what my own labour can bring me.'[30] Her previous Sedley campaign brings together all her techniques. She has to be loved by all those in any sort of relationship with the man she has in mind, which needs considerable flair and psychological insight. At the Sedleys Becky lays siege to Jos, the chosen one, to different members of the family and to the servants, always by means adapted to the nature of each. After beleaguering one of the approaches to the fortress Becky plays the innocent young girl convinced of the superiority of the male sex. Her modest demeanour, her lowered eyes, her white dress are all designed to express the female image sought by future husbands and mothers-in-law. The siege is systematic. At the summit Becky feigns altruism and devotion, staying at Amelia's bedside when she has a migraine, laughing at Mr Sedley's threadbare jokes; at the lower levels, the cook's talent for making jam is the subject of her liveliest interest; the manservant is invested with unusual titles like 'Sir' and 'Mr', and the maidservant gets endless apologies. She employs a similar strategy in the Crawley family to soften all the inhabitants, her pupils whom she allows to devour endless novels and go bird-nesting, Mr Crawley whom she treats respectfully and submissively, paying homage to his superior knowledge and virtue, the Baronet to whom she becomes indispensable, and the authorities of the kitchens and stables towards whom she behaves modestly and politely.[31]

Becky's actions are dictated by an appraisal of the forces ranged against her. Unlike other young people of her own age – spoiled and kept in leading-strings – she has already acquired an experience of human beings. With this knowledge she knows how to harness all kinds of weakness to her own ends: coquetry, men's appetite for superiority, the hunger for deference among the highest placed and the lowliest. Her profound opportunism reveals at the same time the values of the society in which she moves.[32] Her most determined enemies are the women who, apart from Amelia and Lady Jane, try to crush her by the weight of their snobbery. But Becky continually proves the superiority of the education she has received or rather acquired for herself. French and music are not simple accomplishments, ornaments of the future wife, but solidly understood. To stress Becky's superiority over the wife-mothers of the novel[33] not only in intelligence but also strength of character, Thackeray endows her with a tenacity, vitality and competence which throw into relief the passivity of Amelia and Lady Crawley. She even beats them on their own ground, in point of the hypocritical attentions required from every 'good housewife',[34] and which she knew how to lavish on Rawdon. Thackeray uses her to debunk snobbery. Never missing an opportunity to take her revenge on condescension, snobbery and contempt, Becky gives the reader the pleasure of seeing vice punished or intelligence triumph over stupidity. When George Osborne puts on airs towards the governess, quick as a flash she puts him in his place by reminding him that City money cannot take the place of high birth, and turns the tables; she exploits Jos's cowardice when he flees from Brussels, and takes revenge for the slights endured from Countess Bareacres.[35] She is the agent of a certain poetic justice.[36]

The victim of social injustice, alone in the world, Becky rises to fight the unequal fight against the other inhabitants of Vanity Fair who are in pursuit of the same objectives, and is used by the Manager of the Performance as a Punch and Judy policeman to denounce the bluster of her brothers and sisters. In this role she is explicitly defended by the author in the novel and in his letters. In a famous passage[37] Becky observes the relative nature of all virtue and the different meanings of 'temptation' for rich and poor. The narrator seems to agree with her entirely when he questions absolute morality and virtue, and suggests the influence of socio-economic factors. The subversive implications of this passage did not escape G. H. Lewes who was indignant that the author portrayed 'honesty [as] ... the virtue of abundance', and who saw this page as a gratuitous affront to the poor 'who ... die for want of bread, yet who prefer death to stealing'.[38] In reply Thackeray set out the mode of life of a 'respectable' woman according to the norms of *Vanity Fair*. If she had been rich and highly placed from the start, Becky, without shocking anyone, could have

increased her fortune, advanced her family in the world: tied up treasures for herself in the shape of 3 percents, social position, reputation etc ... What satire is so awful as lead us not into temptation![39]

The author suggests that with £5,000 a year all the shocking aspects of Becky's existence would vanish: the plots to catch a good husband, the well-placed connections, the endless calculations and pretences to mould herself into a product acceptable to society, the greed, the avarice, and all the manifestations of insecurity and need.

When the author wonders about the nature of virtue, when the critics invoke the circumstances of her childhood, her poverty, they observe that Becky is not an 'honest' woman in the vague and widely accepted meaning of the word, and that her acts require justification and explanation. At this point one should see whether beyond her realistic dimension Becky is not given a deeper significance.[40] Elizabeth Rigby calls Becky the *'ideal* of feminine wickedness',[41] investing her with an exemplary surreality and a breadth that takes her out of the world of everyday life. Critics will continue to argue. But what one can try to establish is whether, as some think, the defence weighs little beside the case for the prosecution.[42] Can one uncover in Thackeray's conception and treatment of Becky a more marked will to criticize? Is Becky's baseness of a completely different order from the general run of immorality in the novel? In his portrait of the adventuress does the moralist at bottom take precedence over the realist?

Vanity Fair was conceived as a novel without a hero. But critics have constantly judged Becky in relation to Amelia. And even though Amelia's negative characteristics confuse the issue, the opposition between the two women is both the narrative thread of the novel and the author's vision of the world. The contrast between the two destinies was accentuated by the effect of publication by instalment. The moral and philosophical implications are complex and ironic.[43]

Right from the start, while Becky is baiting her trap for Jos Sedley Amelia can only suffer and sigh as she waits for George to fall in love with her. While Becky does not allow George his superiority and gains the upper hand Amelia patiently puts up with the rebuffs and scorn of her sister-in-law. The two women stand out as two on the departure to the war of the two husbands, George and Rawdon. Amelia, whose love renders her totally vulnerable, is wild with despair. Nothing counts for her but the presence or absence of the loved one. Rebecca, on the other hand, remains in perfect command of herself and the situation: her vital functions, Thackeray indicates not without malice, are no more disturbed than her future projects, including what to do in the event of Rawdon's death.[44] This revolting composure is implicitly contrasted with the generosity of Rawdon who has made all the necessary arrangements for his wife in case of his death. Later on Amelia is reborn by sinking herself into a blind, deranged love for her son, whereas in the presence of *her* son Becky sees only an obstacle encumbering the realization of her ambitions. In these different episodes, Amelia with her love, sacrifice, passive suffering, masochism and spontaneous generosity is contrasted with the energy and ingeniousness Becky uses in the fight for life, her calculations involving her in hypocrisy and duplicity, and utter selfishness towards husband, lover, child, friends. The love compounded of illusions, the total fidelity to an unworthy creature on the part of the one brings out the lucidity and detachment of the other. Thackeray's pessimism, and perhaps too the serial form in which this novel was written, led him to create two completely opposite characters: 'Becky knows no love; Amelia is all love.'[45] For Thackeray,[46] the supreme value, love, redeems Amelia from all her faults, for despite its blindness, love in the godless world of *Vanity Fair* is sacred and purifies those who are endowed with it, especially the 'good woman' worshipped by the novelist. The contrast with Amelia is always in one way unfavourable to Becky who, to underline the point, is also explicitly condemned by the three positive characters, Amelia, Lady Jane and Dobbin. Amelia accuses her in an uncharacteristically violent way of wanting to steal her husband's love.[47] Dobbin, one of the rare men whose head is not turned by Becky,[48] is disgusted by her hypocrisy and resolutely opposes her influence over Amelia. Finally, Lady Jane, the embodiment of the good spouse and mother, departs in the end from her usual sweetness and charity and refuses to let her set foot in the house.

Some critics assert Becky is irremediably impeached even from the beginning.[49] When she is presented to the reader in the first instalment, she spitefully throws the dictionary out of the window. The successive expressions on her face are 'an almost livid look of hatred' and 'a smile that was perhaps scarcely more agreeable'. After revealing her grievances, she remarks 'I'm no angel'. The narrator caps: 'She certainly was not.' Then follow some remarks on the responsibility of misanthropists in general, and of Becky in particular, for the rebuffs others inflict on them. Finally, 'she was never known to have done a good action in behalf of anybody'.[50] Whatever the explanations brought to bear later on, the remarks about her family and the social injustice of which she is a victim, it is difficult for her to recover from such categorical condemnation. Through the other characters and through the narrator's comments the author equates Becky with vengeance, hatred and selfishness.[51] Among the traits thrown into relief by Amelia and Lady Jane nothing is more shocking – in view of Thackeray's sensibility and the prevailing ideal of woman – than her attitude towards children in general and her own son in particular. This behaviour is carefully articulated:[52] the slap in the face that Becky gives her son is logical for a character who formerly found no pleasure in looking after little girls in her school. Her indifference towards him punctuates the narrative, underlined on occasion by the narrator: 'here was one who was worshipping a stone'.[53] The lack of feeling worsens into hypocrisy when, out of sheer opportunism, Becky pretends to adore Amelia's and Lady Jane's children, and later her indifference turns into malice when she refuses the adoration her son confesses for her.

Wasn't Thackeray betraying unnecessary hostility (on his part, not hers) when he depicted Becky forcing her eight-year-old son to travel outside in mid-winter?[54] But even taking Thackeray's general attack on unworthy parents into account it is the absence of motherly love, more than anything else, that makes Becky odious. Given the maternal love of Lady Jane and Amelia, the novelist's own love for children, the contemporary mother-fixation and Thackeray's worship of the image, Becky as anti-mother must have been quite enough to ensure the average reader's antipathy.

Thus Becky is the subject of diverse and concerted attack: her character is shown up in a round-about way by contrasting her with other women who submit to the values of the time; and more directly by the narrator's sarcastic remarks, his reference to one 'wretched woman',[55] his propositions about women in general – 'some are made to scheme, and some to love'[56] – and finally his museum of pejorative images. The word 'writhing' is used for the first time by Dobbin but recurs regularly as Becky sinks deeper and deeper into debauchery. This is how Thackeray describes Becky's desperate attempts to convince Lord Steyne of her innocence: 'she clung hold of his coat, of his hands; her own were all covered with serpents and rings, and baubles.'[57] The same association is exploited to the full in the famous passage about the siren where 'the monster's hideous tail' rises up.[58] Becky is constantly called a siren. The word sums up all the aspects of her character. The beauty is there only to bewitch, deceive and destroy. Beneath the surface, beyond the smile, lie convulsions 'diabolically hideous and slimy'.

Thackeray the 'showman', the omniscient novelist, ever in the wings, can easily distort: at the level of plot, in the development of a career marked by bad if not heinous actions; at the level of narration by comments, epithets, insinuations. In the scene with Lord Steyne,[59] all these methods come together. The facts are that Becky is surprised at an intimate supper with Lord Steyne, not without having got rid of her husband first. The description runs – 'The wretched woman was in a brilliant full toilet; her arms, and all her fingers sparkling with bracelets and rings; ... she tried a smile, a horrid smile, as if to welcome her husband.' Metaphors provoke the reader's repulsion: '(her hands) were ... covered with serpents'. The showman comments: 'Was she guilty or not? She said not; but who could tell what was truth which came from those lips; or if that corrupt heart was in this case pure?'

Sentence is passed before the facts have been examined. And, finally, the problem whether Becky is guilty of adultery no longer matters one way or another when seen in the full light of her betrayal and her lies to her husband. Thackeray the writer and Thackeray the illustrator hold slightly discordant discourse on the same subject. The penultimate illustration in the first edition of the novel (1848) accompanies the dialogue between Jos Sedley and Dobbin. Sedley begs Dobbin not to abandon him to Becky. What in the story is an insinuation, a simple fear on Jos's part, becomes the visually dramatic sign of Jos's murder in the illustration and title. The image is of a dark silhouette with dishevelled hair and a sinister grin who, hidden behind the curtain, spies on her victim. Its title is 'Becky's second appearance in the character of Clytemnestra'.[60] If Thackeray has conceived her as a siren from the very beginning, a malificent person who descends the fatal path, one cannot complain, as some critics have done, that the insinuations about Jos Sedley's murder are not in the logic of the character.[61]

Should Becky be seen as the 'impure woman' once again? She certainly is in the sexual sense,[62] for though Thackeray is content merely to insinuate her adultery with Lord Steyne, and with the German students and the numerous other men she attracts, the

18. 'Becky's second appearance in the character of Clytemnestra.' Illustration from Thackeray's *Vanity Fair*

vagueness of the accusations appears no more than compromise with the readers' prudishness. What other meaning could the introduction to chapter 64 have, where Thackeray ironically boasts that he has evoked the 'existence of wickedness' by allusion and wit alone, and where he describes metaphorically and vividly the siren playing among corpses? And when he asserts finally that '... when Becky is out of the way, be sure that she is not particularly well employed, and that the less said about her doings is in fact the better'.[63]

A realistic novelist of society is, however, bound to see sexual impunity as relative. Such perspective destroys the myth of the impure woman placing her within two contexts, on the one hand her personal guilt and on the other hand the corruption of a whole society. In the two scenes where the question is clearly posed (with Lord Steyne in Chapter 53) the issue is sidestepped when Becky is accused and found guilty of other crimes: indifference tainted with hatred for her son, and emotional and material betrayal of her husband. The notion of impurity in any case takes on all its force only if contrasted with purity. While the second term is present in the person of Amelia it is not an absolute pole of reference. His attitude towards Amelia is ambiguous, even though one cannot doubt that she is meant to be a positive character.[64]

Whatever the circumstances Becky is however formally condemned, if not 'damned',[65] even though after all her tribulations she devotes herself to good works and the church in a provincial town,[66] contrary to the tradition which demands the sinner's disappearance or exile. In contrast to Amelia[67] Becky, with her relentless egotism, represents the anti-mother and anti-wife. To the extent that woman, in the mythology of the period, is identified with the figure of the wife and mother, and that Thackeray, despite his fierce criticism of this position,[68] subscribed to the myth emotionally if not intellectually,[69] Becky even embodies the anti-woman. The contemporary ideal prescribed sacrifice to family and society; Becky's nature is essentially predatory. The ideal woman serves her husband and guides him towards good; Becky subjugates Rawdon and drags him down with her. Becky cannot be contained within the formula of the fallen woman; but despite the breadth of Thackeray's social satire and the non-heroic nature of the characters she still represents an opposite to the image of the wife-mother. Her ambiguity expresses the author's desire to transgress the laws of respectability in order to paint a truthful portrait, and also his inability to act on his intentions.

To appreciate the author's attitude towards the characters, we must not forget the evolution of his conception of the novelist's role. Before 1845 Thackeray did not think that moral teaching was within the province of the writer. 'If we want instruction ... (he wrote) ... we prefer to take it from fact rather than from fiction. We like to hear sermons from his reverence at church.'[70] With *Vanity Fair* he modified his views. Whether he experienced at this time an inner crisis, a conversion brought about by events in his private and family life, or whether the role of novelist was deepened with the very conception of his first great novel, it remains true that the writer's moral responsibility towards a vast public became clear in his eyes. His letter to Mark Lemon on 24 February 1847 leaves no doubt about it. 'A few years ago I should have sneered at the idea of setting up as a teacher ... our profession seems to be as serious as the parson's own.'[71] It is unthinkable that the 'parson' would not totally and irremediably condemn the anti-woman.

Seduction in Elizabeth Gaskell and George Eliot

Literary critics and historians have more than once described Elizabeth Gaskell as a social writer. Her interest in social problems was bound up with Manchester, a cross-roads of ideas and events in the 1840s. After marrying the Reverend William Gaskell, she went to live there on 29 September 1832,[1] and she stayed there until she died in 1865.

Mid-nineteenth century Manchester struck English and foreign observers by its industrial character. In the heart of Lancashire, it was then the capital of cotton. The conjunction of a particularly dynamic capitalism and a huge and poverty-stricken working population (not less than 80,000 people worked in the cotton-mills)[2] were responsible for the acute industrial conflicts, demands for labour legislation, and that characteristically mid-nineteenth-century political philosophy, the Manchester School, which was individualistic, radical, for free trade and laissez-faire. Testimonies to the ugliness and wretchedness of the slums, the great inequality of wealth and the general cruelty of the industrial system are legion.[3]

'Tomorrow I meant to have dragged you through mills and manufactures without end, by way of getting one's duty done to Manchester',[4] Mrs Gaskell wrote to a friend. However, as a result of her husband's interests and functions, Elizabeth Gaskell was more than a simple spectator of the industrial phenomenon. The son of a Lancashire sail-cloth manufacturer, Gaskell, a great philanthropist, combined the functions of Unitarian minister and teacher – both in schools and privately – and editor of the *Unitarian Herald*. In the early years of their married life he introduced his wife to the local slums. 'My husband has lately been giving four lectures to the very poorest of the weavers in the very poorest district of Manchester.'[5] In 1852 Catherine Winkworth referred to two of his main philanthropic activities: organizing beerhouses and places of public entertainment and sanitary commissions to fight cholera.[6]

Elizabeth Gaskell was another philanthropist in her own right. She taught in Sunday schools, busied herself with 'soldiers' homes', with poor dressmakers and evening classes.[7] Her activity must have brought her into contact with the ill-treated and unprivileged, with many prostitutes, unmarried mothers and illegitimate children. She was therefore better placed than Dickens, George Eliot and Thackeray to tackle prostitution and the tribulations of children realistically against the background of overcrowding in slums, industrialization and a demoralized working class.

Mary Barton, heroine of that novel, nearly falls for the guiles of a seducer. Although situated in the modern framework of woman's industrial work, she is along with worthy suitor and cruel seducer part of an eternal triangle. Critics have been struck by the heroine's lack of complexity. Whether because of rudimentary psychology or unexploited thematic possibilities Mary seems even less convincing than Emily in *David Copperfield* or Florence and Edith Dombey. She is an apprentice in a dressmaker's workshop – her father believes that factory work is fatal for girls and Mary herself believes that domestic service is a 'species of slavery'.[8] At one point she is attracted by Carson, the son of an important cotton manufacturer, despite the loyal affection of young Jem Wilson, a man of her own class, a good son and a virtuous sailor. Mary's temptation has more than one point in common with Emily's in *David Copperfield*. Like Emily, Mary is endowed with beauty, good taste in clothes and aspirations. Like Dickens, Elizabeth Gaskell associates beauty and dress with vanity and sees in them the seeds of ruin. Like Emily, Mary has lost her mother, and her father immures himself more each day in his sorrow and in his desperate Chartist and trade-union revolt. Driven by social ambition and family isolation, Mary, in this too like Emily, sees Carson as the man who can help her escape from a world without hope and the instrument of a social advancement which will give her the power to do good. Even if one concedes that Mary's yearning for escape is more justified than Emily's, the way it is described until this point owes nothing in particular to the urban setting, and belongs to stereotype. Mary's reversal when she suddenly realizes she loves Jem Wilson is neither prepared for in the plot nor integrated into the narrative thread.[9] The superficiality of it all is less surprising when one knows that Mrs Gaskell never conceived her as the heroine: it was at the publisher's request that she gave up the original title, 'John Barton'. 'Round the character of John Barton all the others formed themselves; he was my hero, *the* person with whom all my sympathies went.'[10]

The hardly glimpsed seducer, Harry Carson, is also singularly misty. Although in some ways he represents the typical seducer of the new England – a textile manufacturer born of working parents – he is more archaic and oversimplified than such traditional upper-middle-class or aristocratic seducers as Steerforth or Arthur Donnithorne.

Mary's tribulations, her temptation, the first stages of her seduction, unfold against the ominous fate of her aunt Esther. As in *David Copperfield*, where Martha's destiny melodramatically prefigures Emily's, Esther, the prostitute, points to the sword of Damocles that hangs over Mary's head. Esther is neither an innocent young peasant nor a fisherman's daughter, nor a pretty milkmaid, but a Mancunian working girl. Seduced by an officer, she finds herself alone with a child and without resources after three years as his mistress. While the author vaguely and arbitrarily associates immorality and female labour she does not enter upon any details of Esther's fall; but her later experiences match the contemporary testimonies of Mayhew, Ryan and others. They were picked up by W. R. Greg in his 1850 article in the *Westminster Review* on prostitution, where in support of the same arguments he also quoted Mayhew's letters in the *Morning Chronicle*.[11] The approval of W. R. Greg (the brother of Samuel Greg, the enlightened Manchester manufacturer), is noteworthy in view of his hostility to the general inspiration of the novel.[12]

The redemption of fallen women was not one of Mrs Gaskell's favourite charities, and prostitution as a social problem was not much described in her letters (to my knowledge she does not allude either to Greg's article or to Mayhew's letters).[13] But she had some experience all the same. On 8 June 1850 she asked Dickens and Angela Burdett-Coutts to help her organize the emigration to Australia of a young apprentice dressmaker who had been seduced, abandoned and imprisoned for theft.[14] This episode is possibly the origin of *Ruth*, but certainly not of *Mary Barton*. 'The whole tale grew up in my mind as imperceptibly as a seed germinates in the earth.'

But even though the unfolding of Esther's fall corresponds in certain ways to observation, and even though this pitiful creature is supposed, like the work of Greg, Mayhew and Acton, to incite readers to pity and philanthropy,[15] Esther is not part of a realistic vision. Arthur Pollard has compared the portraits of demoralization that emerge from Mrs Gaskell's novel with other contemporary works[16] (but leaving aside Engel's). Compared with their testimonies Esther remains the fallen woman of the moralist. From the very beginning of the book she is inextricably linked with prejudices about female frivolity and coquetry, and female factory labour. She is the 'stereotyped outcast'.[17] Like Emily and above all Martha in *David Copperfield*, like Nancy in *Oliver Twist*, like the heroine of *Lizzie Leigh*, Esther loses her child and is doomed to suffering and death. Victim of her own error and the cruelty of a fellow-creature, like the others she finds a reason for living in sacrifice to loved ones. The melodramatic touches often recall Dickens. She generally appears in the setting familiar to Nancy and Martha: a dark, rainy and windy night, inclemencies that only those with nothing more to hope for – the sinful woman, the trade-unionist, and the police – have to endure. The young woman is hardly recognizable and turns away from the lamplight[18] like Lizzie Leigh who 'grovelled among the bedclothes'.[19] Like Dickens, Mrs Gaskell does not scorn apostrophizing her readers with eloquent homilies.[20] The anachronistic *and* eternal side of Esther's character struck Maria Edgeworth. She wrote that Esther 'may be in every town in the Empire ... her faults are not the result of manufacturing wrongs from masters or evils of men'.[21]

Yet in its time and place *Mary Barton* was a modern novel, or at least original. The reactions to it, whether favourable or hostile, proved this. While some industrialists and other supporters of the Manchester School, often connected with Mrs Gaskell,[22] in particular W. R. Greg, were indignant, the novel received the approval not only of Dickens and Carlyle but of such eminent philanthropists as Lord Shaftesbury, Kingsley, F. D. Maurice, and even Cobden and Bright.[23] But it is not in the treatment of the sinful woman or of seduction that we must seek the new note. Female frivolity, the puerile aspiration to become a lady, are still seen as being the principal causes of the fall. The modern element was the dangerous and suspect independence of female factory workers.

Ruth was published by Chapman and Hall in January 1853. Its genesis is difficult to establish. Elizabeth Gaskell had already touched lightly on the topic of the unmarried mother in *Lizzie Leigh*.[24] According to A. Rubenius, Mayhew's articles in the *Morning Chronicle* in 1848 and 1849 could have put her on the trail; but as noted earlier, there are no allusions to Mayhew in the correspondence or to Greg's articles to support this. 'I never spoke much on the subject of the book before',[25] she wrote to Anna Jameson. The cholera epidemic, reminiscent of the last part of the novel, was mentioned by her in 1854 only.[26] The only mention of prostitution is in the series of letters to Dickens on the subject of the young delinquent in 1850.[27] Certain details recall Ruths's seduction. Like Ruth, the girl is an apprentice in a dressmaker's workshop deprived of her family and above all her mother. It was society's indifference and the employers' irresponsibility that pushed her down. The similarities in the two stories end there.

The novel, which deals with illegitimacy – an unusual subject in England at least (Prosper Merimée disputed its originality)[28] – provoked numerous contrary reactions. But the reception was generally favourable. Despite some reservations G. H. Lewes greeted the novel in the *Westminster Review* with a rave review.[29] Catherine Winkworth and the family friend, 'Chevalier Bunsen', were enthusiastic.[30] Greg this time admired the 'beautiful and touching tale'.[31] But in Mrs Gaskell's letters we find the echo of an hostility which so wounded her that she temporarily forbad people to write to her. She alluded to 'the hard things people said of Ruth' and the insults of the *Spectator*, the *Literary Gazette* and *Sharp's Magazine*,[32] One London library withdrew the novel as 'unfit for family reading'. The criticism, which she had foreseen, affected her more than the widespread admiration. She compared herself to Saint Sebastian riddled with arrows, fell ill with a 'Ruth fever', forbad her daughters to read novels and ended by practically identifying with the sinner – accusing herself of being an 'improper woman'.[33] This disarray reveals what a deep unconscious reaction the scabrous subject brought about and her ambivalent attitude towards it. This time she had tackled the subject with a new audacity. In the earlier works, *Lizzie Leigh* and *Mary Barton*, while permitting repentance and a return to lost innocence, she still killed off the sinful woman and the child.

In *Ruth* the seduction is rapidly recounted, and the novel deals at length with the trials, rehabilitation and apotheosis of the mother, her relations with society and her son. The author invokes all possible attenuating circumstances: Ruth's innocence, her naïveté, the way her family deserted her psychologically and materially. Her mother, like Mary Barton's, is dead, leaving the family without a moral guide. Her consequent isolation is also due to the indifference of the owner of the workshop where she is apprenticed. The responsibility is emphasized of Mrs Mason – guilty of ruling her workers with a rod of iron – for leaving them completely to their own devices on Sunday, then through her hardness and lack of understanding throwing Ruth into the arms of the seducer. Elizabeth Gaskell picks up here one of her favourite themes: the employer's responsibility towards the worker, a belief shared in Manchester by her friend, Samuel Greg, the cotton manufacturer.[34] Seducer, family and employer, all responsible for the tragedy, are representative of the society that Mrs Gaskell held liable.

She contrasts two types of men in this allegedly Christian society, Benson and Bradshaw. Benson lives according to the precepts of Christ and the Sermon on the Mount. Like Christ to Mary Magdalene, he says to Ruth 'Go and sin no more'. He risks his job and reputation to give her the means to regain a place in society. In Bradshaw, on the other hand, Mrs Gaskell created a caricature of Christianity reduced to a purely conformist hypocrisy. Mr Bradshaw embodies the type of pharisee vehemently denounced by W. R. Greg in *The Great Sin of Great Cities* who, 'forgetting our own heavy portion in the common guilt', closes his eyes to the sins of the stronger sex and turns away from the 'weeping and kneeling Magdalene'.[35] Fear of contagious vice characterizes those Christians who divide humanity into two categories, the just and the damned. One of the major themes of the work is the critique of this attitude which Mrs Gaskell illustrates in the development of Bradshaw's daughter; the clash between reality (Ruth's kindness and real purity) and the abstract system obeyed by her father (damnation of the sinner) provokes in her a crisis, and then maturation. She will have to learn to see the reality of human beings beyond superficialities and conventions, the human worth of the sinner whom Bradshaw and his like consign to outer darkness. The extenuating circumstances of sin, collective responsibility, exhortation to charity and authentic Christianity, all these themes merged in the novels and inquiries of the period, and met the approval of Mrs Gaskell's friends and the public.

The originality is in Ruth's relationship with Bellingham. Through her refusal to marry her seducer Ruth denies the presupposition which more or less underpinned the conception of sinful women and of females in general. The frivolity and the exclusive aspiration of single women to marry. This refusal, this challenge to the social conventions, which Jane Eyre did not dare make, asserts Ruth's moral superiority over both the father of her child and over her judges. Contempt for the easy solution in accord with the code of middle-class respectability relates Ruth to George Eliot's heroines, in particular to Maggie Tulliver. Catherine Winkworth, among others, got the point[36] – Bellingham's moral degradation paralleled Ruth's spiritual progression, this despite the very heavy punishment inflicted on her by society. The inversion of generally accepted notions in Bellingham's fall constitutes an interesting variation on the double standard.

To the refusal of marriage is linked the problem of the illegitimate child. Just as Mrs Gaskell emphasizes that there are values and objectives more important than marriage, even for women, she also implies – more and more clearly from *Mary Barton* to *My Lady Ludlow* (1858) via *Ruth*[37] – that society must reconsider its judgement on the child's illegitimacy, that it has no right to treat an innocent victim as a scapegoat.[38] This argument is somewhat artificially put forward in *Ruth* through the illegitimate birth of the doctor who nonetheless becomes a respected member of the community.

Does this boldness[39] mean that the author is moving away from the sterotype of the sinful woman and the traditional portraying of seduction? Or, on the contrary, do the contradictions in the characters lead the reader to find her wavering between an inclination to escape contemporary conventional values and the acceptance of the contemporary myth of the fallen woman?

Bellingham, a rich young man as spoiled by life as Steerforth, Arthur Donnithorne and Harry Carson, is not a melodramatic traitor. But he is singularly lacking in substance and complexity. As for Ruth and Leonard, they never succeed in emerging from the fundamental contradictions that contemporaries already noticed. The apparent intention in relating Ruth's temptation and fall is to justify her. Elizabeth Gaskell never ceases to emphasize both the responsibility of the protagonists and the innocence of Ruth, her mental and physical youthfulness. Motherhood does not seem to have affected either her looks or her virginity. Even the cutting of her long hair by the old servant Sally does not succeed in ageing her; beneath her widow's cap her pale face appears even younger and more childlike.[40] Ruth the sinner is not only innocent and pure but good, beautiful and intelligent. G. H. Lewes would have preferred her 'more homely, and less richly endowed in good qualities and good looks'.[41] But this innocent victim whose physical and psychological purity is constantly suggested and emphasized, is considered not only by society but by herself to be guilty of a horrible misdeed.

This first contradiction betrays the author into a second. The hardly formed adolescent is also a woman of character, a devoted and courageous mother, who triumphantly resists the temptation of integration through marriage, and who becomes a town heroine during the cholera epidemic. The epidemic was necessary in order to provide Ruth with the opportunity for glorious public redemption and a credible cause of death. Opinions as to the necessity of this traditional sinner's end were divided. Charlotte Brontë and Emma Shaen[42] were against it. Lewes made no objection. The Winkworths' friend, Chevalier Bunsen, totally supported Mrs Gaskell's 'Ruth *must needs* perish, but atoned and glorified.'[43]

Death and glorification, the vision of 'light', mark the acme of 'the process of ... purification',[44] and the transfiguration of the saint. From the beginning Ruth was an embodiment of the ideal of the young virgin thrown to the lions and doomed to a heroic destiny. To satisfy convention she must illustrate the law that death is the wages of sin. Carried away by her desire to reveal the mechanisms of seduction and humanize the sinner, Elizabeth Gaskell went to the opposite extreme and turned Ruth into a saint. To attempt to weld such contradictory and antagonistic images into the same character was an enterprise doomed to failure, and as W. R. Greg observed, at the same time weakened the case for the Magdalene.[45] The two faces of the myth of woman – sinner and saint – are united in the character of Ruth. The unlikely congruence betrays Mrs Gaskell's deep unease about sexuality, seduction, prostitution and adultery.

The conflict between sin and innocence, purity and impurity, is particularly acute in Leonard and is apparent in the relationship between mother and son, especially when Ruth must both convince him of the enormity of her sin and keep his love for her. Leonard's role is not only to influence public opinion on a social problem – the fate of illegitimate children. Even before his birth Benson (who represents the positive moral pole in the novel), after mature consideration and a debate with his conscience has decided that this child could be the instrument of redemption and expiation for his mother's sin.[46] It is love for Leonard that inspires Ruth to work, study, develop her personality and refuse all dealings with Bellingham. The disembodied and transcendental nature of Ruth's maternal love is first suggested negatively; we have seen how, before and after the seduction, she is constantly associated with purity. Any suggestion of contact or physical attraction for Bellingham is out of the question in the novel. On the other hand the mystical nature of her maternal love is shown in two characteristic scenes. During her son's baptism Ruth seems to stand before God with her child, her gaze fixed on the Infinite. In another scene, which could be called 'The Virgin and the Child in the Garden', Ruth interrupts her innocent games with the cherub when church bell and hymn reaffirm God's presence.[47] Thus the sacrament of motherhood and the child's providential role are constantly emphasized not only by the sermons of the minister Benson, but also by means of religious imagery which turns the pure mother into a Blessed Virgin.

To sum up Mrs Gaskell's treatment of the sinner – more than the authors of earlier chapters she insists on the extenuating circumstances of the seduced woman's sin above all in the world of work. Despite her limited horizons, she does take into account the psychological and social factors that can lead a young girl of humble background to err. She attacks the very foundations of the double standard by denouncing the excessive severity of the world's judgement on the guilty woman – whose superiority over the seducer is shown. This stand corresponds to that of the novelists, investigators and social critics who have appeared in this book. But one is still struck by the traditional attitude to the impure woman here as well as in Margaret (*North and South*), Cynthia (*Wives and Daughters*), Miss Matty (*Cranford*). Virgin and Sinner co-exist with great implausibility in all of them. In Ruth the figure of the sinner at the end of her calvary turns into an imposing statue of the Virgin Mary and the Immaculate Conception.

With George Eliot's Hetty Sorrel in *Adam Bede*, there is a substantial departure from Edith Dombey, 'Little Em'ly' and Ruth. Hetty can be seen as the main character in an individual and collective tragedy, even though critics have often refused to grant such far-reaching significance to this first important novel of George Eliot.

Kebbel in 1881 responded only to the idyll and lingered over the harmony of village life described by Eliot.[48] Gregor and Nicholas on the other hand argue that the pastoral charm and Hetty's character, all of which blur over conflicts and confrontations, do not merge into the moral tragedy which tests and ennobles Adam, Arthur and Dinah.[49] But at least though in my opinion they minimize the complexity of the novel's social reality they recognize the tragic dimension of the seduction. F. R. Leavis reduces this part of the plot to an episode grafted more or less artificially on to an original group: Mrs Poyser, Adam and Dinah.[50]

For Leavis the love of Hetty and Arthur is nothing more than the somewhat dull tribute to a pastoral convention and to George Eliot's delight in moral and psychological themes. But this view probably overestimates the role of Dinah Morris in the plot and of George Eliot's Methodist aunt, in the genesis of the novel.[51]

The novel was originally supposed to end with Hetty's execution (Henry James's preference);[52] and it was at the instigation of G. H. Lewes who was captivated by the character of Dinah that the author decided to marry her off to Adam.[53] Dinah dominates the last section as a result of a change grafted on as an afterthought.

Hetty had an early defender in Henry James who saw her as the central figure in the work and George Eliot's most successful young female character.[54] From his reading of the early pages of the manuscript the publisher Blackwood perceived the relationship of Hetty and Arthur as an essential element in the tragedy.[55] Though rarely labelled as a conventionally dull character Hetty's frivolity and the author's marked antipathy towards her weaken the tragic impact of the seduction, even for those who, like Henry James, admire her as a fictional creation.[56] The critics who rehabilitate Hetty see in her the passive unconscious victim of a tragedy in which all the characters of *Adam Bede* participate to different degrees, of a 'Pilgrim's Progress' towards a wider and profounder vision of existence, and an enrichment through suffering and resignation.[57] But because they consider *Adam Bede* and its characters as the first serious endeavour of a relatively unskilled novelist, and because they are hypnotized by George Eliot as the moralist, they minimize the portrayal of society in this novel. To see *Adam Bede* as a village idyll or as a modernized version of *Pilgrim's Progress* leads to nonsenses like C. T. Biswell's assertion that 'Hetty's plight and Arthur's predicament are not given a social setting'.[58]

George Eliot wrote *Adam Bede* in 1859 after *Scenes of Clerical Life*. Though she began her novelist's career at a time when the other authors discussed here were well into theirs[59] she had behind her considerable intellectual activity including translating, philosophy and criticism. Schooled by her work with the *Westminster Review* and her contacts with the intellectual and philosophical avant-garde of her time she embarked on fictional creation with a background that makes Dickens, the Brontës and Thackeray look illiterate.[60] While she is clearly not at the height of her powers in *Adam Bede* she handles such diverse groups as artisans, farmers, methodists and the gentry in a reasonably convincing way. Her capacity for simultaneous identification and detachment which enables her 'to see the village church not only as the centre of a pastoral landscape but as part of European religious history'[61] is already present. Like the other characters, Hetty is conceived both as an individual and as an element in a particular environment, itself defined in relation to a still wider one. In this context, seduction is not at all an idyllic pastoral convention but a mechanism that releases multidimensional characters which illuminate both the double standard and the overlapping of classes in a feudal society.

Is pretty Hetty, the soap-opera milkmaid, conventional figure out of a pastoral idyll, a character who is psychologically and socially situated within precise limits, is she the victim of a tragedy affecting the whole community? To answer the character has to be seen in each of two stages, before and after the seduction and the revelation of her pregnancy.

The passages that introduce Hetty already throw some light. She is mentioned for the first time by Lisbeth, Adam's mother, with some irritation, as the subject of her son's affection. 'That Hetty Sorrel' is spontaneously condemned by the mother of the virtuous artisan for her inability to save money and her lack of respect for the mother. In the same dialogue between Lisbeth and Seth Bede Hetty is compared pejoratively to a flower, 'as is o' no more use nor the gillyflower on the wall'.[62] Thus while the artisan Adam lives out his time as participant in the divine plan[63] Hetty is the useless ornament. A little later, in the sixth chapter, 'The Hall Farm', Hetty is again on stage for a few moments. The author has already placed Mrs Poyser at the hub of the farm, in a framework where intense activity – emphasized by the restlessness of the time and season – reigns along with tyrannical cleanliness. Unseen by her aunt, Hetty preens herself in the polished surface of the oak table and in the huge pewter dishes. The poles of Mrs Poyser's life are 'cleanliness' – inner and outer – severity (she blasts poor Molly for her innocent attempt to flirt) and a lay gospel of work which contrasts with the contemplative mystical methodism of her niece, Dinah.[64] Hetty, whom Lisbeth has already felt a useless pretty flower basking in the pleasures of the moment, admires herself in surfaces others have spent hours polishing. Narcissism, the foundation of her personality, is hinted at for the first time, and filled out later in the other related images of the mirror and the pond. Her furtive gesture violates in some way the spirit of cleanliness.

Thus before the chapter on 'Hetty's World' George Eliot has in a few strokes succeeded in establishing her relationship with the various groups in the novel. With great economy of means – some gestures of Hetty, comments by the other characters, the counterpoint of these elements within the narrative thread – George Eliot places Hetty within and outside her context. Included in the work of the farm as a member of the family she also remains foreign to this environment whose values she unconsciously denies and destroys.

Once the geographical and psychological background has been established for Hetty as a likely victim, how does the author enter more deeply into this 'tragedy of the little soul'?[65] The key passage is the reverie[66] which contains the seed of the dramatic development of the seduction: the dream of wealth and idleness and the brief aspiration for the state of a lady. While uniting with another human being represents for many of George Eliot's heroines (Dorothea, Romola, and to a certain extent Maggie Tulliver) a step towards the realization of their aspirations for a better life, marriage for Hetty – whether the one she dreams of with Arthur or the one she envisages with Adam – is a means of escape. The entire ambition of this creature of limited sympathies and imagination is to flee her actual condition and also duty, work and the trials that are the lot of every human being. Hetty lives within a world encircled by a 'barrier of dreams'. With some cruelty[67] George Eliot insists on this alienated vision, in particular in the scene where Hetty gives herself up to a secret rite of self-adoration in a disguise that feeds her dream of grandeur.[68] The mirror is indeed the one and only dimension of the contemplation of Hetty whose gaze, unlike that of Dinah at the same moment, lingers neither on herself nor on the outside world but only on the reflection of herself in a narcissism which represents a total locking-out of the world. For Hetty does not only sin by refusing the burden of suffering and the stoic attitude that seems to be second nature to George Eliot's positive characters. During her period of prosperity before the ordeal she seems to shift into an emotional void: her imagination is entirely monopolized by dreams; and in the real world around her neither the death of Adam's father nor the ordeal of her uncle and aunt seem to move her. The scenes with Hetty, the narrator's analysis, the commentaries and contextual presentation, all these means are used by George Eliot to illustrate the narrow narcissism that blinds her to the laws of the world. Absorbed by her vision of herself transformed into a lady she does not hear the mirror fall, a noise that attracts Dinah's attention. It is by means of the images borrowed from animal and vegetable life and from the psychological world of children, that George Eliot characterizes her.[69] All the facts provided about the character, her lack of education, her egotism, her intellectual and emotional shutting-off, her desire to escape, add up to a seducer's dream victim.

Arthur Donnithorne very naturally materializes as prince charming. With the same facility as Emma Bovary, whose imagination was deformed and developed by her sentimental Catholic education, Hetty abandons herself defenceless to her narcissistic dreams. That Arthur does remain the squire and she a simple peasant are for Hetty facts of no significance.[70] The gulf separating them, whose dangerous depths she does not suspect, consolidates the dream and makes Arthur all the more desirable because he is objectively more inaccessible.

In comparison with Lovelace, Thornhill (*The Vicar of Wakefield*), and Steerforth – Machiavellian characters or melodramatic traitors – Arthur is a comparatively congenial seducer. But just as Hetty is not endowed with the intellectual and moral breadth that would allow her to accept her condition and the ordeal that strikes her Arthur, although he has a richer nature, lacks the necessary willpower and discipline to fight his inclinations. George Eliot does not portray Arthur according to any stereotype, but convincingly, as a young man conditioned by his class, aware of the consequences of his acts and prey to an interior dilemma. Each of his meetings with Hetty is preceded by a struggle with himself and followed by a firm resolve to break away. The reality of the conflict is inescapable and the author follows it sympathetically.

In short if, as Barbara Hardy suggests, Adam Bede is a new style artisan in 'the new pastoral', slotted into an industrial context,[71] Arthur Donnithorne, who foreshadows Tito in *Romola*, is the very figure of the modernized seducer. Having the best intentions towards his 'dependents', he is anxious to deserve their esteem and affection. But, weak as he is, Arthur overestimates his willpower and readily imagines himself in great roles: romantic hero, prince charming. He carries Hetty off without caring enough for the consequences. Lacking stoicism, he feels reluctant to confront hard reality until Adam forces him to do so.

But Arthur Donnithorne is above all a well portrayed representative of a social class: as demonstrated in his talk, his physique, and even his dreams. He is in a situation where the least suspicion of flirtation with a woman at once near and far can lead to disaster. All the land of Hayslope belongs or will belong to him on his grandfather's death, a traveller is told. He is 'the young Squire, the heir, the captain'.[72] These expressions of the power and distance separating the sovereign from his subjects as well as his pursuits – hunting, horses, organizing a feast, reading novels – sum up the idleness, pleasure and extroversion of an aristocrat's life. His expectations nourish his dream life. As well as being Father Christmas towards his subjects Arthur sees himself as the one who will make Adam his right hand; just as he had dreamed when he was a child to raise him to the high position of Grand Vizier.[73] When flanked by the clergyman he crosses the threshold of the farm he is received as master; he reacts protectively and benevolently towards the bustling zeal and deference of Mrs Poyser. No wonder the young squire invested with power, with the beauty and charm that only a long tradition of aristocratic privilege can confer, should appear to Hetty as an allpowerful young god, a mirage whose dangers she, unlike Mrs Poyser and Adam, is unable to perceive.

Through the few glimpses into Arthur's inner life, in particular in the dialogue with Adam who surprises him with Hetty in the woods (Chapter 27), George Eliot makes admirably clear how Arthur experiences the adventure with Hetty as a 'bit of thrilling' in the world of a flighty aristocrat for whom life is basically a game. In this dialogue,[74] George Eliot shows the sharpness of the clash between the world of Arthur, for whom some intimate gestures are of no more consequence than his usual pastimes, and the world of Adam and the Poysers from which flirtation, games and fun are excluded. These humble folk are completely absorbed by their daily work. It is a simple world where all gestures and words, kissing and courting[75] are meaningful. When in order to play down his sin Arthur explains that a kiss is a meaningless gesture, he denies Adam's vision. For Adam the kiss, the object of his desires, is the reward that he labours to deserve and the symbol of an irreversible commitment. His anger conveys their mutual lack of understanding and his powerlessness faced with the injustice of their respective relations to Hetty, as well as indignation at Arthur's irresponsibility. It is also a protest against the double standard. Adam is well aware that any sanction will weigh more heavily on Hetty than on her partner. The social implications of Hetty's drama are stressed by the complex network of relations between Adam and Arthur, now subject and benevolent suzerain, now artisan and aristocrat, violently opposed in their rivalry for a woman who causes their divergent moralities to explode against each other.

At the outset George Eliot stresses Hetty's connection with her humble country environment and also her isolation within it. In Hetty's relation to 'the sternly prosaic life of the good people about her, their wholesome decency and their noonday probity'[76] Henry James saw one of the seeds of the tragedy. The Poysers belong to the class of tenant farmers who rent land from the landowner, the Bedes to a working class in which the industrious artisan could hope to become his own master. Mrs Poyser and her children, Seth, Lisbeth and Adam, are not in financial difficulties. Mrs Poyser is helped on the farm by three girls and Poyser employs agricultural labourers. Adam could pay for a servant for his mother. Both enjoy a certain prosperity by comparison with the labourers, the rural proletariat of Stonyshire who are hardly mentioned in the novel. But their wellbeing depends on unending and desperately hard work that alone allows the Poysers to acquire and keep their reputation as good tenants and Adam to hope to equip a small business or to administer the squire's realm. Work, as a vital necessity and a way of life, implies a rigid ethic of respectability, and special punctiliousness in relations between the sexes.[77]

While the microcosm of Hayslope, as Kebbel wrote in an early article on George Eliot, was effectively 'relieved ... from all the harsher elements of feudalism',[78] the system continued to be a permanent threat to farmers. Adam's promotion, for example, depends solely on the whim of the old squire, a threatening figure whose silhouette is always behind Arthur. It is the prince's favour as well as the diligence of the Poysers that allows them to live in the parish of their ancestors. When the squire, an irresponsible landlord who still punctually demands the rent, threatens not to renew their lease, the Poysers' only strong points in this unequal battle are their reputation in the parish as good tenants and respectable people, and their hard work. The rigid dogmatism of this class is therefore a function of their objective vulnerability. In the scene where the landlord is contrasted with Poyser the squire is felt as a physical threat; he has the power to tear them from their roots.[79] But worse still Arthur's code of values threatens these weak people's most precious possession – their respectability. The link between work and a good reputation, the notion of waste[80] which is the very basis of dissolute ways, and the contrast between lower-middle-class and aristocratic ethics, are summed up in a single paragraph when Mrs

Poyser shows her repugnance at letting the Squire's servants into her farm.[81] The strict ethic resulting from precariousness is one of the main factors in Hetty's tragedy.

The presence of the Methodist preacher Dinah in Stonyshire gives the Hayslope community an extra dimension. In the first part of the plot Dinah is simultaneously set against the Poysers and Hetty. Hetty and Dinah represent two extremes: Hetty, enclosed in her narcissistic dream, lacking imaginative vision and an inner life, is contrasted with the saintly Methodist who can only achieve her spiritual aspirations in a world of suffering and distress. Dinah (who is a realized Dorothea) fights for a great cause and Hetty is included in the weak and suffering humanity she feels called upon to comfort. Nowhere is the opposition between the two girls so skilfully indicated as in the scene ('The Two Bed Chambers' – Chapter 15) where a totally self-admiring Hetty celebrates the rites of a narcissistic cult, while Dinah is absorbed in contemplation of the landscapes which envelops in the same mystical love the people of Hayslope, the unfortunates of 'bleak Snowfield' and finally, close to her, that poor lost soul, Hetty. In Dinah, who preaches conversion to the miserable working masses of Stonyshire, 'the hungry country', George Eliot introduces an element that is profoundly alien to the religion of the minister Irwine which is 'established', i.e. integrated into the feudal structure. The worlds both of Stonyshire and the new industrial hell are evoked through Dinah as well as the fervour and enthusiasm of a Methodist preaching to the masses,[82] a fervour that, as we shall see, is alone able to plumb the depths of Hetty's distress in prison.

In the preparation of the story Hetty's discovery that she is pregnant, her whole character, both as an individual and as a member of the group, is therefore portrayed in such a way as to suggest and fill out the social drama of seduction. Hetty, the pretty milkmaid who flirts with the young squire in the shadow of the underwood, becomes first the 'seduced girl' who, later, leaves her people in search of her seducer, and then a hunted animal driven to infanticide. The flight belongs to the internal logic of the egocentric and irresponsible character portrayed by George Eliot. All through the novel Hetty has fled from the unpleasant aspects of existence. By resigning herself to marrying Adam after Arthur's departure she would have chosen a solution within her reach, one capable of wiping out the past through a sort of opportunism that George Eliot despised. Hetty follows Saint-Ogg in *The Mill on the*

Floss and Maggie if she had married Stephen. The flight and finally the attempt to murder the child, the tangible consequence of a sin, which would bring down public opprobrium on her, are a rejection of reality taken to an extreme. These acts are dictated by an instinct for self-preservation; they contrast with the willpower driving Jane Eyre, Ruth and Maggie Tulliver into the service of a transcendental moral order. Maggie, after an escapade of no consequence, does not only submit to the community's verdict but chooses the hardest road by refusing to derive the least personal advantage from the suffering of others. Hetty, adrift and with no emotional roots or principles of conduct, has recourse only to flight and a gesture of destruction. Within her social and psychological context it is the natural reaction of a creature lacking in internal resources and determined in some way by the moral limits of the community. Once this code has been transgressed, she has nothing left.[83] *Adam Bede* is indeed the tragedy of a 'little soul', incapable of taking such a heavy affliction upon itself.

Can one however agree with those who deny that Hetty has any share in the moral progress through suffering which characterizes the development of the main characters, Adam and Arthur?[84] Hetty is obviously incapable of the inner development of Adam or the heroines of the later novels. One can speak of the tragedy of the 'little soul'. But tragedy is no less acute for being suffered passively. 'Animal Consciousness'[85] does not exclude being shocked into awareness. This happens on two occasions. The first is when Hetty haunted by the child's cry is driven by an outburst of unconsidered, instinctive pity to go and seek him. Although there is no question here of a tragic choice but of a reflex momentarily more powerful than the desire to flee, the gesture heralds the later acceptance of her responsibility. The second is her confession – occurring after a withdrawal into herself and a quasi-schizophrenic isolation – which in a way is also accepting her fate. Thus to a certain extent Hetty emerges from her egoism and rediscovers a human community from which she had been cast out.

But Hetty's tragedy is not an individual event. The novel's construction aims at stressing the interdependence of the whole and the parts, the characters and the context. Acts such as the flight and the aborted infanticide derive, on the one hand, from the rigid world and deep hidden fragility of the Hayslope environment, on the other from the mediocrity of Hetty which makes the flight and infanticide logical and probable if not inevitable.[86] The reaction of the groups in the novel would confirm, if it were necessary, that Hetty's seduction – not only in its origins but also in its unfolding - is a collective tragedy, a 'social disaster'.[87] The news of Hetty's drama strikes Hayslope like a thunderbolt. Adam and the Poysers are the most severely hit. For Adam, a simple soul who nevertheless gets closest to the condition of a tragic hero, the suffering is the ferment of inner progress. His growing resignation, his magnanimity towards Hetty and, finally, Arthur are steps towards a wider and deeper vision for a man who had selfishly enclosed himself in his good conscience. For the Poysers Hetty's tragedy is 'a misfortune ... worse than death'[88] to which they can only react, in a sense like Hetty herself, with denial and a closing of their ranks. Lower-middle-class morality, the more inflexible as the farmers' status in a still feudal society was precarious, opposed any transgression. Hetty's wrong destroys all the efforts of the Poysers and their ancestors to consolidate their fragile rooting in Hayslope and reduces to nothingness centuries of labour and moral severity intended to ensure security for themselves and their children. Through the reaction of Hetty's uncle, who totally rejects her, the author brings to light the limitations of a mixture of strictness, traditionalism and secular morality which was unsuited to coping with extremism in attitude or act. The Poysers do not have any of the spirituality of the Vicar of Wakefield who saw the seduction of his daughter by the Squire as an ordeal inflicted by God on the Christian.

Dinah is the only one to forgive immediately, to comfort and finally to be the instrument of conversion. It is striking that among all the people involved – passive, hostile, suffering spectators – the only one able to face the crisis is the Methodist preacher from an industrial setting. Her mystic fervour is enriched by another type of experience. For Dinah desertion of the child and even infanticide are acts that if not widespread certainly do occur (for example in the agricultural proletariat which does not appear in the novel).[89]

The reaction of the Poyser circle to the seduction conforms with their place on the social chessboard. The fate of Arthur Donnithorne is just as typical. Like Adam, Arthur undergoes a moral mutation. For him the drama signifies a dream ended by contact with reality. The man who dreamed of being the benefactor of a happy kingdom sees himself responsible for a collective tragedy. Arthur goes some way towards expiating his crime by attempting to limit its consequences: his voluntary exile and temporary renunciation of all his hopes allows the people he has wronged not to be torn from their setting. But the difference in punishment meted out to Arthur and Hetty is still striking. After his voluntary and temporary exile, his illness and remorse, Arthur returns to the scene of his crime, it seems forgiven. The conclusion implies a reintegration – albeit conditional and disenchanted – and the forgiveness of the community he has so grievously wounded. Hetty on the other hand is convicted if not executed and dies on her return journey.

G. H. Lewes, who dissuaded George Eliot from her original intention of ending the novel with Hetty's execution,[90] has a responsibility for the conventional happy end in the marriage of Adam and Dinah. With Hetty, George Eliot makes no concession. No reconciliation for her, despite the suggestion of a return to the village. Prefiguring the fate of Maggie Tulliver, the author by means of a providential death destroys Hetty's chance of reintegrating with her community, a denouement that Arthur's return would make even more unlikely. One can also consider the disparity between her fate and Arthur's as a realistic perception of the working of the double standard. The epilogue and certain episodes in the novel such as Adam's raging against Arthur suggest as much. Adam is not only the hard Puritan incapable of understanding the temptation of the young squire. He is also aware of the unequal risks run by the protagonists[91] and the crying injustice committed when Hetty moves towards the supreme punishment. He is the only one to express open indignation against it. 'It's *his* doing ... Let 'em put *him* on his trial ... is *he* to go free, while they lay all the punishment on her ?'[92] Doubtless this protest, with its social resonances, is shortlived, Adam's moral development coincides with his acceptance of the social order. But it is no less evocative of the growing condemnation of the double standard.[93]

This analysis of the counterpoint between Hetty and the others dismisses the idea that Hetty is a character imposed on the plot, that the novel is a pastoral idyll placed in an eternal world of the imagination,[94] or the study of a moral and psychological problem.[95] Hetty hardly bears comparison with the later heroines of George Eliot partly because she plays a less important part in the book and is quite different from her colleague, Gwendolen Harleth (*Daniel Deronda*), partly because she embodies everything George Eliot hates in a woman. The author's sympathy is severely tried when she draws a character with whom she cannot identify in any way, in complete contrast to the stoic resignation and aspiration for a heroic destiny of Maggie, Romola and Dorothea. Hence the reproach of 'caricature' formulated by numerous critics.[96] Hetty certainly suffers from George Eliot's inability to paint the real sensuality that ought to be one of her essential dimensions. It is here that Flaubert's superiority with Emma Bovary is perhaps most striking. But in Hetty, George Eliot has attempted and to a certain extent succeeded in painting a realistic portrait of a selfish character with limited imagination, sensibility and intelligence, of a rough creature crushed by a social structure which both exposes her to irresistible temptation and rejects her pitilessly when she yields to it. Hetty is a more convincing character than Ruth – whom Elizabeth Gaskell constantly sought to idealize – or than Edith Dombey and Emily who remain sinful women in a melodrama. George Eliot has killed off the *deus ex machina* of providential solutions that ended the careers of sinful women or transported them into purity: marriage with a virtual seducer (*Pamela*), marriage without the seducer's knowledge (*Vicar of Wakefield*), an edifying death (*Clarissa*), exile or death at the end of a life of charity in Australia or England (Emily in *David Copperfield*, and Ruth).

Arthur and Hetty are actors and victims in a tragedy which affects the entire community. *Adam Bede* is, in one of its aspects, a study of the coexistence of social groups in a still feudal rural system that unites and opposes the landed nobility and the small farmers and artisans. It is seduction, the taboo communication between two classes with divergent interests and morality, that ignites the latent violence which underlies the alleged intimacy and identity of interest of this rural community. Despite its archaic resonances *Adam Bede* is no longer the world of 'feudal harmony'. George Eliot suggests in many ways the context of the new era of the industrial revolution and the fissures in this feudal rural structure.

A Christian and chaste middle class is developing an attitude against the double standard. The Poysers do not see their niece's seduction with the resignation of the Vicar of Wakefield who, like Job, welcomes all the calamities that it pleases God to inflict on him. In the same way Arthur is no longer the incontestable representative of an arbitrary, cruel and total power, possessing the daughter of the vicar as he possesses his lands, his house, his flocks. Arthur's punishment is not providential: he is temporarily exposed to the opprobrium of his circle. His remorse, his moral progress, the internalization of the penalty, attest (as Stephen Marcus has observed about *My Secret Life*),[97] to a fundamental change in society's attitude.

Because the characters are not fully aware of the social conflicts and the class struggle (I have tried to show that they are more aware than is generally recognized) and accept the social order, people have wanted to see *Adam Bede* as a nostalgic paean to an order that has gone for ever. On the contrary, could not this novel be seen in the same perspective as Engels saw Balzac's *La Comedie Humaine*?[98] Independently of the opinions and intentions of the author, the book is a critical portrait of an anachronistic social order, weakened by internal contradictions, in which seduction experienced as a collective tragedy is a striking epitome.

The most extreme vision is of course that of Dickens. Fallen women in his novels have a primarily symbolic function, conveying contemporary values and, in the popular language of the time, melodrama. But the sinful woman is also part of a society dehumanized by its obsession with acquisitions. More complex, with values less clearcut, Becky Sharp also illustrates the criticism by a realistic novelist of the primary objectives of a mercantile and competitive society. The ambiguity of her character betrays the author's hesitations about the ideal of woman. But overall Becky is a negative character, anti-woman, the siren of the propertied classes. Mrs Gaskell's impure women come from a different environment, from the work and exploitation which she knew, relatively speaking, better than the other novelists. But her victims are not far removed from the stock figure. George Eliot is more subtle. She deals in a complex way with the dialectic of seduction and its new social implications.

The pictures are different. But can one see a kinship between the reactions of the various Victorian novelists towards prostitution, towards the fallen woman, more generally towards any sexual behaviour not consecrated by marriage? And if such a kinship exists to what extent do the novelists correspond to the investigators and social critics?

The first point is that the fallen woman always belongs with a critique of society. In Dickens and Thackeray she is part of their condemnation of a social system governed by the cash-nexus. Louisa Gradgrind, Edith Dombey and Becky Sharp appear victims of the marriage-mart, as waste-products of the struggle for material and social prestige. Just like certain old maids or wives they help to build up the case against the 'respectable social system'.[99] This view of the ravages of a growing materialism is shared by the researchers. It is expressed in particular by William Acton and the author of *The Times* article on 'The Other Side of the Picture'.[100]

Such attacks against materialism had been made before in the eighteenth-century novel. Defoe's heroes stand out against a back-cloth of puritanical economic individualism.[101] Even at the price of crime and her body which, in the words of Christopher Hill, 'she could trade either in the open market or on the black market'[102] Moll Flanders is driven by the need for financial independence. Anti-materialism and the rehabilitation of sentimental values were made even more explicit after 1740 in the novels of Richardson. It was not for money that Pamela (1741) held out skilfully against her seducer, but for marriage, the condition of respectability. *Clarissa* (1749) was an eloquent plea against marriages of interest and the disposal of a young girl for profit.

When the fallen woman is low on the social scale, anti-materialist protest combines with philanthropy. The seduced girl, a factory worker or an apprentice dressmaker, is then seen as a victim of circumstance and of society. But the Victorian novel remained vague about those aspects of the wretchedness of the exploited which, in workplace and slum, encouraged promiscuity or what was modestly called the demoralization of the poor. Protest in Dickens and even more in Mrs Gaskell is primarily a call for compassion, for the practice of authentic Christian charity. The same inspiration appears in the sermons of Carter, vicar and principal of a House of Refuge, which he called 'Mercy for the Fallen'.[103] The attitude is the same alloy of Christian charity and 'Respectable sublimation'[104] as the rescue work recommended or practised by individuals or charitable organizations. In a painting of 1854 entitled 'Found', Dante Gabriel Rossetti expressed a similar sentimentality. The young farmer, bursting with physical and moral health, bends down to raise up a woman he has recognized and whose rich and disordered clothing, and humiliated posture, reveal who she is. One of the preliminary sketches for the picture bore these verses from Jeremiah, 11,2: 'remember thee, the kindness of thy youth, the love of thine espousals',[105] which sum up the patronizing message.

The plea for charity towards fallen women which characterizes both contemporary studies and novels goes with condemnation of the double standard. Novelists and critics dwell constantly on the male's responsibility. Dickens morally condemns the seducer in the person of Carker, the instrument of Alice Marwood's and Edith Dombey's ruin, and Steerforth, by sending them both to a violent death. In the same way, in order to emphasize more clearly the iniquity of the double standard, Elizabeth Gaskell insists in *Ruth* on the spiritual superiority of her fallen woman. In *Adam Bede* George Eliot studies it again: the disproportionate punishments continue, more realistic doubtless than the poetic justice which condemns the seducer or canonizes the sinful woman. But the reactions of the seducer and the social group reflect the change in public opinion.

The propagation of an ethic which was lower-middle class to begin with, preaching work and asceticism, progressively consolidated the demand for a single norm of judgement common to men and women. There were contradictions in Greg and Acton who called both for the seducer's punishment and for compulsory control for prostitutes, through the Contagious Diseases Acts. In other words they accepted the institutionalization of the double standard. When the acts were repealed, this was one step towards an achievement of a common standard of sexual respectability for men as well as women.[106]

Criticism of the two standards was closely associated with condemnation of aristocratic life and values. In *David Copperfield* Steerforth is an ambivalent figure both for the author and the other characters. In Arthur Donnithorne George Eliot recreated a type of aristocratic landowner whose way of life undermined a whole community. The same condemnation had already been made in many eighteenth-century novels, *Pamela, Clarissa* and *The Vicar of Wakefield*. Lovelace in particular parades his taste for the dissolute aristocratic ways, his contempt for marriage and for lower-middle-class morality. The image he has of himself in relations with women, the 'eagle' in pursuit of choice game (other characters see him as a 'panther' or 'hyena'), foreshadows that of the Walter of *My Secret Life* who, a century later, treats all servants as fair game. Richardson, the middle-class novelist, expresses the aristocrat's contempt for the lower classes and the male's for the female. As middle-class respectability spreads in the eighteenth and nineteenth centuries, so does criticism of this kind of behaviour. The Victorian novel shows this, as does the condemnation of the private lives of celebrated roués.[107]

The class criticism is not different from that of the publicists and investigators. But in the novel the image of the fallen woman reveals the existence of another model. Her destiny evolves according to a consistent plan. The seduction is, in general, only outlined, except in *Adam Bede*. The fall happens unexpectedly and with no psychological or sensual motivation. The only intervening factors are rudimentary, like the desire to rise in the social scale or emerge from exploitation. After the fall sanctions descend on the sinful woman in the shape of illness, wretchedness, destitution, the wandering and solitary life of the outcast, or – supreme punishment – the death of the child. It all recalls Augustus Egg's pictorial representation of 'adultery'. Egg, the friend of Holman Hunt and Millais, did a series of three pictures entitled 'Past and Present' depicting the sin of the adulteress. Shown in 1858, the work bore the following note in the catalogue: 'Have just heard that B— has been dead for more than a fortnight … I hear that *she* was seen on Friday last near the Strand, evidently without a place to lay her head. What a fall hers has been!'[108]

The punishment society inflicts on the fallen woman, however cruel, is much less painful than the torments of her own conscience. Emily, Martha, Esther, Ruth and Lady Dedlock are consumed with remorse. Only a heroic action, sometimes demanding the sacrifice of their own life, can redeem them in their own eyes, whether this be saving Oliver Twist from the claws of Fagin, Emily from the hell of prostitution, Mary Barton from the most terrible temptation of all. Ruth sacrifices her own life during the cholera epidemic for the sake of the very people who have persecuted her; in Rossetti's picture, 'Found', the sinful woman huddles against the wall to resist the charitable efforts of the young farmer.

The fallen woman's masochistic ruminations are often accompanied by a nostalgic vision of the purity of childhood, a theme admirably portrayed in Holman Hunt's famous picture, 'The Awakened Conscience', finished in 1853. The tune the seducer is playing unawares on the piano, 'Oft in the Stilly Night', [109] all of a sudden recalls her lost innocence to his mistress, sitting on his knee. 'The Awakened Conscience' aims to show 'The manner in which … the spirit of heavenly love calls a soul to abandon the lower life'. He brings into play notions of sin, salvation and lost purity – all components of the stereotype in the novel. The picture's detailed inventory of the costly and tasteless furniture of a *demi-mondaine*'s 'gilded cage', [110] the very gestures, are certainly more developed than in the novel. But as Ruskin and other art critics noted (and this is equally true of 'Found' and 'Past and Present') the kinship between Hunt's picture and the novel is felt not only through the theme, but through the technique, which makes heavy use of symbol.

Pursued by a society that has forgotten or deformed Christ's teaching the sinful woman is doomed to a swift and cruel death, even when she is beatified like Ruth or, like Hetty, is the subject of searching social analysis. At a pinch she can be sent to Australia. The novel never admits the reintegration of the guilty woman into society through work or marriage. The image of the sinful woman is marked (as we have seen) in its conception and presentation by melodrama. Whether of lowly or noble birth, her stereotyped gestures and attitudes express without any nuance a restricted range of feelings: arrogance, pride, challenge, remorse, despair, humility. She creeps along furtively by walls, turns her face away from the light and expresses herself in inflated rhetoric.

Thus the image in the novel makes a very marked contrast to the reality described by the investigators, Mayhew, Acton and Ryan. Their observations differ in several important ways. The fallen woman who as Greg pointed out, had not often fallen from very high was not necessarily pursued by the Furies. Among women of the exploited classes prostitution, which brought in an appreciable income, was often considered a less shameful activity than work. Professional prostitution or occasional deviations were frequently accepted with resignation and fatalism, sometimes even with relative satisfaction and not with burning remorse. Reintegration into society and family through work or marriage was frequent. Contrary to the novel, in reality the supreme punishment was unusual.

By exception, in Elizabeth Barret Browning's *Aurora Leigh* the character and fate of the fallen woman are closer to the truth than in the usual fictional model. On the one hand, Marian Erle's fall is reduced to its economic and social components: the daughter of poor peasants she flees before being sold to the squire. The primitive feudalism of rural sexual mores, the wretchedness and prostitution in great cities – both social evils being accurately described[111] – leave her stranded in a Paris brothel. On the other hand, far from wallowing in remorse and expiation she proudly assumes her maternity. The child is not seen by author or mother as an instrument of redemption or punishment.[112] Marian has grown through her ordeals. A woman entirely apart, proud and worthy, she refuses the hand of Romney Leigh, the blameless hero whom she admires to distraction but does not love. The demystification of the image goes hand in hand with verbal audacity. The poetess, who is not afraid to use words such as brutal 'bastard' or 'harlot' in the poem,[113] explicitly breaks the literary and social conventions of silence.[114]

Although they naturally had certain common attitudes the gap between investigators and novelists was large. From their exploration in depth of 'The Other England' Mayhew, Ryan, Gilbert and Acton inferred a certain relativity of values that the novelists set up as absolute. Novelists fabricated a stereotype of the sinful woman by exaggerating and dramatizing the tragic consequences of the woman's deviations from the ideal of purity and chastity within marriage. But the two images coincide on one essential: the absence of a sexual dimension. Sociologists and novelists completely ignored sex in the other sense of the word. Paradoxically, the sinful woman was as lacking in this appetite as other kinds of women. There was no escape from the belief, given the backing of science, in the asexual nature of the other sex.

[15]

Conclusion

The Victorian woman as she actually was, in fact and in idea, was far from the model woman outlined in the Introduction. The woman in the home who blossoms exclusively as wife-mother is an ideal, or, I should say, only an ideal. The theory that her very weakness was also her power may have been a self-fulfilling prophecy, up to a point. But as well as that the middle-class married woman suffered from legal and social inferiority and from a lack of education. Far from celebrating her role of wife-mother she often seemed to suffer it and, at the same time, do her best to go beyond it towards greater freedom of action. The 'helpmate' theory of woman, of equality through difference, however suspect it may have been, served at this stage in the history of female emancipation to widen woman's sphere and to justify her education and instruction. Among the working classes there was little sign of the future. As wives they were illtreated in surroundings which were a mockery of a home; as mothers they had to tend children threatened constantly by undernourishment, sickness and death.

In a century when owing to male migration there was a surplus of women, middle-class spinsters, deprived of education, professional training and openings, and with no financial support from family or husband, became more and more numerous. They had to fight to earn a living, exposed to every kind of exploitation. It was, however, during this period that traditionally philanthropic female activities, teaching, care of children, of the sick and the poor, began to become 'professional'. At the same time innumerable working-class women worked under atrocious conditions in sweatshops, mines and factories. During this period, however, legislation began to regulate the conditions and working hours of women and children.

To the ranks of enclosed wife-mothers, vegetating spinsters and exploited workers can be added the prostitutes recruited for the most part from women engaged in these same degrading jobs. These many victims of the industrial revolution, in town and country, quite often resigned themselves to an existence which did not last, and, while it did, was easier than the lot of working women.

In the face of all this, is it possible to make out common features in the visions of the various novelists, despite their differences of temperament and sensibility? The unmarried woman, spinster or worker, is generally conceived either as a creature without an identity, an object of sarcasm or pity, or as a virtual and virtuous heroine who will later find fulfilment in marriage. Even with Charlotte Brontë work does not loom large in their lives. The working woman was not entitled to be heroine unless her professional life was seen as a more or less painful prelude for the future wife-mother, as in the works of Charlotte and Anne Brontë. As for the working-class working woman, she rarely appeared. Authors refrained from depicting her, unless, like Mrs Gaskell they were content to join the humanitarian protest which was linked to the belief that the woman's place was in the home. The novelists were even more scared when faced with the realities of unsanctioned sex and prostitution. Their inhibitions produced heavily symbolic characters. With the exception of Becky Sharp and Hetty Sorrel, a woman who strays from the path of virtue is frozen by the novelist in the artificial role of the sinful woman, unless like Ruth she is idealized beyond belief in order to awaken the reader's pity. It is in Dickens's imaginary world that the ideal and stereotype come closest to the contemporary model. His working women were also the most caricatured.

The fact that spinsters and impure women in the novels of this period are despised contrasts for the wife-mothers does not mean that the latter escape criticism. Thackeray went furthest. He seems obsessed by the theme of the husband's tyranny, the abject submission of the wife and by the petty slave mentality which society builds into these oppressed creatures. But his protests did not go beyond decorous limits. While he rose against the injustice of divorce procedures he seemed to accept discrimination against the divorced or 'sinning woman'. Like Anne Brontë, Mrs Gaskell and the majority of feminist reformers, he blamed husbands abusing their powers and the law rather than accuse the powers and the law themselves. He also preferred to blame the lack of women's education rather than the very ideal of the woman in the home. The sympathy of the commentator, and the moralist, if not of the artist, always went out to these 'rose-water women'.

Woman was only one in her trappings. Single, theoretically free women, sinful and impure women, display no more physical or amorous passion than did the Virgin mother and the guardian angel. They move in a world where characters and authors frequently confuse filial, conjugal, fraternal and passionate love, sublimate passion into chaste fraternal love, convert paternal love into conjugal love. This negation of the sexual dimensions of love (absent from French and Russian novels of the same period) is a testimony to the inhibitions and emotional immaturity of the authors and their characters and perhaps of their class in society: adults persisting in living their relationships in an infantile world.

The novelists naturally had reservations about society itself. The denunciation of the marriage-market, for example, which was held to be largely responsible for the unhappiness of spouses and for prostitution, is also a denunciation of a social system that was subjected to the demands of the business ethos and the cash-nexus: a world where the individual's integrity and spirituality are sacrificed to the acquisition of money and prestige. The anti-materialist protest, associated with the exhortation to genuine Christian charity, echoes the warnings of Victorian thinkers like Carlyle, Arnold, Mill and Ruskin against the egoistic philistinism of the age of laissez-faire. But the contemporary female ideal in the main weathered this protest. This was for two reasons. The first is the key role of chastity in the value system of the epoch. The protestant middle-class ethic required the man to repress his instincts and manifestations of pleasure and eroticism; he was thereby wasting precious energy required for work and production. Providentially woman was a pure spirit deprived of sensuality who only used her body for legitimate procreation within Christian marriage or to satisfy male appetites. If she did the latter outside marriage, she became an outcast from society exposed to eternal damnation. The growing condemnation of the double standard emphasized the responsibility of the male partner and brought similar disapproval down on his head. Such in broad outline, according to P. Cominos, was the process by which woman's desexualization contributed to the abstinence of the man. This image of her is one of the instruments for repression of the pleasure principle which is according to Freud a demand made by civilization and one of the causes of its malaise. It was this repression that Wilhelm Reich and Herbert Marcuse found tyrannical and excessive.

The use of the female ideal for repressive ends did not only operate through the denial of sexuality. In the working classes the wife's virtue, resignation and spirituality contributed to acceptance of the social order and the status quo. The wife who exhorted her husband to resign himself to suffering down below with the hope of a reward up above, in the next world, weakened the force of protest and rebellion. Moreover, when one examines the conception of woman's mission in Mrs Ellis and Ruskin and its manifestations in the novel, it appears that woman, the symbol of transcendence, is a cornerstone in a certain Victorian idealism. Woman is to oppose the moral corruption propagated by a materialistic system of laissaz-faire which Victorian thinkers denounced in the name of Christianity and culture. They wanted her to contribute to the maintenance of spiritual values in a century and a country given over to money, profit and competition.

The ideal of the woman in the home, as the intermediary of salvation, was at once a magnet for the increasingly numerous middle-class novel readers and the fulcrum of the novelist's mission to educate the public. At a time when some still denied the dignity of the novel which was relatively recent compared with poetry, novelists often felt obliged to defend themselves. Dickens, Thackeray, Charlotte Brontë, Mrs Gaskell, George Eliot and Trollope all proclaimed their faithfulness to reality. Dickens, it may be remembered, wanted to portray authentic thieves and criminals in *Oliver Twist*; Thackeray, to create a novel without a hero, in *Vanity Fair*, without the usual poetic justice at the end; Elizabeth Gaskell, to depict sectors of urban and industrial life till then unknown in literature; Charlotte Brontë, to create heroines of a new type, independent and impassioned. The will to transcend fictional conventions like those of the Newgate novel or the pastoral was general. But while disapproving didactic tendencies, that is to say the direct transmission of an intellectual message or a moral teaching, criticism generally agreed that the novel should be serious. We have seen that as regards female characters the real could not be separated off from the ideal. The forces limiting the faithful reproduction of contemporary reality were indeed powerful. Belief in art's edifying function, essential to the world-view of the time, was common to painters, writers and critics. According to Ruskin and Holman Hunt the work of art must dispose of its elements as realistically as possible in the service of a high moral purpose. G. H. Lewes echoed this demand in his analysis in the *Westminster Review*[1] of the 'Madonna di San Sist.' of Raphaël. This picture, where the Madonna is given the traits of a Roman peasant, but

Conclusion

expresses awareness of her noble mission, and where the cherubim are at once children and angels, combined according to Lewes an intense naturalism of presentation with idealism of conception. For Dickens, George Eliot and Charlotte Brontë, the novelist had a great moral responsibility towards the public. Thackeray judged it to be as important as the preacher's. Although they refrained from direct admonishment the moral principle dominated in this version of realism, thus resulting too often only in observance of reigning conventions. Moreover, most novelists thought, as Dickens did, that every great novelist must speak to the public as a whole and avoid shocking it too much by confronting it with a reality that is too sordid and cruel (*Oliver Twist*) or with tragic endings like those of Mrs Gaskell. Thackeray saw his responsibilities towards the public in a censorial way when, as editor of a magazine, he refused to publish a poem of Elizabeth Barrett Browning and a story. They might have shocked mothers and young girls. The Victorian novelist in his mission and his relations with the public rejected any romantic notion of the rebellious fringe artist. In order not to alienate his all-powerful public the novelist must strictly limit his disputes with the established order and not lay too much stress on the cruel and shocking sides of life.

Reviews of novels were often spiced with demands for pleasant and wholesome subjects. Harriet Martineau in a rather eulogistic article on *Villette*[2] reproached the author for inflicting useless pain on the reader through her 'subjective' and tragic vision of life. G. H. Lewes, perhaps the most serious and coherent critic of the epoch, after going on at great length about the universality of the mother's mission, criticized Charlotte Brontë's *Shirley*[3] for the characters' lack of politeness, the heroine's insolence, unbecoming for a young girl, and for her 'Yorkshire roughness'. This evaluation of the work according to certain assumptions about the nature of good taste and female refinement is a perfect illustration of the way Victorian realism conformed to contemporary norms within the limits of respectability.

While with Stendhal, Flaubert and Balzac realistic elaboration varied with the choice of subject, none of them had such regard for the public's feeling; and, from 1864, the Goncourts were already exploring underprivileged classes and the uncompromising portrayal of vice. When George Eliot refused, despite her publishers' representations, to play down the unpleasing side of Janet Dempster's character (alcoholism), when she linked the mediocrity of a certain feminine literary production to the Victorian domestic ideal and to the unfathomable general ignorance of women in England,[4] she showed the twofold awareness that was a necessary, but not sufficient condition for dealing a blow to the stereotype. Her work is marked by a complex, relatively intransigent and less prescriptive conception of realism, and an intense awareness, arising probably from personal circumstances, of specifically social phenomena. In a country lacking an intellectual and political tradition of revolt, and having the domestic ideal as a cornerstone of the system of values of the predominant middle class the novelist who made these values his own was generally not in a position to question deeply the foundations of the female. Female emancipation would have to define itself and become more aggressive; middle-class evangelical protestantism, especially the cult of the family and sexual repression, would have to be put down by protest; naturalism would have to sacrifice prescription to description, before a new idea could begin to breathe.

Notes

INTRODUCTION

1. *Histoire de la littérature anglaise*, iv, p. 42.
2. A. Wilson, 'The Heroes and Heroines of Dickens', *Dickens and the Twentieth Century*, ed. J. Gross and G. Pearson, p. 4.
3. *Histoire de la littérature anglaise*, iv, pp. 43–4.
4. Stendhal, *La Chartreuse de Parme*, 1839; Balzac, *Illusions perdues*, 1837 and *Splendeur et misère des courtisanes*, 1839–47; Flaubert, *Madame Bovary*, 1857; Eugène Sue, *Les mystères de Paris*, 1842; Zola, *Thérèse Raquin*, 1867; Turgenev, *On the Eve*, 1859, and *Fathers and Sons*, 1861; Dostoevsky, *Crime and Punishment*, 1866; Tolstoy, *War and Peace*, 1863–9.
5. *The Brontës, their Lives, Friendships and Correspondence*, ii, pp. 179–81.
6. The London Working Men's Association was founded in 1836 by Lovett and Hetherington. 1838 was the year of the National Charter, one version of which – short-lived – included women as part of universal suffrage.
7. 'The Factory Act Extension Act' and 'The Workshop Act', B. L. Hutchins and A. Harrison, *A History of Factory Legislation*, ch. 8.
8. B. Hardy, *The Novels of George Eliot*, p. 47.
9. *Continuities*, pp. 137–9.
10. See *The Life and Struggles of William Lovett*, p. 32, and a poem written in 1856, 'Woman's Mission'.

PART ONE
1
CONTEMPORARY IDEOLOGIES

1. M. J. Quinlan, *Victorian Prelude*, p. 65.
2. See *The Habits of Good Society, A Handbook of Etiquette for Ladies and Gentlemen*.
3. But, as Simone de Beauvoir points out in *The Second Sex*, this conception of woman was already present in the philosophies of antiquity and in Judaism.
4. Mrs John Sandford, *Woman in her Social and Domestic Character*, p. 13.
5. ibid., pp. 23–5.
6. John Maynard, *Matrimony: or what Marriage Life is, and how to Make the Best of it*, pp. 167–8.
7. S. Ellis, *The Daughters of England*, p. 21.
8. *Poems of Tennyson*, 'The Princess', Oxford University Press, 1912, p. 321.
9. D. Greenwell, 'Our Single Women', *North British Review*, xxxvi (Feb. 1862), p. 73.

Notes

10. 'Of Queen's Gardens', *The Works of John Ruskin*, xviii, p. 211.
11. S. Ellis, *The Wives of England*, pp. 70–1.
12. W. R. Greg, 'Why are Women Redundant?', *Literary and Social Judgments*, p. 303.
13. S. Ellis, *The Women of England*, p. 155.
14. S. Ellis, *The Daughters of England*, pp. 93, 95.
15. J. Ruskin, 'Of Queen's Gardens', *The Works*..., xviii, p. 123.
16. S. Ellis, *The Wives of England*, p. 345.
17. 'The Crown of Wild Olive', *The Works*..., xviii, p. 490.
18. C. Kingsley, *His Letters and Memories of his Life*, ii, p. 330.
19. 'The Crown of Wild Olive', *The Works*..., xviii, p. 491.
20. 'Of Queen's Gardens', p. 121.
21. C. Patmore, *The Angel in the House*, pp. 93, 95.
22. 'The Princess' and 'Isabel', *Poems of Tennyson*, pp. 5, 351.
23. J. Ruskin, *Fors Clavigera*, *The Works*..., xxviii, p. 82.
24. S. Ellis, *The Mothers of England*, pp. 382–4.
25. S. de Beauvoir, *Le deuxième sexe*, i, p. 276.
26. S. Ellis, *The Women of England*, p. 50; *The Mothers of*..., pp. 46–9.
27. N. Spain, *Mr. and Mrs. Beeton*, p. 89.
28. I. Beeton, *The Book of Household Management*, p. 1.
29. S. Ellis, *The Daughters of*..., pp. 7, 82, 83, 252, 253, and *The Wives of*..., p. 260.
30. S. Ellis, *The Mothers of*..., pp. 205, 207, 334.
31. P. Bensimon, 'La femme anglaise à l'époque romantique', pp. 175, 176, 180.
32. J. Ruskin, 'Of Queen's Gardens', p. 136.
33. In 1869 the Reverend G. Butler still based his argument in favour of education and professional training for women on the dogma of their particular aptitudes and functions which fitted them for distribution and administration rather than production. *See* 'Woman's Work and Woman's Culture', p. 50.
34. F. P. Cobbe, 'The Final Cause of Woman', *Woman's Work and Woman's Culture*, J. Butler, ed., p. 10.
35. J. Ruskin, 'Of Queen's Gardens', *The Works*..., xviii, p. 122.
36. S. Ellis, *The Women of*..., p. 14.
37. ibid., p. 52.
38. ibid., p. 53; see also Baldwin Brown's sermon in W. S. Houghton, *The Victorian Frame of Mind*, p. 345.
39. S. Ellis, *The Education of the Heart*, pp. 156–7.
40. W. R. Greg, *The Great Sin of Great Cities*, p. 10.
41. H. Mayhew, *London Labour and the London Poor*, iv, p. 212.
42. S. Marcus, *The Other Victorians*, p. 13.
43. These passages do not occur in the first two editions of *Functions and Disorders*... 1857 and 1858, but only, to the best of my knowledge, in the third edition (1862).
44. W. Acton, *Functions and Disorders*..., (3rd edn), p. 102.
45. '... a most painful and distressing climax to her other agitations': ibid., pp. 74, 75.
46. ibid., p. 102.

47. ibid., p. 102.
48. ibid., p. 103.
49. J. Killham, *Tennyson and The Princess*, ch. 5 and 6.
50. J. A. and O. Banks, *Feminism and Family Planning in Victorian England*, pp. 37–41.
51. D. M. Stenton, *The English Woman in History*, p. 319.
52. J. Killham, *Tennyson...*, p. 41.
53. P. Fryer, *The Birth Controllers*, ch. 4, 5, 6.
54. J. A. and O. Banks, *Feminism...*, p. 21.
55. H. Martineau, *Society in America*, i, p. 205.
56. B. R. Parkes, *Remarks on the Education of Girls*, p. 17.
57. Mrs Hugo Reid, *A Plea for Woman*, pp. 11–15.
58. 'Woman in France, Madame de Sablé', *The Westminster Review*, vi (Oct. 1854), p. 451.
59. Mrs H. Reid, *A Plea for Woman*, pp. 31, 32, 46.
60. B. Bodichon, *Women and Work*. p. 7.
61. B. Bodichon, 'The Position of Women in Barbarism and Among the Ancients', *The Westminster Review*, viii (Oct. 1855), p. 379.
62. J. W. Kaye, 'Employment of Women', *North British Review*, xxvi (Feb. 1857), p. 305.
63. B. Bodichon, 'The Position of Women...', pp. 379, 431.
64. F. P. Cobbe, 'The Final Cause of Woman', *Woman's Work and Woman's Culture*.
65. Manuscript by H. Taylor in M. Packe, *John Stuart Mill*, p. 125.
66. Those working now on the edition of the complete works of Mill doubt whether Harriet Taylor wrote the article and attribute it to Mill himself.
67. M. Packe, *John Stuart Mill*, pp. 124–5, 137, 347.
68. Mrs H. Reld, *A Plea for Woman*, pp. 48, 56–52.
69. M. Packe, *John Stuart Mill*, p. 493.
70. J. Kamm, *Rapiers and Battleaxes*, pp. 127–32.
71. See p. 10. Mill's speech profoundly impressed Kate Amberley. His personality and oratorical talents also impressed Lady Frederick Cavendish, despite her conservative and anti-feminist tendencies, when she heard him on 13 April 1866. See *The Amberley Papers*, 1, p. 299 and *The Diary of Lady Frederick Cavendish*, 1, p. 304.
72. *The Diary of Lady Frederick Cavendish*, ii, p. 22.
73. Ida, in *The Princess*, Elpsie in the *Bothie of Tober-na Vudich* (A. H. Clough), The heroine of *The Angel in the House* (Coventry Patmore).
74. Owenite trends and birth-control propaganda. See note 100, chapter 3.

2

THE LEGAL POSITION

1. H. Taine, *Notes sur l'Angleterre*, pp. 102, 103, 106.
2. F. A. Hayek, *John Stuart Mill and Harriet Taylor*, p. 168.
3. E. Reiss, *Rights and Duties of Englishwomen*, p. 6.
4. 'Treatment of Women', *Eliza Cook's Journal*, 9 August 1851, p. 225.
5. 'A man and wife are one person in law; the wife loses all her rights as a single woman, and her existence is entirely absorbed in that of her

husband.' B. Bodichon, *A Brief Summary in Plain English Language of the Most Important Laws Concerning Women*, p. 3.

6. '... her being is absorbed in that of her husband', C. Norton, *A Letter to the Queen on Lord Chancellor Cranworth's Marriage and Divorce Bill*, p. 8.

7. J. W. Kaye, 'The Non-Existence of Women', *North British Review*, xxiii (August 1855), pp. 537–9.

8. C. Norton, *Letter to the Queen...*, p. 4.

9. E. Reiss, *Rights and Duties of English Women*, pp. 7, 45, 47.

10. ibid., p. 47.

11. ibid., p. 48.

12. By the editors of the complete works of J. S. Mill, notably J. W. Robson.

13. J. S. Mill or H. Taylor [Leader], *Morning Chronicle*, 31 May 1860, p. 4.

14. Even after seventeen years of separation, Caroline Norton did not have the right to sign a lease. C. Norton, *Laws for Women in the 19th Century*, p. 161.

15. E. Reiss, *Rights and Duties ...*, p. 31.

16. C. Norton, *A Review of the Divorce Bill of 1856*, p. 13; C. Norton sums up her situation: 'If she be robbed, she cannot prosecute. If she be libelled or slandered, she cannot prosecute. If she earn money, she cannot sue for it. She can make neither deed nor will.' ibid., p. 15.

17. E. Reiss, *Rights and Duties ...*, pp. 21, 32.

18. Mrs H. Reid, *A Plea for Woman*, p. 171.

19. B. Bodichon, *A Brief Summary*, p. 4.

20. J. W. Kaye, 'The Non-Existence of Woman', *North British Review*, xxiii, (August 1855), pp. 552–3; 'The Marriage and Divorce Bill', *North British Review*, xxvii (August 1857), p. 164.

21. C. Norton, *A Letter to the Queen*, pp. 84–5.

22. C. Cornwallis, 'The Property of Married Women', *Westminster Review*, x (October 1856), pp. 342–4.

23. It is significant that a handbook of etiquette of the period, urged prudence in a veiled way on engaged girls, in the shape of a marriage-settlement that would protect them from the possible risks of a husband's passion for gambling or speculation. *The Habits of Good Society*, p. 366.

24. J. W. Kaye, 'The Marriage and Divorce Bill', *North British Review*, xxvii (August 1857), p. 165; C. Cornwallis, 'The Property of Married Women', *Westminster Review*, x (October 1856), p. 337.

25. E. Reiss, *Rights and Duties ...* pp. 24–5 and 31–4.

26. Her 1854 tract, *A Brief Summary in Plain English Language ...* (reissued in 1858) caused a sensation with its simplicity and brutality. Following on from it she organized committees to support a bill, the Law Amendment Society, with a view to protecting the wife's property, and drew up a petition to Parliament signed among others by Elizabeth Barrett Browning, Jane Carlyle, Elizabeth Gaskell, Mary Howitt, Anna Jameson, G. Jewsbury, Harriet Martineau etc. It insisted on the fact that the legislation which still attributed sole responsibility to the husband to support the family was anachronistic at a time when married women were entering the spheres of literature and art in order to earn money for their families. See C. Cornwallis art. cit. *Westminster Review*, pp. 336–8 and J. Kamm, *Rapiers and Battleaxes*, pp. 83–90.

Notes

27. E. Reiss, op. cit., p. 127, J. W. Kaye, 'The Marriage and Divorce Bill', *North British Review*, xxvii (August 1857), p. 167, 'The New Law of Divorce', *The English Woman's Journal*, i (May 1858), p. 187.

28. 'The Workings of the New Divorce Bill', *English Woman's Journal*, i (July 1858), p. 340.

29. 'Property of Married Women', *English Woman's Journal*, i (March 1858), p. 59.

30. ibid., p. 59.

31. E. Reiss, *Rights and Duties* ..., pp. 17–18.

32. T. H. Lister in 'Rights and Conditions of Women', *Edinburgh Review*, lxxiii (April 1841), p. 207, states that in the event of separation, even when caused exclusively by the *husband*'s vices, the children, even very young ones, can be torn away from the *wife*. He can appoint his mistress to look after them instead of the mother, and, doubly wronged, the wife and mother cannot see them without the husband's permission.

33. C. Norton, *The Separation of Mother and Children*, pp. 45–93. J. G. Perkins, *The Life of Mrs Norton*, pp. 97–100, 140.

34. T. H. Lister, 'Rights and Conditions of Women', *Edinburgh Review*, lxxiii (April 1841), p. 208.

35. J. G. Perkins, op. cit., pp. 145–6.

36. E. Reiss, *Rights and Duties* ..., pp. 97–8.

37. E. Reiss, ibid., p. 12.

38. J. S. Mill, *Morning Chronicle*, 31 May 1850, 'Protection of Women', *The Sunday Times*, 24 August 1851, p. 2.

39. 'Wife Torture in England', *Contemporary Review*, April 1878.

40. E. Reiss, op. cit., p. 85, and O. R. McGregor, *Divorce in England*, pp. 22–3.

41. J. W. Kaye, 'The Marriage and Divorce Bill', *North British Review*, xxvii (August 1857), p. 163.

42. O. R. McGregor, *Divorce in England*, p. 17 and J. W. Kaye, ibid., p. 166.

43. E. Reiss, op. cit., p. 14 and C. Norton, *Letter to the Queen*, p. 11.

44. K. Thomas, 'The Double Standard', *Journal of the History of Ideas*, 1959, p. 201.

45. O. R. McGregor, *Divorce in England*, pp. 10–11, 17–18.

46. J. W. Kaye, 'The Non-Existence of Women', *North British Review*, xxiii (August 1855), p. 546.

47. O. R. McGregor, op. cit., pp. 18 and 22.

48. 'Report from the Select Committee', quoted by C. Norton, *A Review of the Divorce Bill of 1856*, p. 113.

49. C. Norton, *A Letter to the Queen* ..., p. 65.

50. K. Thomas, 'The Double Standard', pp. 210–11.

51. E. Reiss, *Rights and Duties* ..., p. 55.

52. O. R. McGregor, *Divorce in England*, p. 18.

53. K. Thomas, 'The Double Standard', pp. 199, 200 and 205.

54. C. Norton, *A Plain Letter to The Lord Chancellor* ..., p. 8.

55. O. R. McGregor, *Divorce* ..., pp. 19 and 20.

56. J. W. Kaye, 'The Marriage and Divorce Bill', *North British Review*, xxvii (August 1857), pp. 170–1 and 'The Non-Existence of Women', *North British Review*, xxiii (August 1855), pp. 173, 543 and 544.

57. O. R. McGregor, *Divorce* ..., p. 20.

3

DAILY LIFE

Aristocratic and Middle-Class Women

1. *The British Mothers' Magazine*, iii–iv (March 1847), p. 66.
2. ibid., iii–iv (November 1847), p. 246.
3. J. A. Banks, *Prosperity and Parenthood*, p. 33.
4. See H. Mayhew, *Whom to Marry and How to get Married or, the Adventures of a Lady in Search of a Good Husband*, illustrated by George Cruikshank, and this passage in *The Comic Almanack*, in 1845, p. 66: 'Gardening for Ladies. The mamma's calendar for July. You daughters now demand serious attention. Dress and plant them in rows for evening parties. Weed poor relations.'
5. *The Economy for the Single and Married by One Who Makes Ends Meet*, p. 26, *How to Woo, How to Win* ..., p. 6.
6. *The Ladies' Companion at Home and Abroad*, 20 April 1850, p. 264.
7. J. A. Banks, *Prosperity* ..., pp. 41–3.
8. J. A. Banks, *Prosperity* ..., p. 41.
9. W. Acton, *Prostitution* ..., p. 171.
10. E. B. Browning, *Elizabeth Barrett to Miss Mitford* ..., p. 264, January and February 1846.
11. *Twenty-two Unpublished Letters*, pp. 71–3.
12. *The Letters of Elizabeth Barrett Browning*, ed. F. G. Kenyon, ii, pp. 72–3, 2 June 1852.
13. *The Amberley Papers*, ed. Bertrand and Patricia Russell, i, p. 290.
14. As in the case of the lady in waiting, Lehzan, see E. Longford, *Victoria R.I.*, pp. 184, 198–203.
15. *The Letters of Elizabeth Barrett Browning*, i, 19 December 1846, p. 312 and 5 November 1846, p. 306.
16. R. Fulford, *Dearest Child*, 16 May 1860, p. 254.
17. ibid., p. 150.
18. *The Letters of R. Browning and E. Browning*, i, 24 December 1845, p. 353.
19. ibid., i, 12 May 1847, p. 330.
20. '... Edward has no taste for the company of wife and children by themselves ...' *The Ladies of Alderley*, ed. M. Mitford, 5 October 1841, p. 25.
21. '... I have been a desolate female most of the autumn', ibid., 4 December 1846, p. 144 – 'I am getting weary of my widowhood, I have now been alone three months out of four ...' ibid., 26 November 1846, pp. 133–4, 143.
22. ibid., 10 March 1846, p. 141.
23. *The Letters of Mrs Gaskell*, p. xii–xiv; contrary to A. B. Hopkins, A. Rubenius insists on the tensions between the couple. A. Rubeinius, *The Woman Question in Mrs Gaskell's Life and Work*, ch. 2 and A. B. Hopkins, *Elizabeth Gaskell, her Life and Work*, p. 376.
24. *The Letters of Mrs. Gaskell*, (418), p. 537 and (570), p. 759. Also (510), p. 690, 'Mr Gaskell is away on his annual wanderings, ... so I neither know where to find him, nor when he will return.'

25. ibid., (191), p. 280.
26. ibid., (69), p. 109.
27. ibid., (70), p. 113.
28. ibid., (305), pp. 470–8, (282), (305), (326), (386).
29. ibid., (89), p. 142.
30. ibid., (394), p. 506, (40), p. 513, (418), p. 534, (553), p. 736.
31. ibid., (557), (584).
32. *The Letters of Mrs. Gaskell*, (276), p. 379.
33. *Mary Howitt, an Autobiography*, ii, pp. 114–17.
34. T. Holme, *The Carlyles at Home*, pp. 140–1.
35. ibid., p. 143.
36. ibid., pp. 146–50.
37. *The Ladies of Alderley*, p. 108.
38. ibid., pp. 134, 135, 199.
39. ibid., p. 199.
40. 'There is no place like home', *The British Mothers' Magazine*, i and ii (July 1845), pp. 145–6.
41. See the astonishing analysis of this phenomenon that Margaret Grey, Josephine Butler's aunt, made as early as 1853. J. E. Butler, *Memoirs of John Grey of Dilston*, pp. 326–7.
42. J. A. Banks, *Prosperity and Parenthood*, p. 101.
43. J. A. Banks, *Prosperity ...*, pp. 85 and 101, *Feminism and Family Planning*, p. 65.
44. 1,172 pages with 500 wood-engravings and 50 colour-plates, which appeared in 24 monthly instalments from November 1858 to October 1861 and as one volume in 1961, republished two years later. M. M. Hyde, *Mr and Mrs Beeton*, p. 89.
45. Servants were a favourite theme for satire. See in particular Mayhew's tale illustrated by G. Cruikshank, *The Greatest Plague of Life, or the Adventures of a Lady in Search of a Good Servant*, and *The Comic Almanack*.
46. *The Diary of Lady Cavendish*, J. Bailey ed., i (4 October 1866), p. 243.
47. ibid., p. 262.
48. M. G. Jeune, *Pages from the Diary of an Oxford Lady, 1843–1862*, pp. 25, 29, 60, 73.
49. *The Letters of Mrs. Gaskell*, (468), p. 617.
50. T. Holme, *The Carlyles at Home*, p. 14.
51. ibid., pp. 152 and 172.
52. ibid., pp. 15–33.
53. A. Hayter, *A Sultry Month ...*, pp. 26–7.
54. Mary Howitt, *an Autobiography*, i, p. 258.
55. See the passage in a letter to C. E. Norton where she lists all the interruptions in a day, the time to put the boiled beef on, flower arrangement, lengthening a skirt, wages and day off for the governess. *The Letters of Mrs Gaskell*, (383), p. 189.
56. ibid., (421), p. 544.
57. *Letters and Memorials of Jane Welsh Carlyle*, iii, letter 214, pp. 19–20, ii, letter 109, p. 38.
58. 'This was the year (only the first year, alas!) of repairing our house ... My own little heroine was manager, eye, inventress, commandress

guiding, head and soul of everything ... She feared no toil howsoever unfit for her, had a masked "talent in architectury" ... Meanwhile, to escape the horrors of heat and dust, I fled (or indeed was dismissed) ...', ibid., ii, letter 140, p. 517.

59. ibid., iii, letter 235, pp. 77–8.

60. ibid., iii, letter 259, p. 136.

61. T. Holme, op. cit., pp. 42, 49, 54–5.

62. 'Do not go to Mr Carlyle for sympathy, do not let him dash you with cold water. You must respect your own work and your own motives, ... So begin, begin! half your loneliness comes from having no outlet for your energies, and no engrossing employment ... You ought to have a dozen daughters – and I am sure they exist somewhere, ... So let your work be dedicated to your "unknown daughters".' *Letter of G. E. Jewsbury to J. W. Carlyle*, letter 121, pp. 426–7.

63. A. Hayter, *A Sultry Month* ..., p. 122.

64. 'Chapters on Maternal Associations'. *The British Mothers' Magazine*, i and ii (July 1845), p. 163.

65. Blessedness of the Sabbath, Brief Remarks on Infant Salvation, The Child's Occupations for the Sabbath, Children Reading the Scripture, Choice of Pious Domestics, Conversion of a Servant, etc., ibid., v and vi, (1849).

66. *The Letters of Mrs Gaskell*, (101).

67. *Prosperity and Parenthood*, p. 3.

68. *The Letters of Charles Dickens*, 16 June 1837, i, p. 113.

69. 'Kate was taken very ill on the way from this place to Glasgow, on Tuesday – a miscarriage, in short, coming on, suddenly, with railway carriage.' ibid., ii. New Year's Day 1848, p. 69.

70. 'Mrs Dickens is ... in that uninteresting condition which makes visiting irksome to her,...', ibid., ii, 4 August 1858, p. 113.

71. A. A. Adrian, *Georgina Hogarth and the Dickens Circle*, p. 50.

72. E. Johnson, *Charles Dickens, his Tragedy and Triumph*, i, pp. 266–7, and ii pp. 906–8.

73. *The Ladies of Alderley*, letter 86, p. 76.

74. ibid., letter 174a, pp. 145–6.

75. R. Fulford, *Dearest Child*, p. 78.

76. ibid., 21 April 1858, p. 94.

77. ibid., p. 94.

78. '... – aches and sufferings and misery and plagues ... and enjoyments, etc. to give up – constant precautions to take ...' ibid., 24 March 1858, p. 77.

79. '... one feels so pinned down – one's wings clipped in fact, at the best ... only half oneself –' ibid., 24 March 1858, p. 78.

80. ibid., 15 June 1858, p. 115.

81. E. Longford, *Victoria R.I.*, pp. 191, 231–2.

82. R. Fulford, *Dearest Child*, 15 June 1858, p. 115.

83. *The Letters of Queen Victoria*, i, p. 32.

84. R. Fulford, *Dearest Child*, pp. 195–6.

85. *The Ladies of Alderley*, ed. N. Mitford, 26 August 1862, p. 336.

86. *Twenty-two Unpublished Letters*, 7 January 1847, p. 23.

87. ibid., March 1855, p. 80.

88. J. A. Banks, *Prosperity* ..., p. 5.

89. O. McGregor, *Divorce in England*, pp. 82–3.

90. Malthus is often wrongly associated with birth-control. He envisaged limits on the size of families only through abstention from marriage and through chastity and absolutely repudiated methods to prevent conception. See P. Fryer, *The Birth-Controllers*, pp. 70–1 and G. Himmelfarb, *Victorian Minds*, p. 103.

91. 'The Diabolical Handbills', 'To the Married of Both Sexes', and 'To the Married of Both Sexes of the Working Population' (1823).

92. *Every Woman's Book; or What is Love?* sold five thousand copies and in 1826, the year it appeared, was reissued three times; see J. A. Banks, *Prosperity* ..., pp. 24–6, P. Fryer, *The Birth-Controllers*, pp. 43–5, 77, and M. J. Packe, *The Life of John Stuart Mill*, pp. 56–9.

93. P. Fryer, *The Birth-Controllers*, ch. ii.

94. See P. and B. Russell; *The Amberley Papers*, ii, and P. Fryer, *The Birth-Controllers*, ch. 12, 16, 17.

95. J. A. Banks, *Prosperity* ..., ch. 10, and P. Fryer, *The Birth-Controllers*, ch. 16 and 17.

96. J. A. and O. Banks, *Feminism and Family Planning in Victorian England*, pp. 105–6, 124.

97. It should be noted that, as early as 1847, a writer in the *British Mothers' Magazine* reckoned that large families were far from being a blessing, above all when resources were limited, iii, iv (July 1847), p. 149.

98. J. A. Banks and O. Banks, *Feminism and Family-Planning* ..., pp. 86–7.

99. It is strange that this episode, so astonishing for that era, is not mentioned by the Banks, nor P. Fryer, nor stressed by the editor of the letters, Nancy Mitford.

100. Edward wrote to Henrietta on 9 November 1847: 'This your last misfortune is indeed most grievous ... What can you have been doing to account for so juvenile a proceeding, it comes ... to distress all your family arrangements & revives the nursery ... I only hope it is not the beginning of another flock for what to do with them I am sure I know not ... it is too late to mend...'
H. Stanley replied the same day:
'A hot bath, a tremendous walk & a great dose have suceeded but it is a warning ... I feel not too well.'
E. Stanley to Henrietta, 10 November 1847:
'I hope you are not going to do yourself any harm by your violent proceedings, for though it would be a great bore it is not worth while playing tricks to escape its consequences. If however you are none the worse the great result is all the better.'
Henrietta to Lord Stanley, 10 November 1846:
'I was sure you would feel the same horror I did at an increase of family but I am reassured for the future by the efficacy of the means.'
N. Mitford, *The Ladies of Alderley*, pp. 169–71.

101. ibid., p. 249.

102. H. Taine, *Notes sur l'Angleterre*, pp. 268–9.

103. M. G. Jeune, *Pages from the Diary of an Oxford Lady, 1843–62*, p. 73, *passim*

104. ibid., p. 73.

105. *The Diary of Lady Frederick Cavendish*, i, pp. 254 and 263.

106. *The Letters of Mrs. Gaskell*, (131), (102), (100), (134), (352).

107. P. Thomson, *The Victorian Heroine*, pp. 17–24.

108. *The Letters of Mrs. Gaskell*, (61), (62), (63).

109. ibid., (154), (480).

110. ibid., (494a), (630).

111. *Mary Howitt, An Autobiography*, i, p. 251.

112. *The Diary of Lady Frederick Cavendish*, i, pp. 252–4.

113. ibid., ii, p. 5.

114. Sarah Austin was great friends with J. S. Mill whom she aided on several occasions. See M. St. J. Packe, *The Life of John Stuart Mill*, pp. 50, 74, 87, 163, 178, etc. and J. Ross, *Three Generations of English Women*, i, p. 97.

115. ibid., i, p. 129.

116. ibid., i, p. 130. She also corresponded with J. S. Mill, Carlyle, Layard, Sir Robert Peel, Guizot, A. Court, Vigny, Tocqueville, the Brothers Grimm.

117. *The Ladies of Alderley*, p. 190.

118. ibid., p. 204.

119. ibid., p. 208.

120. *The Stanleys of Alderley*, N. Mitford, p. XII.

121. *The Amberley Papers*, i, pp. 387–8.

122. ibid.

123. *The Amberley Papers*, i, p. 403.

124. *The Diary of Lady Frederick Cavendish*, i, pp. 250, 261 and 304.

125. ibid., i, p. 304.

126. *The Ladies of Alderley*, pp. 2, 32, 131.

127. *The Amberley Papers*, i, p. 386.

128. *The Diary of Lady Frederick Cavendish*, i, pp. 243–51.

129. M. Lockhead, *Elizabeth Rigby, Lady Eastlake*, pp. 22, 45–63.

130. ibid., pp. 106, 109, 128.

131. J. Ross, *Three Generations of Englishwomen*, i, p. 137 and ii, p. 151.

132. *The Letters of Mrs. Gaskell*, (418), p. 534.

133. 'I look forward to a real life's work for us both. I shall do all – under your eyes and with your hand in mine – all I was intended to do : may but you as surely go perfecting – by continuing – the work begun so wonderfully – a rosetree that beareth seven times seven – ...' *The Letters of Robert Browning and Elizabeth Barrett Browning*, i, p. 457, 6 February 1846.

134. *The Letters of Elizabeth Barrett Browning*, i, p. 354–5, ii, pp. 195, 228, 229.

135. *Letters of the Brownings to George Barrett*, ii, p. 258.

136. ibid., i, p. 471, ii, p. 258.

137. *Mary Howitt, An Autobiography*, ii, pp. 22 and 23.

138. ibid., ii. p. 39.

139. ibid., i, p. 284, ii, pp. 58 and 63, ii, p. 46.

140. '... – a set of shilling books to be sold at all the railway stations in the kingdom, for railway travellers.' ibid., ii, p. 48.

141. '... I must be a little religious, and I mean to have a death in it, as the readers of the tract, I have been told, always ask for "a pretty tract with a death-bed in it".' ibid., ii, p. 45.

142. ibid., ii, p. 46.
143. ibid., ii, p. 46.
144. *The Letters of Mrs Gaskell*, (308), p. 411.
145. ibid., (308), p. 411; ibid., (137), p. 205; ibid., (384), p. 492.
    'It is hard work writing a novel all morning, spudding up dandelions all afternoon and writing again at night', she writes, ibid., (465), p. 614.
146. *The Letters of Elizabeth Barrett Browning*, ii, pp. 195–6.
147. Mary Howitt, *An Autobiography*, ii, p. 86.
148. *The Letters of Elizabeth Barrett Browning*, i, p. 84.
149. *Mrs. Browning*, pp. 142–4.
150. '... daily small Lilliputian arrows of peddling cares; it keeps them from being morbid...' *The Letters of Mrs Gaskell*, (68), p. 106.
151. 'One thing is pretty clear, *Women*, must give up living an artist's life, if home duties are to be paramount.' ibid., (68), p. 106.
152. '... I am every day more convinced that *we women*, if we are to be *good* women, *feminine* and *amiable* and *domestic*, are not *fitted to reign*; at least it is *contre gré* that they drive themselves to the work which it entails.' *The Letters of Queen Victoria*, ii, 17 February 1852, p. 444. 'We women are not *made* for governing – and if we are good women, we must *dislike* these masculine occupations.' ibid., ii, 3 February 1852, p. 438.
153. Of whom Jane Carlyle maliciously remarked: '... an air of moral dullness ...', A. B. Hopkins, *Elizabeth Gaskell ...*, p. 314.
154. E. Gaskell, *The Life of Charlotte Brontë*, pp. 102–5, 216.
155. *The Letters of Mrs. Gaskell*, (72), p. 118.
156. E. Gaskell, *The Life of Charlotte Brontë*, p. 238.
157. Her friend Susanna Winkworth confirmed this: 'Her books indeed were only written when all possible domestic and social claims had been satisfied.' *M. J. Shaen, Memorials of Two Sisters, Susanna and Catherine Winkworth*, p. 242.
158. *The Letters of Elizabeth Barrett Browning*, ii, p. 189.
159. *The Letters of Elizabeth Barrett Browning*, ii, pp. 444 and 445.

The Working Classes

1. In the opinion of O. McGregor, for example, in his work *Divorce in England*, p. 77, and in his bibliography to the *British Journal of Sociology*.
2. J. W. Kaye, 'Outrages on Women', *North British Review*, xxv (May 1856); pp. 234–5.
3. *The Morning Chronicle*, 13 March 1850, p. 5.
4. J. B. Owen, 'Popular Investments', *in Meliora: or, Better Times to Come*, ed. Viscount Ingestre, p. 131.
5. J. W. Kaye, 'Outrages on Women', *North British Review*, xxv (May 1856), p. 234.
6. J. S. Mill, *The Morning Chronicle*, 29 March 1850, p. 4.
7. J. S. Mill, 'A recent Magisterial Decision', *The Morning Post*, 8 November 1854, p. 3.
8. J. S. Mill, 'Protection of Woman', *The Sunday Times*, 24 August 1851, p. 2.
9. 'Treatment of Women', *Eliza Cook's Journal*, v (9 August 1851), p. 225.

Notes

10. W. Gilbert, *Dives and Lazarus*, p. 41.
11. ibid., p. 170.
12. M. Hewitt, *Wives and Mothers* ..., p. 50.
13. ibid.
14. J. W. Kaye, 'Outrages on Women', *North British Review*, xxv (May 1856), p. 240.
15. *Dives and Lazarus*, p. 178, *Meliora: or Better Times to Come*, ed. Viscount Ingestre, pp. 164–5, and 187–90.
16. H. Mayhew, art. cit., *Meliora:* ..., pp. 262–3, 280.
17. F. Engels, *The Condition of the Working Class in England in 1844*, p. 166.
18. H. Taine, *Notes sur l'Angleterre*, p. 184.
19. J. W. Kaye, 'Outrages on Women', *North British Review*, xxv (May 1856), pp. 249–50.
20. J. W. Kaye, art. cit., pp. 249–51.
21. January, February, March 1848.
22. Concerning the homilies exhorting the poor to virtue, piety, the worship of work and sobriety, see Mary Howitt on the aims of *Howitt's Journal*, *Mary Howitt, An Autobiography*, ii, p. 39.
23. 'How to make the best of everything. Extract of a Working Man's Wife', in *The British Mothers' Magazine*, i and ii (1845), p. 35.
24. *The British Mothers' Magazine*, i and ii (September 1845), p. 205.
25. *The Conditions of the Working Class in England in 1844*, pp. 165–6.
26. 'Why are Women Redundant', in *Literary and Social Judgements*, p. 311.
27. M. Hewitt, *Wives and Mothers* ..., pp. 21–31.
28. ibid., pp. 77–8.
29. W. Gilbert, *Dives and Lazarus*, pp. 39–43.
30. M. Hewitt, *Wives and Mothers* ..., pp. 35–6.
31. ibid., pp. 92–3.
32. ibid., pp. 96–8.
33. ibid., p. 94.
34. Hansard, T. C., *The Parliamentary Debates* ..., House of Commons, Lord Ashley, 7 June 1842, col. 1329.
35. *Sybil* ..., ii, ch. 10, p. 121.
36. M. Hewitt, op. cit., p. 107.
37. See tables in M. Hewitt, op. cit., pp. 101, 104, 107–22.
38. ibid., pp. 130–8.
39. F. Engels, *The Condition of the Working-Class* ..., p. 160.
40. The best known were 'Godfrey's Cordial', 'Infants' Cordial', M. Hewitt, op. cit., pp. 141–7, and F. Engels, op. cit., p. 161.
41. W. Gilbert, *Dives and Lazarus*, pp. 68–72.
42. See this work, i, ch. VI.
43. M. Hewitt, *Wives and Mothers* ..., pp. 156, 164–5.

4

THE MYTH IN THE NOVEL

1. C. Dickens, *Sketches of Young Couples*, pp. 90–1.
2. J. Butt and K. Tillotson, *Dickens at Work*, p. 193.
3. E. Johnson ed., *Letters from Charles Dickens to Angela Burdett-Coutts*, p. 15.

Notes

4. *Bleak House*, pp. 35–6.
5. *Great Expectations*, p. 190.
6. *Bleak House*, p. 100.
7. ibid p. 46, compare the meals lovingly prepared by Bella Wilfer for John Rokesmith in *Our Mutual Friend*, and by Ruth Pinch for her brother in *Martin Chuzzlewit*.
8. '... you had better murder him than marry him – if you really love him ...', he says to Caddy, ibid., p. 414.
9. ibid., pp. 39–40, 418.
10. *Bleak House*, pp. 44, 184, 418.
11. *Martin Chuzzlewit*, p. 298.
12. Mill to H. Taylor, 20 March 1854, MS. Letter in King's College Library, Cambridge. Quoted by M. Packe, *John Stuart Mill*, p. 311, note.
13. 'She must agitate, agitate, agitate ... She must go in to be a public character. She must work away at a Mission.' C. Dickens, 'Sucking Pigs', *Household Words*, 8 November, 1851, p. 146.
14. ibid., p. 145.
15. *Bleak House*, pp. 537 and 872.
16. ibid., p. 421.
17. ibid., ch. 8.
18. P. Thomson, *The Victorian Heroine*, pp. 17, 25–7.
19. C. Rover, The Punch Book of Women's Rights, pp. 40–1. In a number of *The Comic Almanack* by Thackeray, H. Mayhew etc., there is a satirical poem accompanying a caricature by George Cruickshank (1847); an unprepossessing looking woman sitting at her work table, waves away with an imperious gesture her weeping husband and howling children. pp. 159, 160.
20. *Bleak House*, pp. 40–2.
21. *Sketches of Young Couples*, pp. 63, 64.
22. 'The legs of the bird slide gently down into a pool of gravy, the wings seem to melt from the body, the beast separates into a row of juicy slices ...', ibid., p. 64.
23. '... the prettiest little figure conceivable. She has the neatest little foot, and the softest little voice, ... etc.', ibid., p. 62.
24. *Martin Chuzzlewit*, pp. 605–7.
25. 'Such weighing and mixing and chopping and grating, such a dusting and washing and polishing, such snipping and weeding and trowelling ... Such making and mending and folding and airing ...', accompanied by a perusal of 'The Complete British Housewife'. *Our Mutual Friend*, p. 770.
26. 'Amos Barton', *Scenes of Clerical Life*, i, pp. 29, 97.
27. J. Mitchell, 'Women: The Longest Revolution', *New Left Review*, No. 40 (Nov.–Dec. 1966), p. 17, note.
28. B. Friedan, *The Feminine Mystique*.
29. See John Forster, *The Life of Charles Dickens*, pp. 10, 25–30.
30. ibid., i, p. 130, ii, pp. 905–6.
31. *Sketches of Young Couples*, p. 62.
32. '... I have almost repulsed and crushed my better angel into a demon ...' *Hard Times*, p. 688.
33. *Our Mutual Friend*, p. 767.

34. '... I am the most mercenary little wretch ... I have made up my mind that I must have money, Pa. I feel that I can't beg it, borrow it, or steal it; and so I have resolved that I must marry it.' *Our Mutual Friend*, pp. 46 and 360–1.

35. J. W. Stedman, 'Child-Wives of Dickens', *The Dickensian*, May 1963, p. 118.

36. *Our Mutual Friend*, p. 511.

37. J. W. Stedman, art. cit., p. 118.

38. Butt and Tillotson, *Dickens at Work*, pp. 130–1.

39. S. Monod, *Dickens romancier*, p. 254.

40. *David Copperfield*, pp. 534–5.

41. 'a thing of light, and airiness, and joy', *David Copperfield*, p. 538.

42. *David Copperfield*, pp. 686–7.

43. ibid., p. 692.

44. *David Copperfield*, p. 692.

45. A. Lucas, 'Some Dickens Women', *Yale Review*, xxix (1940), p. 709.

46. *David Copperfield*, p. 761.

47. ibid., pp. 222, 223, 231.

48. 'Quiet and peace were there, Rachel was there ...' *Hard Times*, p. 563.

49. 'Thou changest me from bad to good ... Thou'rt an angel; ... thou has saved my soul alive !' says Stephen to Rachel. *Hard Times*, pp. 568, 571.

50. *David Copperfield*, pp. 266, 362, 363, 607, 833.

51. 'Ever pointing upwards, Agnes, ever leading me to something better; ever directing me to higher things ! ... until I die my dearest sister, I shall see you always before me pointing upwards!' *David Copperfield*, p. 837.

52. '... the once deserted girl shone like a beautiful light upon the darkness of the other.' *Hard Times*, p. 798. Florence burns with 'the sacred fire from heaven', *Dombey and Son*, p. 248. 'She [Ada] shone in the miserable corner like a beautiful star.' *Bleak House*, p. 813.

53. W. S. Harvey, 'Chance and Design in Bleak House', in *Dickens and the Twentieth Century*, Gross and Pearson, pp. 147–9.

54. Ed. K. J. Fielding, *The Speeches of Charles Dickens*, pp. 55–6.

55. '[He] has spoken of them [women] ... as always inspired by a love of domesticity, by fidelity, by purity, by innocence, by charity and by hope, which makes them discharge under the most difficult circumstances their duty, and which brings over their path in this world some glimpses of the light of heaven ...' J. Forster, *The Life of Charles Dickens*, p. 177.

56. Angus Wilson, is very violent in respect of them: '... the least pleasing, most frumpy, and smug vision of ideal womanhood that he produced. Esther Summerson ..., ... this wise, womanly, housekeeping, moralizing, self-congratulating, busy little creature ...', is striking for '... complete lack of physical body – a deficiency so great that Esther's small-pox spoilt face jars us because she has no body upon which a head could rest.' A. Wilson, 'The Heroes and Heroines of Dickens', in *Dickens and the Twentieth Century*, ed. J. Gross and G. Pearson.

57. 'He spoke so tenderly and wisely to me, ... I believe I had never loved him so dearly ...' *Bleak House*, p. 604.

58. E. Gaskell, *Wives and Daughters*, p. 156.

Notes

59. *North and South*, pp. 138, 142, 211.
60. Anne Brontë, *The Tenant of Wildfell Hall*, i, pp. 266–8.
61. G. Eliot, 'Amos Barton', *Scenes of Clerical Life*, i, p. 24.
62. 'Janet's Repentance', *Scenes of Clerical Life*, ii, p. 186.
63. C. Brontë, *Jane Eyre*, ii, pp. 38, 39.
64. C. Brontë, *The Professor*, pp. 260, 263.
65. ibid., pp. 237–9.
66. ibid., pp. 265–9.
67. *Pendennis*, i, p. 17. See *The Letters and ... Papers*, ii, letter of 6 March 1846, p. 231 and iii, 3 March 1853, p. 244.
68. 'Sketches and Travels in London', in *Contributions to Punch*, ii, pp. 246–9, 351–2.
69. Thackeray, *Vanity Fair*, ed. Tillotson, pp. 108, 377, 540.
70. *The Letters and ... Papers*, i, pp. 469, 476.
71. ibid., iv (19 June 1855), p. 440.
72. Thackeray, *The Adventures of Philip*, ii, pp. 225–6 and i.
73. *Pendennis*, ii, pp. 82–8.
74. *Esmond*, pp. 6 and 7.
75. ibid., pp. 71–3.
76. *Pendennis*, ii, pp. 422, 434.
77. *Newcomes*, ii, p. 252.
78. ibid., ii, p. 162.
79. *Pendennis*, ii, p. 250.
80. ibid., i, p. 25.
81. G. Tillotson, *Thackeray, the Novelist*, Appendix I, p. 278. Reviews in the *Leader*, the *Scotsman*, *The English Women's Domestic Magazine*, in G. N. Ray, *Thackeray*, ii, pp. 117–18.
82. A. Trollope, *Autobiography*, ch. XII, pp. 225–6.
83. J. Y. T. Greig, *Thackeray*, p. 124.
84. *Oeuvres Complètes, Correspondance*, Paris 1926–33, ii, p. 304.
85. G. N. Ray, *The Buried Life*, p. 123.
86. *The Letters and ... Papers*, i, p. 268.
87. ibid., i, pp. 320, 420.
88. G. N. Ray, *The Buried Life.* p. 22.
89. *The Letters and ... Papers*, i, pp. 463, 466, 473.
90. ibid., i, Appendix VII, 'The psychiatric case history of Isabella Shawe', pp. 518–20.
91. ibid., ii, pp. 429, 440.
92. '... I have a natural hang dog melancholy within – very likely it's a woman I want more than any particular one: ... – It is written a man should have a mate above all things. The want of this natural outlet plays the deuce with me.' ibid., ii, p. 813.
93. ibid., iii, p. 619.
94. G. N. Ray, *The Buried Life*, pp. 50–1.
95. G. N. Ray, *Thackeray*, i, p. 111.
96. 'All sorts of recollections of my youth came back to me; ... dark and sad and painful with my dear good mother as a gentle angel interposing between me and misery.' *The Letters and ... Papers*, ii, p. 361. *The Buried Life*, p. 14.

97. *The Letters and ... Papers*, iii, pp. 12–13.

98. G. N. Ray, *The Buried Life*, p. 95 and J. Y. T. Greig, *Thackaray*, pp. 160–3.

99. G. N. Ray, *Thackeray*, ii, pp. 73 and 74; G. N. Ray, *The Buried Life*, pp. 80–1.

100. *The Letters and ... Papers*, iv, p. 419.

101. 'Her innocence, look, angelical sweetness and kindness charm and ravish me to the highest degree ...' ibid. ii, pp. 271–2, or again 'that almost angelical loving nature', ibid., iii, p. 225.

102. 'No Sister': ibid., ii, p. 475. 'My dear Sister': ibid., ii, p. 530. 'I whisper to you *ma soeur*, full of love and awe ...': ibid., ii, p. 710. '... God bless you my sister ...': ibid., iv, p. 425. 'O my sister', : ibid., iv, p. 426.

103. ibid., iv, p. 437.

104. ibid., iv, p. 341.

105. *The Letters and ... Papers*, ii, p. 471.

106. G. N. Ray, *Thackeray*, ii, p. 70.

5

THE COUNTERVAILING CRITICISM

1. *Dombey and Son*, p. 2.

2. Trollope, *The Vicar of Bullhampton*, p. 259.

3. Cockshut, *Trollope*, pp. 114–15.

4. *The Vicar of Bullhampton*, ch. LXVII, LXXI.

5. Trollope, *Autobiography*, ch. X, pp. 181–2.

6. 'Essay on the Newcomes', *Oxford and Cambridge Magazine*, i, (January 1856), pp. 56–7, quoted by G. N. Ray, *Thackeray*, ii, p. 242.

7. *The Book of Snobs* in *Contributions to Punch*, ii, pp. 41 and 160.

8. ibid., ii, pp. 20–1.

9. *Contributions to Punch*, ii, pp. 311–18, 335.

10. *The Newcomes*, i, p. 304.

11. J. Y. T. Greig, *Thackeray*, pp. 60 and 70.

12. Thackeray, *The Adventures of Philip* ..., ii, p. 204.

13. *The Letters and ... Papers*, iv, p. 145.

14. ibid., iii, pp. 523–4.

15. *The Newcomes*, i, pp. 363–9; *Pendennis*, ii, pp. 4–5, etc.

16. See *The Newcomes*, i, Introduction, pp. XLVII, XLVIII. We know that Ethel was inspired by Blanche Airlie and Sally Baxter. Thackeray said he was struck by the resemblance between Sally and Beatrix. See *The Letters and . . . Papers*, iii, pp. 149 and 183, and G. N. Ray, *Thackeray*, ii, p. 242.

17. *Henry Esmond*, pp. 288, 391, 400–1, 439–40.

18. ibid., p. 372.

19. ibid., p. 378.

20. *The Newcomes*, ii, p. 42.

21. *ibid.*, ii, pp. 63 and 92.

22. ibid., i, p. 429.

23. ibid.

24. ibid., i, pp. 440–1.

25. *Henry Esmond*, p. 514.

26. *The Virginians*, i, p. 43.

Notes

27. *The Newcomes*, ii, pp. 372–3 and 505.
28. 'Madame Sand and the New Apocalypse', *The Paris Sketch Book*, pp. 231–2.
29. 'Sketches and Travels in London', in *Contribution to Punch*, ii, p. 305.
30. ibid., p. 306.
31. 'The Ravenswing', *Yellow Plush Papers*, pp. 225–6, 302.
32. *Pendennis*, i, p. 259.
33. *Vanity Fair*, ed. Tillotson, pp. 82–3 and 'The Ravenswing', pp. 226–7.
34. *The Buried Life*, pp. 95–6.
35. *Henry Esmond*, pp. 122–3.
36. 'He is master of property, happiness – life almost. He is free to punish, ... – to ruin or to torture. He may kill a wife gradually, ... He may make slaves and hypocrites of his children; ...', writes Thackeray, ibid., p. 164.
37. *Barry Lyndon*, pp. 282–3, 265, 279.
38. ibid., pp. 260, 308.
39. *The Newcomes*, ii, p. 268.
40. ibid., ii, pp. 268, 269.
41. ibid., ii, p. 269.
42. ibid., ii, p. 269.
43. J. Y. T. Greig, *Thackeray*, p. 150.
44. P. Thomson, *The Victorian Heroine*, p. 98.
45. *North British Review*, xxiii (August 1855), p. 553.
46. 'Treatment of Women', *Eliza Cook's Journal*, 9 August 1851, p. 226. See *David Copperfield*, pp. 682–3.
47. Anne Brontë, *The Tenant of Wildfell Hall*, i, pp. 190, 196–7, 276.
48. ibid., i, p. 196 and ii, p. 256.
49. Harrison and Stanford, *Anne Brontë*, p. 223.
50. A. Brontë, *The Tenant of Wildfell Hall*, Preface by C. Brontë to the second edition, p. x.
51. 'The Brontë Novels', *The Nineteenth Century*, March 1903, p. 489.
52. 'Janet's Repentance', *Scenes of Clerical Life*, ii, 1878, p. 212.
53. ibid., p. 102.
54. *The George Eliot Letters*, ii, p. 344.
55. ibid., ii, pp. 347 8.
56. MS.: fol. 11–12, in G. S. Haight, *George Eliot*, p. 238.
57. *Bleak House*, pp. 105 and 106, 109.
58. ibid., p. 626.
59. '– an exquisite slave is what we want for the most part: ...', he writes in 'On Love, Marriage, Men and Women', in *Sketches and Travels in London*, pp. 306–7.
60. *Vanity Fair*, ed. Tillotson, p. 165.
61. *The Memoirs of Barry Lyndon*, p. 204.
62. Sarah Ellis, *The Wives of England*, pp. 78 and 117.
63. *The Virginians*, i, pp. 184–5, 276.
64. *Pendennis*, i, pp. 281–2.
65. ibid., ii, pp. 337 and 460.
66. ibid., ii, p. 494.
67. H. Martineau, *Autobiography*, ii, p. 376.
68. *Henry Esmond*, pp. 164–5.

69. H. O. Brogan, 'Rachel Esmond ...', *Journal of English Literary History*, xxiii (September 1946), pp. 224, 225–6.
70. J. Y. T. Greig, *Thackeray*, pp. 163–4, and G. N. Ray, *Thackeray*, ii, p. 192.
71. *The Letters and ... Papers*, iii, p. 175.
72. G. N. Ray, *Thackeray*, ii, pp. 180, 181, 183.
73. G. N. Ray, *The Buried Life*, p. 53.
74. H. Taine, *Histoire de la Littérature anglaise*, iv, p. 102.
75. *Pendennis*, i, p. 94.
76. *Pendennis*, ii, pp. 171–4.
77. ibid., ii, p. 189.
78. MS. letter, June 1850 in G. N. Ray, *The Buried Life*, p. 95.
79. *The Letters and ... Papers*, ii, p. 661.
80. 'Biographical Introduction', *The Letters and ... Papers*, iii, pp. xxxv–xxxvii.
81. ibid., ii, 381.
82. On this question see the detailed analysis of the contrast in each of these chapters, in Myron Taube, 'Contrast as a Principle of Structure in *Vanity Fair*', *Nineteenth Century Fiction*, xviii (Sept. 1963), pp. 119–26. J. Y. T. Greig, *Thackeray*, pp. 111 and 112 and chapter on Becky Sharp.
83. *Vanity Fair*, p. 476.
84. *The Letters and ... Papers*, ii, p. 309.
85. *Vanity Fair*, p. 114.
86. ibid., p. 540.
87. See the comments of Mario Praz, *The Hero in Eclipse in Victorian Fiction*, pp. 217–24.
88. *Vanity Fair*, p. 651, but Thackeray does not seem to approve of their moral code.
89. ibid., pp. 322–3, 601.
90. See *The Letters and ... Papers*, ii, p. 474, passage noted by M. Taube in 'The Character of Amelia in *Vanity Fair*', *Victorian Newsletter*, No. 18 (Autumn 1960), pp. 6–7.
91. *Vanity Fair*, pp. 600–1, see article by J. K. Mathieson, 'The German Sections of *Vanity Fair*', *Nineteenth Century Fiction*, xviii (December 1963), pp. 237–46.
92. G. N. Ray, *The Buried Life*, p. 36, and J. K. Mathieson, art. cit., p. 236.
93. *The Letters and ... Papers*, i, pp. 315 and 318.
94. ibid., i, p. 479.
95. ibid., ii, pp. 41–2.
96. *The Newcomes*, ii, p. 66.
97. ibid., ii, pp. 324–5.
98. 'her cruel yellow face, and her sharp teeth and her grey eyes', *The Adventures of Philip* ..., ii, p. 88.
99. See E. Wagenknecht, 'The Selfish Heroine: Thackeray ...', *College English*, (Chicago), Feb. 1943, p. 294, and J. W. Dodds, 'Thackeray in the Victorian Frame of Mind', *Sewanee Review*, xlviii (1940), p. 475, and *Thackeray*, p. 129.
100. H. Taine, *Histoire de la Littérature anglaise*, iv, p. 105.
101. '... for the reader it is merely a matter of going on and on, ...' – F. R. Leavis, *The Great Tradition*, p. 21.

Notes

102. A. Pollard, *Mrs. Gaskell*, p. 121.
103. *Wuthering Heights*, Preface, p. X.
104. See G. H. Lewes's article in the *Leader* of 28 December 1850, quoted by A. R. Brick, 'Lewes's Review of *Wuthering Heights*', *Nineteenth Century Fiction*, xiv (March 1960), p. 357.
105. R. Strange, *The Theory of the Novel in England, 1850–1870*, pp. 219–21.
106. *Wuthering Heights*, p. 90.
107. *Wuthering Heights*, pp. 59, 60, 61.
108. Balthus, op. cit., 62.10, p. 90.
109. *Wuthering Heights*, p. 131.
110. J. H. Mitter, 'Emily Brontë', *The Disappearance of God*, p. 175.
111. *Wuthering Heights*, p. 131.
112. *Wuthering Heights*, p. 143.
113. J. Blondel, *Emily Brontë* ..., p. 338.
114. *Wuthering Heights*, p. 94.
115. ibid., p. 172.
116. *Wuthering Heights*, p. 158.
117. *Wuthering Heights*, p. 173.
118. *Wuthering Heights*, pp. 208, 222.
119. ibid., p. 263.
120. A. Kettle, *An Introduction to the English Novel*, i, p. 150.
121. The hypothesis of a resemblance with the heroines of Charlotte Brontë seems more debatable to me. See E. Wright, op. cit., p. 179.
122. *Sylvia's Lovers*, pp. 351–2 (see A. B. Hopkins, *E. Gaskell*, p. 267).
123. 'I know I'm for ever trying and trying to be a good wife to him, and it's very dull work ...' ibid., p. 390.
124. See E. Wright, op. cit., pp. 184–5.
125. *Sylvia's Lovers*, pp. 364–82.
126. B. Hardy, *The Novels of George Eliot*, p. 48.
127. 'George Eliot', *A Century of George Eliot Criticism*, p. 189.
128. *The George Eliot Letters*, ii, p. 9.
129. ibid., ii, p. 104.
130. ibid., ii, p. 174.
131. ibid., ii, p. 225.
132. ibid., ii, p. 227.
133. ibid., ii, p. 436.
134. E. Simcox, 'George Eliot', *Nineteenth Century*, May 1881, p. 798.
135. E. Simcox, art. cit., p. 796.
136. L. Lerner, *The Truth-tellers*, 967, p. 42. See also G. Himmelfarb, *Victorian Minds*, pp. 302–3.
137. For Henry James this hardly natural and indeed superfluous creature conveys a lack of equilibrium between her emotional significance and her role in the plot. Leavis on the other hand reckons that with this character whom she was not tempted to identify with, George Eliot gave proof of an exceptional emotional maturity in the Victorian sensibility. H. James, 'Felix Holt the Radical', *A Century of George Eliot Criticism*, p. 42. F. R. Leavis, *The Great Tradition*, pp. 68–70.
138. B. Hardy, *The Novels of George Eliot*, p. 93.
139. *Felix Holt*, i, 40.

Notes

140. ibid., i, p. 42.
141. *Felix Holt* ..., i, pp. 31–2.
142. ibid., i, p. 166.
143. 'Janet's Repentance', *Scenes of Clerical Life*, ii, p. 124.
144. ibid.
145. *Felix Holt* ..., ii, p. 200.
146. B. Hardy, *The Novels of George Eliot*, p. 57.
147. ibid., p. 62.
148. *Felix Holt* ..., ii, p. 356.
149. G. S. Haight, *George Eliot*, p. 387.
150. *The George Eliot Letters*, iv, pp. 245, 265.
151. 'George Eliot', *A Century of George Eliot Criticism*, p. 280.
152. *A Century of George Eliot Criticism*, p. 91.
153. *Romola*, i, p. 269.
154. ibid., ii, pp. 18–19, 42.
155. *Romola*, ii, p. 321.
156. ibid.
157. ibid, ii, p. 146.
158. *Romola*, ii, p. 410.
159. Tessa sees her, like the poor of Florence, as a supernatural apparition. *Romola*, p. 423.
160. George Eliot replied: '... the various *strands* of thought I had to work out forced me into a more ideal treatment of Romola than I had foreseen... – though the "Drifting away" and the Village with the Plague [ch. 61 and 68] belonged to my earlier vision of the story ...' *The George Eliot Letters*, iv, pp. 103, 104.
161. ibid., iv, pp. 97, 301.
162. *A Century of George Eliot Criticism*, p. 29.
163. F. R. Leavis, *The Great Tradition*, p. 61.
164. *The George Eliot Letters*, i, p. 268.
165. V. Woolf, 'George Eliot', *A Century of George Eliot Criticism*, p. 189.

PART TWO

6

FROM THE WOMAN'S SPHERE TO THE PRACTICE OF A PROFESSION

1. A. Clark, *Working Life of Women in the Seventeenth Century*, pp. 290–308.
2. I. Watt, *The Rise of the Novel*, p. 145.
3. B. Bodichon (Leigh-Smith), *Women and Work*, pp. 8, 9.
4. I. Watt, op. cit., p. 141.
5. E. Reiss, *Rights and Duties of Englishwomen*, pp. 131, 137.
6. *Women and Work*, p. 6.
7. D. Greenwell, 'Our Single Women', *North British Review*, xxxvi (February 1862), pp. 62–6.
8. *Women and Work*, p. 9.
9. J. Butler, ed., *Woman's Work and Woman's Culture*, pp. xvi, xxii, xxiii, xxxi.

Notes

10. H. Martineau, 'Female Industry', *Edinburgh Review*, cix (April 1859), pp. 294–8.
11. *Autobiography, with Memorials by M. W. Chapman*, ii, p. 419.
12. J. D. Milne, *Industrial and Social Position of Women*, p. 171.
13. H. Martineau, 'Nurses Wanted', *The Cornhill Magazine*, xi (April 1865), p. 409.
14. 'Woman and her Social Position', *The Westminster Review*, xxxv (January 1841), p. 164.
15. *Society in America*, iii, ch. 2.
16. H. Martineau, *Autobiography*, i, pp. 141–2.
17. P. Séjourné, *Aspects généraux du roman féminin en Angleterre de 1740 à 1800*, p. 95.
18. ibid., pp. 378–9.
19. *British and Foreign Review*, November 1836.
20. 'Women Artists', *The Westminster Review*, xiv (July 1858), p. 164.
21. H. Martineau, *Autobiography*, i, p. 145.
22. *The Brontës, Their Lives and Friendships in Correspondence*, ii, pp. 79–80.
23. *The George Eliot Letters*, ed. G. S. Haight, iii, 30 June 1859, p. 106.
24. E. Gaskell, *The Life of Charlotte Brontë*, pp. 102–3.
25. ibid., p. 104.
26. ibid., pp. 233–4.
27. G. H. Lewes, 'Currer Bell's Shirley', *The Edinburgh Review*, xci (January 1850), and F. R. Gary, 'Charlotte Brontë and G. H. Lewes', *PMLA*, li (1936).
28. F. R. Gary, art. cit., p. 536.
29. *The Brontës, Their Lives …*, 1 November 1849, iii, p. 31.
30. E. Gaskell, *The Life of Charlotte Brontë*, pp. 254–6, 283–4.
31. *The George Eliot Letters*, iii, p. 106, 30 June 1859.
32. W. R. Greg, 'False Morality of Lady Novelists', *National Review*, viii (January 1859), pp. 147–8.
33. George Eliot, 'Silly Novels by Lady Novelists', *The Westminster Review*, x (October 1856), pp. 442–61.
34. I. S. Ewbank, *Their Proper Sphere*, ch. 1.
35. J. Kamm, *Hope Deferred: …*, p. 170, note.
36. 'Governesses', *Eliza Cook's Journal*, No. 20 (15 September 1849), p. 305.
37. 'Schools' Inquiry Commission', *Parliamentary Papers*, 1867 8, xxviii, part iii, p. 693.
38. E. Gaskell, *The Life of Charlotte Brontë*, p. 141.
39. A. Jameson, *Memoirs and Essays*, p. 254 and J. D. Milne, *Industrial … Position of Women*, p. 130.
40. F. D. Maurice, *Lectures to Ladies in Practical Subjects*, pp. 8, 9.
41. J. Kamm, *Hope Deferred …*, p. 170.
42. H. Martineau, 'Middle-Class Education in England – Girls', *The Cornhill Magazine*, x (November 1864), p. 554.
43. 'Schools' Inquiry Commission', *Parliamentary Papers*, 1867–8, xxviii, part iv, p. 246 and p. 700.
44. F. Nightingale, *Nightingale Papers*, MS. 'Autobiographical and other Memoranda by F. N. 1845–1860', No. of MS.: 43402 (*c.* 1851), pp. 81–2.

Notes

45. E. Gaskell, *The Life of Charlotte Brontë*, p. 122.
46. H. Martineau, *Autobiography*, i, p. 149.
47. J. Kamm, *Hope Deferred* ..., p. 170.
48. B. Bodichon, *Women and Work*, p. 17.
49. 'Governesses', *Eliza Cook's Journal*, 15 September 1849, No. 20, p. 306.
50. See note 37.
51. 'Governesses', *Eliza Cook's Journal*, 15 September 1849, No. 20, p. 306.
52. E. Rigby, *Journal of Correspondance of Lady Eastlake*, i, p. 125.
53. C. Woodham-Smith, *Florence Nightingale, 1820–1910*, p. 124.
54. A. Jameson, *Memoirs and Essays*, p. 235.
55. See E. Gaskell, *The Life of Charlotte Brontë*, pp. 114–17, 139.
56. E. Rigby, '*Vanity Fair* ...; *Jane Eyre*, ...', *The Quarterly Review*, lxxxiv (December 1848), p. 177.
57. See W. F. Neff, *Victorian Working Women*, pp. 158–60.
58. A. Jameson, *Memoirs and Essays*, pp. 251–98.
59. See E. Rigby, art. cit., pp. 181–3.
60. *Saint-James's Magazine*, vi, pp. 505–7; see also W. F. Neff, *Victorian Working Women*, pp. 176–7, and J. Kamm, *Hope Deferred* ..., pp. 172–3.
61. For details of the beginnings of 'Queen's College', see 'Queen's College', *The Quarterly Review*, lxxxvi (March 1850), pp. 364–83, J. Kamm, *Hope Deferred* ..., p. 173, and J. Kilham, *Tennyson and the Princess*, pp. 130–1.
62. H. Martineau, 'Middle-class Education ...', *The Cornhill Magazine*, x (November 1864), p. 567.
63. See J. Kamm, *Hope Deferred* ..., pp. 210–12, and F. Basch, 'La femme en Angleterre depuis l'avènement de Victoria jusqu'à la première guerre mondiale', *Histoire mondiale de la femme*, iv, pp. 214–15.
64. F. R. Parkes, *Remarks on the Education of Girls*, p. 13.
65. B. Harrison, 'Victorian Philanthropy', *Victorian Studies*, ix, No. 4 (June 1966), p. 360.
66. D. Owen, *English Philanthropy 1660–1960*, pp. 413–19.
67. F. R. Parkes, *Remarks* ..., p. 13.
68. F. D. Maurice, *Lectures to Ladies in Practical Subjects*, p. 13.
69. A. Jameson, *Sisters of Charity*, ch. 4 and 8, p. 4.
70. In this poem, female beauty is revealed to Philip Hewson when, one day, he sees a young woman tear up potatoes; henceforth he exalts the useful tasks of women, washing, cooking, cleaning, etc. which emphasize the mockery and futility of worldly life. Contrary to what Paul Veyriras writes in his remarkable work on the poet, I do not think 'Clough's daring thought' is to be hailed. For according to Clough, female labour is entirely dedicated to the service of man and thus does not differ in essence from the paid activities of Caddy Jellyby in *Bleak House* or Frances Henri in *The Professor*, which we have discussed earlier. See Paul Veyriras, *A. H. Clough*, p. 266.
71. S. de Beauvoir, *Le Deuxième Sexe*, i, p. 24.
72. F. D. Maurice, *Lectures to Ladies* ..., pp. 16, 92–3.
73. H. Martineau, 'Nurses Wanted', *The Cornhill Magazine*, xi (April 1865), p. 416.
74. J. W. Kaye, 'Employment of Women', *North British Review*, xxvi (February 1857), p. 297.

Notes

75. All this must be seen in the context of the sanitary and hospital conditions of the country which the commissions of inquiry were beginning to study: in 1838 Doctors Southwood-Smith, Arnott and Kay presented a report to the Poor Law Commissioners on the inhabitants of the East End of London. In 1840 the first report on the sanitary conditions of the working classes appeared; in 1844 the first report of the Commission of Urban Health.
76. M. A. Nutting and L. L. Dock, *History of Nursing*, ii, pp. 73, 76.
77. ibid., ii, p. 88, and C. Woodham-Smith, *Florence Nightingale*, pp. 143–4.
78. *The Times*, 13 and 14 October 1854, in C. Woodham-Smith, op. cit., pp. 134–5.
79. ibid.
80. F. D. Maurice, *Lectures to Ladies* ..., A. Jameson, *The Communion of Labour*, D. Greenwell, 'Our Single Women', *North British Review*, xxxvi (February 1862), pp. 80–3.
81. F. Nightingale, *Nightingale Papers*, MS, 'Reports by F. N. on her Crimean Nurses' (*c.* 1854) – 1856, No. of MS. 43402.
82. Furthermore the nurses had the habit of eating the food of the sick and drinking their wine. This state of affairs was not surprising, said a witness, since nurses were hired in the street; people working during the day and recruited as night nurses slept instead of working. (*Lincolnshire Chronicle*, October 1866).
83. 'You would not think it, ma'am, but a week ago I was in silks and satins... dancing at Woolwich. Yes! ma'am, for all I am so dirty I am draped in silks and satins sometimes. Real French silks ...' *The Letters of Mrs. Gaskell*, (217), p. 319, and C. Woodham-Smith, p. 39.
84. C. Woodham-Smith, *Florence Nightingale*, p. 461.
85. A. Jameson, *The Communion of Labour*, pp. 88 93.
86. C. Woodham-Smith, op. cit., p. 58.
87. ibid., pp. 142–3.
88. F. Nightingale, *Nightingale Papers*, MS. 'Reports by F. N. on her Crimean Nurses', May 1856: Nurses returning. Report No. 1, No. of MS. 43402.
89. 'The prostitutes come in perpetually-poor creatures staggering off their beat! It took worse hold of them than any', said F. Nightingale to Mrs Gaskell. *The Letters of Mrs. Gaskell*, (217), p. 318.
90. C. Woodham-Smith, op. cit., p. 464: 'Una and the Lion', published in *Good Words*, 1868.
91. ibid., p. 137, letter of 15 October 1854.
92. ibid., pp. 147, 185.
93. F. Nightingale, *Nightingale Papers*, 'Reports by F. N. on her Crimean Nurses, May 1856: Nurses returning'. Report No. 1, No. of MS. 43402.
94. C. Woodham-Smith, op. cit., pp. 145–6.
95. F. D. Maurice, *Lectures to Ladies* ..., pp. 48, 49.
96. A. Jameson, *The Communion of Labour*, pp. 128–32.
97. See F. Nightingale, *Notes on Hospitals*.
98. F. Nightingale, *Notes on Nursing*, p. 192.
99. F. Nightingale, *Method of Improving the Nursing Service* ..., p. 3.
100. ibid., p. 11.

101. F. D. Maurice, *Lectures to Ladies* ..., p. 14; R. Strachey, *The Cause*, pp. 166, 175, 179; F. Basch, art. cit., pp. 223–5.
102. R. Strachey, op. cit., ch. 5; B. Bodichon, *Women and Work*, p. 16.

7

WORKSHOP, MINE AND FACTORY

1. A. Jameson, *Memoirs and Essays*, p. 213.
2. 'The Wrongs of Englishwomen', *Eliza Cook's Journal*, 5 October 1850, pp. 354–5.
3. See also H. Beecher-Stowe, *Sunny Memories of Foreign Lands*, p. 298.
4. J. D. Milne, *The Industrial ... Position of Women*, pp. 182–6.
5. *Reports from Commissioners*: Children's Employment (Trades and Manufactures), *Parliamentary Papers*, 1843, xiv, part iii, pp. 555–6.
6. ibid., pp. 546, 556–7.
7. See W. F. Neff, *Victorian Working Women*, pp. 122–3 and *Reports from Commissioners*: Children's Employment (Trades and Manufactures), *Parliamentary Papers*; 1843, xiv, part iii, pp. 541, 558.
8. *Reports from Commissioners*: Children's Employment (Trades and Manufactures), *Parliamentary Papers*, 1843, xiv, part iii, pp. 833–7.
9. J. D. Milne, op. cit., pp. 185–6.
10. W. F. Neff, op. cit., p. 131.
11. H. Martineau, 'Female Industry', *Edinburgh Review*, cix (April 1859), pp. 327–8.
12. R. Strachey, *The Cause*, p. 51.
13. H. Beecher-Stowe, *Sunny Memories of Foreign Lands*, p. 299–300.
14. K. Marx, *Kapital*, ed. Dona Torr, pp. 239, 240.
15. ibid., p. 240 (*Morning Star*).
16. *The Times*, 22 June 1863.
17. *The Times*, 24 June 1863.
18. J. D. Milne, *The Industrial ... Position of Women*, p. 202; see also H. Martineau, 'Female Industry', *Edinburgh Review*, cix (April 1859), p. 320.
19. T. C. Hansard, *The Parliamentary Debates* ..., 15 March 1844, col. 1092.
20. F. Engels, *The Condition of the Working Class in England in 1844*, p. 158.
21. I. Pinchbeck, *Women Workers and the Industrial Revolution, 1750–1850*, pp. 187–8, and note 2, p. 188.
22. I. Pinchbeck, *Women Workers* ..., p. 187.
23. T. C. Hansard, *The Parliamentary Debates* ..., 15 March 1844, lxxiii, col. 1077, 1078, 1079.
24. *Reports of the Inspectors of Factories* ..., *Parliamentary Papers*, 1843, xxvii, part xvi, pp. 306–7.
25. T. C. Hansard, op. cit., 15 March 1844, col. 1081–4.
26. *Reports of the Inspectors of Factories* ..., J. L. Saunders, *Parliamentary Papers*, 1843, xxvii, pp. 353–4.
27. I. Pinchbeck, *Women Workers* ..., p. 193.
28. See note 24.
29. J. D. Milne, *The Industrial ... Position of Women*, p. 202.
30. For the hours of work, see I. Pinchbeck, op. cit., pp. 255, 256 and *Report from Commissioners*: Children's Employment (Mines), (*Parliamentary*

Papers, 1842, xv, part 1), pp. 118–37; for salaries, see I. Pinchbeck, op. cit., pp. 257–9.

31. ibid.

32. See *Reports from Commissioners*: Children's Employment (Mines), (*Parliamentary Papers*, 1842, xv, part 1), pp. 86–96 and 103–7.

33. According to Adam Smith's theories the natural identity of needs was supposed to produce spontaneous adjustment in supply and demand of labour and salaries; as a rule nature operated in such a way as to bring about justice and satisfaction of all individual interests without the need for legislative intervention. Halévy points out that although Adam Smith did not believe in a complete identity of interests between capitalists, landowners and salaried workers, he was however hostile to State intervention in these mechanisms, as well as to coalitions of workers. A supporter of the free play of economic and industrial forces, he was opposed to any State action aimed at controlling or protecting one or other of the parties. E. Halévy, *La Formation du radicalisme philosophique*, iii, p. 387 and i, pp. 171 and 185.

34. See W. O. Ayedelotte, 'The Conservative and Radical Interpretations of Early Victorian Social Legislation', *Victorian Studies*, xi (Dec. 1967), pp. 228, 232–4.

35. B. L. Hutchins and A. Harrison, *A History of Factory Legislation*, pp. 69, 90–1, 95.

36. R. C. Hansard, op. cit., 3 May 1844, col. 615–33.

37. See the MS. letters of T. Chapman to Harriet Martineau, exposing his reasons for refusing to publish a pamphlet by her in the review.

38. S. Greg, *Two Letters to Leonard Horner, Esq. on the Capabilities of the Factory System*.

39. W. F. Neff, *Victorian Working Women*, p. 43.

40. T. C. Hansard, op. cit., 3 May 1844, col. 615–33.

41. ibid., col. 615, 616, 618.

42. ibid., 14 July 1842, col. 101 and 119.

43. D. R. McGregor, *Divorce in England*, p. 61.

44. N. W. Senior, *Letters on the Factory Act ...*, p. 819.

45. B. L. Hutchins and A. Harrison, *A History of Factory Legislation*, pp. 113–18; for the clauses of the 1844 Act see pp. 85–7.

46. The nuanced position of Chapman and *The Westminster Review* on labour legislation, and his scepticism concerning the disinterestedness of manufacturers are revealed in his letters to Harriet Martineau when he refused to publish her pamphlet in the magazine. See the 'letter from J. Chapman to H. Martineau', 6 November 1855, MS.: Martineau Collection, Birmingham University. The letters are to be edited by S. K. Rosenberg.

47. When Dickens was editor of *Household Words* articles by Henry Morley were published on the question on 14 April, 12 May, 23 June and 28 July. They were based on the reports of the Inspector L. Horner (1785–1864), explaining that the number and frequency of accidents caused by machines had hardly diminished since 1844 as a result of the reluctance of manufacturers to implement the regulations.

48. Hutchins and Harris, op. cit., p. 122.

49. R. Blake, *Disraeli*, pp. 170–2.

50. Hutchins & Harrison, *A History of Factory* ..., pp. 40–2.

51. J. L. and B. Hammond, *Lord Shaftesbury*, pp. 289–90.

52. J. L. and B. Hammond, *Lord Shaftesbury*, p. 21.

53. I. Pinchbeck, *Women Workers* ... pp. 267–8.

54. For the alliance of Ashley with the 'Young England' group against Peel on the ten-hour day, see R. Blake, *Disraeli*, pp. 179, 242.

55. Hutchins & Harrison, *A History of Factory* ..., pp. 85–6.

56. I. Pinchbeck, op. cit., p. 190.

57. Hutchins & Harrison, op, cit., pp. 43, 48, 49, 109.

58. ibid., pp. 97–100.

59. The relay system permitted the employer to apportion as he pleased the ten hours legal work of protected categories in a factory operating longer. Marx compared this timetable to that of actors who, although they are not always on stage, are mobilized for the entire performance. See Hutchins and Harrison, op. cit., pp. 100–4. Ibid. pp. 108 and 112 and J. L. and B. Hammond, *Lord Shaftesbury*, note 1, p. 149.

60. T. C. Hansard, op. cit., 7 June 1842, col. 1335 on 15 March 1844, col. 1096–9, and also Engels, *The Condition of the ... Working-class* ..., p. 305.

61. W. F. Neff, op. cit., see pp. 54–5 (Cooke-Taylor, P. Gaskell and F. Engels) and p. 259, notes 145–8.

62. *Reports ... Labour of Children in Factories, Parliamentary Papers*, 1831–2, xv, part xi, pp. 218–19, 320, 374, 381. See also W. F. Neff, op. cit., pp. 55–6.

63. T. C. Hansard, op. cit., 7 June 1842, col. 1335.

64. F. Engels, *The Condition of the Working-class* ..., p. 162.

65. It was an extreme case since, according to the estimates quoted by Engels in 'Statement of Facts ...' (*Manchester Guardian*, 1 May 1844, p. 5) in 412 factories employing 10,731 women, 821 had unemployed husbands; *The Condition* ... p. 165 note 1 and 162–4.

66. T. C. Hansard, op. cit., 7 June 1842, col. 1348.

67. F. Engels, op. cit., pp. 162–4.

68. P. Gaskell writes: 'Nothing would tend more to elevate the moral condition of manufacturing population, than the restoration of woman to her proper social rank: ... No great step can be made until she is snatched from unremitting toil and made what Nature meant she should be – the centre of a system of social delight. Domestic avocations are those which are her peculiar lot.' P. Gaskell, *The Manufacturing Population of England*, pp. 166–7.

69. T. C. Hansard, op. cit., 14 July 1842, col. 108.

70. T. C. Hansard, op. cit., 15 March 1844, col. 1097.

71. ibid., 15 March 1844, col. 1099.

72. ibid., 15 March 1844, col. 1906.

73. ibid., 3 May 1844, col. 630.

74. ibid., 3 May 1844, col. 657.

75. It is interesting to see the same metaphysical arguments about 'woman's nature' being unfitted for work and dedicated to the family and domestic occupations used in 1841 by workers to hide, this time, their fear of a competing labour-force making less demands.

Notes

76. W. R. Greg, 'Juvenile and Female Labour', *Edinburgh Review*, lxxiv (January 1844).
77. H. Martineau, 'Female Industry', *Edinburgh Review*, cix (April 1859), p. 325.
78. J. D. Milne, *The Industrial ... Position of Women*, pp. 211, 224–50.
79. I. Pinchbeck, *Women Workers ...*, pp. 199–200.
80. H. Martineau, 'Female Industry', *Edinburgh Review*, cix (April 1859), p. 335.

8
CHARLES DICKENS'S ANTI-WOMAN

1. *Great Expectations*, pp. 40, 69.
2. *The Old Curiosity Shop*, p. 65.
3. *Our Mutual Friend*, p. 246.
4. *Dombey & Son*, pp. 100–1.
5. See the controversy about the Yorkshire schools resulting from Dotheboys Hall in *Nicholas Nickleby*, in P. Collins, *Dickens and Education*, ch. 5 and 6.
6. ibid., pp. 137, 241, note 18.
7. D. Greenwell, 'Our Single Women', *North-British Review*, xxxvi (February 1862), p. 62.
8. *Dombey & Son*, p. 7.
9. *The Old Curiosity Shop*, pp. 259, 286.
10. *David Copperfield*, p. 46.
11. ibid., p. 389.
12. ibid., pp. 127, 129, 211.
13. The model for Sarah Gamp was a nurse who looked after Miss H. Meredith, friend of Miss Burdett-Coutts, and whose eccentricities both women described to Dickens. See M. Cardwell, 'Rosa and Mrs Brown', *The Dickensian*, lvi (January 1960) and a letter from Dickens to Miss Burdett-Coutts in October 1848. See Edgar Johnson, *Charles Dickens...*, i, p. 453.
14. *Martin Chuzzlewit*, p. 416.
15. ibid., p. 713.
16. ibid., p. 416.
17. *Martin Chuzzlewit*, p. 249.
18. *Nicholas Nickleby*, p. 20.
19. 'Betsy Trotwood herself is perfectly in the tradition of the fairy godmother – omnipotent, wilful and kind. She has no human need to conform herself to reality. All her prejudices, some of which are cruel, are treated as admirable.' A. D. J. Cockshut, *The Imagination of Charles Dickens*, p. 121.
20. E. Johnson, *Charles Dickens ...*, ii, p. 906.
21. A. A. Adrian, *Georgina Hogarth and the Dickens Circle*, pp. 24–8, 48.
22. J. Lindsay, 'Charles Dickens and Women', *Twentieth Century*, cliv (November 1953), p. 382.
23. A. A. Adrian, *Georgina Hogarth ...*, p. 74, and *The Letters of Charles Dickens*, iii, p. 160.
24. E. Johnson, *Charles Dickens ...*, ii, p. 918.
25. See *Harper's Weekly*, 27 July 1858 in A. A. Adrian, *Georgina Hogarth ...*, p. 58.

26. ibid., p. 131.
27. *Little Dorrit*, ii, p. 681.
28. M. Cardwell, 'Rosa Dartle and Miss Brown', *The Dickensian*, lvi (January 1960), pp. 30, 31.
29. *David Copperfield*, p. 289.
30. *David Copperfield*, p. 467.
31. ibid., p. 712.
32. ibid., p. 794.
33. *Great Expectations*, pp. 53, 54.
34. E. Wilson, *The Wound and the Bow*, p. 64; E. Johnson, 'Ada Nisbet's Dickens and Ellen Ternan', *Nineteenth Century Fiction*, vii (March 1953).
35. *Great Expectations*, p. 236.

9

REVOLT AND DUTY IN THE BRONTËS

1. E. Rigby, '*Vanity Fair*; ..., *Jane Eyre*; ...', *The Quarterly Review*, lxxxiv (December 1848), p. 176.
2. *Eliza Cook's Journal*, No. 202, 12 March 1853.
3. A. Harrison and D. Stanford, *Anne Brontë*, pp. 55–7, and *The Brontës, their Lives* ..., i, p. 129.
4. ibid., i, pp. 141, 162.
5. ibid., i, p. 177.
6. ibid., i, pp. 110, 226.
7. ibid., i, p. 180.
8. ibid., i, p. 240.
9. *The Brontës, their Lives* ..., i, pp. 260, 266–7, 290.
10. ibid., ii, pp. 3, 12.
11. W. Gérin, *Charlotte Brontë*, pp. 11, 102–3.
12. ibid., p. 260.
13. ibid., p. 53.
14. *The Brontës, their Lives* ..., ii, p. 52.
15. Harrison and Stanford, *Anne Brontë*, p. 237.
16. *The Brontës, their Lives* ..., ii, p. 162.
17. A. Brontë, *Agnes Grey*, p. 11.
18. ibid., pp. 21, 68, 153.
19. I. S. Ewbank, *Their Proper Sphere*, p. 34.
20. *Shirley*, ii, pp. 64, 65.
21. *Jane Eyre*, i, p. 111.
22. *Villette*, i, p. 92.
23. ibid., ii, pp. 59–60.
24. ibid., i, p. 225.
25. ibid., ii, p. 310.
26. *The Brontës, their Lives* ..., i, p. 173.
27. See H. Martineau, *Autobiography*, i, p. 133.
28. *The Brontës, their Lives* ..., i, p. 174, ii, p. 38.
29. ibid., i, p. 296.
30. ibid., i, p. 173.
31. ibid., ii, p. 77.

Notes

32. *Shirley*, i, p. 198.
33. ibid., ii, p. 82, i, p. 193.
34. G. H. Lewes, '*Shirley*', *The Edinburgh Review*, xci (January 1850), pp. 164, 165, 166.
35. *Jane Eyre*, i, pp. 138, 139.
36. '*Jane Eyre*', *Dublin University Magazine*, xxxi (May 1848), p. 611.
37. *Villette*, ii, p. 131.
38. W. Gérin, *Charlotte Brontë*, pp. 209–10.
39. C. Brontë, *Villette*, i, p. 255.
40. W. Gérin, *Charlotte Brontë*, p. 260.
41. *The Brontës, their Lives* ..., iii, pp. 5, 6.
42. ibid., ii, pp. 215–16.
43. ibid., iii, p. 104. Mary Taylor defended work for women in a series of articles in *The Victorian Magazine*, 1865–70.
44. E. Gaskell, *The Life of Charlotte Brontë*, p. 313.
45. The article by H. Taylor appeared in July 1851 in *The Westminster Review*. See M. St. J. Packe, *The Life of J. S. Mill*, p. 347, and E. Gaskell, *The Life* ..., p. 344.
46. R. Offor, *The Brontës: their Relations to the History and Politics of their Time*, p. 7.
47. *The Brontës, their Lives* ..., ii, p. 236.
48. ibid., iv, pp. 14–34.
49. R. Offor, *The Brontës* ..., pp. 4–6. She had seen the issues of the *Mercury* for 1812–1813–1814.
50. C. Shorter, *The Brontës and their Circle*, p. 111.
51. *The Brontës, their Lives* ..., ii, p. 202.
52. '*Jane Eyre*', *Revue des Deux Mondes*, xxiv (October–December 1848), p. 475.
53. E. Rigby, '*Vanity Fair;* ..., *Jane Eyre;* ...'; *Quarterly Review*, lxxxiv (December 1848), p. 173.
54. E. Rigby, art. cit., p. 173. Matthew Arnold condemned the spirit of *Villette* equally severely and says that the reason why *Villette* is an unpleasant work is because the author's spirit contains nothing but hunger, revolt and rage, which was all she knew to put in her book. *Letters*, i, 14 April 1853, p. 29.
55. *Villette*, i, pp. 68–70.
56. *The Brontës, their Lives* ..., iii, pp. 85, 101. The 'Scenes from the Life of an Unprotected Female' appeared in *Punch* from 3 November 1849 to 20 April 1850.
57. *Jane Eyre*, i, p. 167.
58. '*Shirley*', *The Times*, 7 December 1849, in *Brontë Society Transactions*, xi (1950), p. 363.
59. I. S. Ewbank, *Their Proper Sphere*, pp. 44–6.
60. G. H. Lewes, '*Shirley*', *The Edinburgh Review*, xci (January 1850), pp. 160–1.
61. V. Woolf, '*Jane Eyre* and *Wuthering Heights*', *The Common Reader*, First Series, pp. 198–9.
62. George Smith, *Poets and Novelists*, p. 249: 'Her genius is intense but not broad, and it is breadth alone which distinguishes the loftiest minds.'

Notes

63. *Villette*, ii, p. 308.
64. *Shirley*, ii, p. 256.
65. H. Martineau, 'Villette', *Daily News*, 3 February 1853, and E. Gaskell, *The Life of Charlotte Brontë*, pp. 373–5.
66. *The Professor*, pp. 261, 266, 267.
67. David Cecil, *Early Victorian Novelists*, p. 123.
68. 'I knew my traveller with his broad and jetty eyebrows; his square forehead, made squarer by the horizontal sweep of his black hair. I recognized his decisive note, more remarkable for character than beauty; his full nostrils denoting, I thought, choler; his grim mouth, chin, and jaw – yes, all three were very grim, and no mistake. .... I suppose it was a good figure in the athletic sense of the term – broad chested and thin flanked, though neither tall nor graceful.' *Jane Eyre*, i, p. 115.
69. ibid., ii, p. 94.
70. *The Brontës, their Lives* ..., i, p. 174.
71. ibid., i, p. 206.
72. ... *Letters of G. E. Jewsbury to J. W. Carlyle*, pp. 4–7.
73. *The Brontës, their Lives* ..., i, p. 221.
74. W. Gérin, *Charlotte Brontë*, appendix A, pp. 568–75.
75. ibid., ch. 15 and 16.
76. *The Brontës, their Lives* ..., ii, p. 67. NB. This letter was written in French.
77. ibid., i, pp. 256, 260.
78. ibid., ii, p. 35.
79. ibid., ii, p. 148.
80. *The Brontës, their Lives* ..., iv, p. 29.
81. ibid., iv, pp. 30, 57.
82. W. Gérin, *Charlotte Brontë*, p. 471.
83. *The Brontës, their Lives* ..., iv, pp. 115 and 119.
84. ibid., iv, pp. 112, 114.
85. ibid., iv, pp. 145, 152.
86. *The Letters and ... Papers of W. M. Thackeray*, iii, p. 233.
87. *The Brontës, their Lives* ..., iv, pp. 117–18, 164.
88. C. Kingsley, 'A Country-Parish', in *Lectures to Ladies on Practical Subjects*, F. D. Maurice, ed.
89. *Jane Eyre*, ii, pp. 276, 278.
90. K. Tillotson, *Novels of the Eighteen-Forties*, pp. 309–10.
91. *Eliza Cook's Journal*, No. 202, 12 March 1853.
92. 'Le roman contemporain en Angleterre: *Shirley*', *Revue des Deux Mondes*, October–December 1949, pp. 719–20.
93. A contemporary commented: 'Notwithstanding the author's protest on woman's behalf, it is clear that she recognizes marriage as the highest destiny of her sex on earth.' *Eliza Cook's Journal*, No. 40, 2 February 1850, p. 221.
94. L. Dooley, 'Psychoanalysis of Charlotte Brontë, as a Type of the Woman of Genius', *The American Journal of Psychology*, xxxi (July 1920), pp. 248–58.
95. F. E. Ratchford, 'Brontës' Angrian Cycle of Stories', *PMLA*, xliii (June 1928), p. 496.
96. W. Gérin, op. cit., pp. 3–89.

Notes

97. F. E. Ratchford, art. cit., pp. 495–500. See also F. E. Ratchford, *The Brontë's Web of Childhood*, pp. 209–12.
98. W. Gérin, *Charlotte Brontë*, p. 135.
99. L. Dooley, art. cit., p. 234.
100. P. Cominos, 'Late Victorian Sexual Respectability', *International Review of Social History*, viii (1963), pp. 243–50.
101. *Jane Eyre*, ii, p. 100, 'I was experiencing an ordeal: a hand of fiery iron grasped my vitals. Terrible moment ...'
102. *The Brontës, their Lives* ..., ii, p. 170.
103. K. Tillotson, *Novels of the Eighteen-Forties*, p. 306.
104. '... If I were so far to forget myself and all the teaching that had ever been instilled into me, – as under any pretext – with any justification – through any temptation – to become the successor of these poor girls, he would one day regard me with the same feeling which in his mind desecrated their memory.' *Jane Eyre*, ii, p. 95.
105. '... But I remembered caresses were now forbidden. I turned my face away, and put his aside.' *Jane Eyre*, ii, p. 79.
106. 'And what a distortion in your judgement, what a perversity in your ideas, is proved by your conduct! Is it better to drive a fellow-creature to despair than to transgress a mere human law – no man being injured by the breach.' *Jane Eyre*, ii, p. 102.
107. *The George Eliot Letters*, i, p. 268.
108. David Cecil, *Early Victorian Novelists*, p. 127.
109. *The Brontës, their Lives* ..., iv, p. 19.
110. *Jane Eyre*, ii, p. 101.
111. *Jane Eyre*, ii, p. 159.
112. *Jane Eyre*, ii, p. 281.
113. M. Arnold, *Culture and Anarchy*, pp. 131, 137.
114. J. Blondel, *Emily Brontë* ..., Avant-propos, p. 11.
115. W. Gérin, *Charlotte Brontë*, pp. 34–5, 101.
116. J. Blondel, op. cit., pp. 99–100.
117. She wrote to a girl who hesitated between two opposed paths: stay with her old mother or depart to be a governess in a family: '... I will show you candidly how the question strikes me. The right path is that which necessitates the greatest sacrifice of self-interest – which implies the greatest good to others; and this path, steadily followed will lead, I believe, in time, to prosperity and to happiness: though it may seem, at the outset, to tend quite in a contrary direction.' E. Gaskell, *The Life of Charlotte Brontë*, p. 208.
118. *The Brontës, their Lives* ..., iii, pp. 189, 285.
119. ibid., ii, p. 115.
120. W. Gérin, *Charlotte Brontë*, pp. 467–72.
121. G. Bataille, *La Littérature et le mal*, p. 21.

10
A MORE REALISTIC PORTRAYAL

1. *My Lady Ludlow*, Knutsford Edition, ch. 13.
2. ibid., p. 188.

3. 'Libbie Marsh's Three Eras', in *Lizzie Leigh and Other Stories*, ed. Clement Shorter, p. 394.
4. *My Lady Ludlow*, p. 129.
5. *Wives and Daughters*, p. 482.
6. *Cranford*, p. 96.
7. *Wives and Daughters*, pp. 326, 327, 328.
8. ibid., p. 165.
9. See *Cranford* and *Wives and Daughters*, p. 164.
10. *Wives and Daughters*, ch. 14.
11. ibid., p. 523.
12. ibid., pp. 578–9.
13. See M. Dodsworth, 'Women Without Men at Cranford', *Essays in Criticism*, xiii (April 1963).
14. *Wives and Daughters*, p. 185.
15. 'Mr Harrison's Confessions' in *Cousin Phyllis and Other Tales*, p. 120.
16. *Cranford*, p. 159.
17. *My Lady Ludlow*, p. 143.
18. J. A. V. Chapple and A. Pollard, *The Letters of Mrs. Gaskell*, (86), p. 138.
19. See letter from C. Winkworth to his sister Emily in M. J. Shaen, *Memorials of two Sisters ...*, p. 93 : 'Mr Gaskell is doing a great deal now ... in two committees. One is for the better regulation of beer houses and places of public amusement, the other a Sanitary Committee to prepare the town for the next visit of the cholera', and F. Basch, 'Mrs Gaskell vue à travers ses lettres', *Études Anglaises*, xxi, No. 3 (1968), pp. 263–5.
20. Chapple and Pollard, *The Letters of Mrs Gaskell*, (384), p. 488.
21. *Wives and Daughters*, pp. 110–11.
22. ibid., p. 35.
23. ibid., p. 254.
24. See *The Letters of Mrs Gaskell*, (217).
25. A. Rubenius, *The Woman's Question in Mrs Gaskell's Life and Work*, p. 132.
26. A. W. Ward, 'Introduction to *Ruth*', Knutsford edition.
27. *The Letters of Mrs Gaskell*, (217), pp. 320–1.
28. R. D. Waller, 'Letters addressed to Mrs Gaskell by Celebrated Contemporaries', *Bulletin of the John Rylands Library* (Manchester 1935), p. 107.
29. D. Shusterman, 'W. R. Greg and Mrs Gaskell', *Philological Quarterly*, xxxvi (April 1957), p. 268, see W. R. Greg, 'Mary Barton', *The Edinburgh Review*, lxxxix (April 1849).
30. A. Rubenius, *The Woman's Question ...*, p. 165.
31. *North and South*, pp. 118–20.
32. A. Rubenius, *The Woman's Question ...*, p. 144.
33. *Mary Barton*, pp. 138–9.
34. *North and South*, p. 121.
35. In an article, mentioned in note 19, I have examined the limitations of Mrs Gaskell's feminism and social demands.
36. *North and South*, p. 80.
37. *Coningsby* (1844), *Sybil or the Two Nations* (1845), *Tancred* (1847) form a trilogy. The first two novels expound the philosophy of history of Dis-

raeli and the ideas of the Young England Movement. See R. Blake, *Disraeli*, ch. 9.
38. *Coningsby*, Bk. 4, p. 151.
39. *Ibid.*, p. 153.
40. R. Blake, *Disraeli*, p. 121, note 2.
41. S. M. Smith, 'Willenhall and Wodgate: Disraeli's Use of Blue Books Evidence', *Review of English Studies*, New Series, xiii, 52 (November 1962), pp. 368–84.
42. One of the members of the Commission of Enquiry on Children's labour in mines and factories, set up on 20 October 1840. The first report on work in mines appeared in 1842, and Willenhall is mentioned in the 2nd part of the appendix to the 2nd report of the commission. Cf. S. M. Smith, art. cit., pp. 368–9 and notes.
43. *Sybil*, pp. 174–5, 203.
44. See *Reports from Commissioners*, Children's Employment (Mines), *Parliamentary Papers*, xv (1842, part 1, pp. 86–96 and 105–7).
45. *Sybil* ..., p. 121.
46. Which did not prevent him for political reasons from intervening against a Bill of Ashley about inspection of mines in 1850. See R. Blake, *Disraeli*, pp. 179 and 296.
47. Lord Ashley, *Hansard*, House of Commons, 14 March 1844, col. 1096 and 1097.
48. *Sybil* ..., pp. 142–5.
49. ibid., p. 112.
50. ibid., pp. 123–4.
51. ibid., pp. 124–5.
52. ibid., p. 113.
53. H. Martineau, *Autobiography*, i, p. 133.
54. *The Letters of Elizabeth Barrett Browning*, ii, p. 189.

PART THREE

11

THE GREAT SOCIAL EVIL

1. O. McGregor, 'The Social Position of Women in England, 1850–1914', A Bibliography, *British Journal of Sociology*, No. 1, 1955, pp. 48–60; F. Engels, *The Condition of the Working Classes in England in 1844*, p. xxvi; B. Harrison, 'Underneath the Victorians', *Victorian Studies* (March 1967), p. 240.
2. *Sinks of London Laid Open*, p. 89.
3. O. McGregor, art. cit. p. 59, note 63.
4. M. Ryan, *Prostitution in London*, 1833; W. Tait, *Magdelinism* ..., 1840; W. Acton, *Prostitution* ..., 1857; J. Greenwood, *The Seven Curses of London*, 1863; H. Mayhew, *London Labour and the London Poor*, 1861, the chapter on prostitution in London is by Bracebridge Hemyng; W. R. Greg, *The Great Sin of Great Cities*, 1850.
5. The number of prostitutes identified by the police was nothing like the real number. Thus Acton speaks of 8,600 prostitutes registered by the

Notes

Metropolitan Police in 1857 (pp. 16, 18); but Ryan in 1839 (pp. 89, 168) quoting Talbot gave a total of 80,000 prostitutes for London. Mayhew in 1861 followed Ryan (iv, p. 213). Engels in 1844 speaks of 40,000 prostitutes in London, without giving any other information (p. 144), and Taine in 1872 50,000 (p. 47). R. Vaughan in his apologia for the great cities and industrial England (p. 227), deliberately used these gaps between estimates, to jeer at the exaggeration in the estimates of immorality. As for the unmarried mothers, William Acton estimated there were 2,449,669 in England and Wales (p. 18).

6. Michael Ryan quoted a report of the London Society for the Protection of Young Females of 18 October 1836 according to which there were 1,500 brothels in the city but more probably twice that number. Acton in 1857 gave the figures of the report of the Metropolitan Police: 2,825 brothels. M. Ryan, op. cit., p. 132. W. Acton, *Prostitution* ..., p. 16.

7. H. Mayhew, *London Labour* ..., iv, p. 220.

8. T. C. Hansard, *Parliamentary Debates*, Lord Ashley in the Commons, 7 June 1842, 'Employment of Women and Children in Mines and Collieries', col. 1349 and 1350.

9. H. Mayhew, *London Labour* ..., iv; J. Greenwood, *The Seven Curses* ..., pp. 287–9; S. Marcus, *The Other Victorians*, pp. 99, 100, 156; *My Secret Life*, ii, ch. 9, iii, pp. 8, 54, 151, 161.

10. Julia Desmond, a young prostitute, told how on leaving hospital she had been accosted by 'a nice motherly woman ...' who offered to help her. In a fine apartment '... I saw many young ladies, elegantly dressed, who all called her "mother", and to whom she seemed very kind.' That evening, presented to several 'clients', Julia learned the truth. The procuress who had given her a present of jewellery threatened to denounce her to the police for theft if she fled. *Doings in London* ... p. 84.

11. M. Ryan, *Prostitution* ..., pp. 188, 189.

12. W. Acton, *Prostitution* ..., pp. 108, 117.

13. 'The Greatest of our Social Evils', *The Times*, 6 May 1857.

14. W. Acton, *Prostitution* ..., p. 169 and note.

15. J. Greenwood, *The Seven Curses of London*, pp. 316–17, 319.

16. J. Greenwood, op. cit., pp. 321–2.

17. W. Acton, *Prostitution* ..., p. 99, etc.

18. Taine, *Notes* ..., p. 48.

19. W. Acton, *Prostitution* ..., ed. P. Fryer, p. 235, note 24.

20. *My Secret Life*, iv, p. 199.

21. Taine, *Notes* ..., p. 48.

22. W. Acton, *Prostitution* ..., ed. P. Fryer, pp. 103, 234, note 20.

23. F. Tristan, *Promenades dans Londres*, p. 7.

24. E. Montégut, 'Un missionnaire de la cité de Londres', *Revue des Deux Mondes*, viii (1 November 1854), pp. 491–4.

25. *Sinks of London* ..., p. 89.

26. L. Enault, *Londres*, p. 104.

27. M. Ryan, *Prostitution* ..., p. 74; H. Mayhew, *London Labour* ..., iv, p. 255.

28. I. Pinchbeck, *Women Workers and the Industrial Revolution*, p. 212.

29. H. Mayhew, *London Labour* ..., iv, p. 262.

308

Notes

30. M. Ryan, op. cit., p. 180.

31. '... How did I come to get this sort of life? It's easy to tell. I was a servant gal away down in Birmingham. I got tired of workin' and slavin' to make a livin', and getting a – bad one at that; what o' five pun' a year and yer grub, I'd sooner starve, I would.' H. Mayhew, *London Labour* ..., iv, p. 223.

32. ibid., p. 258.

33. W. Gilbert, *Dives and Lazarus*, pp. 75–6.

34. Walter had countless adventures with servants in his family or, later, at home: Mary, the cook, Charlotte the chambermaid, Sarah and Susan two sisters whom he impregnated almost simultaneously. *My Secret Life*, i, ch. 4, 5, 12.

35. W. R. Greg, 'Why are Women Redundant?' in *Literary and Social Judgments*, p. 303.

36. W. R. Greg, 'Juvenile and Female Labour', *Edinburgh Review*, lxxix (January 1844), pp. 138–45.

37. F. Engels, *The Condition of the Working Classes* ..., pp. 108–9, p. xx.

38. ibid., pp. 135, 136, 144, 166, 167, 168.

39. W. R. Greg, *The Great Sin* ..., pp. 16, 17.

40. W. Gilbert, *Dives and Lazarus*, p. 150.

41. *My Secret Life*, ii, ch. 8.

42. H. Mayhew, *London Labour* ..., iv, p. 257.

43. I. Pinchbeck, *Women Workers* ..., p. 212.

44. W. R. Greg, *The Great Sin* ..., p. 11.

45. *Doings in London* ..., p. 83.

46. *My Secret Life*, ii, p. 128, iii, p. 82.

47. H. Mayhew, op. cit., pp. 256, 257.

48. W. R. Greg, *The Great Sin* ..., p. 17, Report to H.M.G.'s Principal Secretary of State for the Home Department from the Poor Law Commissioners on an Inquiry into the Sanitary Condition of the Labouring Population (by Edwin Chadwick), p. 18.

49. W. Gilbert, *Dives* ..., p. 151.

50. W. R. Greg, *The Great Sin* ..., p. 19.

51. H. Mayhew, *London Labour* ..., iv, p. 257.

52. W. Tait, *Magdelinism* ..., p. 112.

53. H. Mayhew, *London Labour* ..., iv, p. 212.

54. W. R. Greg, *The Great Sin* ..., pp. 12, 13.

55. As well as the original, *My Secret Life*, which can only be consulted in the British Museum Reading Room with special permission, it is necessary to read Stephen Marcus's study, *The Other Victorians* and B. Harrison's 'Underneath the Victorians', *Victorian Studies* (March 1967).

56. *My Secret Life*, viii, p. 230.

57. K. Thomas, 'The Double Standard', *Journal of the History of Ideas*, 1959, pp. 212–13.

58. M. Ryan, *Prostitution* ..., p. 171.

59. W. Acton, *Prostitution* ..., pp. 57, 62.

60. ibid., p. 169.

61. *The Times*, 5 May 1857.

62. W. Acton, *Prostitution* ..., p. 170.

63. ibid., p. 171.
64. See H. Mayhew, *London Labour* ..., iv, pp. 212 and 233, W. Acton, op. cit., p. 33, and M. Ryan, op. cit., part II.
65. W. R. Greg, *The Great Sin* ..., p. 36.
66. W. E. H. Lecky, *History of European Morals*, ii, pp. 282–3. Francis Newman called these laws 'Safe Harlot Providing Acts'. See G. Himmelfarb, *Victorian Minds*, p. 309.
67. H. Mayhew, *London Labour* ..., iv, p. 212.
68. M. Ryan, *Prostitution* ..., pp. 160–3.
69. H. Mayhew, *London Labour* ..., iv, p. 213.
70. ibid., iv, pp. 240–1.
71. ibid., iv, pp. 215–17.
72. *The Times*, 6 May 1857.
73. W. Acton, *Prostitution* ..., p. 73.
74. H. Mayhew, *London Labour* ..., iv, p. 219.
75. J. W. Kaye, 'Employment of Women', *North British Review* (February 1857), pp. 324–7.
76. H. Mayhew, *London Labour* ..., iv, p. 219.
77. ibid., p. 226.
78. W. Acton, *Prostitution* ..., p. 72.
79. *My Secret Life*, viii, p. 229, v, p. 332. See also K. Thomas, 'The Double Standard', p. 206.
80. F. Engels, *The Condition of the Labouring Classes* ..., pp. 144–5.
81. M. Ryan, *Prostitution* ..., p. 209.
82. David Owen's book *English Philanthropy, 1660–1960*, almost entirely neglects this aspect of Victorian good works.
83. M. Ryan, op. cit., p. 90, etc., and H. Mayhew, *London Labour* ..., iv, p. 210.
84. H. Mayhew, ibid., pp. 268–9. D. Owen quotes 25 or 30 establishments of this kind, op. cit., p. 163.
85. *The Times*, 'The Greatest of our Social Evils', 6 May 1857.
86. T. T. Carter, *The First ten Years of the House of Mercy, Clewer*
87. John Blackmore, *London by Moonlight*, Nos. 1 and 2.
88. P. Magnus, *Gladstone*, pp. 106–8; see too the summary of interrogations at the Marlborough Street Police Court, in *The Times*, 14 May 1853, as well as a letter to the paper signed 'J.S.' about the philanthropic nocturnal tours of Gladstone, 13 May 1853. See M. R. D. Foot, *Gladstone Diaries*.
89. P. Collins, *Dickens and Crime*, p. 111.
90. ibid., pp. 101, 102.
91. *Letters from Charles Dickens to Angela Burdett-Coutts*, pp. 98, 103, 167–8.
92. T. T. Carter, *The First Ten Years* ..., p. 40.
93. *Letters from Charles Dickens* ..., pp. 78–9, 124–7.
94. ibid., pp. 153, 228, 250, 267.
95. *Letters from Charles Dickens to Angela Burdett-Coutts*, pp. 178–9.
96. ibid., pp. 78, 85, and '... there could be little or no hope in this country for the greater part ... That they came there to be ultimately sent abroad, ...' 'Home for Homeless Women', *Household Words*, 23 April 1853, p. 169.
97. 'Home for Homeless Women', p. 170.

Notes

98. P. Collins, *Dickens and Crime*, p. 108.
99. *Letters from Charles Dickens* ..., pp. 98–9.
100. C. Dickens, 'The Ruffian' in *The Uncommercial Traveller*, Nonesuch Dickens, p. 633 (*All The Year Round*, 10 October 1868).
101. 'Female Penitentiaries', *The Quarterly Review*, September 1848, p. 364.
102. 'London by Moonlight'.
103. H. Mayhew, op. cit., p. 268.
104. M. Ryan, op. cit., pp. 125–30.
105. T. T. Carter, op. cit., p. 39.
106. 'Home for Homeless Women', *Household Words*, 23 April 1853, p. 169.
107. J. Butler, *Personal Reminiscences of a Great Crusade*, pp. 24–9, 30, 31, etc. B. Harrison, 'Beneath the Victorians', *Victorian Studies*, x, No. 3 (March 1967), p. 261.

12
DICKENS'S SINNERS

1. K. Hollingsworth, *The Newgate Novel, 1830–1847*, ch. 1 and 2.
2. In her book K. Hollingsworth studies in detail the dates of appearance of the instalments of *Oliver Twist* in *Bentley's Miscellany* and how they relate to Dickens's work as a journalist and the dates of Bills to reform the penal code, pp. 111–14.
3. K. Hollingsworth, op. cit. pp. 114–16, and C. Dickens, 'The Hospital Patient', *Sketches by Boz*, p. 243. S. Marcus points out that one of the sources for the character would be Madge Wildfire in *The Heart of Midlothian*, Dickens, p. 76, note 2.
4. *Oliver Twist*, pp. xi and xix. The categorical tone confirms the hypothesis of Hollingsworth, whereby the incident related in 'The Hospital Patient' is at the origin of the conception of Nancy.
5. *Oliver Twist*, Preface of 1841, p. ix.
6. Thackeray. 'Going to See a Man Hanged', *Fraser's Magazine*, xxii (August 1840), in Hollingsworth, *The Newgate Novel* ..., pp. 128–9.
7. 'Catherine: a Story', *Fraser's Magazine*, xxi (February 1840), p. 211.
8. The word is cut in other editions, cf. P. Collins, *Dickens and Crime*, p. 96.
9. *Oliver Twist*, p. 305.
10. ibid., p. 141.
11. K. Tillotson, *Novels of the Eighteen Forties*, p. 66. But H. House, writes: 'He did not escape in his language ... but he did not escape in his ideas either.' *The Dickens World*, p. 219.
12. H. House, *The Dickens World*, pp. 216, 217.
13. *Oliver Twist*, pp. 89 and 90.
14. ibid., pp. 302 and 303.
15. ibid., p. 304.
16. ibid., p. 305.
17. ibid., p. 308.
18. S. Marcus sees in Nancy's hallucinations – images of flames of hell, of shroud, of coffin, both the language of melodrama and of an evangelical tradition, *Dickens*. 69–71.
19. Z. Raafat, *Melodrama in Charles Dickens's Writings*, p. 245.

20. E. Wilson, 'Dickens and the two Scrooges', *The Wound and the Bow*, p. 62.
21. A. Nicoll, *History of the English Drama*, p. 97.
22. E. Johnson, *Charles Dickens* ..., ii, pp. 1103 and 1104.
23. See Z. Raafat, op. cit., p. 244.
24. H. House, *The Dickens World*, ch. 6 and p. 63.
25. H. House, op. cit., p. 165.
26. *Dombey and Son*, p. 2.
27. J. Moynahan, 'Dealings with the Firm of Dombey and Son', in *Dickens and the Twentieth Century*.
28. S. Marcus, *Dickens* ..., p. 339.
29. See J. Holloway, 'Hard Times ...' in *Dickens and the Twentieth Century*.
30. H. House, *The Dickens World*, p. 69.
31. *Hard Times*, p. 687.
32. E. Wilson, art. cit. in *The Wound and the Bow*, p. 42.
33. *Hard Times*, p. 489.
34. *Dombey and Son*, pp. 292, 278.
35. J. Butt and K. Tillotson, *Dickens at Work*, p. 103.
36. *The Letters of Charles Dickens*, ii, pp. 17, 18.
37. *Dombey* ..., p. 754.
38. A. O. J. Cockshut, op. cit., pp. 106, 107.
39. Butt and Tillotson, op. cit., p. 103, note 3.
40. ibid., p. 109.
41. *Dombey* ..., pp. 566, 660–1.
42. *Hard Times*, p. 606: 'Cheerless and comfortless, boastfully and doggedly rich, there the room stared at its present occupants, unsoftened and unrelieved by the least trace of womanly occupation.'
43. *Dombey* ..., p. 292.
44. ibid., pp. 374, 392, 425. It appears to me difficult to speak, as does K. Tillotson, of the complexity of Edith's character, and to think that the conventions of melodrama are only superimposed on the character. *Novels of the 1840s*, p. 177.
45. See Angus Wilson's analysis, 'The Heroes and Heroines of Dickens', *A Review of English Literature*, July 1951, p. 16.
46. *Hard Times*, p. 606.
47. *Dombey* ..., pp. 566, 613, 664, 764.
48. ibid., see the illustration by 'Phiz'. *Dombey* ..., pp. 761–2.
49. ibid., p. 664, see illustration.
50. *Bleak House*, pp. 507, 508.
51. *Dombey* ..., pp. 652, 653.
52. K. Tillotson, *Novels* ..., p. 179.
53. *Dombey* ..., illustrations pp. 496, 576, 762.
54. M. Praz, *The Hero in Eclipse* ..., p. 129.
55. E. Wilson, 'Dickens and the two Scrooges', in *The Wound and the Bow*, p. 60.
56. K. Tillotson, *Novels* ..., p. 180.
57. Butt and Tillotson, *Dickens at Work*, p. 95, note 1.
58. *Dombey* ..., p. 424.
59. *Hard Times*, p. 698.
60. *Bleak House*, p. 507.

Notes

61. *Dombey* ..., pp. 424, 425.
62. *Hard Times*, p. 698.
63. *Bleak House*, p. 508. See also illustrations, pp. 762, 766, 806.
64. *Hard Times*, pp. 683, 684.
65. *Dombey* ..., p. 873.
66. *Hard Times*, p. 765.
67. *The Letters of Charles Dickens*, ii, 10 March 1847, pp. 17, 18.
68. *David Copperfield*, pp. 102, 139, 142.
69. P. Collins, *Dickens and Crime*, p. 97.
70. *David Copperfield*, p. 289.
71. ibid., pp. 141, 142.
72. ibid., ch. 7 and p. 231.
73. A. Wilson, 'The Heroes and Heroines of Dickens', in *Dickens and the Twentieth Century*, p. 9.
74. *David Copperfield*, p. 35.
75. ibid., p. 302.
76. *David Copperfield*, pp. 103, 464.
77. ibid., pp. 662, 664.
78. P. Collins, *Dickens and Crime*, p. 98.
79. ibid., see also Butt and Tillotson, *Dickens at Work*, pp. 148, 149.
80. *The Letters of Charles Dickens*, ii, 23 January 1850, p. 201.
81. See the articles in *Household Words*, of 30 March and 26 June 1850 quoted by Butt and Tillotson, op. cit., pp. 166, 167, note 1.
82. M. Praz, *The Hero in Eclipse* ..., p. 131.
83. P. Collins, *Dickens and Crime*, p. 97.
84. *David Copperfield*, pp. 303, 437.
85. *David Copperfield*, p. 448.
86. For details of the pathetic and sentimental style of these letters, see S. Monod, *Dickens romancier*, p. 339.
87. *David Copperfield*, pp. 622, 623, 719–22.
88. *David Copperfield*, p. 863.
89. P. Collins, *Dickens and Crime*, p. 114.
90. *Charles Dickens*, iii, 2 January 1869, p. 697.
91. *David Copperfield*, pp. 321, 322.
92. ibid., p. 330.
93. ibid., pp. 322–36. Arnold Kettle emphasizes humorously the artificial side of this scene: 'It is true that Em'ly and Martha protest too much, presumably for the benefit of Miss Burdett-Coutts's charitable efforts on behalf of the prostitutes. If their misery and remorse is so continuous – Em'ly's begins *before* she goes off with Steerforth – it is hard to understand why the prospect of sexual freedom should have held such a strong attraction.' 'Thoughts on *David Copperfield*', *A Review of English Literature*, ii, No. 3 (July 1961), p. 74.
94. *David Copperfield*, pp. 673, 674.
95. *David Copperfield*, ch. 47, 'Martha'.
96. ibid., p. 863.
97. Butt and Tillotson, *Dickens at Work*, p. 118.
98. *David Copperfield*, p. 36, from 'You're quite a sailor ...' to 'This may be premature'.

99. *Letters ... to Angela Burdett-Coutts*, 4 February 1850, p. 165.

100. See *Crazy Jane*, 1827, *Michael Erle, the Maniac Lover*, 1839, *Richard Plantagenet*, 1836, M. Booth's study, *The English Melodrama*, pp. 123, 124.

101. M. Booth, op. cit., *The English Melodrama*, pp. 121, 122.

102. ibid., pp. 153, 154.

103. M. Booth quotes words which seem to have come out of the mouth of Martha or Nancy or extracts from 'An Appeal to Fallen Women', *Letters from Charles Dickens to Angela Burdett-Coutts*, pp. 98–100: 'What word is strong enough to paint the misery of the betrayed, abandoned broken-hearted woman? The good scorn her – daylight will not brook her – sin alone opens a door of refuge, and the yells of a wolfish world are in her ears, ... Look at her now in the spotted livery of shame, the prey of every drunken ruffian! Behold her cheek; the foul breath of lust has poisoned the innocent bloom that once bore witness to the health within.' *Lilian, the Show Girl*, 1836, M. Booth, op. cit., p. 142.

104. 'Nineteenth Century Drama', *Victorian Studies*, xii, No. 21 (September 1968), p. 94.

13

THE SIREN AND THE LADDER

1. See W. M. Thackeray, 'Novels by Eminent Hands', 1846, in *Contributions to Punch*, i.

2. Thackeray, 'William Ainsworth and Jack Sheppard', *Fraser's Magazine*, xxi (February 1840), p. 228.

3. See *The Letters and Private Papers* ..., ii, pp. 281, 282.

4. ibid., iv, pp. 206, 207, 227, 228.

5. 'Catherine: a Story', *Fraser's Magazine*, xxi (February 1840), p. 211.

6. G. N. Ray, *Thackeray* ..., i, p. 385. J. E. Baker, 'Vanity Fair and the Celestial City', *Nineteenth Century Fiction*, x (September 1955), p. 89.

7. K. Tillotson, *Novels* ..., p. 226; G. N. Ray, *Thackeray* ..., i, pp. 389–93.

8. *Vanity Fair*, pp. 14, 114.

9. 'But Captain Dobbin does become the hero, and is deficient. ... why is he so shamefully ugly, so shy, so awkward? Why was he the son of a grocer? Thackeray in so depicting him was determined to run counter to the recognized taste of novel readers.' Trollope, *Thackeray*, p. 93.

10. Thackeray explains his taste for reality as opposed to the heroic in *The Letters and Private Papers* ..., ii, May 1851, pp. 772, 773.

11. *The Letters and Private Papers* ..., ii, pp. 312, 313.

12. A Hayward, 'Thackeray's Writings', *The Edinburgh Review*, lxxxvii January 1848), p. 50.

13. E. Rigby, 'Vanity Fair ..., Jane Eyre ...', *The Quarterly Review*, lxxxiv December 1848), pp. 153–85.

14. *The Examiner*, 22 July 1848, p. 468, quoted in *The Letters and Private Papers* ..., ii, p. 424.

15. R. Bell, in *Fraser's Magazine*, September 1848, quoted in *The Letters and Private Papers* ..., ii, p. 423, note 165.

16. G. N. Ray, *The Buried Life*, pp. 48, 49. H. Martineau, *Autobiography*, ii, p. 376.

Notes

17. Trollope, *Thackeray*, pp. 93, 94.
18. *Vanity Fair*, p. 250.
19. A. E. Dyson, 'Vanity Fair', *Critical Quarterly*, vi (Spring 1964), p. 16.
20. *The Letters and Private Papers* ..., ii, pp. 309, 473. See note on the same page which quotes Bell in *Fraser's Magazine*, September 1848.
21. J. E. Baker, 'Vanity Fair and the Celestial City', *Nineteenth Century Fiction*, x (September 1955), p. 90.
22. W. C. Roscoe, cited by K. Tillotson, *Novels* ..., p. 235.
23. *Vanity Fair*, p. 55.
24. ibid., pp. 109, 124.
25. ibid., p. 469.
26. ibid., pp. 85, 86.
27. E. D. Forgues, 'Poètes et romanciers modernes de la Grande-Bretagne: W. M. Thackeray et ses romans', *Revue des Deux Mondes*, 1 September 1854, p. 1018.
28. E. Rigby, art. cit., p. 157.
29. 'If a person is too poor to keep a servant, though ever so elegant, he must sweep his own room: if a dear girl has no dear Mamma to settle matters with the young man, she must do it for herself.' *Vanity Fair*, pp. 33-4.
30. *Vanity Fair*, p. 88.
31. ibid., p. 92.
32. R. A. Fraser, 'Pernicious Casuistry ...', *Nineteenth Century Fiction*, xii (1941), pp. 144-5.
33. *Vanity Fair*, p. 474.
34. ibid., pp. 164-5.
35. ibid., pp. 133, 138, 306-8.
36. K. Tillotson, *Novels* ..., p. 246.
37. *Vanity Fair*, pp. 409-10.
38. *The Morning Chronicle*, 6 March 1848, in *The Letters and Private Papers* ..., ii, 353.
39. ibid., ii, p. 354.
40. E. Rigby, art. cit., p. 157.
41. Becky's French origins allow her, she believes, to provide a comfortable explanation for this difference: 'The only criticism we would offer is one which the author has almost disarmed by making her mother a French-woman. The construction of this little clever monster is diabolically French ... France is the land for the real Siren, with the woman's face and the dragon's claws.' E. Rigby, p. 160, 'Vanity Fair ..., Jane Eyre ..., *The Quarterly Review*, lxxxiv (December 1848).
42. G. Saintsbury, *A Consideration of Thackeray*, pp. 168-9.
43. K. Tillotson, *Novels* ..., pp. 240-4. M. Taube, 'Contrast as a Principle of Structure in Vanity Fair', *Nineteenth Century Fiction*, xviii (September 1963).
44. *Vanity Fair*, pp. 286-7.
45. M. Taube, art. cit., p. 120.
46. 'But she [Amelia] has at present a quality above most people ...: Love – by wh. she shall be saved.' *The Letters and Private Papers* ..., ii, p. 309.
47. *Vanity Fair*, p. 298.

Notes

48. Despite Trollope's reservations (see the beginning of the chapter), Dobbin is the only character, with Amelia, to find grace in the eyes of Thackeray. See *The Letters and Private Papers* ..., ii, p. 381, and R. Las Vergnas, *W. M. Thackeray* ..., p. 283.

49. R. A. Fraser, art. cit., p. 142 and J. E. Tilford, 'The Degradation of Becky Sharp', *South Atlantic Quarterly*, lviii (Autumn 1959), p. 605.

50. *Vanity Fair*, pp. 18, 19.

51. A. E. Dyson, who has also been struck by this portrayal, writes: '... Thackeray goes out of his way to blacken her character in the opening pages, ...' *Vanity Fair* ..., *Critical Quarterly*, vi (Spring 1964), p. 18.

52. See H. A. Talon, *Two Essays on Thackeray*, p. 19.

53. *Vanity Fair*, p. 369.

54. ibid., p. 433.

55. '... Thackeray continually indicates his distaste for her ... shrill voice ... livid hatred ... demoniacal laughter ... this angel ... Poor little Becky ...' Cf. J. E. Tilford, art. cit., p. 605, and *Vanity Fair*, p. 515.

56. *Vanity Fair*, p. 114.

57. ibid., p. 515.

58. ibid., p. 617.

59. ibid., pp. 514–17.

60. ibid., p. 662.

61. J. E. Tilford, art. cit., p. 607.

62. M. Talon does not share this opinion! 'I do not believe that she ever slept with Lord Steyne, or with any other man except her husband.' op. cit., p. 11.

63. *Vanity Fair*, pp. 617–18. We can catch Thackeray here red-handed in a contradiction. Did he not reproach Dickens with taking risks in the portrayal of one of his characters, Nancy, in *Oliver Twist*, whose most important activities ought to have been hushed up? 'We had better pass them by in utter silence; for, as no writer can or dare tell the *whole* truth concerning them, and faithfully explain their vices, there is no need to give *ex-parte* statements of their virtues.' 'Catherine: a Story', *Fraser's Magazine*, xxi (February 1840), p. 211.

64. Thackeray's ambivalence towards Becky and Amelia, the discordance between the values professed by the narrator and the action of the novel have been interpreted as symptoms of a neurosis in a recent study inspired by the theories of Karen Horney and Erich Fromm. R. J. Paris, 'The Psychic Structure of *Vanity Fair*', *Victorian Studies*, x (June 1967). No. V.

65. R. D. Fraser, art. cit., p. 146.

66. K. Tillotson suggests that to have to play this last part was the supreme punishment for Becky. See *Novels* ... p. 233.

67. See the study of Amelia in this book.

68. ibid., i, pp. 205–11 and *passim*, *Vanity Fair*, p. 165. The account of the visit to the Brays, in *The Letters and Private Papers* ..., ii, note 46, pp. 437–8, an attack against men seeking submissive wives and therefore hypocritical wives, in 'Sketches and Travels in London', *Contribution to Punch*, ii, pp. 306–8. See letter to Isabella Shawe on education, in *The Letters and Private Papers* ... p. 317. See 'The Lion-huntress of Belgravia', in *Miscellanies*, p. 236.

69. See *The Letters and Private Papers* ..., i, pp. 460 and iv, appendix XXVI, p. 419: 'Some More Words About Ladies' in 'Sketches and Travels in London', *Contributions to Punch*, ii, pp. 245–9.

70. *Morning Chronicle*, 3 April 1845, quoted by G. N. Ray, '*Vanity Fair*, one Version of the Novelist's Responsibility', *Essays by Diverse Hands*, xxv (1950), p. 90.

71. *The Letters and Private Papers* ..., ii, p. 282.

14

SEDUCTION IN ELIZABETH GASKELL AND GEORGE ELIOT

1. A. B. Hopkins, *Elizabeth Gaskell* ..., p. 52.

2. A. Briggs, *Victorian Cities*, pp. 122–4, 130.

3. ibid., pp. 98, 111–12, and *Report on the Sanitary Condition of the Labouring Population of Great Britain*.

4. *The Letters of Mrs Gaskell*, (52), p. 87.

5. *The Letters of Mrs Gaskell*, (12), p. 33.

6. S. and C. Winkworth, *Memorials of Two Sisters*, p. 93; A. Pollard, *Mrs Gaskell*, p. 15.

7. F. Basch, 'Mrs Gaskell vue à travers ses lettres' *Études Anglaises*, xxi, No. 3 (1968), p. 263.

8. *Mary Barton*, p. 26.

9. K. Tillotson has noted how, through the language and conventional formulae of Mary the scene of the rupture becomes melodrama, *Novels* ..., p. 214.

10. *The Letters of Mrs Gaskell*, (39), 5 January 1849, (42), 1843, p. 74.

11. W. R. Greg, *The Great Sin of Great Cities*, pp. 4–8.

12. W. R. Greg, 'Mary Barton', *Mistaken Aims* ... and *The Great Sin of Great Cities*, p. 23: W. R. Greg gives 700 prostitutes for Manchester.

13. Unlike her friend Catherine Winkworth. *Memorials of Two Sisters*, p. 62.

14. *The Letters of Mrs Gaskell*, (61–62–63–42).

15. *Mary Barton*, pp. 143, 185; K. Tillotson, *The Novels* ..., pp. 204–6.

16. A. Pollard, *Mrs Gaskell*, pp. 38–9.

17. K. Tillotson does not agree: 'She is a warning, but never the stereotyped "outcast".' *The Novels* ..., p. 65.

18. *Mary Barton*, pp. 142–4.

19. *Lizzie Leigh*, p. 35.

20. 'To whom shall the outcast prostitute tell her tale? Who will give her help in the day of need? Hers is the leper-sin, and all stand aloof dreading to be counted unclean.' *Mary Barton*, p. 185.

21. R. D. Waller, 'Letters Addressed to Mrs Gaskell', *Bulletin of the John Rylands Library*, xix (1935), p. 110.

22. *The Letters of Mrs Gaskell*, 'Half the masters here are bitterly angry with me.' (37).

23. K. Tillotson, *The Novels* ..., pp. 206–8; A. Pollard, *Mrs Gaskell*, p. 59.

24. 'Lizzie Leigh' appeared in *Household Words*, on 20 March, and 6 and 13 April 1850.

25. *The Letters of Mrs Gaskell*, (153).

26. ibid., (211).

27. ibid., (61, 62, 63).

Notes

28. He writes: '... I fear that the subject is not as new for me as it must be for an Englishman ... What passes in England for boldness is something very simple in France'. Letter from Mérimée to Mrs William Senior (shortly after the appearance of E. Mortégut's 'Le roman social en Angleterre', *Revue des Deux Mondes*, April–June 1853). A. B. Hopkins, 'Mrs Gaskell in France', *P.M.L.A.* liii, 1938, p. 562.

29. G. H. Lewes, 'Ruth and Villette', *Westminster Review*, iii (April 1853), pp. 474–91.

30. C. and S. Winkworth, *Memorials of Two Sisters*, pp. 98–101.

31. W. R. Greg, 'False Morality of Lady Novelists', *Literary and Social Judgments*, p. 110.

32. *The Letters of Mrs Gaskell*, (150), (151).

33. *The Letters of Mrs Gaskell*, (148) and (150).

34. See the two letters from Samuel Greg to Leonard Horner the factory inspector about his philanthropic activities in his own factory: Sunday school, drawing lessons, singing lessons, organized games. *Two Letters to Leonard Horner, Esq. on the Capabilities of the Factory System.*

35. W. R. Greg, *The Great Sin ...*, p. 20.

36. '... one of Mrs Gaskell's objects was to make her readers feel how much worse he was in every way that Ruth, although the world visited her conduct with so much heavier a penalty than his.' *Memorials of Two Sisters*, p. 101.

37. E. Wright traces this evolution in *Mrs Gaskell*, pp. 70–1.

38. G. H. Lewes observed that in this matter no illegitimate child would be exposed to an opprobrium as cruel as that imagined by Mrs Gaskell. 'Ruth and Villette', p. 485.

39. A. B. Hopkins, *Elizabeth Gaskell ...*, p. 130.

40. *Ruth*, p. 146.

41. G. H. Lewes, 'Ruth and Villette', *The Westminster Review*, iii (April 1853), p. 480.

42. A. Pollard, *Mrs Gaskell*, p. 102 and C. and S. Winkworth, *Memorials of Two Sisters*, p. 103.

43. ibid., pp. 99 and 103: 'sie musste untergehen, ...'

44. A. Pollard, op. cit., p. 102.

45. W. R. Greg, 'False Morality ...', in *Literary and Social Judgments*, p. 112.

46. *Ruth*, pp. 120–1.

47. ibid., pp. 180, 191.

48. Kebbel, 'Village Life of George Eliot', *Fraser's Magazine*, xxiii (February 1881), pp. 274–5.

49. I. Gregor and B. Nicholas, 'The two Worlds of *Adam Bede*', in *The Moral and the Story*, pp. 16–19, 24. Barbara Hardy, *Adam Bede* a 'new pastoral', *The Novels of George Eliot*, p. 34.

50. F. R. Leavis, 'George Eliot', in *A Century of George Eliot Criticism*, G. S. Haight, ed., p. 239.

51. *The George Eliot Letters*, ii, pp. 502–3.

52. H. James, 'The Novels of George Eliot', *A Century of ...*, p. 47.

53. *The George Eliot Letters*, ii, p. 503.

54. H. James, 'The Novels of George Eliot', *A Century of George Eliot Criticism*, p. 47. H. James, 'Felix Holt the Radical', in *A Century of ...*, p. 41.

Notes

55. 31 March 1858, *The George Eliot Letters*, ii, p. 446.
56. H. James, 'Felix Holt the Radical', *A Century of* ..., p. 41.
57. Gregor & Nicholas, ch. cit.; R. Stump, *Movement and Vision in George Eliot's Novels*, I. W. Adam, 'Restoration through Feeling in George Eliot's Fiction, A new Look at Hetty Sorrel', *Victorian Newsletter*, February 1962.
58. C. T. Bissell, 'Social Analysis in the Novels of George Eliot', *Journal of English Literary History*, September 1951, p. 231.
59. See Introduction.
60. B. Willey, 'George Eliot', *A Century of George Eliot Criticism*, p 260.
61. G. Hough, 'Novelist-philosophers – xii George Eliot', *Horizon*, xvii (January 1948), p. 54.
62. *Adam Bede*, pp. 45, 46.
63. See the first chapter of the novel. Adam working sings a hymn:

    Awake my soul, and with the sun
    Thy daily stage of duty run;
    Shake off dull sloth ...

    See his tirade about the sanctity of labour and works, artisanal and instructional. *Adam Bede*, ch. I.
64. ibid., pp. 72–8.
65. B. Hardy, *The Novels of George Eliot*, p. 26.
66. *Adam Bede*, p. 98.
67. The majority of critics reckon that George Eliot has 'loaded' her character: W. J. Harvey, op. cit., pp. 86 and 116; G. Hough, art. cit., p. 60 writes that for a woman to have the right to be beautiful she must be a holy methodist or a drowning Jewess.
68. *Adam Bede*, pp. 146–7.
69. W. J. Harvey, op. cit., pp. 230–1.
70. See the passage (Adam Bede, pp. 98–9) where George Eliot describes how Arthur, a creature of flesh and bones, is integrated with Hetty's dream world.
71. B. Hardy, op. cit., p. 34.
72. *Adam Bede*, pp. 18, 61.
73. ibid., p. 62.
74. ibid., pp. 288–9.
75. ' "I don't know what you mean by flirting", said Adam, "but if you mean behaving to a woman as if you loved her, and yet not loving her all the while", ...' *Adam Bede*, p. 288. ' "And you've been kissing her, and meaning nothing, have you?" ' ibid., p. 289.
76. H. James, 'The Novels of George Eliot', *A Century of* ..., p. 50.
77. See K. Thomas, 'The Double Standard', *Journal of the History of Ideas*, 1959, p. 204.
78. Kebbel, 'Village Life of George Eliot', *Fraser's Magazine*, xxiiii (February 1881), p. 274.
79. *Adam Bede*, p. 337.
80. See the suggestions of Stephen Marcus about the meaning of the expression in *The Other Victorians*, pp. 21–2.
81. ' "... I've never been used t' having gentlefolks's servants coming about my back places, a-making love to both the gells at once, and keeping 'em

Notes

with their hands on their hips listening to all manner o' gossip when they should be down on their knees a-scouring." ' *Adam Bede*, p. 334.

82. It should be noted that the Methodists indeed had female preachers. William Lovett describes the persuasive eloquence and religious enthusiasm of these preachers of the Bryanite sect who incited the adolescent to convert. *The Life and Struggles of William Lovett*, p. 18.

83. Gregor and Nicholas, *The Moral and the Story*, p. 26: 'Hetty lives ... by the coercive morality of the community and when this is broken, she is destroyed; she has no life apart from this.' D. Van Ghent, 'On Adam Bede', *The English Novel*, p. 179.

84. Gregor and Nicholas, op. cit., pp. 20–4 and H. James, 'The Novels of George Eliot', *A Century of ...*, p. 50.

85. B. Hardy, *The Novels ...*, pp. 26–7, and pp. 178–9; compare 'the claustrophobic economy' of this tale with the melodramatic trumpetings of Dickens every time it is a question of an impure woman.

86. This is well analysed by D. Van Ghent: 'Hetty is lost because she is more fragile than others and therefore more dependent than others on the community discipline ...; lost from the only values that can support her mediocrity, she sinks in the chaos of animal fear, ...' *The English Novel* p. 179.

87. B. Hardy, *The Novels ...*, p. 40.

88. *Adam Bede*, p. 397.

89. It is also within the framework of Methodism that Dinah can exercise the profession of preacher and thus resolve Dorothea's dilemma and that of countless women of the time in search of a spiritual and independent activity.

90. J. S. Diekoff, 'The Happy Ending of *Adam Bede*', *Journal of English Literary History*, iii (1936).

91. *Adam Bede*, 'A Crisis', pp. 288–9.

92. ibid., p. 393.

93. K. Thomas, 'The Double Standard', *Journal of the History of Ideas*, 1959, pp. 204–6.

94. T. T. Kebbel, 'Village Life ...', and Gregor and Nicholas, *The Moral and the Story*.

95. F. R. Leavis, 'George Eliot', *A Century of George Eliot Criticism*.

96. W. J. Harvey, *The Art of George Eliot*, p. 85.

97. S. Marcus, *The Other Victorians*, pp. 138–9.

98. See the letter from F. Engels to M. Harkness, April 1888, in Marx and Engels, *On Literature and Art*, 1956, pp. 37–8.

99. P. Cominos, 'Late Victorian Sexual Respectability ...', *International Review of Social History*, viii (1963), p. 28.

100. P. Cominos writes: 'Perceptive late Victorians understood prostitution to be an integral part of the whole matrimonial system', art. cit., p. 230. However, Dickens and Thackeray, Mayhew and Acton or Theophrastus, the author of 'the other side of the picture', had made this analysis at the beginning or in the middle of the period.

101. I. Watt, *The Rise of the Novel*, ch. 3 and 4.

102. C. Hill, 'Clarissa Harlow and her Times', *Puritanism and Revolution*, p. 388.

Notes

103. T. T. Carter, *Mercy for the Fallen*, pp. 17, 18.
104. P. Cominos, op. cit., p. 31.
105. R. Ironside and J. Gere, *Pre-raphaelite Painters*, pp. 32–3.
106. P. Cominos, 'Late Victorian ...', pp. 47–8.
107. ibid., p. 226.
108. A. G. Reynolds, *Painters of the Victorian Scene*, pp. 18, 78, figs. 48, 49, 50.
109. *Oxford History of English Art*, x, p. 286.
110. Mayhew, *London's Underworld*. Intro. p. 13. Inspired by the concern for detail and the extremely professional but debatable attitude of the pre-raphaelite artists, the painter visited on several occasions a brothel in St John's Wood.
111. E. Browning, *Aurora Leigh*, pp. 126 and 271–3.
112. ibid., pp. 252, 253. Elizabeth Browning puts into the mouth of Marian Erle opinions that some would find advanced in the twentieth century; she is proud for example of her child's love for his mother, however sinful the latter may be, and declares that the father's absence is less pernicious for the child than some fathers like him.
113. ibid., p. 377.
114.   'We wretches cannot tell out all our wrong,
                Without offence to decent happy folk.
            I know that we must scrupulously hint
                With half-words, delicate reserves, the thing
                Which no one scrupled we should feel in full.'
            E. Browning, *Aurora Leigh*, p. 273.

15
CONCLUSION

1. *The Westminster Review* (October 1858).
2. *Daily News* (3 February 1853).
3. *Edinburgh Review* (January 1850).
4. 'Woman in France: Madame de Sablé', *Westminster Review* (October 1854).

Bibliography

LITERARY SOURCES

ANNE BRONTË 1820–49: CHARLOTTE BRONTË 1816–55: EMILY BRONTË 1818–48

Works

The Shakespeare Head Brontë, ed. T. V. Wise and J. A. Symington, 19 vols, London, 1931–8. It comprises: the novels, 13 vols; *The Brontës, Their Lives and Friendships in Correspondence*, 4 vols, 1932; *The Miscellaneous and Unpublished Writings of Charlotte and Patrick Branwell Brontë*, 2 vols, 1938.

BRONTË, EMILY JANE, *Five Essays/written in French*, trans. and ed. F. E. Ratchford, Austin, Texas, 1948.

— *Hurlemont*, trans. Sylvère Monod, Paris, 1963.

Critical Works

ANON., '*Jane Eyre*', *Dublin University Magazine*, xxxi (May 1848), pp. 608–14.

ANON., '*Shirley*', *Eliza Cook's Journal*, No. 40 (2 February 1850), pp. 219–21.

BLONDEL, JACQUES, *Emily Brontë: Expérience Spirituelle et Création Poétique*. Paris, 1955.

BRICK, ALLAN R., 'Lewes's review of *Wuthering Heights*', *Nineteenth Century Fiction*, xiv (March 1960), pp. 355–9.

BRIGGS, ASA, 'Private and social themes in *Shirley*', *Brontë Society Transactions*, pt. 68, 1958, pp. 203–19.

BURCKART, CHARLES, 'C. Brontë's *Villette*', *The Explicator*, item 8 (September 1962).

COLBY, R. A., '*Villette* and the life of the mind', *PMLA*, lxxv (September 1960), pp. 410–19.

DAY, M. S., 'Central concepts in *Jane Eyre*', *The Personalist*, iv (Autumn 1960), pp. 495–505.

DOBELL, SIDNEY, 'Currer Bell', *The Palladium* (September 1850), pp. 62–75.

DOOLEY, L., 'Psychoanalysis of Charlotte Brontë as a type of the woman of genius', *The American Journal of Psychology*, xxxi (July 1920), pp. 221–72.

DUPONT, VICTOR, 'Trois notes sur les Brontës', *Études anglaises*, vi, No. i (February 1953), pp. 16–27.

EWBANK, INGA-STINA, *Their Proper Sphere – a Study of the Brontë Sisters as Early Victorian Female Novelists*, London, 1966.

FORCADE, E., '*Jane Eyre*', *Revue des Deux Mondes*, xxiv (October–December 1848), pp. 471–94.

— 'Le roman contemporain en Angleterre: *Shirley*', *Revue des Deux Mondes*, October–December 1849, pp. 714–35.

Bibliography

GARY, FRANKLIN, 'Charlotte Brontë and G. H. Lewes', *PMLA*, li (1936), pp. 518–42.

GÉRIN WINIFRED, *Charlotte Brontë: The Evolution of Genius*, Oxford, 1967.

HARRISON, A. and STANFORD, D., *Anne Brontë: Her Life and Work*, London, 1959.

HINKLEY, LAURA L., *The Brontës: Charlotte and Emily*, London, 1947.

HOWELLS, W. D., 'The Brontë novels', *The Nineteenth Century*, liii (March 1903), pp. 484–95.

KETTLE, ARNOLD, 'Emily Brontë: *Wuthering Heights* (1847)', *An Introduction to the English Novel*, London, 1951, pp. 139–55.

KORG, JACOB, 'The problem of unity in *Shirley*', *Nineteenth Century Fiction*, No. 2, xxii (September 1957), pp. 125–36.

LANE, MARGARET, *The Brontë Story: a Reconsideration of Mrs Gaskell's Life of Charlotte Brontë*, London, 1953. . .

LANGBRIDGE, ROSAMOND, *Charlotte Brontë: a Psychological Study*, London, 1929.

LEWES, G. H., '*Wuthering Heights* and *Agnes Grey*', *The Leader*, 28 December 1850, p. 953.

— '*Ruth* and *Villette*', *The Westminster Review*, iii (1853), pp. 474–91.

LEWES, J. H., '*Shirley*', *Edinburgh Review*, xci (January 1850), pp. 153–73.

MARTIN, R. B., *The Accents of Persuasion: Charlotte Brontë's Novels*, London, 1966.

— 'Charlotte Brontë and Harriet Martineau', *Nineteenth Century Fiction*, vii (December 1952), pp. 198–201.

[MARTINEAU, HARRIET] 'Death of Currer Bell', *Daily News*, 6 April 1855.

[MARTINEAU, HARRIET] '*Villette*', *Daily News*, 3 February 1853.

MASON, LEO, '*Jane Eyre* and *David Copperfield*', *The Dickensian*, xliii, pt 4 (1947), pp. 172–9.

MILLER, J. H., 'Emily Brontë', *The Disappearance of God*, London, 1963, pp. 157–211.

MONOD, SYLVÈRE, 'L'imprécision dans *Jane Eyre*', *Études anglaises*, xvii, No. 8 (1964), pp. 21–9.

MOORE, GEORGE, *Conversations in Ebury Street*, London, 1936.

OFFOR, DR RICHARD, *The Brontës: Their Relations to the History and Politics of Their Time*, reprinted from the *Publications of the Brontë Society*, pt. 53 (1943).

RALLI, AUGUSTUS, 'Charlotte Brontë', *The Fortnightly Review*, xliv (2 September 1913), pp. 524–38.

RATCHFORD, F. E., 'Charlotte Brontë's Angrian cycle of stories', *PMLA*, xliii (June 1928), pp. 494–501.

— *The Brontës' Web of Childhood*, New York, 1941.

SANDWITH, M. E. I., '*Jane Eyre* and *Eugénie Grandet*', *The Nineteenth Century*, xcii (August 1922), pp. 230–40.

SCARGILL, M. H., 'All Passion Spent': a revaluation of *Jane Eyre*', *The University of Toronto Quarterly*, xix, No. 2 (January 1950).

SCHORER, MARK, 'Fiction and the matrix of analogy', *The Kenyon Review*, xi (Autumn 1949), pp. 539–60.

SHORTER, CLEMENT K., *Charlotte Brontë and Her Circle*, London, 1896.

SOLOMON, ERIC, 'The incest theme in *Wuthering Heights*', *Nineteenth Century Fiction*, xiv (June 1959), pp. 80–3.

Bibliography

SWINBURNE, A. L., *A Note on Charlotte Brontë*, London, 1877.

WARING, S. M., 'Charlotte Brontë's Lucy Snowe', *Harper's Magazine*, xxxii (February 1866), pp. 366–71.

WATSON, MELVIN R., '*Wuthering Heights* and the Critics', *The Trollopian*, iii (March 1949), pp. 243–63.

— 'Tempest in the soul: The theme and structure of *Wuthering Heights*', *Nineteenth Century Fiction*, iv (September 1949), pp. 87–100.

WEIR, EDITH M., 'Contemporary reviews of the first Brontë novels', *Brontë Society Transactions*, xi (1957), pp. 88–96.

WOOLF, VIRGINIA, '*Jane Eyre* and *Wuthering Heights*', *The Common Reader* (1st series), London, 1925; pp. 196–204.

CHARLES DICKENS 1812–70

Works

The Nonesuch Dickens, ed. A. Waugh, H. Walpole, W. Dexter, T. Hatton, 23 vols, London, 1937.

The Letters of Charles Dickens, ed. Walter Dexter, 3 vols, London, 1938.

Letters from Charles Dickens to Angela Burdett-Coutts – 1841–1865, ed. Edgar Johnson, London, 1955.

The Speeches of Charles Dickens, ed. K. J. Fielding, Oxford, 1960.

Sketches of Young Couples, London, 1840.

(anonymously) 'Home for Homeless Women', *Household Words*, vii (23 April 1853), pp. 169–75.

'Sucking Pigs', *Household Words*, No. 85, 8 November 1851, pp. 145–7.

Critical works

ADRIAN, ARTHUR A., *Georgina Hogarth and the Dickens Circle*, London, 1957.

BUTT, JOHN and TILLOTSON, KATHLEEN, *Dickens at Work*, London, 1957.

BUTT, JOHN, '*Bleak House* once more', *Critical Quarterly* (Winter 1959), pp. 302–7.

— '*Bleak House* in the context of 1851', *Nineteenth Century Fiction*, x (June 1955), pp. 1–21.

CANNING, A. S. G., *Dickens and Thackeray Studied in Three Novels*, London, 1911.

CARDWELL, M., 'Rose Dartle and Mrs Brown', *The Dickensian*, lvi (January 1960), pp. 29–33.

COCKSHUT, A. O. J., *The Imagination of Charles Dickens*, London, 1961.

COLLINS, P. A. W., *Dickens and Education*, London, 1963.

— *Dickens and Crime*, London, 1965.

DABNEY, ROSS H., *Love and Property in the Novels of Dickens*, London, 1967.

DENEAU, D. P., 'The brother-sister relationship in *Hard Times*', *The Dickensian*, (September 1964), pp. 173–7.

DREW, A. P., 'Structure in *Great Expectations*', *The Dickensian*, lii (June 1956), pp. 123–7.

FIELDING, K. J., *Charles Dickens: a Critical Introduction*, London, 1965 (1st ed. 1957).

— 'The recent reviews: Dickens in 1858', *The Dickensian*, li–liv (December 1955), pp. 25–32.

Bibliography

— 'Women in the home: an article Dickens did not write', *The Dickensian*, xlvii, Pt 3 (June 1951), pp. 140–2.

FORD, GEORGE, H., *Dickens and his Readers, Aspects of Novel-Criticism Since 1836*, Princeton, 1955.

FORD, G. H. and LANE L., ed. *The Dickens Critics*, New York, 1961.

FORSTER, JOHN, *The Life of Charles Dickens*, ed. J. W. T. Ley, London, 1928.

GARIS, R., *The Dickens Theatre: a Reassessment of the Novels*, Oxford, 1965.

GISSING, G., *Charles Dickens, a Critical Study*, London, 1926.

GROSS, JOHN and PEARSON, GABRIEL, ed., *Dickens and the Twentieth Century*, London, 1962.

HOLLINGSWORTH, KEITH, *The Newgate Novel, 1830–1847, Bulwer, Ainsworth, Dickens and Thackeray*, Detroit, 1963.

HOUSE, HUMPHREY, *Dickens's World: Novels as Material for Nineteenth Century Social History in Great Britain*, London, 1942.

— 'Introduction' to *Oliver Twist* (*Oxford Illustrated Dickens*), pp. v–xiv, London, 1949.

JACKSON, T. A., *Charles Dickens: The Progress of a Radical*, London, 1937.

JOHNSON, EDGAR, 'Ada Nisbet's *Dickens and Ellen Ternan*', *Nineteenth Century Fiction*, vii (March 1953), pp. 296–8.

— '*Bleak House*: the anatomy of society', *Nineteenth Century Fiction*, vii (September 1952), pp. 73–89.

— 'Dickens and Shaw: critics of society', *The Virginia Quarterly Review*, xxxiii (Winter 1957), pp. 66–79.

— *Charles Dickens. His Tragedy and Triumph*, 2 vols, London, 1953.

JONES, HOWARD MUMFORD, 'On re-reading *Great Expectations*', *South West Review* (Dallas, Texas), (Autumn 1954), pp. 328–35.

LEVINE, GEORGE, 'Communication in *Great Expectations*', *Nineteenth Century Fiction*, xviii (September 1963), pp. 175–81.

LINDSAY, J., 'Charles Dickens and women', *Twentieth Century*, cliv (November 1953), pp. 375–86.

LUCAS, AUDREY, 'Some Dickens women', *Yale Review*, xxix (1940), pp. 706–28.

MARCUS, STEVEN, *Dickens: From Pickwick to Dombey*, London, 1965.

MILLER, HILLIS, *Charles Dickens: the World of His Novels*, Cambridge, Mass., 1958.

MILLER, WILLIAM, *The Dickens Student and Collector: A List of Writings Relating to Charles Dickens and His Works, 1836–1945*, London, 1946.

MONOD, SYLVÈRE, *Dickens Romancier*, Paris, 1953.

MOSES, BELLE, *Charles Dickens, His Girl-Heroines*, London, 1911.

NISBET, ADA, *Dickens and Ellen Ternan* with a Foreword by Edmund Wilson, Berkeley and Los Angeles, 1952.

ORWELL, GEORGE, *Charles Dickens. Critical Essays*, London, 1946.

PHILLIPS, WALTER C., *Dickens, Reade and Collins: a Study in the Condition and Theories of Novel Writing in Victorian England*, New York, 1919.

RAAFAT, ZENA, 'Melodrama in Charles Dickens's writings', unpublished M.A. thesis, University of South Wales, Swansea, 1962.

RIDEAL, CHARLES F., *Charles Dickens' Heroines and Women-folk*, London, 1896.

STEDMAN, JANE W., 'Child-wives of Dickens', *The Dickensian*, lix (May 1963), pp. 112–18.

Bibliography

TRILLING, LIONEL, 'Introduction' to *Little Dorrit*, (*Oxford Illustrated Dickens*), London, 1953.

WILSON, ANGUS, 'The heroes and heroines of Dickens', *A Review of English Literature* (July 1961), pp. 9–18.

WILSON, EDMUND, 'Dickens: the two Scrooges', in *The Wound and the Bow*, London, 1961, pp. 1–93.

WOOLF, VIRGINIA, '*David Copperfield*' in *The Moment*, London, 1947, pp. 65–9.

BENJAMIN DISRAELI 1804–81

Works

Sybil or the Two Nations, London, 1913.
Coningsby, London, 1931.

Critical Works

BLAKE, ROBERT, *Disraeli*, London, 1966.

MAITRE, RAYMOND, *Disraeli*, 2 vols, Paris, 1957.

MASEFIELD, MURIEL, *Peacocks and Primroses, A Survey of Disraeli's Novels*, London, 1953.

SMITH, SHEILA M., 'Willenhall and Wodgate: Disraeli's use of Blue Book evidence', *Review of English Studies*, New Series, xiii, 52 (November 1962), pp. 368–84.

GEORGE ELIOT 1819–80

Works

The Works of George Eliot, Cabinet Edition, 20 vols, London, 1878–80.

The George Eliot Letters, ed. G. S. Haight, 7 vols, New Haven and London, 1954–55.

Adam Bede, London, 1960.

'Silly novels by women novelists', *The Westminster Review*, New Series, x (October 1856), pp. 442–61.

'Woman in France: Madame de Sablé', *The Westminster Review*, vi (October 1854), pp. 448–73.

Critical Works

ADAM, I. W., 'Restoration through feeling in George Eliot's fiction: a new look at Hetty Sorrel', *Victorian Newsletter* (February 1962), pp. 9–12.

ALLEN, WALTER, *George Eliot*, London, 1964.

ANON., 'Review of 1. *Scenes of Clerical Life*. 2. *Adam Bede*. 3. *The Mill on the Floss*', *Quarterly Review*, cviii (1840), pp. 469–99.

BENNETT, JOAN, *George Eliot, Her Mind and Her Art*, Cambridge, 1962.

BISSELL, C. T., 'Social analysis in the novels of George Eliot', *Journal of English Literary History*, xviii (September 1951), pp. 227–39.

DIEKHOFF, JOHN S., 'The Happy Ending of *Adam Bede*', *Journal of English Literary History*, iii (1936), pp. 221–7.

FERANDO, LLOYD, 'George Eliot, Feminism and Dorothea Brooke', *Review of English Literature*, iv, pt. 1 (January 1963), pp. 76–90.

HAIGHT, G. S., ed., *A Century of George Eliot's Criticism*, London, 1966.

Bibliography

— *George Eliot, A Biography*, Oxford, 1968.

— *George Eliot and John Chapman. With Chapman's Diaries*, New Haven, 1940.

Hardy, Barbara, *The Novels of George Eliot: a Study in Form*, London, 1959.

Harvey, W. J., *The Art of George Eliot*, London, 1961.

HOUGH, GRAHAM, 'Novelist-Philosophers – xii George Eliot', *Horizon*, xvii (January 1948), pp. 50–62.

HUSSEY, M., 'Structure and imagery in *Adam Bede*', *Nineteenth Century Fiction*, x (1955), pp. 115–29.

KEBELL, T. T., 'Village life of George Eliot', *Fraser's Magazine*, xxiii (February 1881), pp. 263–76.

KITCHEL, A. T., *George Lewes and George Eliot*, New York, 1933.

LERNER, LAURENCE, *The Truthtellers. Jane Austen, G. Eliot. D. H. Lawrence*, London, 1967; New York: Schocken Books, 1967.

MCKENZIE, K. A., *Edith Simcox and George Eliot*, London, 1961.

SIMCOX, EDITH, 'George Eliot', *Nineteenth Century*, (May 1881), pp. 778–801.

STUMP, REVA, *Movement and Vision in George Eliot's Novels*, Seattle, 1959.

THALE, JEROME, *The Novels of George Eliot*, New York, 1959.

ELIZABETH C. GASKELL 1810–65

Works

The Works of Elizabeth Gaskell, ed. Clement Shorter, *World's Classics*, 11 vols, London, 1906–19.

The Life of Charlotte Brontë, *Everyman's Library*, London, 1958.

POLLARD, A. and CHAPPLE, J. A. V., ed. *The Letters of Mrs. Gaskell*, Manchester, 1966.

Critical Works

DODSWORTH, MARTIN, 'Women without men at Cranford', *Essays in Criticism*, xiii (April 1963), pp. 132–45.

GREG, W. R., 'The licence of modern novelists', *Edinburgh Review*, cvi (July 1857), pp. 124–6.

— 'Mary Barton', *Edinburgh Review*, April 1849, pp. 402–35.

HALDANE, E., *Mrs Gaskell and Her Friends*, London, 1930.

HOPKINS, A. B. '*Mary Barton*: a Victorian best seller', *The Trallopian*, iii (July 1948), pp. 1–18.

HOPKINS, A. B., 'A Letter of Advice from the Author of *Cranford* to an Aspiring Novelist', *Princeton University Library Chronicle*, xv (Spring 1954), pp. 142–50.

— *Elizabeth Gaskell: Her Life and Work*, London, 1952.

— 'Mrs Gaskell in France, 1849–1890', *PMLA*, liii (1938), pp. 545–74.

— 'Liberalism in the social teachings of Mrs Gaskell', *Social Service Review*, 1931, pp. 57–73.

LEHMANN, ROSAMOND, 'A neglected Victorian classic', *Penguin New Writing*, xxxii (1947), pp. 89–101.

MONTÉGUT, EMILE, 'Le roman social en Angleterre', *Revue des Deux Mondes*, (April–June 1853), pp. 894–926.

MOUY, CHARLES DE, 'Romanciers anglais contemporains – Mistress Gaskell', *Revue européenne*, xvii (1 September 1861), pp. 138–64.

Bibliography

POLLARD, A., *Mrs. Gaskell, Novelist and Biographer*, Manchester, 1969.

— 'The novels of Mrs Gaskell', *Bulletin of the John Rylands Library*, xliii (March 1961), pp. 403–25.

RUBENIUS, AINA, *The Woman Question in Mrs Gaskell's Life and Works*, Uppsala, 1950.

SHUSTERMAN, DAVID, 'William Rathbone Greg and Mrs Gaskell', *Philological Quarterly*, xxxvi (April 1957), pp. 268–72.

SMITH, G. B., 'Mrs Gaskell and her novels', *The Cornhill Magazine* (February 1874), pp. 191–212.

WALLER, ROSS D., ed. 'Letters addressed to Mrs Gaskell by celebrated contemporaries', *Bulletin of the John Rylands Library*, xix (1935), pp. 102–69.

WHITEHILL, JANE, ed., *Letters of Mrs Gaskell to Charles Eliot Norton 1855–1865*, London, 1932.

WRIGHT, EDGAR, *Mrs Gaskell. The Basis for Reassessment*, London, 1965.

CHARLES KINGSLEY 1819–75

Works

Alton Locke, London, 1900.

Yeast, a Problem, Everyman's Library, London, 1912.

Charles Kingsley: His Letters and Memories of His Life, ed. by his wife, 2 vols, London, 1877.

Critical Works

BALDWIN, STANLEY E., *Charles Kingsley*, London, 1934.

MARTIN, ROBERT BERNARD, *The Dust of Combat: A Life of Charles Kingsley*, London, 1959.

THORP, MARGARET FARRAND, *Charles Kingsley, 1819–1875*, Princeton, 1937.

W. M. THACKERAY 1811–63

Works

The Works of W. M. Thackeray, Centenary Biographical Edition, 26 vols, London, 1910–11.

The Letters and Private Papers of W. M. Thackeray, ed. G. N. Ray, 4 vols, London, 1945–6.

Vanity Fair, ed. K. and G. Tillotson, London, 1953.

'William Ainsworth and Jack Sheppard', *Fraser's Magazine* (February 1840), pp. 227–45.

Critical Works

ANON., 'Enter Becky Sharp', *Times Literary Supplement*, 4 January 1947.

ANON., 'Thackeray's writings', *Edinburgh Review* (January 1848), pp. 46–67.

BAKER, JOSEPH E., '*Vanity Fair* and the Celestial City', *Nineteenth Century Fiction*, x (September 1955), pp. 89–98.

BROGAN, HOWARD A., 'Rachel Esmond and the dilemma of the Victorian ideal of womanhood', *A Journal of English Literary History*, xiii, no. 3, Baltimore (September 1946), pp. 223–32.

BROWNELL, W. C., *Victorian Prose Masters*, London, 1902.

Bibliography

CAREY-TAYLOR, A., 'Balzac and Thackeray', *Revue de Littérature Comparée*, xxxiv, No. 2 (1960), pp. 354–69.

CHASLES, PHILARÈTE, 'Le roman de moeurs en Angleterre: La Foire aux Vanités', *Revues des Deux Mondes* (15 February and 1 March 1849), pp. 537–71 and 721–59.

CHESTERTON, G. K., 'Vanity Fair' in *A Handful of Authors*, London, 1953, pp. 56–65.

DODDS, JOHN W., *Thackeray: a Critical Portrait*, London, 1941.

— 'Thackeray in the Victorian frame', *Sewanee Review*, xlviii (1940), pp. 466–78.

DYSON, A. E., '*Vanity Fair*: an irony against heroes', *Critical Quarterly*, vi (Spring 1964), pp. 11–31.

FORGUES, E. D., 'Poètes et romanciers modernes de la Grande-Bretagne, W. M. Thackeray et ses romans', *Revue des Deux Mondes*, (1 September 1854), pp. 1001–32.

FRASER, RUSSELL A., 'Pernicious casuistry: a study of character in *Vanity Fair*', *Nineteenth Century Fiction*, xii (September 1957), pp. 137–47.

— 'Sentimentality in *The Newcomes*', *Nineteenth Century Fiction*, iv (December 1949), pp. 187–96.

GREENE, D. J., 'Becky Sharp and Lord Steyne – Thackeray or Disraeli?', *Nineteenth Century Fiction*, xvi (September 1961), pp. 157–64.

GREIG, J. Y. T., *Thackeray: A Reconsideration*, London, 1950.

HAYWARD, A., 'Thackeray's writings', *The Edinburgh Review*, lxxxvii (January 1848), pp. 46–67.

LAS VERGNAS, R., *W. M. Thackeray. L'homme, le penseur, le romancier*, Paris, 1932.

MAITRE, R., 'Balzac, Thackeray et Charles de Bernard', *Revue de Littérature Comparée*, xxiv, No. 2 (1950), pp. 279–93.

MATHISON, JOHN K. 'The German sections of *Vanity Fair*', *Nineteenth Century Fiction*, xviii (December 1963), pp. 235–46.

MONOD, SYLVÈRE. 'La fortune de Balzac en Angleterre', *Revue de Littérature Comparée*, 1950, pp. 181–210.

MOTTI, R., *A Few Words on Thackeray's Portraiture of Women*, Piacenza, 1913.

PACEY, W. C., 'Balzac and Thackeray', *The Modern Language Review*, xxxvi (1941), pp. 212–24.

PARIS, BERNARD J., 'The psychic structure of *Vanity Fair*', *Victorian Studies*, x, No. 4 (June 1967), pp. 389–410.

RAY, G. N., *The Buried Life, A Study of the Relation Between Thackeray's Fiction and his Personal History*, London, 1952.

— '*Vanity Fair*: one version of the novelist's responsibility', *Essays by Diverse Hands (Transactions of the Royal Society of Literature of the United Kingdom)*, xxv (1950), pp. 87–101.

— *Thackeray: A Biography: The Use of Adversity, 1811–1846*, London, 1955; *The Age of Wisdom, 1847–1863*, London, 1958.

RIGBY, E., '1. *Vanity Fair*; by W. M. Thackeray, London, 1848. 2. *Jane Eyre*; an Autobiography, Edited by Currer Bell, 3 vols, London, 1847. 3. Governesses' Benevolent Institution – Report for 1847', *Quarterly Review*, lxxxiv (December 1848), pp. 153–85.

SAINTSBURY, GEORGE, *A Consideration of Thackeray*, London, 1931.

Bibliography

SPILKA, MARC, 'A note on Thackeray's Amelia', *Nineteenth Century Fiction*, x (September 1955), pp. 203–10.

STEVENSON, A. L., '*Vanity Fair* and Lady Morgan', *PMLA*, xlviii (1933), pp. 547–51.

SUDRANN, JEAN, 'Thackeray and the use of time', *Victorian Studies*, x, No. 4 (June 1967), pp. 359–88.

TALON, HENRI A., *Two Essays on Thackeray*, Faculté des Lettres et des Sciences Humaines, Dijon.

TAUBE, MYRON, 'The character of Amelia in the meaning of *Vanity Fair*', *Victorian Newsletter*, No. 18 (Autumn 1960), pp. 1–7.

— 'Contrast as a principle of structure in *Vanity Fair*', *Nineteenth Century Fiction*, xviii (September 1963), pp. 119–35.

TAYLOR, A. CAREY, 'Balzac et Thackeray', *Revue de Littérature Comparée*, xiii, No. 2 (1960), pp. 354–69.

TILFORD, J. E., 'The Degradation of Becky Sharp', *South Atlantic Quarterly* (Durham, North Carolina), lviii (Autumn 1959), pp. 603–8.

TILFORD, J. E., JR, 'The love-theme of *Henry Esmond*', *PMLA*, lxvii (September 1952), pp. 684–701.

TILLOTSON, GEOFFREY, *Thackeray the Novelist*, Cambridge, 1954.

TROLLOPE, A., *Thackeray*, London, 1880.

WAGENKNECHT, E., 'The selfish heroine: Thackeray and Galsworthy', *College English* (Chicago), iv (February 1943), pp. 293–8.

ANTHONY TROLLOPE 1815–82

Works

Autobiography, ed. M. Sadleir and F. Page, 1950.

Barchester Towers, 2 vols, London, 1953.

Can You Forgive Her? 2 vols, London, 1948.

He Knew He Was Right, London, 1948.

The Last Chronicle of Barset, 2 vols, London, 1932.

The Kellys and the O'Kelleys, London, 1929.

'Higher education of women', *Four Lectures*, London, 1938.

The Letters of Anthony Trollope, ed. Bradford Booth, London, 1951.

Miss MacKenzie, London, 1924.

Orley Farm, 2 vols, London, 1935.

Rachel Ray, London, 1924.

The Small House at Allington, London, 1939.

The Vicar of Bullhampton, London, 1924.

The Warden, London, 1952.

Critical Works

ADAMS, RUTH M., 'Miss Dunstable and Miss Coutts', *Nineteenth Century Fiction* (December 1954), pp. 231–5.

COCKSHUT, A. O. J., *Trollope*, London, 1955.

GEROULD, WINIFRED and J. T., *A Guide to Trollope*, Princeton, 1948.

JAMES, HENRY, 'Anthony Trollope', in *Partial Portraits*, London, 1888, pp. 97–133.

SADLEIR, MICHAEL, *Trollope: A Bibliography*, 2 parts, London, 1928.

— *Trollope: A Commentary*, London, 1927.

Bibliography

GENERAL STUDIES

ALLEN, WALTER, *The English Novel*, Harmondsworth, 1965.

ALLOTT, MYRIAM, *Novelists on the Novel*, London, 1959.

ALTICK, RICHARD D., *The English Common Reader, A Social History of the Magazine-reading Public, 1800–1900*, Chicago.

ARNOLD, MATTHEW, *Culture and Anarchy*, ed. J. Dover-Wilson, Cambridge, 1963.

— *Letters 1848–1888*, ed. George W. E. Russell, 2 vols, London, 1895.

BAKER, E. A., *The History of the English Novel – The Age of Dickens and Thackeray*, vii, London, 1936.

BAKER, JOSEPH E., ed., *The Reinterpretation of Victorian Literature*, Princeton, 1950.

BALD, MARJORIE A., *Women-writers of the Nineteenth Century*, Cambridge, 1923.

BASCH, FRANÇOISE, 'Socialisme et critique littéraire en Angleterre autour de 1900', *Le Mouvement Social*, No. 59 (April–June 1967), pp. 70–88.

BATAILLE, GEORGES, *La Littérature et le Mal*, Paris, 1957.

BATHO, E. C. and DOBRÉE, B., *The Victorians and After, 1830–1914*, London, 1950.

BATTISCOMBE, GEORGINA and LASKI, MARGHANITA, ed., *A Chaplet for Charlotte Yonge*, London, 1965.

BONNELL, H. H., *Charlotte Brontë, George Eliot, Jane Austen: Studies in Their Works*, New York, 1902.

BOOTH, MICHAEL R., *English Melodrama*, London, 1965.

BROWNING, ELIZABETH B., *Aurora Leigh*, London, 1857.

BUCKLEY, JEROME HAMILTON, *The Victorian Temper: A Study in Literary Culture*, Cambridge, Mass., 1951.

CABAU, JACQUES, *Thomas Carlyle ou le Prométhée enchaîné. Essai sur la genèse de l'œuvre de 1795 à 1834*, Paris, 1968.

CAZAMIAN, LOUIS, *Le Roman social en Angleterre 1830–1850. Dickens–Disraeli–Mrs Gaskell–Kingsley*, Paris, 1904.

CECIL, LORD DAVID, *Early Victorian Novelists ...*, London, 1934.

CHESTERTON, G. K., *The Victorian Age in Literature*, London, 1913.

CLOUGH, ARTHUR H., *The Poems of Arthur Hugh Clough*, ed. H. F. Lowry, Q. L. P. Norrington, F. L. Mulhausen, Oxford, 1951.

COURTNEY, W. L., *The Feminine Note in Fiction*, London, 1904.

CRUSE, AMY, *The Victorians and Their Reading*, Boston and New York, 1935.

DALZIEL, MARGARET, *Popular Fiction 100 Years Ago. An Unexplored Tract of Literary History*, London, 1957.

DAVIES, BERNICE F., 'The social status of the middle-class Victorian woman as it is interpreted in representative mid nineteenth century novels and periodicals', unpublished Ph.D. dissertation, Stanford University, 1943.

DECKER, C. R., *The Victorian Conscience (An English Criticism of Nineteenth Century European Literature)*, New York, 1952.

DELAFIELD, E. M., *Ladies and Gentlemen in Victorian Fiction*, London, 1937.

DEVONSHIRE, M. G., *The English Novel in France, 1830–1870*, London, 1929.

DOWDEN, EDWARD, *Studies in Literature: 1789–1877*, London, 1878.

DUNCAN, HUGH DALZIEL, *Language and Literature in Society*, Chicago, 1953.

Bibliography

ELWIN, MALCOLM, *Victorian Wallflowers. Studies in Nineteenth Century English Literature*, London, 1934.

FAVERTY, E. F., *The Victorian Poets. A Guide to Research*, Cambridge, Mass., 1968.

FORD, BORIS, ed., *From Dickens to Hardy, A Guide to English Literature*, vi, London, 1963.

FROUDE, J. A., *Thomas Carlyle: A History of His Life in London, 1834–1881*, 2 vols, London, 1884.

— *The Nemesis of Faith*, London, 1849.

GOLDMANN, LUCIEN, BERNARD, M. and LALLEMAND, R., ed., *Littérature et Société: Problèmes de méthodologie en sociologie de la littérature*, Bruxelles, 1967.

GOLDMANN, LUCIEN, *Pour une Sociologie du roman*, Paris, 1964.

GREG, W. R., 'False morality of lady novelists', *National Review*, viii (January 1859), pp. 144–67.

— *Mistaken Aims and Attainable Ideals of the Artisan Class*, London, 1876.

GREGOR, IAN and NICHOLAS, BRIAN, *The Moral and the Story*, London, 1952.

HARDY, BARBARA, *The Appropriate Form. An Essay on the Novel*, London, 1964.

HARRISON, FREDERIC, *Studies in Early Victorian Literature*, London, 1895.

HAYTER, ALATHEA, *A Sultry Month: Scenes of London Literary Life in 1846*, London, 1965.

— *Mrs. Browning: A Poet's Work and its Setting*, London, 1962.

HILL, CHRISTOPHER, 'Clarissa Harlowe and her times' in *Puritanism and Revolution*, London, 1958; New York: Schocken Books, 1964.

HILL, G. B. and POWELL, L. F., *Boswell's Life of Johnson*, 6 vols, Oxford, 1934–50.

HOLLOWAY, C. JOHN, *The Victorian Sage*, London, 1962.

HORNE, R. H., ed., *A New Spirit of the Age*, 2 vols, London, 1844.

HOUGHTON W. E., *The Victorian Frame of Mind, 1830–1870*, New Haven, 1964.

HOWELLS, W. D., *Heroines in Fiction*, 2 vols, New York, 1901.

JAMES, LOUIS. *Fiction for the Working Man, 1830–1850. A Study of the Literature Produced for the Working Classes in Early Victorian Urban England*, London, 1963.

JOHNSON, R. BRIMLEY, *The Women Novelists*, London, 1918.

JOHNSON, WENDELL STACEY, '"The Bride of Literature": Ruskin, The Eastlakes, and mid-Victorian theories of art', *The Victorian Newsletter*, No. 26 (February 1964), pp. 23–8.

KERMODE, FRANK, *Continuities*, London, 1968.

KETTLE, ARNOLD, *An Introduction to the English Novel*, 2 vols, London, 1951.

KILLHAM, JOHN, *Tennyson as The Princess. Reflections of an Age*, London, 1958.

LEAVIS, F. R., *The Great Tradition. George Eliot, Henry James, Joseph Conrad*, Harmondsworth, 1962.

LEAVIS, Q. D., *Fiction and the Reading Public*, London, 1965.

LEVIN, HARRY, 'What is Realism?', *Comparative Literature*, iii (Summer 1951), pp. 193–9.

LEWES, G. H., 'Currer Bell's *Shirley*, *Edinburgh Review*, xci (January 1850), pp. 153–73.

— 'Realism in art: recent German fiction', *The Westminster Review*, New Series, xiv (October 1858), pp. 488–518.

LEWIS, NAOMI, *A Visit to Mrs. Wilcox*, London, 1957.

Bibliography

LOCHHEAD, MARION, *Young Victorians*, London, 1959.

LUKACS, GEORG, trans. Edith Bone, *Studies in European Realism. A Sociological Survey of the Writings of Balzac, Stendhal, Zola, Tolstoy, Gorki and Others* ..., London, 1950.

— *Balzac et le Réalisme Français*, Paris, 1967.

HOWARD, D., LUCAS J., GOODE, J., *Tradition and Tolerance in Nineteenth Century Fiction*, London, 1966.

MAISON, MARGARET M., 'Adulteresses in agony' (discussion of the sensational novel in the context of the Divorce Act 1857), the *Listener*, 14 January, 1961, p. 133.

MARANDON, S., *L'image de la France dans la conscience anglaise, 1848–1900*, Paris, 1967.

MARE, MARGARET and PERCIVAL, ALICIA, *Victorian Best-Seller. The World of Charlotte M. Yonge, etc.*, London, 1947.

MARX, KARL and ENGELS, FREDERICK, *Literature and Art*, Bombay, 1956.

MONTÉGUT, E., *Écrivains modernes de l'Angleterre:* première série, Paris, 1885; deuxième série, Paris, 1889, troisième série, Paris, 1892.

MOORE, KATHERINE, *Cordial Relations. The Maiden Aunt in Fact and Fiction*, London, 1967.

NICOLL, ALLARDYCE, *History of English Drama 1660–1900*, 5 vols, Cambridge, 1955.

PAGE, H. A., 'The morality of literary art', *Contemporary Review*, v (June 1867), pp. 161–89.

PATMORE, COVENTRY, *The Angel in the House. The Victories of Love*, London, 1905.

PRAZ, MARIO, *The Hero in Eclipse in Victorian Fiction*, trans. Angus Davidson, London, 1956.

RAYMOND, MICHEL, *Le Roman depuis la Révolution*, Paris, 1967.

RIGBY, ELIZABETH, '1. Vanity Fair; a Novel Without a Hero, by William Makepeace Thackeray. 2. Jane Eyre; an Autobiography. Edited by Currer Bell. 3. Governesses' Benevolent Institution. Report for 1847', *The Quarterly Review*, lxxxiv (December 1848), pp. 153–85.

ROSA, MATTHEW W., *The Silver-Fork School. Novels of Fashion Preceding Vanity Fair*, New York, 1936.

RUSKIN, JOHN, *The Diaries of John Ruskin*, selected and edited by Joan Evans and John Howard Whitehouse, 3 vols, Oxford, 1956.

— *The Works of John Ruskin*, ed. E. T. Cook and A. Wedderburn, 39 vols, London, 1903–12.

SADLEIR, MICHAEL, *Excursions in Victorian Bibliography*, London, 1922.

SCHLATTER, F. M., *The Puritan Element in Victorian Fiction*, Zürich, 1940.

SCRIMGEOUR, G. L., 'Nineteenth century drama', *Victorian Studies*, xii, No. 1 (September 1968), pp. 91–100.

SÉJOURNÉ, PHILIPPE, *Aspects généraux du roman féminin en Angleterre de 1740 à 1800*, Paris, 1966.

SENIOR, N. W., *Essays on Fiction*, London, 1864.

SILOTE, BERNICE, ed., *Myth and Symbol: Critical Approaches and Applications* (by Northrop Frye etc.), Lincoln (Nebraska), 1963. (C. I. Dougherty, 'Of Ruskin's Gardens', pp. 141–51.)

SMITH, G. B., *Poets and Novelists. A Series of Literary Studies*, London, 1875.

Bibliography

STANG, RICHARD, *The Theory of the Novel in England 1850–1870*, London, 1959.

STEVENSON, LIONEL, *The English Novel: a Panorama*, London, 1961.

STEVENSON, LIONEL, ed., *Victorian Fiction. A Guide to Research*, Cambridge, Mass., 1964.

TAINE, H., *Histoire de la Littérature anglaise*, 5 vols, Paris, 1866.

TENNYSON, ALFRED, *Poems of Tennyson 1830–1870*, ed. H. Frowde, with 91 illustrations by Millais, Rossetti ..., London, 1912.

THOMSON, PATRICIA, 'The three Georges', *Nineteenth Century Fiction*, xviii (September 1963), pp. 137–50.

— *The Victorian Heroine. A Changing Ideal, 1837–1873*, London, 1956.

TILLOTSON, KATHLEEN, *Novels of the Eighteen Forties*, London, 1954.

UTTER, R. P. and NEEDHAM, G. B., *Pamela's Daughters*, London, 1937.

VAN GHENT, DOROTHY, *The English Novel: Form and Function*, New York, 1961.

VEYRIRAS, PAUL, *Arthur Hugh Clough (1819–1861)*, Paris, 1964.

VILLARD, LÉONIE, *La femme anglaise au dix-neuvième siècle et son évolution d'après le roman anglais contemporain*, Paris, 1920.

WATT, IAN, *The Rise of the Novel. Studies in Defoe, Richardson and Fielding*, London, 1957.

WEBB, R. K., *The British Working Class Reader 1790–1848. Literary and Social Tension*, London, 1955.

WELLEK, RENÉ, 'The concept of realism in literary scholarship', *Neophilologus*, xlv–xlvi (January 1961), pp. 1–20.

WILLEY, BASIL, *Nineteenth Century Studies. Coleridge to Matthew Arnold*, Harmondsworth, 1964.

WILLIAMS, ALEXANDER M., *Our Early Female Novelists and Other Essays*, Glasgow, 1904.

WOOLF, VIRGINIA, *Granite and Rainbow*, London, 1958.

— *A Room of One's Own*, London, 1929.

— *The Common Reader*, London, 1925.

— *The Common Reader* (Second Series), London, 1932.

WRIGHT, A. H., *Jane Austen's Novels: a Study in Structure*, London, 1961.

GENERAL SOURCES

HISTORICAL, SOCIOLOGICAL, BIOGRAPHICAL AND ART STUDIES

ACTON, WILLIAM, *The Functions and Disorders of the Reproduction Organs in Youth, in Adult Age, and in Advanced Life*, London, 1857; 2nd edn., 1858; 3rd edn., 1862; 4th edn., 1865.

— *Prostitution Considered in its Moral, Social and Sanitary Aspects. In London and Other Large Cities*, London, 1857.

— *Prostitution*, ed. Peter Fryer, London, 1968. Excellent introduction and notes.

ANON., *Lincolnshire Chronicle*, Stamford (October 1866).,

— 'A few words on imprudent marriages', *The Ladies' Companion at Home and Abroad*, i (20 April 1850), p. 264.

— 'Chapters on maternal associations', *The British Mothers' Magazine*, i and ii (July 1845), pp. 162–4.

Bibliography

— 'Cottage readings', *The British Mothers' Magazine*, iii–iv (January 1848), pp. 12–15; iii–iv (February 1848), 35–8; iii–iv (March 1848), pp. 53–7.

— 'The cottager's chapter', *The British Mothers' Magazine*, i and ii (September 1845), pp. 205–6.

— (T. G.), *Doings in London or Day and Night Scenes of the Frauds, Frolics, Manners, and Depravities of the Metropolis, with 33 engravings, by Bonner from designs by Mr R. Cruikshank*, London, 1840.

— 'The duty of mothers in reference to war', *The British Mothers' Magazine*, iii–iv (March 1847), pp. 66–7.

— *The Economy for the Single and Married; by One 'Who Makes Ends Meet'*, London, 1845.

— 'Female penitentiaries', *The Quarterly Review*, lxxxiii (September 1848), pp. 359–76.

— 'Governesses', *Eliza Cook's Journal*, No. 20 (15 September 1849), pp. 305–9.

— *The Habits of Good Society: A Handbook of Etiquette for Ladies and Gentlemen*, London, 1859.

— 'How to make the best of everything. Extract from the working man's wife', *The British Mothers' Magazine*, i and ii (February 1845), pp. 35–9.

— *How to Woo; How to Win and How to Get Married*, 1856.

— 'Letter of advice from an experienced matron to a young married lady', *Fraser's Magazine*, xxxix (April 1849), pp. 397–405.

— *London in the Sixties (With a Few Digressions) by 'One of the Old Brigade'*, London, 1848.

— 'Milliners' apprentices', *Fraser's Magazine*, xxxiii (March 1846), pp. 308–16.

— 'The new law of divorce', *The English Woman's Journal*, i (May 1858), pp. 186–8.

— 'Passing events', *The English Woman's Journal*, i (August 1858), pp. 429–32.

— 'Property of married women', *The English Woman's Journal*, i (March 1858), pp. 58–9.

— 'Queen's College – London', *The Quarterly Review*, lxxxvi (March 1850), pp. 374–83.

— *Sinks of London Laid Open ...*, illustrated by G. Cruikshank, London, 1848.

— 'There is no place like home', *The British Mothers' Magazine*, i and ii (July 1845), pp. 145–6.

— 'Treatment of women', *Eliza Cook's Journal*, v (9 August 1851), pp. 225–7.

— 'The vocations of women', *Eliza Cook's Journal*, No. 56 (25 May 1850), pp. 59–63.

— 'Woman, and her social position', *The Westminster Review*, xxxv (January 1841), pp. 24–52.

— 'Women artists', *The Westminster Review*, xiv (July 1858), pp. 173–85.

— 'The working of the new divorce bill', *The English Woman's Journal*, i (July 1858), pp. 339–41.

— 'The wrongs of English women', *Eliza Cook's Journal*, (5 October 1850), pp. 354–55.

AYDELOTTE, W. O., 'The conservative and radical interpretations of early Victorian social legislation', *Victorian Studies*, xi (December 1967), pp. 225–36.

Bibliography

BAGEHOT, WALTER, *The Love-Letters of Walter Bagehot and Eliza Wilson ... 10 November, 1857 to 23 April, 1858*, London, 1933.

BAILEY, D. S., *The Man-Woman Relation in Christian Thought*, London, 1959.

BAILEY, JOHN, ed., *The Diary of Lady Frederick Cavendish*, 2 vols, London, 1927.

BAMFORD, SAMUEL, *Bamford's Passages in the Life of a Radical, and Early Days*, 2 vols, London, 1893.

BANKS, J.A., *Prosperity and Parenthood. A Study of Family Planning Among the Victorian Middle Classes*, London, 1954.

BANKS, J. A. and OLIVE, *Feminism and Family Planning in Victorian England*, Liverpool, 1964; New York: Schocken Books, 1964.

BARTON, MARGARET and SITWELL, OSBERT, *Sober Truth. A Collection of Nineteenth Century Episodes, Fantasies, Grotesque and Mysterious*, London, 1930.

BARTON, MARGARET and SITWELL, OSBERT, *Victoriana*, London, 1931.

BASCH, FRANÇOISE, 'La Femme en Angleterre de l'avènement de Victoria (1837), à la première guerre mondiale (1914)', *Histoire Mondiale de la Femme*, iv (Paris, 1966), pp. 187–251.

BEAUVOIR, SIMONE DE, *Le Deuxième Sexe*, 2 vols, Paris, 1949.

BEBEL, AUGUST, *La Femme et le Socialisme*, trans. Claude Prévost, Berlin, 1964; *Woman Under Socialism*, New York: Schocken Books, 1971.

BEETON, MRS ISABELLA, *The Book of Household Management*, London, 1961.

BENSIMON, PAUL, 'La femme anglaise et l'époque romantique', *Histoire Mondiale de la Femme*, iv (Paris 1966), pp. 163–85.

BENSON, A. C. and VISCOUNT ESHER, ed., *The Letters of Queen Victoria: A Selection from Her Majesty's Correspondence Between the Years 1837 and 1861*, 3 vols, London, 1907.

BEVINGTON, MERLE MOWBRAY, *The Saturday Review, 1855–1868. Representative Educated Opinion in Victorian England*, New York, 1941.

BLACKMORE, JOHN, *The London by Moonlight Mission: Being an Account of Midnight Cruises on the Streets of London During the Last Thirteen Years*, London, 1860.

— *London by Moonlight: or Missionary Labours for the Female Temporary Home*, pamphlets Nos. 1–5; series 2, No. 1, London, 1853–4.

BLAKE, ROBERT, *Disraeli*, London, 1966.

BOASE, T. S. R., *English Art 1800–1870*, Oxford History of English Art, 10 vols, London, 1959.

BODICHON, BARBARA (LEIGH-SMITH), 'The position of woman in barbarism and among the ancients', *The Westminster Review*, viii (October 1855), pp. 378–436.

— *A Brief Summary in Plain English Language of the Most Important Laws Concerning Women*, London, 1854.

— *Women and Work*, London, 1857.

BREWER, LESLIE, *The Good News. Some Sidelights on the Strange Story of Sex-Education*, London, 1962.

BRIGGS, ASA, *The Age of Improvement*, London, 1959.

— *Victorian Cities*, London, 1963.

— *Victorian People. Some Reassessments of People, Institutions, Ideas and Events. 1851–1867*, London, 1934.

BRIGGS, ASA and SAVILLE, JOHN, ed., *Essays: Labour History in Memory of*

Bibliography

J. D. H. Cole., 25 September 1889–14 January 1959, London, 1960.

BROWNING, E. B., *Elizabeth Barrett to Miss Mitford: The Unpublished Letters of Elizabeth Barrett Browning to Mary Russell Mitford*, ed. Betty Miller, London, 1954.

— *The Letters of Elizabeth Barrett Browning*, ed. F. G. Kenyon, 2 vols, London, 1897.

— *The Letters of Robert Browning and Elizabeth Barrett Browning. 1845–1846*, 2 vols, London, 1899.

— *Letters of the Brownings to George Barrett*, ed. P. Landis, Urbana, Illinois, 1958.

— *Twenty-two Unpublished Letters of Elizabeth Barrett Browning and Robert Browning Addressed to Henrietta and Arabella Moulton-Barrett*, New York, 1935.

BULWER-LYTTON, E. L., *England and the English*, 2 vols, London.

BUTLER, JOSEPHINE E., *An Autobiographical Memoir*, ed. G. W. and L. A. Johnson, London, 1909.

— *Memoir of John Grey of Dilston*, London, 1869.

— *Personal Reminiscences of a Great Crusade*, London, 1896.

— *Woman's Work and Woman's Culture*, London, 1869.

CARLISLE, HENRY E., ed., *A Selection From the Correspondence of Abraham Hayward, Q.C. From 1834 to 1884*, 2 vols, London, 1886.

CARLYLE, J. W., *Letters and Memorials of Jane Welsh Carlyle*, ed. James Anthony Froude, 3 vols, London, 1883.

CARTER, T. T., *Harriet Monsell, A. Memoir*, London, 1884.

— *The First Ten Years of the House of Mercy, Clewer* London, 1861.

— *Mercy for the Fallen. Two Sermons in Aid of the House of Mercy, Clewer*, London, 1856.

CHAPMAN, JOHN, unpublished letters to Harriet Martineau, Martineau MSS. Collection, Birmingham University Library.

CLARK, ALICE, *Working Life of Women in the Seventeenth Century*, London, 1919.

COBBE, FRANCIS P., 'Wife torture in England', *Contemporary Review*, xxxii (April 1878), pp. 55–87.

COLE, G. D. H., *The Life of Robert Owen*, London, 1930.

— *A Short History of the British Working-Class Movement 1789–1947*, London, 1948.

COMINOS, PETER T., 'Late-Victorian sexual respectability and the social system', *International Review of Social History*, viii, pt 1, pp. 18–48; pt 2 (1963), pp. 216–250.

CORNWALLIS, CORNELIA, 'The property of married women', *Westminster Review*, x (October 1856), pp. 331–60.

CUNNINGTON, C. W., *English Women's Clothing in the Nineteenth Century*, London, 1937.

DEACON, RICHARD, *The Private Life of Mr Gladstone*, London, 1965.

DEVEY, LOUISA, *Life of Rosina, Lady Lytton*, London, 1887.

EASTLAKE, LADY (E. RIGBY), *Journals and Correspondence of Lady Eastlake*, ed. Charles Eastlake Smith, 2 vols, London, 1895.

ELIADE, M., *Mythes, rêves et mystères*, Paris, 1957.

ELLIS, SARAH (STICKNEY), *The Daughters of England*, London, 1845.

Bibliography

— *The Education of the Heart: Woman's Best Work*, London, 1869.

— *The Home Life and Letters of Mrs Ellis*, compiled by her nieces, London, 1893.

— *The Mothers of England*, London, 1843.

— *The Wives of England, Their Relative Duties, Domestic Influence, and Social Obligations*, London, 1843.

— *The Women of England*, London, 1839.

ENAULT, LOUIS, *Londres*, illustrated with 174 wood engravings by Gustave Doré, Paris, 1876.

ENGELS, FRIEDRICH, *The Condition of the Working Class in England in 1844*, ed. W. H. Chaloner and W. O. Henderson, Oxford, 1958. (1st edn, 1845.)

— *The Origin of the Family ...*, trans. Alick West and Dona Torr, London, 1940.

FARR, DENNIS L. A., *William Etty*, 96 plates, London, 1958.

FORSTER, E. M., *Marianne Thornton 1797–1887*, London, 1956.

FRIEDAN, B., *Feminine Mystique*, New York, 1963.

FRYER, PETER, *The Birth Controllers*, London, 1965.

— *Mrs. Grundy. Studies in English Prudery*, London, 1963.

FULFORD, ROGER, ed., *Dearest Child. Letters Between Queen Victoria and the Princess Royal, 1858–1861*, London, 1964.

GARRISON, WILLIAM LLOYD, *W. L. G. 1805–1879 ... the Story of His Life Told by His Children*, 4 vols, New York, 1955.

GASKELL, P., *The Manufacturing Population of England, its Moral, Social, and Physical Conditions, and the Changes Which Have Arisen From the Use of Steam Machinery; with an examination of infant labour*, London, 1833.

GILBERT, WILLIAM, *Dives and Lazarus (or the Adventures of an Obscure Medical Man in a Poor Neighbourhood)*, London, 1858.

GLASS, D. V., *Population Policies and Movements in Europe*, Oxford, 1940.

GREEN, SAMUEL G., *The Working Classes of Great Britain: Their Present Condition, and the Meaning of Their Improvement and Elevation*, London, 1850.

GREENWELL, DORA, 'Our single women', *North British Review*, xxxvi (February 1862), pp. 62–87.

GREENWOOD, JAMES, *The Seven Curses of London*, London, 1869.

GREG, SAMUEL, *Two Letters to Leonard Horner, Esq. on the Capabilities of the Factory System*, London, 1840.

GREG, W. R., 'Juvenile and female labour', *Edinburgh Review*, lxxix (January 1844), pp. 130–56.

GREG, W. R., *Literary and Social Judgments*, London, 1869. (Four particularly interesting essays: 'False morality of lady novelists', pp. 82–112; 'French fiction: the lowest deep', pp. 146–83; 'Why are women redundant', pp. 280–316; 'Truth v. edification', pp. 317–36.)

— *The Great Sin of Great Cities* (reprint of article 'Prostitution' in *Westminster and Foreign Quarterly Review*, July 1850), London, 1853.

GRIMAL, PIERRE, ed., *Histoire mondiale de la femme*, 4 vols, Paris, 1965–7.

HALÉVY, ÉLIE, *La Formation du radicalisme philosophique*, 3 vols, Paris, 1901–4.

— *Histoire du peuple anglais au dix-neuvième siècle*, 5 vols, Paris, 1918–32.

HAMMOND, J. L. and BARBARA, *The Age of the Chartists. 1832–1854. A Study of Discontent*, London, 1930.

Bibliography

— *Lord Shaftesbury*, London, 1936.

HANSARD, THOMAS C., *The Parliamentary Debates From the Year 1803 to the Present Time* ...

HARRISON BRIAN, 'The power of drink', the *Listener*, lxxxi (13 February 1969), pp. 204–6.

— 'Underneath the Victorians', *Victorian Studies*, x, No. 3 (March 1967), pp. 239–62.

— 'Victorian philanthropy', *Victorian Studies*, ix, No. 4 (June 1966), pp. 353–74.

HAYEK, F. A., *John Stuart Mill and Harriet Taylor. Their Correspondence and Subsequent Marriage*, London, 1951.

HENDERSON, MRS., *The Young Wife's Own Book. Her Domestic Duties and Social Habits*, Glasgow, 1857.

HEWITT, MARGARET, *Wives and Mothers in Victorian Industry*, London, 1958.

HILL, FREDERIC, *Crime: Its Amount, Causes, and Remedies*, London, 1853.

HIMES, N. E., *Medical History of Contraception*, London, 1936; New York: Schocken Books, 1970.

HIMMELFARB, G., *Victorian Minds*, London, 1968.

HOBSBAWM, E. J., *Labouring Men. Studies and the History of Labour*, London, 1964.

HODDER, EDWIN, *The Life of Samuel Morley*, London, 1887.

HOLME, THEA, *The Carlyles at Home*, London, 1965.

HOUGHTON, W. E., ed., *The Wellesley Index to Victorian Periodicals 1824–1900*, i, Toronto and London, 1966.

HOUSE, HUMPHREY, *All in Due Time. The Collected Essays and Broadcast Talks of Humphrey House*, London, 1955.

HOUSE, HUMPHREY and BEALES, H. L., *Ideas and Beliefs of the Victorians. An Historic Revaluation of the Victorian Age*, London, 1949.

HOWITT, MARY, *An Autobiography*, ed. Margaret Howitt, 2 vols, London, 1889.

HUTCHINS, B. L. and HARRISON, A., *A History of Factory Legislation*, preface by Sidney Webb, London, 1926.

HYDE, HARTFORD M., *Mr and Mrs Beeton*, London, 1951.

INGESTRE, VISCOUNT, *Meliora: or Better Times to Come*, London, 1852.

IRONSIDE, R. and GERE, J. A., *Preraphaelite Painters*, 94 plates, London, 1948.

JAEGER, MURIEL, *Before the Victorians*, Harmondsworth, 1967.

JAMESON, ANNA B., *The Communion of Labour. A Second Lecture on the Social Employments of Women*, London, 1856.

JAMESON, ANNA B., *Memoirs and Essays*, London, 1846.

— *Sisters of Charity. Catholic and Protestant Abroad and at Home*, London, 1856.

— *Winter Studies and Summer Rambles in Canada*, London, 1838.

JEUNE, MARGARET GIFFORD, *Pages From the Diary of an Oxford Lady. 1843–1862*, Oxford, 1932.

JEWSBURY, G. E., *Selections From the Letters of Geraldine Endsor Jewsbury to Jane Welsh Carlyle*, London, 1892.

JUMP, J. D., 'Weekly reviewing in the 1850's', *Review of English Studies*, xxiv, No. 93 (January 1948), pp. 42–57.

— 'Weekly reviewing in the 1860's', *Review of English Studies*, New Series, iii, No. 11 (July 1952), pp. 244–62.

KAMM, JOSEPHINE, *Hope Deferred – Girls' Education in English History*, London, 1965.

Bibliography

— *Rapiers and Battleaxes. The Women's Movement and its Aftermath*, London, 1966.

KAYE, J. W., 'Employment of women', *North British Review*, xxvi (February 1857), pp. 291–338.

— 'The Marriage and Divorce Bill', *North British Review*, xxvii (August 1857), pp. 163–93.

— 'The non-existence of women', *North British Review*, xxiii (August 1855), pp. 536–62.

— 'Outrages on women', *North British Review*, xxv (May 1856), pp. 233–56.

KELLETT, E. E., *As I Remember*, London, 1936.

KITSON-CLARK, G., *The Making of Victorian England*, London, 1962.

LECKY, W. E. H., *History of European Morals From Augustus to Charlemagne*, 2 vols, London, 1869.

LISTER, T. H., 'Rights and conditions of women', *Edinburgh Review*, lxxiii (April 1841), pp. 189–209.

LOCHHEAD, MARION, *Elizabeth Rigby, Lady Eastlake*, London, 1961.

— *The Victorian Household*, London, 1964.

LONGFORD, ELIZABETH, *Victoria R. I.*, London, 1964.

LOUDON, J. W., 'How should girls be educated?', *The Ladies' Companion at Home and Abroad*, i (23 March 1850), p. 184.

LOUDON, J. W., 'Leader', *The Ladies' Companion at Home and Abroad*, i (29 December 1849), p. 8.

LOVETT, WILLIAM, *Life and Struggles of William Lovett*, ed. R. H. Tawney, London, 1967. (1st edn, 1876.)

— *Social and Political Moralists*, London, 1853.

— *Woman's Mission*, London, 1856.

MACKAY, CHARLES, ed., *The Home Affections Portrayed by the Poets*, engraved by the brothers Dalziel, London, 1858.

MCGREGOR, O., *Divorce in England. A Centenary Study*, London, 1957.

— 'The social position of women in England. 1850–1914. A Bibliography', *British Journal of Sociology*, No. 1 (1955), pp. 48–60.

MAGNUS, PHILIP, *Gladstone: A Biography*, London, 1954.

MARCUS, STEVEN, *The Other Victorians*, London, 1966.

MARIENSTRAS, RICHARD, 'L'Anglaise sous le règne d'Elizabeth', *Histoire mondiale de la femme*, ii, Paris, 1966, pp. 397–454.

MARSHALL, D., *The English Domestic Servant in History*, London, 1949.

MARTINEAU, HARRIET, *The Factory Controversy; a Warning Against Meddling Legislation*, issued by the National Association of Factory Occupiers, Manchester, 1855.

— 'Female industry', *Edinburgh Review*, cix (April 1859), pp. 293–336.

— 'Modern domestic service', *Edinburgh Review*, cxv (April 1862), pp. 409–39.

— *Harriet Martineau's Autobiography, with Memorials by M. W. Chapman*, 3 vols, London, 1877.

— 'Middle-class education in England – girls', *The Cornhill Magazine*, x (November 1864), pp. 549–68.

— 'Nurses wanted', *The Cornhill Magazine*, xi (April 1865), pp. 409–33.

— *Society in America*, 3 vols, London, 1837.

MARX, KARL, *Capital. A Critical Analysis of Capitalist Production*, ed. and trans. Dona Torr, London, 1938.

Bibliography

MAURICE, F. D., KINGSLEY, C., etc., *Lectures to Ladies on Practical Subjects*, London, 1855.

MAURICE, F. D., *The Life of Frederick Denison Maurice*, 2 vols, London, 1884.

MAYHEW, HENRY, *London Labour and the London Poor*, 4 vols, London, 1861–3. (The author of vol. IV on prostitution was Bracebridge Hemyng.)

— *The Greatest Plague of Life: or the Adventures of a Lady in Search of a Good Servant*, illustrated by George Cruikshank, London, 1847.

MAYHEW, HENRY and AUGUSTUS, *Whom to Marry and How to Get Married... or the Adventures of a Lady in Search of a Good Husband*, illustrated by George Cruickshank, London, 1848.

MAYNARD, JOHN, *Matrimony: or, What Marriage Life is, and How to Make the Best of it*, London, 1866.

MILL, J. S., *Autobiography*, ed. H. J. Laski, London, 1924.

[MILL, J. S.], 'A recent magisterial decision', *Morning Post*, 8 November 1854, p. 3.

[MILL, J. S. or TAYLOR, HARRIET], leader in *Morning Chronicle*, 31 May 1850, p. 4.

[MILL, J. S.], leader in *Morning Chronicle*, 13 March 1850.

[MILL, J. S.], leader in *Morning Chronicle*, 29 March 1850.

[MILL, J. S.], 'Protection of women', *Sunday Times*, 24 August 1851, p. 2.

[MILL, J. S.], *The Subjection of Women*, ed. Stanton Coit, London, 1906.

MILNE, J. D., *Industrial and Social Position of Women in the Middle and Lower Ranks*, London, 1867.

MINEKA, FRANCIS E., *The Dissidence of Dissent: The Monthly Repository, 1806–1838*, Chapel Hill, North Carolina, 1944.

MITCHELL, JULIET, 'Women: the longest revolution', *New Left Review*, xl (November–December 1966), pp. 11–37.

MONKHOUSE, W. COSMO, *Pictures by Sir Charles Eastlake*, London, 1875.

MONTÉGUT, E., 'Un missionnaire de la cité de Londres', *Revue des Deux Mondes*, viii (1 November 1854), pp. 483–507.

NEALE, R. S., 'Class and class-consciousness in early nineteenth-century England: three classes or five?', *Victorian Studies*, xii, No. 1 (September 1968), pp. 4–32.

NEFF, WANDA FRAIKEN, *Victorian Working Women, a Historical and Literary Study of Woman in British Industries and Professions. 1832–1850*, London, 1929.

NESBITT, GEORGE L., *Benthamite Reviewing. The First Twelve Years of the 'Westminster Review', 1824–1836*, New York, 1934.

NEWSOME, DAVID, *Godliness and Good Learning. Four Studies on a Victorian Ideal*, London, 1961.

NIGHTINGALE, FLORENCE, a collection of leaflets, photographs, newspaper cuttings and other Papers ... in the British Mueum, 1855?–1945.

— *Method of Improving the Nursing Service in Hospital*, London, 1868.

— *Notes on Hospitals*, London, 1859.

— MS. reports by Florence Nightingale on her Crimean nurses, c. 1854–6, B.M. Add. MS. 43402.

— *Notes on Nursing: What it is, and What it is not*, London, 1860.

NORTON, CAROLINE, *A Letter to the Queen on Lord Chancellor Cranworth's Marriage and Divorce Bill*, London, 1855.

Bibliography

— *A Plain Letter to the Lord Chancellor on the Infant Custody Bill*, London, 1839.

— *A Review of the Divorce Bill of 1856*, London, 1857.

— *English Laws for Women in the Nineteenth Century*, London, 1854.

— *The Separation of Mother and Child by the Law of 'Custody of Infants'*, London, 1838.

NUTTING, M. A. and DOCK, L. L., *A History of Nursing*, 2 vols, New York and London, 1907.

OLIPHANT, MARGARET, 'The condition of women', *Blackwood's Edinburgh Magazine*, lxxxiii (February 1858), pp. 139–54.

— 'The laws concerning women', *Blackwood's Edinburgh Magazine*, lxxix (April 1856), pp. 379–87.

OSBORNE, SIDNEY G., *The Letters of S. G. O. A Series of Letters on Public Affairs ... published in 'The Times' 1844–1888*, ed. Arnold White, 2 vols, London, 1890.

OWEN, DAVID E., *English Philanthropy 1660–1960*, Cambridge, Mass., 1966.

PACKE, MICHAEL ST JOHN, *The Life of John Stuart Mill*, London, 1954.

PAPPE, H. O., *John Stuart Mill and the Harriet Taylor Myth*, Melbourne, 1960.

PARKES, BESSIE RAYNER, *Essays on Woman's Work*, London, 1865.

— *Remarks on the Education of Girls*, London, 1854.

Parliamentary Papers, *Reports From Commissioners – Children's Employment (Mines)*, xv (1842).

— *Reports From Commissioners: Children's Employment (Trades and Manufactures)*, xiv (1843).

— *Reports From the Inspectors of Factories ...*, xxvii (1843).

Reports ... Labour of Children in Factories, xv (1831–2).

— *Schools' Inquiry Commission*, xxviii (1867–78).

— *Supplementary Report ... as to the Employment of Children in Factories*, xix (1834).

PATMORE, C., 'The social position of women', *North British Review*, xiv (February 1851), pp. 515–40.

PATTERSON, CLARA BURDETT, *Angela Burdett-Coutts and the Victorians*, London, 1953.

PERKINS, JANE GREY, *The Life of Mrs Norton*, London, 1909.

PETRIE, SIR CHARLES, *The Victorians*, London, 1960.

PINCHBECK, IVY, *Women Workers and the Industrial Revolution, 1750–1856*, London, 1930.

QUENNELL, P., ed., *London's Underworld*, London, 1960.

QUINLAN, M. J., *Victorian Prelude. A History of English Manners 1700–1830*, New York, 1941.

REID, MRS HUGO (MARION), *A Plea for Woman being a Vindication of the Importance and Extent of her Natural Sphere of Action*, London and Edinburgh, 1843.

REISS, ERNA, *Rights and Duties of Englishwomen: a Study in Law and Public Opinion*, Manchester, 1934.

REYNOLDS, GRAHAM, *Painters of the Victorian Scene*, London, 1953.

RITCHIE, JAMES E., *The Night Side of London*, London, 1857.

ROSENBERG, S. K., *John Chapman and The Westminster Review: 1852–1860*, unpublished M.A. thesis, Birmingham University, 1953.

ROSS, JANET, *Three Generations of Englishwomen. Memoirs and Correspondence*

Bibliography

of Mrs John Taylor, Mrs Sarah Austin, and Lady Duff Gordon, 2 vols, London, 1888.

ROUGEMONT, DENIS DE, *L'amour et l'Occident*, Paris, 1955. 1st edn, 1939.

ROUTH, H. V., *Money, Morals and Manners as Revealed in Modern Literature*, London, 1935.

ROVER, CONSTANCE, *The Punch Book of Women's Rights*, London, 1967.

RUSSELL, BERTRAND and PATRICIA, ed., *The Amberley Papers*, 2 vols, London, 1966.

RYAN, MICHAEL, *The Philosophy of Marriage, in its Social, Moral and Physical Relations*, London, 1837.

RYAN, MICHAEL, *Prostitution in London with a Comparative View of that of Paris and New York*, London, 1839.

SANDFORD, MRS JOHN, *Female Improvement*, 2 vols, London, 1836.

— *Woman in her Social and Domestic Character*, London, 1831.

SARGENT, G. E., *Domestic Happiness; Home Education; Politeness and Good Breeding*, London, 1851.

SAVILLE, JOHN, ed., *Democracy and the Labour Movement*, London, 1954.

SCHÜCKING, LEVIN L., *Die Familie im Puritanismus*, Leipzig and Berlin, 1929.

SENIOR, NASSAU W., *Letters on the Factory Act as it Affects the Cotton Manufacturer, Addressed, in the Spring of 1837 to the Right Hon. The President of the Board of Trade by N.W.S.*, 2nd edn, London, 1844.

SIMEY, M. B., *Charitable Effort in Liverpool in the Nineteenth Century*, Liverpool, 1951.

SIMON, BRIAN, *Studies in the History of Education, 1780–1870*. London, 1960.

— *Studies in the History of Education, Education and the Labour Movement, 1870–1920*, London, 1965.

SMILES, SAMUEL, *Self-Help, with Illustrations of Character, Conduct and Perseverance* (with a centenary introduction by Professor Asa Briggs), London, 1958.

SPAIN, NANCY, *Mrs Beeton and her Husband*, London, 1948.

STANLEY, MARIA J., *The Ladies of Alderley. Being the Letters Between Maria Josepha, Lady Stanley of Alderley ... Henrietta Maria Stanley ... 1841–1850*, ed. Nancy Mitford, London, 1938.

STANLEY, *The Stanleys of Alderley. Their Letters Between the Years 1851–1865*, ed. Nancy Mitford, London, 1939.

STENTON, D. M., *The English Woman in History*, London, 1957.

STRACHEY, RAY, *The Cause: a Short History of The Woman's Movement in Great Britain*, London, 1928.

SUSSMAN, HERBERT, 'Hunt, Ruskin and *The Scapegoat*', *Victorian Studies*, xii, No. 1 (September 1968), pp. 83–90.

TAINE, H., *Notes sur l'Angleterre*, Paris, 1872.

TAIT, WILLIAM, *Magdalenism: an Inquiry into the Extent, Causes and Consequences of Prostitution in Edinburgh*, 1st edn, Edinburgh, 1840.

TAYLOR, GORDON RATTRAY, *The Angel-Makers. A Study in the Psychological Origins of Historical Change, 1750–1850*, London, 1958.

TAWNEY, R. H., *Religion and the Rise of Capitalism*, London, 1926.

THACKERAY, W. M., MAYHEW, H., etc., *The Comick Almanack*, illustrated by George Cruikshank, London, First Series, 1835–43; Second Series, 1844–53.

THOMAS, KEITH, 'The Double Standard', *Journal of the History of Ideas*, 1959, pp. 195–216.

Bibliography

THOMPSON, E. P., *The Making of the English Working Class*, London, 1963.

THRALL, MIRIAM M. H., *Rebellious Fraser's. Nol Yorke's Magazine in the Days of Maginn, Thackeray, and Carlyle*, New York, 1934.

TORR, DONA, *Tom Mann and his Times. 1856–1890*, London, 1956.

TREVELYAN, G. O., *The Life and Letters of Lord Macaulay*, 4 vols, London, 1876.

TRISTAN, FLORA, *Promenades dans Londres*, Paris, 1840.

TROELTSCH, ERNEST, *The Social Teaching of the Christian Churches*, trans. O. Wyon, 2 vols, London, 1931.

VAUGHAN, ROBERT, *The Age of Great Cities; or, Modern Society Viewed in its Relation to Intelligence, Morals and Religion*, London, 1843.

WALSH, J. H., *A Manual of Domestic Economy: Suited to Families Spending from £100 to £1000 a Year*, London, 1857.

'WALTER', *My Secret Life*, 11 vols, Amsterdam, *c.* 1888–94.

WATKINS, HENRY G., *Friendly Hints to Female Servants*, London, 1867.

WEBB, R. K., *Harriet Martineau: a Radical Victorian*, London, 1960.

WEBER, MAX, *The Protestant Ethic and the Spirit of Capitalism*, trans. Talcott Parsons, London, 1930.

WEST, KATHARINE, *Chapter of Governesses, 1800–1949*, London, 1949.

WILLIAMS, RAYMOND, *Culture and Society, 1780–1950*, Harmondsworth, 1961.

WINKWORTH, SUSANNA and CATHERINE, *Memorials of Two Sisters Susanna and Catherine Winkworth*, ed. by their niece M. J. Shaen, London, 1908.

WOODHAM-SMITH, CECIL, *Florence Nightingale 1820–1910*, London, 1950.

WOODWARD, E. L., *The Age of Reform, 1815–1870* (*Oxford History of England*, xiii), Oxford, 1962.

WORDSWORTH, CHRISTOPHER, *Miscellanies, Literary and Religious*, 3 vols, London, 1879.

YOUNG, G. M., *Early Victorian England, 1830–1865*, 2 vols, London, 1951.

— *Victorian England. Portrait of an Age*, London, 1960.

INDEX

Index

abortion, 38

Acton, William, 8–9, 195; *The Functions and Disorders of the Reproductive Organs*, 8–9; *Prostitution* ..., 27, 197, 198, 202–3, 204, 205, 264, 265, 267, 268

adultery: and divorce law, 23–5; in *Felix Holt*, 95, 97; in *Vanity Fiar*, 239–41

Ainsworth, William Harrison, 229

Albert, Prince Consort, 27

alcoholism, female: in the novel, 82, 273–4; among nurses, 119, 120; in the working classes, 136

Amberley, Kate (*née* Stanley), 27, 28, 41, 42

Amberley, Lord, 27, 37, 41, 42

Annuals, 3, 7

Anti-Corn Law League, xvi, 129

anti-feminists, and the professions, 121–2

anti-slavery movement, 40

Argyll Rooms, 198

aristocracy, the: daily life of, 26–47 *passim*: and domestic staff, 31; and double standard, 265; and good works, 41, 114; morals of, 3; and seduction, in *Adam Bede*, 255–8, 260–1, 262–3

Arnold, Matthew, 173, 271

artists, women, 107

Ashley, Lord, *see* Shaftesbury, Anthony Ashley Cooper, 7th Earl of

Ashworth, Henry, 130

Association for the Aid and Benefit of Milliners and Dressmakers, 124–5

Association for the Promotion of Employment of Women, 122

Athenaeum, The, 43

Austen, Jane, xv, 75, 108, 164; *Pride and Prejudice*, 77

Austin, Sarah, 40, 43, 45

Bacon, Sir Frances, 17

Balzac, Honoré de, xiii, 273; *La Comédie Humaine*, 263

Bamford, Samuel, 183

Banks, J. A., 30, 34, 37

Banks, Olive, 30

Baptists, 198

Barbier, Henri-Auguste, 203

Bataille, George, 174

Beale, Dorothea, 14

Bedford College, London, 114

Beecher Stowe, Harriet, 39, 162

Beeton, Mrs, 5, 61; *The Book of Household Management*, 6, 31

Bell, R., 230

Bennett, Arnold, xv

Bentham, Jeremy, 129

birth control, xvi, 37–8, 47; and working classes, 51

birthrate, decline in after 1860s, 37

Bissell, C. T., on *Adam Bede*, 252

Blackwood, John, 82, 97, 252

Blondel, J.: *Emily Brontë* ..., 91, 173

'Bloomerism', 55

Bodichon, Barbara, 10, 94, 158, 189; and enslavement of women, 12; and governesses, 111; and legal status of wives, 17, 21; and Petition of 1856, 21; and women's suffrage, 14; and work for women, 46, 103, 105–6, 121–2

'Bounderby, Louisa' (*Hard Times*), 56, 58–9, 64, 75, 145, 210, 214, 215–16, 217, 219, 220, 224, 263–4

Bradlaugh, Charles, 37

Bradshaw's Railway Library, 44

Branwell, Miss, 173

347

Index

Index

Index

Index

Index

Index

Index

Marcus, Stephen, 195, 197, 263
Marcuse, Herbert, 271
marriage: Acton on consummation of, 9; of convenience, 26, 27, 75–6; decrease in number of, 202–3; delay in, and prostitution, 202–3; economics of, 26–7, 29–30; and legal rights, 16–25; rarity of happy, 27–8; working-class, encouragement of early, 50, 136; Victorian attitude to, xix; *and see* marriage-market, wives
marriage-market, criticized in the novel, 75–9, 215–16, 232, 233–4, 271
Married Woman's Property Act (1870), 16, 22
Married Woman's Property Committee, 22
Married Women's Property Bill (1857), 21–2, 40
Martin, John, 170
Martineau, Harriet, 10, 12 17, 115, 157, 181, 189, 209; on education, 114, 138; on feminine influence, 11; on governesses, 111; literary activity of, 107; on Thackeray, 84, 230; on *Villette*, 165, 273; and work for women, 12, 105, 106, 111, 121–2, 124, 131, 185
'Marwood, Alice' (*Dombey and Son*), 210, 215, 216–19, 220, 265
Mary, the Virgin, myth of, xiii, 6, 8, 84; and the novel, 71, 84, 99, 251; reverse of, 151
Marx, Karl: *Das Kapital*, 125
materialism: attacks on, 264, 271, 272; and role of woman, 7, 8
Maternal Societies, 33
Matrimonial Causes Act (1844), 17
Matrimonial Causes Act (1857), xvi, 16, 20, 21, 22–4
Maurice, F. D.: and educative gifts of women, 110–11, 113–14; and *Mary Barton*, 246; and nurses, 120, 121–2; and role of woman, 46, 115
Mayhew, Henry, 195, 197, 245, 246, 268; 'Home is Home ...', 49;

London Labour..., 195, 199, 200, 201, 202, 204, 205, 207, 209, 267
Maynard, John: *Matrimony*, 4
Mazzini, Giuseppe, 209
medical profession, women's exclusion from, 121–2; *and see* nursing profession
Melbourne, Lord, 20
Meredith, George, xv, xvii, 75
Merimée, Prosper, 247
Metropolitan Police records, 48–9, 195, 199
Middle Ages, 24–5
middle classes: codification of social behaviour of, 3; daily life of wife in, 26–47 *passim;* number of children in, 37; and importance of domestic staff, 31–2; lack of contact with working classes, 191; liberation of from domestic slavery, 3, 6–7, 30–1; morality of, xviii, 265; and philanthropy, 114; rise of, xvi, xviii, 30–1; and work for women, 109–11
Midnight Meeting Movement, the, 207, 209
Mill, John Stuart, 12, 13, 41, 129, 161, 271; and cruelty to wives, 23, 48; on Dickens' attitude to feminism, 55; and female education, xvi; election of to Parliament, xvi–xvii, 14; and the Franchise Bill, xvi, 42; and Great Crusade, 209; and legal rights of wives, 16, 17–18, 23; *The Subjection of Women*, xvii, 4, 10, 13, 14
Milne, J. D.: *The Industrial ... Position of Women*, 138–9
Mine Act (1842), 134
mines, employment of women and children in, 51, 128–9, 269; Disraeli and, 186–7; Lord Ashley and, 132–4; protection of, 129–30, 132–4
Mitford, Mary Russell, 85
Monkton-Milnes, R., 39
Montégut, Emile, 198
Monthly Repository, The, 10

Index

Moore, George, xv, 75
Morning Chronicle, 229, 245
motherhood, 33–8; in G. Eliot, 96; idealized role of, 33, 46, 250–1; idealized role of in the novel, 53, 67–8, 71, 73–4, 250–1; and incestuous connotations in Thackeray, 85–6; legal rights of over children, 22; and marriage-market, in Dickens, 215–16; and unmarried mother in *Adam Bede*, 258–9; and unmarried mother in *Ruth*, 181, 246–51; and working-class mothers, 50–2
mothers-in-law, in Thackeray, 87–8
Mozart, Wolfgang Amadeus, 221
Murray, John, 42
Museum Soirées, 38
My Secret Life, 197, 198, 199, 200, 202, 205–6, 263, 265

'Nancy' (*Oliver Twist*), 210–13, 221, 224, 246
narcotics, children and, 52
National Association of Factory Occupiers, 131
Nicholls, Rev. Arthur, 167–8
'Nickleby, Kate', 141, 145, 224
Nightingale, Florence: cult of, 47; and education, 111; and E. Gaskell, 39; and Great Crusade, 209; and health of governesses, 112; nursing career of, 116, 118–21, 182–3; and nursing conditions, 118
Nightingale School of Nursing, 120–1, 190
North London Ophthalmic Institution, 124
Norton, Caroline, 181; literary work of, 45; and rights of wife, xvi, 17, 19, 20, 22, 25, 28
Nottingham Providence Society, 40
novel, the: criticisms of marriage-market in, 75–9, 215–16, 232, 233–4, 271; and dependence of the wife, 83–6; and fallen women, 210ff., 263–8; and family reading, 42; French, xiii–xiv, 42, 95, 228,

273; idealization of women in, xiii–xv, xix xx, 53 74, 99, 270–4; the Newgate novel, 210, 211, 229, 272; and position of women in society, 75–100 *passim;* and prostitution, 203–4, 205, 210ff., 270; and realism, 272–4; Russian, xiii–iv; seduction in, xiv–xv, 243ff.; and sex, 65–6, 239–41, 263–8, 270–1; spinsters in, 141ff., 270; tyranny of the husband in, 79–83; woman's, mediocrity of, 106–7; working-class woman in, 83, 183–5, 187, 190, 244–8, 270; *and see* Brontë, Anne; Brontë, Charlotte; Brontë, Emily; Dickens, Charles; Disraeli, Benjamin; Eliot, George; Gaskell, Mrs Elizabeth; Thackeray, William Makepeace; Trollope, Anthony
nuns, and nursing orders, 115–16
nursing profession, 106, 115–22; development of, 115–16, 120–2; in Dickens' novels, 145–6, 151; in E. Gaskell's novels, 182–3; privileged classes and, 119–20; women's suitability for, 47, 115; working-class women in, 52, 116–20, 146
Nussey, Rev. Henry, 157, 166

Oastler, Richard, 132, 134
Owen, Robert, 10, 132

Parkes, B. R., 11, 12, 94, 114, 121–2
Patmore, Coventry: *The Angel in the House*, 6
Peel, Sir Robert, 138
periodicals, xvi, 3, 42; and attitude to working classes, 49; feminist, 10; and the home, 30–1; and governesses, 113; and role of mother, 33
Perkins, J. G., 22
Perry, Erskine, 22
Petition of 1856, 20–1, 29
philanthropists: and conception of male and female roles, 137–8,

Index

140; Dickens and, 54–6; and fallen women, 264; and female labour, 7, 52, 124–5, 129–30, 132–40 *passim;* and governesses, 113–14; and *Mary Barton,* 246; and prostitution, 195, 206–9; and seamstresses, 124–5

philanthropy, as female occupation, 39–41, 114–15, 119, 269

Phillips, Watts: *Lost in London,* 227

'Pinch, Ruth' (*Martin Chuzzlewit*), 57, 141, 142–3

Place, Francis, 10, 37

politics, women's interest in, 40, 41–2

Pollard, Arthur: *Mrs. Gaskell,* 245–6

poor laws, 56, 200

Praz, Mario, 219, 224

Proctor, Mrs, 230

professional women: in Dickens, 145–6, 151; in E. Gaskell, 180–3; *and see* governesses

professions, women and, 104, 106–22; anti-feminists and, 121–2; opening-up of, 40–1 122

prostitution, 130, 136, 269–70; and absence of female sexual desire, 8; attitudes of prostitutes to, 204–5, 267; causes of, 199–201, 202–3; Dickens and, 207–9, 216, 223, 225, 245; and double standard, 202–3; and marriage of prostitutes, 205, 267; novelists and, *see below;* philanthropists and, 195, 206–9; studies of, 195–209, 245, 267; and syphilis, 203; and Victorian morality, 201–2, 205–6, 263, 267; working-class wives and, 48

novelists and, 203–4, 205, 210ff., 263, 270; Dickens and, 210, 216, 225–7; E. Gaskell and, 245–6, 247; *and see* fallen women

Protestantism, xix, 3, 7; and nursing orders, 116

psychological disorders, 33, 112

Punch, 38, 56, 76, 113, 124, 163, 229

Quarterly Review, The, 42, 155, 209, 230

Queen's College London, 114, 180, 190

Queen's School, 41

Ratchford, F. E.: 'Brontë's Angrian Cycle of Stories', 170

Ray, G. W.: *Thackeray,* 72–3

Rayner-Parkes, Bessie, *see* Parkes, B. R.

Reich, Wilhelm, 271

Reid, Mrs Hugo, 10, 11; *A Plea for Women,* 13–14, 20

Reform Act (1867), xvi

Revue des deux mondes, La, 162, 169, 233

Richardson, Samuel, xix; *Clarissa Harlowe,* xiv, xv, 262, 264, 265; *Pamela,* xiv, xv, 221, 262, 264, 265

Rigby, Elizabeth (Lady Eastlake): on governesses, 112–13, 152, 155; literary activities of, 42–3; on 'Vanity Fair ... Jane Eyre ...', 162, 230, 233, 236

Ritchie, Lady, 86

Roebuck, economist, 129, 130, 131

Roland, Pauline, 10

Rossetti, Dante Gabriel, 264

Rubenius, A., 246

rural areas, immorality in, 200

Ruskin, John, 271; on Holman Hunt, 266–7; on man's role, 7; *Modern Painters,* 42; and woman's role, 5, 56, 272

Russell, Bertrand, 28

Ryan, M.: *Prostitution ....,* 199, 202, 203, 204, 209, 267, 268

Sadler, Michael, 132, 134, 136

Sadler Report (1933–4), 51

Sadler's Committee and Report, 132, 134, 135

St Leonard, Lord, 24

St Paul, 4

Saint-Simon, Claude Henri, 10

St Thomas's Hospital, 120–1

Sand, George, xiii; *Indiana,* 79

Sandford, Mrs John, 3–4

schoolmistresses: in C. Brontë, 156, 157–8; in Dickens, 141–3

Index

Index

Ternan, Ellen, 60, 148, 151
textile industry, *see* factories
Thackeray, Isabella (*née* Shawe), 71–2, 77, 87–8
Thackeray, William Makepeace: on C. Brontë, 168; and censorship of E. B. Browning, 47, 229, 273; emotional life of, 71–4, 85–6; and Jane Brookfield, 73–4, 80, 85; lectures by, 39; marriage of, 71–2, 77, 87–8; and moral responsibility of the novelist, 229, 242, 273; and his mother, 72–3, 85, 86; on *Oliver Twist*, 211, 229–30; parodies by, 229, 230
novels of, xiv, xvii; ambiguity of female characters in, 53, 84–7, 88, 241–2, 263; and cult of wife-mother, 53, 66, 69–74, 79, 84, 86–7, 88, 237, 238, 241, 270; and female education, 87; and divorce procedures, 80–1, 270; impure women in, 229, 231, 233–42, 263–4, 270; love in, 65, 86–7, 231, 237; and marriage-market, 76–9, 232, 233–4; maternal possessiveness in, 84–6; and money, 231–3, 235–6; mothers-in-law in, 87–8; realism of, 230–1, 272; and subjection of the wife, 79–81, 83–4, 270
works mentioned in text: *The Adventures of Philip* ..., 70, 77, 87, 88; *Catherine*, 229; *Henry Esmond*, 70, 73, 77, 78–9, 80, 84–5, 88, 172; *The Memoirs of Barry Lyndon*, 80, 83; *The Newcomes*, 76, 77–8, 79, 80–1, 87, 88; *Pendennis*, 70–1, 77, 83–4, 85–6, 88; *The Ravenswing*, 79; *Sketches and Travels in London*, 76; *Vanity Fair*, xiv, 70, 78, 79, 86–7, 88, 229, 230–42, 263–4, 270, 272; *The Virginians*, 77, 79, 83; *Yellowplush Stories*, 87
Thomas, Keith, 195
Thompson, William: *Appeal of one Half of the Human Race*, 10
Tillotson, Kathleen: *The Brontës, their*

Lives ... 171; (and Butt, John), *Dickens at Work*, 53, 60, 216; *Novels* ..., 219
Times, The, 26, 27, 109, 111, 116, 125, 197, 201, 202, 204–5, 207, 264
Tolstoy, Alexei N., xiii–xiv, 164, 174
Tristan, Flora, 10; *Promenades dans Londres*, 198
Trollope, Anthony: Thackeray's censorship of, 229; on *Vanity Fair*, 230–1
novels of, xvii; attitude to marriage in, 75–6; realism of, 175, 272; spinsters in, 189
works mentioned in text: *Can You Forgive Her?*, 76; *The Kellys and O'Kellys*, 76; *The Small House at Allington*, 76; *The Vicar of Bullhampton*, 76; *The Warden*, xvii
'Trotwood, Betsy' (*David Copperfield*), 81, 147–8, 149
Turgenev, Ivan, xii–xiv
Twining, Louisa, 39

Unitarian Herald, 28, 243
Unitarianism, 10, 31, 39, 243
Urania Cottage, 207–8, 209, 223, 225

Victoria, Queen: marriage of, 27–8; and pregnancy, 35–6, 37; reign of, xv–xvi; and woman as monarch, 46
virginity: in eighteenth-century novel, xiv; ownership of, 24, 202

Wells, H. G., xv; *Ann Veronica*, xvii
Westminster Review, The, xvii, 10, 13, 16, 99, 129, 161, 245, 247, 252, 272
'Wickfield, Agnes' (*David Copperfield*), 59, 60, 63–4, 65, 141
wife-beating: and the law, 18, 23, 48; in the novel, 83
'Wilfer, Bella' (*Our Mutual Friend*), 57–8, 59–60, 75
Wilson, Angus: 'The Heroes and Heroines of Dickens', xiii, 222
Wilson, Edmund, 219

Index